New Approaches to Resistance in Brazil an

New Approaches to Resistance
in Brazil and Mexico

John Gledhill and
Patience A. Schell, editors

Duke University Press   *Durham & London*
2012

© 2012 Duke University Press
All rights reserved.
Printed in the United States of America on acid-free paper ∞
Typeset in Arnhem Blond by Tseng Information Systems, Inc.
Library of Congress Cataloging-in-Publication Data
appear on the last printed page of this book.

Contents

Acknowledgments

First and foremost, our thanks are due to the Arts and Humanities Research Council of the United Kingdom for funding the interdisciplinary research project on which this book is based. We are also grateful to Dr. Jocélio Teles dos Santos, director of the Center of Afro-Oriental Studies (CEAO) of the Federal University of Bahia, for allowing us to hold the public sessions of our seminars in the CEAO, to Dr. Federico Besserer for doing the same on the first day of our work in Mexico City, at the Anthropology Department of the Metropolitan Autonomous University, Iztapalapa, and to Dr. Jean Meyer for making the facilities of his own institution, the Center for Economic Research and Teaching, available to us during the rest of our stay. In Manchester, we were fortunate to be able to count on the efficient administrative support of Claudia Natteri and Charlotte Jackson in the School of Social Sciences for handling the complex travel, accommodation, and subsistence arrangements necessary to bring an international group of scholars together in the same place at the same time. Charlotte Liddell provided us with valuable editorial support in preparing the manuscript for initial submission to the press, funding for which was provided by Manchester's School of Languages, Linguistics and Cultures. We are also grateful to Parvathi Kumaraswami for helping us arrange translation from Spanish or Portuguese, and we are grateful to our translators: Lucy Lawton, Sarah Magee, Sarah Maitland, Monica Morales Moreno, Tara Plunkett, and Richard Reed. Finally, thanks are due to Valerie Millholland and Miriam Angress at Duke University Press for their support in bringing our thoughts on resistance to publication.

A Case for Rethinking Resistance

JOHN GLEDHILL

This book explores what the notion of "resistance" can contribute to scholarly understandings of the history and contemporary social and political life of Latin America's two largest countries, Brazil and Mexico. Our case studies aim to contribute to broader theoretical debates at the interface between history and the social sciences. This introduction reviews debates about the usefulness of resistance from the perspective of an anthropologist. Alan Knight closes the book with a historian's overview of the broader implications of our findings.

At first sight, our theme might seem anachronistic. Although "resistance studies" became an academic boom industry in the 1980s (D. Moore 1998, 348), the next decade brought a wave of critiques. Some critics, such as Sherry Ortner (1995), remained sympathetic to the idea that resistance studies possessed a worthwhile object of analysis but called for that analysis to become more theoretically nuanced and more grounded in ethnography. Others, however, argued that misplaced moral fervor had driven anthropology toward an obsession with resistance that, by trying to explain everything, ended up explaining nothing (M. Brown 1996; Sahlins 2002). Given such critiques, one anthropologist, Robert Fletcher, confessed to thinking twice about including "resistance" in the title of his paper, for fear of alienating potential readers. Yet he went on to argue that "rethinking" could "resurrect a troubled but significant field of research." "Fundamentally," he insisted, "studies of resistance are concerned with the struggle for equality, the fight to end exploitation and achieve a more just and humane society" (Fletcher 2001, 44).

It also seems important that "resisting" is often what our research subjects say they are doing when they struggle, to defend their lands, culture, or religion, or to achieve *new* rights and social dignity in situations of inequality and discrimination. For example, the people of a Nahua indigenous community that I studied in Ostula, Mexico, took pride in their successful historical resistance to very real threats of genocide and dispossession (Gledhill 2004a). In 2006, newly allied with the Zapatista Army of National Liberation, Ostula was declared a "community in resistance" to government agrarian certification programs (see Baitenmann, chapter fourteen). This was a new move in a longstanding dispute over lands usurped by invading ranchers in the early twentieth century, a dispute made more acute by growing capitalist interest in developing the tourism and mining potential of Ostula's communal territory. The stakes remain high in these conflicts. The village schoolteacher elected to head the commission pursuing the land claim was brutally murdered in July 2008. A year later, following a confrontation in which shots were fired at indigenous men, women, and children, Ostula turned its communal police into a self-defense force and seized control of the disputed terrain. In the face of this spectacular action, which made headlines in national newspapers, the state government agreed to compensate the ranchers for returning the lands to the community, but Ostulans continued to suffer violent reprisals.

This is another good reason to take resistance seriously. Yet Fletcher's case study presented analytical dilemmas that this book demonstrates are ubiquitous in studies of resistance. Although some of his research subjects, Chilean indigenous people threatened with displacement by a hydroelectric dam, mounted a vigorous campaign with the support of indigenous-rights NGOs, environmental and alter-globalization activists, and university intellectuals to defend their land and way of life, the majority not only seemed willing to embrace resettlement as a positive opportunity to experience "development" and "progress," but gave their votes to the political ultraright. This led Fletcher to criticize James Scott's (1985; 1990) paradigmatic formulation of "everyday forms of resistance" for making it difficult to account for actors who do not seem to find their situations as oppressive as outside activists and academics think they should. Understanding why people in apparently similar "situations of domination" react differently is a central issue in rethinking resistance integral to many analyses in this book and systematically explored by Robert Slenes in chapter five in the case of slaves in the Brazilian southeast. Fletcher's argument also raises the issue of possible bias on the part of resistance theorists regarding the types of actors and movements deemed worthy of investigation. Should actors who are not at the bottom of the social scale, such as the Catholic women discussed by Patience Schell in chapter nine, or "subaltern" actors not struggling for a more just and humane society, be included in studies of resistance when they are challenging the will of governments and elites (including, perhaps, "liberal multicultural elites")? These are some of the questions that we asked contributors to this book to address.

One way forward is to expand the discussion of resistance from Scott's everyday forms of resistance to the broader field of what Sidney Tarrow calls "contentious politics." Contentious politics embraces any "collective activity on the part of claimants—or those who claim to represent them—relying at least in part on non-institutional forms of interaction with elites, opponents, or the state." It therefore encompasses the study of social movements, which Tarrow, following Charles Tilly, defines as "sustained challenges to powerholders in the name of a disadvantaged population living under the jurisdiction or influence of those powerholders" (Tarrow 1996, 874). The usefulness of pursuing a broader perspective is illustrated by Jean Meyer's and Schell's discussions of Catholic opposition to the state in postrevolutionary Mexico (chapters eight and nine). Much of the rest of this book shows that we need to look more closely at the interactions and alliances between subaltern groups and other social and political actors. Although the latter are generally less humble social actors who find themselves opposed to those currently exercising power, as illustrated by some of the nineteenth-century alliances described by Marcus de Carvalho in chapter four, we also sometimes find the clandestine hand of the powerful at work in ways that "manage" the rebellious actions of the poor, as Javier Auyero shows in his analyses of the role played by the Peronist political machine and police in the Argentine food riots of 2001 (Auyero 2007). This suggests that the study of resistance should be embedded in more complex accounts of the *practices* of power. Among the lines of analysis that we pursue in this book are the ways in which the exercise of power is furthered by state responses institutionalizing movements that generate "contentious politics," a line of analysis exemplified by Ilka Boaventura Leite's study of the "juridical-formal" *quilombo* in chapter twelve, and the broader role of multicultural policies within contemporary neoliberal techniques of rule. Yet as Guillermo de la Peña concludes in chapter eleven, none of these critical perspectives on the workings of power relations eliminate the need to consider the role of "subaltern projects in the march of history," even if, as Patricia Pessar notes in chapter six, the identities, meanings, and practices that inspire such projects will inevitably shift with the times.

This book is based on intensive discussions between anthropologists and historians in three four-day research seminars funded by the British Arts and Humanities Research Council and held in Salvador, in the Brazilian state of Bahia, Mexico City, and Manchester, England. Our basic question was whether resistance studies could still be revitalized through further new thinking, bearing in mind the volume of new research that has accumulated since the original boom. Although some participants remained skeptical about the value of resistance studies, our discussions did show that asking searching questions about resistance was a productive framework for advancing new interpretations. Indeed, as Felipe Castro Gutiérrez shows in chapter two, a high level of skepticism about the inevitability of indigenous resistance to colonialism, and a wariness of reading the past in terms of present social and political concerns, can stimulate original research on deeper and less obvious manifestations of indigenous "indignation and irritation" that offer interesting parallels to Matthew Gutmann's account in chapter fifteen of the contemporary "compliant defiance" of working-class Mexicans. The remainder of this introduction provides a more detailed review of the evolving debate and the areas in which this book seeks to move it forward.

Resistance Studies in Historical Perspective

In chapter two Castro Gutiérrez suggests that an archeology of the notion of resistance could trace connections between its appearance in modern Latin American movements, such as the "Five Hundred Years of Indigenous and Black Resistance" campaign, and European antecedents such as nineteenth-century anarchist thought and the struggles of the French partisans under Nazi occupation. Nevertheless, the intellectual movement that generated the boom in resistance studies in the 1980s was the product of a more recent historical conjuncture. In the United States, resistance studies emerged, as Gutmann notes in chapter fifteen, in the climate of "diminished expectations" associated with the triumph of Reaganism. In Latin America, the conjuncture was different, with military regimes still in power in many countries until the mid-1980s. A few countries, such as

Guatemala, were still locked in conflicts between Leftist insurgents and authoritarian regimes backed by Washington well into the 1990s. Nevertheless, the experience of dictatorship scarcely enhanced the credibility of revolutionary Left projects, while resistance theory, as a celebration of the decentered "popular subject," subsequently took its place alongside "new social movements theory" as a tool for thinking about more radically democratic alternatives in an era in which democratization generally got off to a cautious start.

Interest in resistance theories in Latin America was, however, further stimulated by the attempt to incorporate indigenous peoples into revolutionary movements. Northern intellectuals wished to show solidarity with the struggles of groups that revolutionary socialists and capitalist modernizers alike had deemed a reproach on national dreams of achieving "modernity" (Beverley 1999). David Stoll (1999) has controversially argued that the solidarity work of U.S. scholars around the iconic *testimonio* book *I, Rigoberta Menchú* actually prolonged violence in Guatemala, since without it the military would have eliminated the guerrilla completely (see Knight, conclusion). From Stoll's perspective, Menchú was a Marxist revolutionary wolf masquerading in the sheep's clothing of a Maya peasant woman, but the resistance theme was taken up by Latin American intellectuals working against the grain of both the assimilationist policies of developmental states and orthodox Left positions in which issues of class override questions of ethnicity, race, and gender. Although Scott's work has been criticized for its focus on "an analytics of class to the exclusion of other productive and social inequalities (notably gender, age and ethnicity)," (D. Moore 1998, 350) Mexican scholars focusing on indigenous issues, such as Adriana López (1996) and Marcela Coronado (2000), found his ideas useful.

Latin American scholarship is not a simple replication of gringo scholarship, even if the Northern academy remains "hegemonic" (Restrepo and Escobar 2005). For example, the Gramsci of Latin American scholars generally looks more like the Italian Communist strategist than the "lite" version appropriated by North American cultural anthropology (Crehan 2002). Nor has the politics of Latin America stood still since the mid-1980s. Yet whether the politics is one of state capture, as achieved by Evo Morales's Movement for Socialism in Bolivia, or pluralistic radical democratization from below that eschews electoral participation, as advocated by the Zapatistas in Mexico, much of it does not seem to be an "infrapolitics" focused on muttered defiance behind the backs of the dominant of the kind on which Scott focused our attention, "an unobtrusive realm of political struggle" based on "the veiled cultural struggle and political expression of subordinate groups who have ample reason to fear venturing their unguarded opinion" (1990, 183–84).

Nevertheless, although the historical conjunctures that gave birth to the resistance theories of the 1980s have passed, some issues that were part of a broader concern with power relations remain at the center of current debates. In particular, we have the influence of Michel Foucault and his contention in the first volume of *The History of Sexuality* that "where there is power, there is also resistance" (1978, 95–96). In a critique of the "romanticism" of first-generation resistance theorists, Lila Abu-Lughod turns Foucault on his head by re-rendering his dictum that "resistance is never in a position of exteriority to power" as "where there is resistance, there is power" (Abu-Lughod 1990, 42). For Abu-Lughod, the advantage for anthropologists' "using resistance as a diagnostic of power" was that they could move away from abstract theories of power to the ethnographic "study of power in particular situations" and the way emancipation from one form of hierarchy or oppression can lead to new forms of hierarchy and oppression. In her ethnographic examination of the apparently safe spaces in which Bedouin women could enjoy a smoke and elaborate their "hidden transcripts" about such matters as male vices and arranged marriages, Abu-Lughod discusses the ambivalent implications of the social and economic changes that led some women to wear makeup and add negligees to their trousseaux. She concludes: "In resisting the axes of kin and gender, the young women who want the lingerie, Egyptian songs, satin wedding dresses, and fantasies of private romance their elders resist are perhaps unwittingly enmeshing themselves in an extraordinarily complex new set of power relations. These bind them irrecoverably to the Egyptian economy, itself tied to the global economy, and to the Egyptian state, many of whose powers depend on separating kin groups and regulating individuals." Nevertheless, after posing the question of whether "certain modern forms and techniques of power work in such indirect ways, or seem to offer such positive attractions, that people do not as readily resist them," she goes on to show how the adoption of modest Islamic dress and participation in Islamic movements represents a reaction to the contradictions that these new entanglements with global capitalism and the state pose for women who remain relatively socially marginalized. But fundamentalist practices not only entail yet another set of disciplines, they tie the participants to new transnational structures, the religious nationalisms of global Islam (Abu-Lughod 1990, 52).

Here, then, Foucault leads us toward a more complex account of the mutual relationships between power and resistance. As Donald Moore (1998, 351) points out, Scott's theory of infrapolitics combines the hidden transcript metaphor with spatial metaphors, in particular the binary opposition, borrowed from Erving Goffman, between "on-stage" and "off-stage." "Hidden" resistance takes place by assumption in places, such as slave quarters, where it is assumed that "power does not saturate or colonize" subaltern consciousness. No consideration can be given to how spaces and places, and the boundaries between them (such as "public" versus "private"), are constructed through the workings of power relations and challenges to them. Following earlier objections to Scott's idea of "power free" spaces of subaltern autonomy (Starn 1992, 94), Moore also points out that Abu-Lughod's position can be seen as one that Gramsci anticipated in speaking of the "limited and partial autonomy" of subaltern groups, which remain subject to the "activity" of dominant groups even when they are struggling against them (D. Moore 1998, 352). In chapter six of this book, Pessar argues against Scott's view of millenarianism as an exclusively subaltern "subculture" by showing how it is also an element of a mutually constituted dominant culture.

However, as Ortner (1995, 174–75) points out, one positive effect of Scott's drawing attention to "everyday forms of resistance" was to foment debate about which acts might reasonably be characterized as resistance and which not. This led to a series of revisions that highlighted the ambiguity of the acts themselves and the ambivalent subjectivities that tended to accompany relations between actors from dominant or subordinate groups. Not only were practices of "collaboration" often co-present with apparent practices of resistance, but it rapidly became apparent that subaltern groups had to be unpacked into actors differentiated by age, gender, status, and other "subject positions" (Ortner 1995, 175–76).

The "subject position" concept is central to poststructuralist and postmodernist thinking, and here Ortner also highlights the difficulties of Scott's tendency to ascribe a single and fixed identity to subalterns within a preconceived and objective "structural grid of class oppositions" (D. Moore 1998, 350). Identities and subjectification are in part the results of being classified and stigmatized by socially superior others (classifications that subalterns, such as slum-dwellers, can either affirm or reject, but not necessarily *escape*, in the practice of their daily lives). In contemporary societies, cultures of consumerism and "lifestyle" expand the possibilities of individuals' constructing their own identities, although they still tend to do so according to current social ideas about what it takes to earn the "respect" of others, and even according to transnational models of what it means to be "cool" or "modern." Yet possible subject positions remain multiple in most contexts: the same woman can be a woman, a poor woman, a peasant woman, a virtuous mother, a Catholic woman, etc. Subject positions are also situational, with one aspect of identity being appropriate for one context and another aspect, possibly contrasting with or even conflicting with the first, more suited to managing different types of social interactions. A canny and well-connected peasant politician will often find it convenient to become a humble and uneducated son of the village, for example. Yet while all this is useful, Ortner also points out that there is a danger, exemplified by the deconstructionist work of Gayatri Spivak, of "dissolving" the subject as living agent in a social context altogether (Ortner 1995, 184–86). Despite resistance theory's apparent expansion of the definition of "political" action, it ironically did not contain enough politics at the end of the day, for the dominant-subordinate dichotomy often concealed the lively internal politics *within* subaltern populations (Ortner 1995, 177). Closer analysis of the internal politics of subalterns is a major theme of this book.

A defender of Scott's pioneering work could, however, argue that these revisions enriched rather than invalidated a paradigm that served as a useful corrective to previous thinking, complementing other seminal contributions such as the work of E. P. Thompson and U.S. and Brazilian historians of slavery (see Slenes, chapter five). Scott challenged distinctions habitually made between "pre-political" forms of action and supposedly more "effective," politically and socially transformative, types of consciousness. Bringing the politics of marginalized social groups onto the analytical agenda encouraged new thinking about dismissing particular forms of infrapolitical practices as "utopian" and "millenarian," in particular those associated with religion. Many of the practices discussed in the resistance literature deserved recognition and study, even if further analysis showed that some that were too hastily identified as resistance were susceptible to more complex readings. There was considerable value in recognizing unvoiced and subterranean practices of resistance in forms of behavior that had not previously been considered in such terms and in contexts where too much had been assumed about the docility of subaltern groups and the depth of their complicity in their own domination. The work of anthropologists such as Jean Comaroff and John Comaroff (1991) might be accused of exaggerating the real challenge to power relations posed by movements such as that of the Zionist churches in southern Africa, but it highlighted the limitations of trying to think about such contexts in terms of occidental Marxist ideas about what "working-class consciousness" should look like and the yardstick of an equally occidental vision of "revolutionary" politics.

Nevertheless, resistance theory produced its own blind spots, as Gutmann (chapter fifteen) shows in his critique of Scott's account of "lower-class politics." Scott presents the subaltern as a deeply knowing, nonmystified elaborator of rich cultural practices of disguised resistance inhibited from more overt action only by a shrewd assessment of its impracticality. Another important bias was the tendency to ignore "popular movements" that appeared to be reactionary by traditional Left standards, as well as forms of resistance that adopted pacific and nonconfrontational forms for reasons other than fear (see Meyer, chapter eight). In the areas where Mexican Catholics did take up arms in the Cristero rebellion, peasant insurgents seemed to be resisting the apparently more progressive agrarian reform movement in the name of an institution that generally seemed to be on the side of the landlords, the Catholic Church. Yet using the label "progressive" immediately betrays judgments on the part of the observer, judgments not only about what counts as "objective class interest" but also about what peasants should want most out of life (see Knight, conclusion). Since people in apparently similar socioeconomic situations could be found in opposing camps, the Cristiada not only returns us to Fletcher's problem of explaining such differences but also forces us to consider which variables might be most relevant in explaining political differences among subalterns.

From Resistance to Power and "Hegemony"

The most trenchant critiques do not stop at critiquing resistance. Marshall Sahlins attacked an obsession with power as "the latest incarnation of Anthropology's incurable Functionalism" (Sahlins 2002, 20–21). Ortner maintained, "Resistance, even at its most ambiguous, is a reasonably useful category, if only because it highlights the presence and play of power in most forms of relationship and activity" (Ortner 1995, 175). Yet Sahlins found such assertions of the pervasiveness of power in human life disturbing, while Michael Brown (1996, 4) argued that Foucault merely offers us "culture as prison, culture as insane asylum, culture as 'hegemonic domination of the [insert Other of choice].'" This is not the view of Abu-Lughod, whom Brown also cites: she simply points out that most forms of emancipation have their price. In a similar way, Sahlins's huffing and puffing overstates its perfectly reasonable case for not trying to explain *everything* in the world of culture as either a product or expression of power relationships by seeming to turn down the opportunities that Ortner welcomes for looking at how power relationships might enter into the production and transformation of culture.

More recently, Foucauldians have, in fact, challenged the kind of critique that Brown makes of their mentor. Diane Nelson (2005) examines two "biopolitical" interventions by the Guatemalan military state, one the counterinsurgency campaign against indigenous communities of the 1980s and the other the "all out war" against malaria declared by the Guatemalan Health Ministry in 1955. Her first step is a rethinking of indigenous insurgency. By 1988, when it was clear that the guerrillas had lost the armed struggle and split into factions, it was also clear that many indigenous people were now rejecting the shared emphasis of the state, nonindigenous guerrilla leaderships, and their (now decimated) indigenous allies on "modernizing the country" by leaving indigenous culture behind. The war itself, and experiences of racism in the guerrilla ranks, encouraged different visions of liberation, including organization around Maya identity and cultural rights (Nelson 2005, 223). The army followed its scorched-earth policy of the early 1980s with a "development pole" strategy that combined discipline and surveillance with food aid, housing, and health care programs that attracted funds from churches and NGOs as well as foreign governments (223–24). Thus, in place of simple opposition between a pure resisting "people" and a brutal military regime, the war revealed more complex alignments and tensions, putting into question whether "collaboration" was simply the result of fear of death, and it ended up delivering more of the things that indigenous people in Guatemala had previously been demanding, such as schools and health care.

In the case of malaria eradication campaigns, a quintessential expression of deployment of the techniques of "modern government" to regulate the "vitality" of a population, there is another kind of two-sidedness in what is at stake in terms of power. The implementation of the programs required intimate knowledge of the population at the level of households (to ensure the success of medication programs), knowledge that could later be put to life-destroying purposes, but which, in this original context, also fostered a new interest among peasants in collaborating with the state (and with each other), even though some refused to cooperate, as they also did in the case of the guerrillas' call to arms (Nelson 2005, 233).

Malaria eradication was not a wholly humanitarian enterprise. The campaigns made the lowland environment and an indigenous labor force weakened by disease more productive for capitalists. Yet malaria eradication cannot be reduced to that one-dimensional sociopolitical explanation, because hygiene is not simply a matter of social control. Although the campaigns strengthened the state in some ways, they did not undermine the case of coastal labor organizers that improved health care was as necessary as better wages and working conditions (obliging the state and the landlords to continue to murder those organizers). Nelson argues that these two biopolitical processes illustrate the principle that new sources of power and legitimacy are constantly introduced into political processes since human actors are neither totally autonomous subjects nor "docile automatons" but are bound up in relations "through which power always flows in more than one direction," obliging the powerful to concede the legitimacy of some popular demands, even if this is often an unintended consequence of their pursuit of other agendas (2005, 234).

If Foucault can be defended against the critiques of Brown and Sahlins, it is also worth following up Moore's suggestion that Foucault's claim that "resistance is never in a position of exteriority to power" was anticipated by Gramsci's account of the politics of subalternity (D. Moore 1998, 353). In making this argument, Moore draws on William Roseberry's critique of Scott's interpretation of Gramscian "hegemony" as a variant of the "dominant ideology" thesis and Roseberry's alternative proposal that hegemony should be explored "not as a finished and monolithic ideological formation but as a problematic, contested, political process of domination and struggle" (351).

As Kate Crehan (2002, 173) points out, anthropological appropriations of Gramsci often reduce hegemony "solely to the domain of ideas, beliefs, meanings and values." The same is true of Scott's arguments, developed as a critique of the idea that subalterns are afflicted by a "false consciousness" produced by "a dominant or hegemonic ideology" (J. C. Scott 1990, 71). On this basis, Scott distinguishes between "thick" and "thin" concepts of hegemony, the former representing a situation in which subalterns simply accept the legitimacy of rule by the dominant, and the latter a situation in which the subalterns are convinced by the dominant that they are powerless to change the system (72). Scott rejects both types of hegemony on the grounds that subalterns are never mystified by the ideologies propagated by their betters and are therefore always predisposed to "resist" exploitation and domination, yet will not rebel against the system if they judge rebellion too costly an option.

Fletcher (2001, 47) follows Timothy Mitchell (1990) and Charles Tilly (1991) in arguing that an individual-rational-actor model lies at the heart of Scott's arguments on hegemony. Rebellion, in Tilly's words, becomes a matter of "crude individualized rationality," while the propensity of all subaltern populations to rebel, given the opportunity, is guaranteed (and therefore put beyond the need for further explanation) by Scott's assumption that there is always a "unitary and shared" hidden transcript that expresses their inevitable "resistance" (Tilly 1991, 599). Tilly concludes that "such an argument displaces to another level the questions that bedevil theories of hegemonic ideology," such as "how do subalterns construct, share and change their discourses?" (598). These problems do not bedevil Gramsci's account of hegemony. Hegemony is never synonymous with ideology in Gramsci's writings, since it "always involves *practical activity*, and the social relations that produce inequality, as well as the ideas by which that inequality is justified, explained, normalized, and so on" (Crehan 2002, 174, emphasis added).

Although Gramsci subscribed to the Marxist thesis of "determination by the economic base in the last instance," he did not think it possible to understand the concrete realities of a country without taking into account a range of social, cultural, political, and institutional variables, all products of a particular history. In place of a simple "dominant-subaltern" binary opposition, he offers us "historical blocs" of differentiated elite groups (such as landowners, merchants, and the officer corps) and institutions (such as the Catholic Church) confronting equally differentiated "popular" classes. Gramsci urged communist militants to strive to understand the "feelings" of the "popular element" in order to understand how people *lived* their class situations, how differences within and between subalterns reflected the impacts of particular forms of domination and ex ploitation on their subjectivities and "contradictory consciousness" (Crehan 2002, 206–7; also see Gutmann, chapter fifteen). Although Gramsci was as antagonistic to "fanaticism" as any Latin American revolutionary, he had no doubt, for example, about the need to understand the way rural people drew on religious values and symbols in the construction of their material and social lives (see Pessar, chapter six). He was equally certain that even subaltern practices that sought to change the social order of things would never be sufficient to create a new society without the guidance of the party and its intellectuals. Yet these practices would have an impact on how rule was accomplished — through the existing hegemony — by affecting the overall balance of social and political forces.

Gramsci's view was that although the actions of subaltern groups influenced the state of power relations, their practices of resistance could not be fully autonomous from those relations. This brings us back to Roseberry's reading of Gramsci, which Pessar (chapter six) and Margarita Zárate (chapter ten) employ in their analyses. Roseberry (1994, 363) argued that "the dominated" are obliged to use the same language as the dominant for their demands to be heard and that this has material consequences. Yet against Scott's treatment of the languages of power and contestation as fixed "scripts" in what Donald Moore (1998, 351) describes as a "static theater of resistance," Roseberry suggested that hegemony should be used to understand struggle rather than consent: "What hegemony constructs, then, is not a shared ideology but a common material and meaningful framework for living through, talking about, and acting on social orders characterized by domination" (Roseberry 1994, 361).

Changing Historical Contexts

This book offers a wide range of historical case studies, and as John Monteiro shows in chapter one, some processes studied in contemporary contexts, such as ethnogenesis, are also relevant to the past. Nevertheless, historical change is important. A recurrent theme in chapters on contemporary situations is the extent to which neoliberalism has reconfigured the possibilities open to "resistance movements" since the 1980s.

Nestor García Canclini (1995b) has argued that neoliberal globalization has brought about a "cultural reorganization of power" in the region that means that power now works more "obliquely" than vertically. One facet of this is the commodification of the production of personhood in contemporary market society. Livio Sansone (2004), for example, has shown how young black men from the poorest districts of Salvador, Bahia, reject the low-paid menial jobs accepted by their fathers, are less likely to seek solace in Afro-Brazilian religion, and less deferential to their white social superiors, but still find ways of participating in a globalized black consumer culture. He argues, however, that their everyday struggles for recognition as "persons" through consumption do not foster an "oppositional consciousness" in relation to dominant social groups (see Schell, chapter nine). As Maria Gabriela Hita shows in chapter thirteen, this reading does not fit all poor young black people in the city, but ambiguities in the way "oppositional consciousness" is expressed do reflect the role of the market in construction of the self.

Many Brazilians and Mexicans do participate in explicitly antineoliberal social movements, including place-based movements supported by transnational activist networks against development projects involving foreign corporations backed by the local state. The people of Atenco, in the state of Mexico, for example, won a famous victory against the expropriation of their farmlands to build a new airport for Mexico City (Stolle-McAllister 2005). Yet the state of Mexico is also one of the parts of the country where lynchings are most common (Vilas 2002). Enraged "self-help" popular justice may be a way of resisting the socially corrosive effects of neoliberalism and defending "community integrity," but it reflects the oblique power effects of living in a deteriorating economic and social situation when the official justice and police systems principally serve the defense of privilege and victimize less powerful citizens.

Another major area of debate concerns the potentially demobilizing effects of neoliberal styles of government. What Nikolas Rose (1999) termed "government at a distance" advanced substantially in Latin America in the 1990s, with transfers of administrative functions and budgetary resources to local government and a heightened role for nongovernmental organizations. Some social movements have been transformed into NGOs, and their leaderships professionalized or incorporated into government, leading analysts such as Joe Foweraker (2001) to argue that "democratization" diminished the force of social movements during the 1990s. From that perspective, neoliberal "inclusion" of the poor and ethnic minorities defuses resistance by creating empty public rituals of participation accompanied by backstage cooptation and continuing political clientelism and hidden behind the rhetoric of "recognizing the capacity of the disadvantaged to exercise their citizenship." Yet such an assessment seems too pessimistic. Even if "socially progressive" NGO interventions often have ambiguous effects, as highlighted by de la Peña, Luis Nicolau Parés, and Hita in this book, and some NGOs and governments actively seek to promote a society of self-reliant, self-disciplining, neoliberal citizens, such projects seem to produce unintended consequences (resistances) that militate against those citizens becoming completely docile, particularly in conditions of extreme social inequality (Postero 2006). To return to Nelson's point, neoliberal governmentality projects seldom produce *simply* the effects that their architects desired.

Nevertheless, although neoliberal ideas about citizen "participation" and "empowerment" offer spaces for subalterns to gain new influence in the public sphere, the potential trap, as Charles Hale (2002) points out in discussing neoliberal multiculturalism, is that institutionalization of these spaces creates a boundary that separates movements and demands that are acceptable from those that are "too radical." As opportunities to "participate" increase, including opportunities for former social movement activists to work within government programs, more people opt to work within that boundary rather than beyond it: as Zárate shows in chapter ten, even "radical" movements now worry about questions of "legality." The logic of neoliberal governmentality is to canalize resistance into manageable channels and to limit the challenge that demands for rights and recognition present to the most politically influential capitalist interests. Yet we still have much to learn about how this works out in practice. As Helga Baitenmann shows in chapter fourteen, the new agrarian tribunals created by President Salinas's neoliberal "reform" of Mexico's landholdings have enabled some subalterns to use new state institutions to contest past state actions, thereby extending the state's role in agrarian affairs after the official end of land redistribution, much of it based on disputes between peasants rather than direct conflicts between peasants and large landowners. Contributions to this book suggest, however, that the artifices of neoliberal governmentality are far from extinguishing popular challenges to the current order of things, despite the fact that where artifices fail, state terror is still an option, as Gutmann reminds us in his discussion of the Popular Assembly of the Peoples of Oaxaca in chapter fifteen. Yet neoliberal artifices do complicate subaltern politics and often, as Parés suggests in chapter seven, oblige us to ask new questions about where we are mostly likely to find practices of resistance that might unsettle power relations.

All contributors to this book agree that historically contextualized analyses that tackle inconvenient facts, such as the way some subalterns ally with the "enemy" while others are rebelling (see Viqueira, chapter three), are essential for providing a response to such questions. Different chapters address the foundational works of resistance theory discussed in this introduction in different ways. Some build on insights that the original wave of resistance theory produced, others largely reject that framework; some address gaps in past work, and others embed the question of resistance within broader analyses of power, hegemony, and contentious politics in order to refocus debate. Yet throughout, the aim of understanding "subaltern politics" remains central. In his concluding discussion, Knight offers some general reflections on how resistance, as a concept, might rise in our conceptual hierarchy to achieve the status of those "big, old concepts," such as power and hegemony, whose status he sees as "bolstered by useful theoretical and practical knowledge." The most productive readings even of "big old" concepts are sometimes still subject to dispute, as I suggested in the case of hegemony, but whatever the ultimate fate of resistance, this book shows that "useful theoretical and practical knowledge" can still emerge from thinking about it, providing that we recognize its limits as well as its possibilities as a force in history and the way that history itself changes the conditions under which subaltern struggles take place.

Brazil and Mexico as a Comparative Framework

The final question that I should address is how and why we have attempted to compare Brazil and Mexico in this project. This is not an attempt to explore how common structural variables relate to each other in different national contexts of the kind that characterized efforts to explain the occurrence or nonoccurrence of agrarian revolutions in literature that preceded the resistance boom, such as that of Jeffery Paige (1975). Nor do we adopt the quantitative multivariate analysis paradigm used by some historians and social scientists to explore questions regarding the impact of economic cycles on social mobilization and political conflict through systematic intercountry comparisons (Tarrow 1996, 877). Our approach is to use case studies to advance theory-building in a way that contributes to the goals of comparative analysis (Lijphart 1971).

Anthropology's method is always implicitly "comparative" in this sense. Anthropologists question the universality of the taken-for-granted assumptions of their societies by holding them up to the mirror of "the other." That is, anthropologists think about what they observe with other possible instances in mind, favoring a view of society and culture as "constructs" reflecting the diversity of humankind. The historical framework of this book reminds us that even the recent past was often different: today's "indigenous people" may be yesterday's "peasants," for example, because claiming an indigenous identity has become a more effective way of capturing resources (see de la Peña, chapter eleven).

Historically and ethnographically grounded case studies offer the virtue of contextualization that is absent from theorizing that assumes, for example, that the experience of being a slave is the same everywhere: as Slenes shows in chapter five, those experiences are not necessarily the same, even in a single region at a single point in time. We recognize that Brazil and Mexico do not exhaust all the variations that Latin America offers with regard, for example, to ideas about "race," *mestizaje*, and "indigeneity." Much of this book highlights the importance of taking into account transnational and transregional processes in all historical periods. Thinking outside conventional national frames and divisions between "North" America and "Latin" America is likely to provide further insights into "hidden histories" of subaltern action (see, for example, Shukla and Tinsman 2007). Nevertheless, there are important cultural, social, and political similarities across Latin America, and by taking examples from two countries that take us from the colonial period to the present day, our project considers similarities and differences to enhance the theory-building potential of the case study approach by drawing the contributors into thinking about how their analyses might play out in the other context.

Brazil and Mexico are both profoundly unequal societies built on foundations of colonial conquest and enslavement. This is the frame in which social movement activists and engaged academics talk of the resistance of indigenous and black people to domination and exploitation, one of the connotations, for example, of the Quilombola movement in Brazil, discussed by Leite in chapter twelve. Yet we can see another kind of resistance in the historical reproduction of cultures and identities with roots in aboriginal America or Africa: resistance as conservation and temporal continuity, a conservative rather than revolutionary process (see Pessar, Parés, and de la Peña, chapters six, seven, and eleven). Although our discussion is not restricted to historical actors who see themselves as "indigenous" or "afro-descendent," it is appropriate that such actors occupy a prominent place in our discussions.

Nevertheless, differences between the countries also have a direct bearing on debates about resistance, society, and politics. Brazil achieved its independence in 1822 as an empire still ruled by a member of the Portuguese royal family and dominated by slave-owning landed classes. The Muslim slave revolt of 1832 in Salvador (Reis 2003) was one of the consequences of the slave owners' ability to resist the extension to society as a whole of the liberal principles to which the empire's constitution paid lip service (see also Slenes, chapter five). Even after British pressure sufficiently strengthened the hand of Brazilian abolitionists to end the Atlantic trade in 1850, it took thirty-eight years for the emancipation of existing slaves to be completed, and freedom did not necessarily imply a great deal of positive change in the lives of rural plantation workers. Slavery had enduring effects on Brazilian society: it affected the status of free lower-class Brazilians, creating a society in which all depended on the "favor" of their social superiors (Schwarz 1992).

Yet despite the legacies of slavery, society in colonial or independent Brazil cannot be reduced to a two-class model of homogeneous agrarian elites dominating an equally homogeneous subaltern population, leaving aside the massive immigrations that made Italian, German, and Japanese Brazilians important constituents of the national population. Not all colonial subalterns were slaves, or former slaves, or "blacks" or mulattos. Many poor backlands people saw themselves as "whites" or as *mestiços* produced by race mixing between the aboriginal inhabitants of Brazil and Europeans. The popular notion that Brazil's Indians largely "died out" or vanished through race mixing will not get us very far in understanding Brazilian history, as Monteiro's and Carvalho's chapters demonstrate. A degree of social mobility was possible, especially for mulattos who followed a "whitening strategy" that affirmed elite values. From the point of view of resistance theory, a crucial problem seems to be that subalterns often seemed to be "collaborating" rather than resisting, although our contributors also show that this distinction is seldom as simple as it seems.

Similar issues emerge in the chapters on Mexico by Castro Gutiérrez and Juan Pedro Viqueira. Yet some differences are striking. Despite the growth of landed estates, the Spanish Crown's prohibition of indigenous enslavement and desire to exploit indigenous people as tribute payers to the greater benefit of the empire entailed a degree of "protection" for the colonially created "indigenous community" that left an indelible mark on Mexican national history. Although Mexico's population is as diverse in its origins as that of Brazil, and it is now becoming politically attractive to valorize the contribution of once-stigmatized immigrants from China and Japan, the country has the largest absolute number of citizens professing an indigenous identity of any Latin American country, despite the efforts of nineteenth-century liberal reformers to abolish the Indian corporate community by denying it legal personality and privatizing communal lands. Liberal efforts to create a new society of individual property-owning (and property-less) citizens "equal before the law" were followed by equally determined efforts on the part of the postrevolutionary state to encourage indigenous people to assimilate culturally into a mestizo national mainstream through land reform and the adoption of "peasant" class identities (Boyer 2003). Why these projects did not fully achieve their goals is a key issue in Mexican history.

The law was also used to limit the access to land of Brazil's former slaves. Brazil has also deployed notions of "mixing" in the building of national identity through a "myth of racial democracy," a myth now challenged by black movements to a degree that has brought significant changes in government policies, even though many Afro-Brazilians continue to reject racialized politics. Yet the absence of a comprehensive land reform in Brazil is a major point of contrast in the modern histories of the two countries. At the end of the first decade of the twenty-first century, it is tempting to see an incipient divergence of historical trajectories, with Brazil increasingly seen as a "rising power" on the world economic and diplomatic stage, and Mexico, with an escalating drug war and an economy more dependent on the United States, seemingly less well placed to face the future. There are also differences in the quality of the democracies that followed the end of military rule in Brazil and the continuous, seventy-year rule of the Institutional Revolutionary Party in Mexico. Yet similarities in political cultures and practices, not to mention underlying social problems, remain striking, and it would be a mistake to assume that authoritarianism has entirely disappeared from democratic Brazil. As this book demonstrates, the affinities between the cases make the detailed analysis of differences and their implications so instructive.

*   *   *

This book is divided into three parts. The first presents historical studies from the sixteenth century through the nineteenth. The second focuses on religious institutions and movements, so often relegated to epiphenomenal status in relation to class oppositions or treated as simply "reactionary," combining historical and contemporary perspectives. The third part focuses on more contemporary, ethnography-based studies. Each part has its own short introduction, and our discussions produced interesting dialogues between the chapters, across the divisions between sections, periods, countries, and disciplines. Nevertheless, some readers may prefer to read Knight's concluding overview before delving into the more detailed studies.

PART ONE

Resistance and the Creation of New Worlds

These chapters shed new light on the kinds of historical agency that indigenous and Afro-descendent people exercised within colonial societies. Leading away from simple assumptions about necessary antagonisms between subalterns and their masters and the pragmatics of overt rebellion versus hidden transcripts of resistance, these chapters seek to understand why some subalterns collaborate while others do not, what shapes these choices and the forms of consciousness that the actors develop at particular times and in particular places, and what shapes the varying relations between subaltern and superordinate actors in different contexts. Answering these questions is central to appreciating the important contributions that Amerindians and Africans made to the shaping of these new worlds.

John Monteiro explores how postinvasion ethnogenesis reflected conflicts within and among indigenous people rather than simply their struggles to build meaningful new identities and ways of life in an environment radically reshaped by colonial structures of domination. He highlights a variety of ways indigenous polities became engaged in the colonial project, as refugees or as allies or enemies of Europeans, frequently borrowing from the colonists' own cultural repertoire. Far from being a symptom of culture loss and incipient extinction, Monteiro suggests that these strategies gave force and meaning to the efforts of native societies and their leaders to remain actors on the colonial stage, whether the outcome of the efforts was the appearance of a titled indigenous dynasty in Portuguese America or a native point of view in which taking on the conqueror's religion, technology, and consumption was a means to domesticate and control the European other. As Luis Nicolau Parés shows in chapter seven, this latter argument has also been made by Andrew Apter in regard to

Afro-Brazilians, whose mimesis of elements of Catholicism in Candomblé could be seen as an embodied way of apprehending and controlling the spiritual universe of the slave masters.

Felipe Castro also emphasizes the need to abandon simplistic stories of the sustained resistance of indigenous Mexicans against their colonial masters, important as those stories are to the contemporary indigenous autonomy movement. His discussion parallels Monteiro's in its inclusion of indigenous actors who advanced their own interests within the colonial order, but he focuses particularly on achieving a deeper understanding of the logic of various forms of riot, protest, and rebellion that, even when ritualized and symbolic, nevertheless expressed the undercurrents of indignation and irritation that lay beneath a colonial environment that appeared relatively tranquil.

Juan Pedro Viqueira's discussion starts from a position of strong skepticism about the Manichean division between homogeneous elites and subalterns that he accuses resistance models of propagating. Taking the Cancuc rebellion in early eighteenth-century Chiapas as a best-case scenario demonstrating history as a simple struggle between Indians and Spaniards, Viqueira shows the complexity of the divisions within Chiapas's indigenous population, emphasizing the need to understand the not always edifying conduct of both the rebels and the range of indigenous actors who opposed the rebellion. Although these sources do not enable us to determine motivations beyond a doubt, they offer insights into rarely recognized aspects of violent confrontation, such as the way that some rebels sought to moderate the suffering of the enemies now under their power.

Marcus de Carvalho's study of the Cabanada rebellion and the ensuing resistance of an armed community led by the "slave thief" Vicente de Paula is set in the forest zone of the frontier of the Brazilian states of Pernambuco and Alagoas more than a century after the Cancuc rebellion. Here we are dealing with "popular" rebels whose access to land depended on clientelistic networks of landowners, while the Indians of Jacuípe, who became the most "ferocious" of the Cabanos, had a long history of collaboration. Yet the transformation of local political arrangements after the exile of Emperor Pedro I brought poor peasants, Indians, and escaped slaves together, making them a rebel community. Although the rebels fought against dispossession by an expanding plantation economy, Carvalho shows that the movement did not represent a withdrawal from society but a continuing effort to change the wider political system. There is a clear parallel between the end of a colonial "pact" in the Bourbon period in Mexico and the war fought by the "people of the forests" against the "Jacobins" who deposed Pedro I.

Robert Slenes explores the political meanings of a plotted slave rebellion discovered by the authorities in 1848 in the state of Rio de Janeiro. Making a broader argument that highlights the necessity of talking about plural "slave societies" in Brazil, he shows how prospects for obtaining freedom, and a social mobility that often involved former slaves' becoming slave owners, differed between small and large plantations in the Brazilian southeast, while relations between slaves and masters in the small holdings and the social world of freed slaves contributed to later developments that dampened hopes for nonracialized citizenship. Although he accepts that Brazilian conditions could promote social divisions within the slave quarters and between slaves and free Afro-Brazilians, he argues that the large plantations of the southeast never offered the same prospects for freedom as the smaller farms, and that in this region rebellious slave movements did not seem to reflect strong divisions found in Bahia between Africans and creoles and slaves and *libertos* (freed slaves). As in Bahia, however, enslaved Africans used their African cultural heritage in adapting to the new conditions they faced: cults of affliction that drew on a widely diffused African cultural patrimony not only served to build a common identity and a matrix of social organization for the enslaved population but also reproduced the governance functions that population had possessed in Africa, leading Slenes to suggest that organized slave rebellions were part of conscious subaltern intervention in the politics of the abolition of the Atlantic trade, and ultimately slavery itself.

CHAPTER ONE

Rethinking Amerindian Resistance and Persistence in Colonial Portuguese America

JOHN MONTEIRO

During his "Philosophical Journey" through Amazonia in the 1780s, Alexandre Rodrigues Ferreira spent time in Monte Alegre and Santarém, Indian towns noted for their ceramics. His account of the *cuias* (ceramic bowls) made by the Indian women remains interesting for its detailed description of production techniques and for the evidence it provides of the volume of bowls produced. Europeans purchased most of the production: "The Indian women who know that the whites will buy them [the *cuias*], make sure to perfect them."[1] But Ferreira seemed particularly interested in one important detail: the Indian women reserved part of their production for their own use, with not only material but symbolic implications:

> The *cuias* are the Indians' plates, cups, and all of their tableware. Each of them reserves one for the Principal [headman] from which to drink water or wine when he visits . . . The bowl is distinguished by a shell ornament, attached by a ball of wax covered with beads, and a *muiraquitã* [a sacred green stone in the form of an animal] on top, which serves as a handle for the Principal. They offer it to him on a tray made from patauá palm shafts. No matter how hard I tried to buy one of these, it was not possible, so great is the esteem that they hold for the bowl from which their chief drinks. (Ferreira 1974, 36–39)

What does this exchange tell us about indigenous resistance in colonial Portuguese America? Ferreira was frustrated by the women's refusal to hand over an object of great ethnographic interest, even for a sum of money. Producing Portuguese-style ceramics for the market, the Indian women appeared to be responding to the economic reforms introduced by the Marquis of Pombal some thirty years earlier. But the persistence of distinctive cultural practices left the uncomfortable feeling that the Indians had something to say about the terms of their own transformation.

Based in part on documentary research and in part on the discussion of contributions to the literature on Indians in colonial Brazil, this chapter traces some of the ways scholars have treated the issue of resistance. One feature that the Brazilian case shares with other parts of the Americas is the ambiguous meanings that resistance acquired in the sixteenth century and the seventeenth. The great Jesuit missionary Antônio Vieira captured that ambiguity in one of his diatribes against Indian slavery in Maranhão, when he contrasted the Indians' lack of resistance to epidemic disease with their readiness to flee from plantations and mission villages (compare with Alencastro 2000, 138). While the problem of population decline invites comparison with other parts of the Americas, another part of Vieira's observations points in a different direction: he explicitly compares Amerindian and African slavery, favoring the latter, a point not lost on generations of historians who have focused attention on African slavery and resistance while largely ignoring the indigenous presence, as if the Amerindians had been totally wiped out. Indigenous peoples indeed survived, and although severe population loss had significant effects on territorial configurations, identity claims and power relations had an important influence on conditions for contesting colonial rule. Furthermore, as Stuart Schwartz and Hal Langfur argue in a provocative article, Amerindian and African histories remain intrinsically bound and demand to be studied together (Schwartz and Langfur 2005).

Another issue worth mentioning is the strong potential for dialogue between processes highlighted in the study of contemporary communities and similar processes taking place during the colonial period. First, contemporary "ethnogenesis"—an outcome of identity politics and their impact on guarantees to land and other rights, discussed by de la Peña for the Mexican case in chapter eleven—has important colonial precursors. Second, recent anthropological studies of myth and history have focused on the "domestication of the Other," part of a larger perspective on how indigenous peoples selectively process their relations with powerful outside forces, sometimes with "subversive" implications. For the colonial period, studies on indigenous uses of Catholicism—and of Calvinism, in the short period of Dutch occupation in the seventeenth century—have benefited from this perspective. Third, indigenous participation in migratory movements, labor markets, urban life, the military, and other activities in which indigenous people do not usually appear relevant also raises questions about the boundary between resistance and other actions involving ethnic markers. Finally, Afro-Brazilian claims on *quilombo* territories, discussed by Ilka Boaventura Leite in chapter twelve, often involve strategies pioneered by indigenous communities in their struggles for land (Arruti 2006; J. H. French 2009). This invites scholars to look into the colonial past for clues to the historical relations between Africans and Indians. Often appearing submerged in national narratives on slavery, *mestiçagem*, and social exclusion, the significance of this surprisingly neglected topic is apparent from Marcus de Carvalho's discussion in chapter four.

Indigenous History and Resistance in Lowland South America

The problem of resistance has gained ground in studies of indigenous peoples in Brazil over the past twenty-five years, accompanying important changes in the ways Indians are perceived in the public sphere. For the better part of five centuries, themes of destruction and disappearance predominated among social thinkers and policymakers alike. A long sequence of colonial, imperial, and federal legislation treated indigenous peoples as transitional entities, whose cultural distinctiveness would inevitably be lost in the processes of "civilization," "acculturation," or "assimilation." Even social anthropologists, who encountered what they considered practically untouched "primitive societies" in remote areas, tended toward pessimism about the effects of "contact." For the better part of the twentieth century, anthropological writing alternated between the scientific study of exotic social universes and melancholic descriptions of their destruction.

While this duality in work on indigenous peoples in Brazil goes back at least as far as Curt Nimuendaju, by the 1940s postcontact dilemmas occupied a large part of the anthropological agenda. North American–style acculturation studies provided a perspective on culture change directly associated with interethnic contact, but also drew criticism from Brazilian anthropologists for failing to recognize conflict (R. C. Oliveira 1964) or the role of state policy in imposing transformations (Ribeiro 1970). They showed little regard for indigenous perspectives, as their focus was on how contact undermined cultural integrity.

It was from a position criticizing the lack of attention to indigenous logics that Florestan Fernandes contributed a pioneering study of Amerindian resistance. Author of several studies on Tupinambá society, including a remarkable monograph on indigenous warfare, Fernandes (1975, 127–29) asserted that in order to understand the logic of indigenous reactions to innovations imposed from the outside it was necessary to "rotate perspective" by deliberately eliding the contact situation in order to grasp the social, political, and symbolic organization of indigenous societies in their own right. This method informed his essay on "the Tupi reaction to conquest" (F. Fernandes 1975, 11–32), which drew from historical evidence but also inferred much from his own structural-functionalist theoretical model of Tupi social organization, warfare, and religion. Fernandes classified resistance into two types: outright rebellion, doomed to failure since the Portuguese military reaction would lead to the disarticulation of Tupi social organization, and mass flight to areas well away from the presence of Europeans, where the Tupi could restore the "equilibrium" needed to reproduce a vigorous society, according to his model.

This account suggested that the survival of Amerindian societies depended on isolation and autonomy. The contrast between fiercely independent, "authentic" Indians and the dependent, culturally impoverished remains of once vigorous societies became commonplace in government policy, as well as in social and scientific thought since the mid-nineteenth century, even if a few prominent thinkers, notably Darcy Ribeiro (1970), underscored the intrinsic relation between misguided policy and the destruction of indigenous societies.

By the late 1970s, the growth of a broad-based Indian rights movement gave rise to a major paradigm shift. A new "Indian history," first developed to support Indian land claims with historical evidence of occupation, subsequently became an academic field in its own right. Current approaches are illustrated by two recent books of note, *Pacificando o branco* (Albert and Ramos 2002) and *Time and Memory in Indigenous Amazonia* (Fausto and Heckenberger 2007), building on pioneer collections such as *Rethinking History and Myth* (Hill 1988) and *História dos Índios no Brasil* (Cunha 1992), as well as articles on Brazil in the *Cambridge History of the Native Peoples of the Americas* (Salomon and Schwartz 1999). In fusing pro-Indian activism with academic research, anthropologists drew inspiration both from the struggles of indigenous peoples and from a growing body of literature that reinscribed history within ethnological research.

In her foreword to *Time and Memory in Indigenous Amazonia*, Manuela Carneiro da Cunha provides a synthesis of the main contributions. Referring to *Pacificando o branco*, she notes: "The authors endeavored to look into the modalities by which different Amazonian indigenous groups captured the invasion that befell them. Our historiography renders the events as their defeat: their narrative renders the same events as their labor of domesticating, of pacifying us together with our germs and our commodities." She emphasizes the important theoretical contribution of Eduardo Viveiros de Castro, who, rethinking Lévi-Strauss's idea about the Amerindians' "openness to the Other," focuses on how different groups consider their relation to Others within a framework of predation, which, according to Carneiro da Cunha, "translates into the regimentation of alterity for the production of identity, assimilating one's enemy as a mode of reproduction." This approach affords new insights into warfare, cannibalism, and other themes treated by Florestan Fernandes, and new readings of indigenous perceptions of colonial domination. "Predation, as Eduardo Viveiros de Castro has eloquently shown, is the basic, given, relational mode. Given such assumptions, conversion to Catholicism can be conversely seen by neophytes as predation on other people's God(s) . . . what the French called civilizing the native, can be reciprocally seen as the appropriation of foreign practices . . . Acculturation can thus be understood as a mode of social reproduction, as a kind of endogenous transformation" (Fausto and Heckenberger 2007, xi–xiv).

While adopting Fernandes's suggestion to rotate perspectives, anthropologists such as Carneiro da Cunha and Viveiros de Castro add history to their approach. For Fernandes, the Tupinambá had to reject all things foreign in order to restore their tribal equilibrium, while according to this alternative understanding, they had to constantly *change* by seeking to capture and domesticate the Other's symbols, material objects, technology, religion, and discourse in order to *remain* Tupinambá.

Identity Politics and Ethnogenesis in the Colonial Period

Over the past decades, ethnohistorical research has proved that the impact of European colonization can no longer be summed up as the decimation of native populations and the destruction of indigenous societies. This impact also produced "new peoples and new *kinds* of peoples," as Stuart Schwartz and Frank Salomon argue (1999, 441). According to Guillaume Boccara (1999), whose work brings new insights to the study of Mapuche ethnogenesis on the southern frontier of Spanish America, "scholars are widely recognizing the constructed nature of social formations and identities, as well as the dynamic character of cultures and 'traditions.'" Boccara replaces the radical opposition between precontact "purity" and postcontact "contamination" with a perspective that underscores continuous processes of cultural innovation through "ethnogenesis," "ethnification," and "*mestizaje*." For Neil Whitehead, these processes include a broad spectrum of possibilities "ranging from the total extinction of some ethnic formations to the endurance and invention of others" (Whitehead 1993, 285).

In these new perspectives, the term "ethnogenesis" captures the articulation between endogenous patterns of change and exogenous forces introduced by European expansion. Jonathan Hill (1996) argues that the term invokes the "simultaneously cultural and political struggles" deployed by colonial-era native actors in their efforts "to create enduring identities in general contexts of radical change and discontinuity." We can no longer treat indigenous societies as local, isolated cultures, but at the same time we cannot understand "specific forms of ethnogenesis" only in terms of relations between subaltern peoples and structures of domination and power: "In addition to a people's struggle to exist within a general history characterized by radical, often imposed changes, ethnogenesis is grounded in the conflicts within and among indigenous and Afro-American peoples" (Hill 1996, 1–2).

Analogous to Boccara's approach, the work of Gary Clayton Anderson (1999) underscores indigenous agency and cultural creativity in responses to the European presence along the northern frontier of Spanish America. Ethnogenesis is rooted in the process by which "bands altered themselves culturally to forge unity with other groups, abandoning languages, social practices, and even economic processes to meet the needs of the new order." This involved integrating people from distinct groups (such as captives) as well as the incorporation and "reinvention" of European goods, technologies, and practices, including trade and the use of horses. Anderson also discusses the problem of the "distribution of resources," showing how social hierarchies developed through the concentration of power and wealth in segments such as elders and chiefs.

While these perspectives emphasize the agency of native actors, the literature is less clear in defining which social units of analysis are relevant to the periods before and after the arrival of Europeans. Viveiros de Castro points out this problem in his critique of *História dos Índios no Brasil*, asserting that "the freezing and isolation of ethnic groups is a post-Columbian sociological and cognitive phenomenon" (1993, 32). The designation of ethnic names "resulted from a complete misunderstanding of the ethnic and political dynamics of the Amerindian *socius*," grounded in a "substantivist and national-territorialist" conception of society, that strayed far from the "relative and relational nature of indigenous ethnic, political, and social categories" (32). The ethnohistorical mosaic of fixed ethnic groups that covers the postcontact map of Brazil stands in stark contrast to a constantly shifting precolonial configuration.

But while the essentialization of ethnic categories reflected an ethnocentric misconception, it was not entirely free of ulterior motives. The classification of subordinated peoples into naturalized and fixed categories was a necessary step in the articulation of colonial domination, as Nicholas Dirks reminds us (1996, xi). Labeled "ethnification" by Boccara and "tribalization" by other authors, this operation not only proved a fundamental tool of colonial statecraft, but also established parameters for the ethnic survival of indigenous peoples, who began to deploy a broad variety of strategies within the constraints dictated by colonial rule. This has encouraged scholars to treat the confused tangle of historical ethnic names with greater caution and precision, especially when tracing the relationship between precolonial social forms and the social units that appear in the early sources, written after the settlement of European, African, and Asian peoples in the Americas.

An intrinsic relation therefore exists between the ethnic and social classifications imposed by the colonial order and the formation of ethnic identities. Indigenous identities developed both in relation to precolonial origins and in relation to other ethnic and social categories that were developing concomitantly in the colonial context. In Portuguese America, this differentiation intensified with the expansion of the Atlantic slave trade and the growth of an Afro-Brazilian population.

New ethnopolitical configurations grew out of the different ways indigenous polities became engaged in the colonial project, whether as allies, enemies, or refugees. Many groups sought to maintain a measure of political autonomy through "collaboration" with advancing colonial powers. "Ethnic soldiering" became a widespread phenomenon, in which specific groups carried out colonial military actions against indigenous enemies, European invaders, and runaway slave communities (Whitehead 1990). Other groups specialized in supplying indigenous slaves to Europeans as part of far-reaching trade networks involving highly prized European commodities, especially iron, firearms, and distilled liquors (Farage 1991; J. Monteiro 1994; J. Fernandes 2004). Yet ethnic soldiering or supplying slaves involved far more than the European manipulation of precolonial rivalries between ethnic groups, as early Brazilian historians would have us believe: these processes often generated new sociopolitical units.

Boccara (1999), for example, traces the transformation of Mapuche warfare from its precolonial form to the postcontact *maloca*, a raiding enterprise that sought to acquire European goods and strengthened the role of chiefs who began to wield "a new type of power." This shift in warlike activities also involved constant attacks against groups allied to the Spanish, who became an important source for horses. The Mapuche "reinvented" themselves in a paradoxical manner, exploiting their peculiar relationship with the colonial sphere in order to remain effectively independent from colonial rule.

In Brazil, much has been written about Tupinambá warfare, but practically nothing has been written about its transformation. Fernandes's study of the "social function of warfare" in the early colonial setting was never developed, since other priorities took precedence. Early colonial documents point towards the reconfiguration of indigenous warfare along the coast, including native testimonies concerned with the increasing sale of war captives, as well as evidence showing the specialization of some groups in supplying slaves directly to the Europeans. Later, situations analogous to the Mapuche example emerged. The cases of the Guaikuru and Paiaguá along the western frontier of Portuguese America in the late seventeenth century and the eighteenth century are well documented, while groups of "corsairs"—such as the Mura along the Madeira River or the Avá-Canoeiro along the Tocantíns—made frequent raids on the Portuguese and their indigenous allies (Vangelista 1991; Amoroso 1992; Sweet 1992). Groups that were of little significance—or even nonexistent—in precolonial times achieved prominence in the colonial context (Whitehead 1993, 297).

During the sixteenth century and the seventeenth, a long sequence of wars contributed to the reshuffling of indigenous polities into fixed ethnic groups: the Tamoio war, wars prosecuted by Mem de Sá in Bahia and Rio de Janeiro, the conquests of Paraíba, Maranhão, and Pará, the Luso-Dutch war, the group of conflicts known as the Guerra dos Bárbaros (War of the Barbarous Indians), and the destruction of the quilombo of Palmares, just to mention the most prominent episodes (Hemming 1978; Puntoni 2002). Potiguar warriors, tough adversaries in the conquest of Rio Grande do Norte, not only later served the Portuguese in fighting against the Aimoré Indians of Porto Seguro and Ilhéus but even fought on the other side of the Atlantic—and on both sides of the conflict—in the Angolan theater of the Luso-Dutch wars (Boxer 1952). Although the literature often paints a stable picture of alliances and adversaries based on pairings of enemy groups— as in the immemorial hatreds between the Tupinambá and the Tupinikin, the Potiguar and the Caeté, or the Botocudo and the Puri—colonial documents offer abundant examples of groups shifting from one alliance to another and adjusting to conditions.

Ethnic names thus took on a relational and historically specific character. The pair of enemies, the Tamoio and the Tememinó, that emerged in sixteenth-century conflicts illustrates this process, as the former adopted a name meaning "ancestors" while the latter means, roughly, grandchild. Such references to kinship or generational relationships developed throughout Portuguese America, especially among Tupi and Guarani groups who often referred to other Tupi and Guarani speakers as relatives. It appears that the term "Tamoio" emerged within the Tupinambá revolt that spread along the coast between the southern captaincies of São Vicente and Rio de Janeiro in the late 1540s. This movement gained strength with the arrival of the French in the mid-1550s, establishing a rival European colony in Guanabara Bay that was bolstered by alliances with the Tupinambá. Significantly, in Hans Staden's (1874) account, written at the beginning of the conflict, there is no mention of either term, "Tamoio" or "Tememinó." Staden's contemporary Jean de Léry (1994, 147– 48) refers to the Tupinambá's northern enemies not as Tememinó but as Maracajá, "wildcats." This name gave way to Tememinó at some point, the new name becoming consolidated once the "Indians of the Cat" sealed a longstanding alliance with the Portuguese. After fighting alongside the Portuguese to oust the French from Guanabara and defeat the Tamoio, the Tememinó received rewards in lands and honorific titles, their leaders maintaining the privileges originally granted to D. Martim Afonso Araribóia well into the eighteenth century (M. R. C. Almeida 2003, 150–67).

Sixteenth-century and seventeenth-century sources reveal a tension between the attempt to establish a unified category for the coastal Tupi (initially in opposition to the Tapuia) and the increasingly fragmented division of the coastal peoples into a large number of local groups, each adopting specific ethnic names. Some accounts offer comments from the indigenous perspective on the ethnification process. In the Jesuit Jácome Monteiro's early seventeenth-century account taken from Tupi informants (published in S. Leite 1938–50, vol. 8), mythical cultural heroes had initially established the division between Tupi and Tapuia: "[The Tupi] also say that this Maíra Tupã divided the languages so that they could wage war on the Tapuias, but they do not know how to explain this any further" (408). But other indigenous narratives reproduced by colonial writers refer specifically to the origins of divisions between Tupi speakers themselves. In explaining "how the Tupinambá Indians established residence on the Island of Maranhão and adjacent areas," Capuchin missionary Claude d'Abbeville fused the Christian notion of earthly paradise with a Tupinambá perspective on the history of conquest. The Indians told him of a "beautiful land that they call Caeté, or great forest," located to the south of Maranhão. The Tupinambá, "the greatest and most valiant warriors," lived in these lands until the Portuguese took control over them, and "preferred to abandon their own country rather than to capitulate to the Portuguese" (d'Abbeville 1614, 261–261v). They wandered for a long time through the interior until they reached the sea again, establishing numerous villages there. Others remained in the interior, living in the Ibiapaba Hills.

In evoking these great migrations, Tupinambá narratives in Maranhão reflected historical events from the second half of the sixteenth century, especially the successive conquests of Bahia, Pernambuco, and Paraíba. The term "Caeté," mentioned above, became a reference to one of the bitterest opponents to Portuguese expansion in northeastern Brazil. These Indians became the main objects of a cruel declaration of "just war" in 1562, leading to their relentless persecution by the Europeans and their indigenous allies. But as the Tupinambá began to "hide themselves in the woods and in the most impenetrable forests," this refuge provided not only escape from the Portuguese but also a space for recreation of internal divisions. As d'Abbeville explained, the Tupinambá established several villages, "spreading themselves around and deriving their names from their places of residence, though maintaining the name Tupinambá, which serves to this day to qualify them." Many of the older Indians still remembered their arrival in Maranhão, when a great celebration took place:

> What happened was that they all became inebriated and one woman clubbed a man in the middle of the celebration, which resulted in a great riot that divided and separated the whole group. Some took sides with the offended victim while others stayed with the woman and the disagreement was so great that they were no longer great friends and allies and became great enemies; since then they have been in a state of permanent warfare, calling each other tobajaras, which means great enemies, or better yet, according to the word's etymology: you are my enemy and I am yours. (d'Abbeville 1614: 261v)

According to most amateur "Tupinologists," who prefer the spelling "Tabajara," this term means "owners of the villages," leading us to believe that the Capuchin writer made a mistake in his etymology. However, this is a linguistic corruption and resignification of a Tupi word much closer to d'Abbeville's definition, incorporating the locational adverb *toway* (or *tobaí*), which means "facing" or "in front of." Tupi specialist Teodoro Sampaio considered the combination *tobaí+yara* to mean "he who is facing, the neighbor in front." But he also added: "This also means competitor, rival, emulator; or a man's brother-in-law" (T. Sampaio 1987, 331).[2] "You are my enemy and I am yours": d'Abbeville captured the relational dimension of this term perfectly. Indeed, the term Tobajara became a name referring to different peoples along the coast, wavering in meaning between ally and enemy, depending on the observer's point of view. Hans Staden, for example, asserted in the mid-sixteenth century that the Tupinambá of São Vicente were called "Tawaijar" by their foes, "which means enemy" (Staden 1874, 50).

By the seventeenth century, however, this ethnic name became associated with specific Tupi populations. In the 1650s, Antônio Vieira summarized the volatile history of the Tobajara of the Ibiapaba Hills, most likely the Tupinambá splinter mentioned in d'Abbeville's account. At the beginning of the century, the Jesuit priests Francisco Pinto and Luiz Figueira had converted them, but the mission was abandoned following the violent death of the charismatic Pinto. When the Dutch occupied Pernambuco in 1630, the once-baptized Tobajara were living like all other heathens, according to Vieira, forming an alliance with the Dutch and fighting against the Portuguese as well as other "Tobajaras of their own nation." Dissatisfied with their Dutch allies, they rebelled and "decided to avenge the lives they had lost during this enterprise" by attacking the Dutch. In spite of this about-face, Vieira did not think any more highly of the Tobajara, considering them to be "the wild beasts that were raised and hidden in those hills." They seemed even wilder following the expulsion of the Dutch in 1654, when Protestant Indian refugees from Pernambuco joined them. "With the arrival of these new guests," observed Vieira, "Ibiapaba truly became the Geneva of the Brazilian backlands" (Vieira 1992, 127–31).

A half-century later, Indians from Ibiapaba provided their own version of their trajectory, offering a different perspective on their ethnogenesis. In sending their petition to King João V, they did not refer to themselves as "Tobajara" but simply as "Indians." The "Indians of the mission village in the Ibiapaba Hills" were experiencing hard times at that moment (around 1720), primarily because they had suffered many losses to warfare and disease, but also because the Jesuit mission had received many new residents, mostly Tapuia survivors from the wars that had raged throughout the northeast since the 1680s. In requesting lands and special privileges for their chiefs, they reviewed their postcontact history. They reminded the Crown that "long ago" their ancestors had left Bahia, which corresponds to d'Abbeville's information but was elided by Vieira. Their migration had been accompanied by "two other chiefs with numerous followers, who became separated after crossing the São Francisco River, and they disappeared into the Araripe Hills where they have hidden for over one hundred years, and they may be more than four thousand souls." But this rebellious past was quickly replaced in the petition by the positive image of faithful vassals who had rendered many services to the Portuguese Crown, "not only in the Restoration of Pernambuco but continually since the Fathers of the Company [of Jesus] had settled them." These petitioners subscribed to a pattern common to most colonists, requesting a *sesmaria* grant on lands "that their fathers and grandfathers had cultivated," but departed from this pattern in their effort to delineate a very particular memory of their colonial experience.[3]

The trajectory of Potiguar leaders in Paraíba and Rio Grande do Norte also illustrates the process of ethnic consolidation within the context of colonial wars. Once again, the name itself is subject to controversy: Were they Petiguar tobacco chewers or Potiguar shrimp eaters?[4] Over time, the latter term gained acceptance and its Portuguese equivalent, *camarão* (shrimp), became the surname of the indigenous dynasty that developed. Before 1599, the Potiguar were staunch enemies of the Portuguese and their Tobajara allies, especially after they garnered support from French

traders who supplied them with firearms, but heavy losses led an important faction to accept baptism and alliance with the Portuguese. Six cara-
vels set sail with 1,300 Potiguar and Tobajara warriors under the command
of Chief Zorobabé to defeat and enslave rebellious Aimoré groups in the
captaincies of Ilhéus and Porto Seguro to the south.

Following Zorobabé's triumphal return to Paraíba, the governor called
on his services to quash a *mocambo* of "runaway Guinea blacks in the palm
groves of Itapicuru." He was able to capture some of the maroons and sold
them to the whites, using the proceeds to buy a "field banner, drums, a
horse and clothes" for an even more triumphal reception in Paraíba. He
even asked the Franciscans to organize "a dance of *curumins* [Indian boys]
and to decorate the church and open its doors to receive him." Yet while
the mimicry of European pomp attracted him, Zorobabé did not abandon desires to "take revenge" on his enemies and began to prepare a war
against Milho Verde (Green Corn), "a chief in the *sertão* who had killed
one of his Christian nephews." Most likely his main objective was to capture Indian slaves to sell to the Portuguese. The Franciscans warned him
that Milho Verde's people "already were the king's vassals and a just war
against them could not be made without their order and consent from
the governor." But Zorobabé enjoyed a great deal of prestige among the
colonists, who showered him with gifts "either to acquire Indians for their
enterprises or because of the fear they had of him rebelling." Apparently
sharing this fear, the governor eventually imprisoned Zorobabé. While incarcerated, he faced several attempts on his life, but seemed immune even
to poison. Increasingly seen as a threat, he was sent to Lisbon, "but since
this was a seaport and every day boats came from Brazil and he could return," authorities dispatched him to the interior town of Évora, where he
died (Salvador 1889, 287–92).

Participation in Colonial Society

As new research unfolds, a picture is emerging of the significant kind of
historical agency achieved by native political and spiritual leaders who
operated within and often against the colonial order. This picture stands
in stark contrast to the more usual approach to resistance, resistance often
portrayed as amorphous, collective actions in stubborn defense of ancestral traditions. By shifting their focus to native strategies and actions, recent studies underscore the need to revise a broad spectrum of questions,

ranging from so-called spiritual conquest to Indian slavery, mission labor, and the impact of late colonial reforms, among others (see, for example, Farage 1991; Cunha 1992; J. Monteiro 1994; Vainfas 1995; Domingues 2000; Sommer 2000; M. R. C. Almeida 2003; J. A. Fernandes 2003).

Mission villages provided an important space for the reconfiguration of indigenous identities throughout the colonial period, as Regina Celestino de Almeida shows for Rio de Janeiro (2003, 129–85, 257–80). While missionaries made great efforts to show that converted Indians had left their pagan pasts behind, their accounts not only reveal the persistence of native religious manifestations but also how Indians reworked their social and symbolic universe in the wake of devastating epidemics, forced migrations, and the imposition of Christian cosmology (Pompa 2003, 339–419). A good example is the Jesuit Fernão Cardim's "Epistolar Narrative," which, in describing Visitor Gouveia's inspection of the Brazilian missions between 1583 and 1590, supplies us with rich details on how the mission Tupinambá adjusted to the new times.

Two elements stand out: the reconfiguration of warfare and the centrality of rituals. On the first front, the Jesuits initially perplexed the Indians, as this episode related by Cardim suggests: "A boy, passing by the Visitor in a canoe, asked in his language: *Pay, marapé guaranîme nande popeçoari*? Father, how can you be unarmed in this time of war and siege?" (Cardim 1997, 259). In fact, the Jesuit Soldiers of Christ felt they were well armed, with the word of God, and this military equivalency did not go unnoticed by the Indians. On the second front, the Jesuits met enthusiastic responses from the Indians to the elaborate rituals the Jesuits prepared, especially when they celebrated certain saints or conducted theater performances. The celebration of *endoenças* (Holy Thursday) was conducted in both Portuguese and Tupi: "Because there were many whites present, the *mandato* [ablution ceremony] was given in Portuguese, and the passion in the native tongue, which caused great devotion and brought tears to the Indians." Tupi was the main language used in devotional performances, although the Jesuits also taught Portuguese, Latin, and even Spanish to the *curumins*. In another ceremony in the same mission of Espírito Santo, "the Indians performed a dialogue in the Brazilian [Tupi] language, Portuguese, and Castillian, and they [were] very graceful in speaking peregrine languages, especially Castillian" (Cardim 1997, 232).

While these accounts tell us more about Jesuit intentions than indigenous responses, they do provide clues about how mission Indians forged their own space within the colonial project. The celebrations organized to receive the Jesuit authorities included the performance of native traditions, such as the ritual sweeping of the visitor's path and the welcome of tears. As they approached the Espírito Santo mission, Indian flute players met Visitor Gouveia's entourage. "The Indian boys," wrote Cardim, "hidden in the fresh forest, chanted several devotional hymns as we dined, which caused great devotion in the midst of those woods, especially along with the play just written to receive the Visitor, their new shepherd." Cardim's description suggests that the mission Indians performed these reception rituals in such a way as to prove their Christian devotion without abandoning their own traditions, which gained new characteristics on each new occasion. This was surprising to the Jesuit: "Everything brought out devotion under those forests, in these strange lands, even more so because such ceremonies were not expected of such barbarous peoples." Indeed, the "Epistolar Narrative" recounts episodes that revealed a clear effort to integrate the new religious activities into pre-Christian patterns. "The *curumins*, or boys, their bows and arrows raised, shouted out their war cry, and painted in various tones, naked, they advanced with their hands raised to receive the father's blessing, saying in Portuguese 'Jesus Christ be blessed.'" Even the devil proved indispensable in the celebrations and theater performances: "An *anhangá*, or devil, did not fail to appear, as he emerged from behind the trees; this was the Indian Ambrósio Pires, who had gone to Lisbon with Father Rodrigo de Freitas. The Indians celebrate this figure with great enthusiasm because of his attractiveness, expressions and caginess; they always put some devil in all their festivities, if these are to be well celebrated" (Cardim 1997, 222).

Sacred music, instructional dialogues, and carefully staged rituals were an important part of the lives of mission Indians. However, this did not mean the end of the native chants and rites that the priests so diligently tried to extirpate. Following one of the devotional ceremonies described in the "Epistolar Narrative," the Indians carried on the festivities on their own, to the rhythm of "gourds filled with stones (not unlike Portuguese boys with their tambourines)" and choreographed so "that they never miss[ed] a step, and stamp[ed] on the ground together in such a way that they [made] the earth shake." Notwithstanding his attempt to relativize the scene through metropolitan analogies, Cardim witnessed a ritual to the sound of the *maracá*, reminiscing about the glories of past warfare and vengeance. "I could not understand what they were chanting," confessed

Cardim, "but some of the priests told me that they were singing in verse about the deeds and deaths their ancestors perpetrated" (Cardim 1997, 234–35). On another such occasion, "the procession was filled with devotion, with many torches and bonfires, and many of the Indians had to be disciplined, since they go at one another in a cruel manner, and this they hold not only to be a virtue, but they also consider it to be an act of bravery to take blood and become *abaetê*, that is, valiant" (247).

In d'Abbeville's *History of the Capuchin Missions in Maranhão*, Tupinambá leader Japiaçu narrates the origins of the radical separation between Indians and whites:

> We lived as one, you and us; but God, sometime after the deluge, dispatched his bearded prophets to teach us his laws. These prophets gave our father, from whom we descend, two swords, one made of wood and the other iron, allowing him to choose between them. He thought the iron sword was too heavy and chose the wooden one. Seeing this, the ancestor from whom you descend, who was cleverer, took the iron sword. Ever since then, we have been miserable, because when the prophets saw that we did not want to believe in them, they returned to the heavens, leaving their footprints inscribed with crosses in the rocks near Potiú. (d'Abbeville 1614, 69v–70)

This speech lends itself to several interpretations. At first sight, it appears to transform the tragic history of contact into myth, offering a native explanation—within an indigenous narrative genre—for the subordinate condition experienced by the Tupinambá in the early seventeenth century. But the most revealing aspect lies in the displacement of the subject: it was the actions of the Indian's ancestor that determined the march of history. Carneiro da Cunha, commenting on this and similar myths, emphasizes that "in the myth, a choice is offered to the Indians, who rather than being victims of some predestined force become agents determining their own fate. Perhaps they made the wrong choice. But at least they saved their dignity in having shaped their own history" (Cunha 1992, 19).

Resisting by Changing

Carneiro da Cunha's emphasis on the need to recognize native leaders as subjects shaping their own history is an advance in Brazilian history. However, postcontact choices were always conditioned by factors related to European expansion. The demographic catastrophe left in its wake a desperate situation. Facing increasingly unfavorable conditions, native leaders often adopted objects, strategies, and discourses introduced by the colonizers. Hence native resistance was not limited to a stubborn clinging to precolonial traditions, but gained force and meaning as indigenous leaders and societies opened themselves to innovation.

European observers, who tended to portray Indians who resisted as savages hostile to whites by nature, did not always recognize this characteristic of indigenous politics. Writing on the Portuguese occupation of the *sertão* in Pernambuco, Sebastião da Rocha Pita (1980) remarks that the landowners who received grants measured in leagues had to conquer that territory palm by palm, so great was the resistance that the barbarous heathen offered. The flip side of this image involved Indians who collaborated with colonial projects.

This second stereotype is exemplified by a mid-eighteenth-century document listing twenty-five examples of "Famous Indians in Arms who contributed to the temporal and spiritual conquest of this State of Brazil." "From these and other similar cases," argued the anonymous writer, "clearly we can infer that the Indians of our Lusitanian America are not as limited, crude, and undisciplined as ordinarily portrayed, where they are treated more like irrational wild beasts and brutes than as men capable of reason."[5] Among others, the author singled out "Pindobuçu, magnanimous, intrepid and brave who, wielding a wooden sword, threatened his own in order to maintain peace with the Portuguese and the favor of the Jesuit priests." He also mentioned "Garcia de Sá, another famous preacher of the Faith, whose spirit resembled that of the Apostle of the Gentiles," and "the celebrated Jacaranha, great friend of the missionaries who dressed in a long blue habit with a red cross embroidered on his breast." The author also describes the participation of Indians in the relocation of indigenous populations from the remote hinterland to colonial settlements. For example, "the famous Indian Arco Verde (Green Bow) . . . proved so zealous in his faith that he traveled 400 leagues into the wilderness in search of his kinsmen in order to bring them under the control of the Church and the priests, with little fear of his enemies, whom he defeated, placing them in retreat and killing many."

Although the anonymous author emphasized the collaborative role of these Indians, their activities show how indigenous subjects adopted some of the symbols and discourse of the Europeans in order to forge their own space within this emerging New World. Much in the same way that the literature on African slavery in Brazil has collapsed the polarity between "accommodation" and "resistance," personified in the Uncle Tom–like "Pai João" and the unyielding rebel "Zumbi," the same must be done with Amerindian social actors (Schwartz 1977; Reis and Silva 1989). In an interesting twist, Patrícia Melo Sampaio (2000, 341) suggests that Indians and mestiços in the colonial Amazon should be read as neither *canicurus*, the despised "traitors" along the Negro river who collaborated with colonial interests, nor *ajuricabas*, in reference to the Manao leader on the same river who preferred killing himself to becoming a slave of the whites.

Indeed, the same language used in the "Famous Indians" manuscript can be found in the rebellious movements that opposed colonial rule. The Tupinambá of Maranhão, for example, in addition to the wooden swords, also used the written word in a conspiracy plotted by a leader named Amaro, supposedly "raised" by the Jesuits in a Pernambuco mission. Brandishing a few Portuguese letters, Amaro pretended to read them to a large meeting of rebellious headmen, asserting that "the subject of these letters [was] that all the Tupinambá [were] to be enslaved." According to Bernardo Pereira de Berredo, "this suggestion was so diabolical that it soon took hold of the brutality of so many barbarians, who agreed unanimously that they should kill all the whites" (Pereira de Berredo 1989).

Antônio Vieira, in his account of the Ibiapaba mission, also noted that rebellious Indians used writing in their efforts to negotiate peace with the Jesuits who were beginning to encroach on this "Geneva of the backlands." One of the local leaders, Francisco, "presented letters to the missionaries, which [the indigenous emissaries] brought from all the headmen, encased in calabashes sealed with wax, so that they would not be damaged when the bearers cross[ed] the rivers." Moreover, "the priests were impressed when they saw that the letters were written on Venice paper, and closed with sealing wax from India" (Vieira 1992, 139–40).

The written word, not unlike the wooden sword, became another alternative from which indigenous leaders could choose. While the myth of the wooden sword appeared to dislocate the critical action deciding the group's fate to a remote past, the content of the narrative referred explicitly to the contemporary situation experienced by the Tupinambá. Japiaçu knew very well who his interlocutors were. After all, the bearded prophets had returned, presenting new choices as challenging as the ones presented to the group's ancestral father. It was at this crossroads, where tradition and innovation met face to face, that the history of the Indians was forged against the strong current of colonial expansion.

Notes

1 All English translations of texts published in other languages are by the author.
2 Carlos Fausto (personal communication with the author) suggests that *toway+ara* could be an agentive nominalization of the locational adverb *toway*, thus meaning "on the other side," even closer to "enemy."
3 "Petição dos Índios da Serra da Ibiapaba," received in Lisbon October 12, 1720, Arquivo Histórico Ultramarino, Ceará cx 1. Doc. 90 (Projeto Resgate CD-Rom, AHU_ACL_CU_006, Cx. 1. D. 65). My thanks go to Professor Francisco Pinheiro of the University of Ceará for making a copy of his transcription available.
4 According to Teodoro Sampaio (1987, 306–7), "Potiguara" meant "eaters of excrement," an offensive term used by enemies. Slightly corrupted, it came to mean "shrimp eaters."
5 "Índios Famosos em Armas que neste Estado do Brasil concorreram para sua conquista temporal e espiritual," anonymous manuscript, Instituto de Estudos Brasileiros, University of São Paulo. On the specific intellectual and political context that generated this account, see Kantor (2004, 108–15, 219–35).

CHAPTER TWO

Rituals of Defiance

Past Resistance, Present Ambiguity

FELIPE CASTRO GUTIÉRREZ

Reactions to the Conquista

Every society remembers the people, institutions, and events of the past by bringing them together into an account that makes them understandable while at the same time pointing—explicitly or implicitly—to models of current behavior within the narratives of the past. In Mexico, indigenous resistance to the Spanish conquest has always been a particularly sensitive theme. Viewed as a traumatic rupture in the country's historical development, the *conquista* remains a controversial subject today. It may be useful, then, to review these successive images of the colonial past and study them in more detail.

The first evangelists and royal officials had a favorable view of Mexico's indigenous peoples, referring repeatedly to their "good and blessed simplicity." To these Spanish settlers, the indigenous peoples were like a soft wax upon which they could easily impress faithfulness to the king and good Christian virtues, without encountering much resistance (Quiroga 1985). They would attribute the occasional rebellion to abuse or excesses on the part of a given official or settler, or perhaps even to the ignorance of the natives themselves. Thus, we are given the impression that such conflicts were seen as either solvable or avoidable with an appropriate level of vigilance by the church or government. This was the origin of several laws that informed the official stance to be taken in relation to uprisings. The *Leyes de Indias* (or "Laws of the Indies," as they have come to be known in English), for example, gave explicit instructions to the viceroys, courts, and governors with regard to rebel Indians:

Try to subdue them and attract them to our royal service with gentleness and peacefulness, without war, robbery or death; maintain the laws given by us for the good government of the Indies and treatment of the natives; should it be necessary to grant them some liberties or exemptions from all kinds of tribute, you can and should do it, for the time and in the form which seems appropriate to you, and pardon the crimes of rebellion which they might have committed, even if they are against us and our service, giving a report later in the Council. (*Recopilación* 1987, iii, iv)[1]

In Spain, by contrast, a "crime against one's country" was particularly serious. It was punishable almost invariably by death, and also saw the offender's home destroyed and his land scattered with salt, rendering it infertile, so that his crime would never be forgotten. It is clear, however, that there was quite a distance between the pious orders of the Spanish monarchs on the one side, and the daily practicalities of Indian governance on the other. Even so, there is no doubt that Spanish rule in New Spain was maintained for three centuries without any great episodes of generalized repression. Indeed, after the Mixtón Rebellion (1540–41), the majority of uprisings were staged along the remote northern frontier and the isolated southeastern Yucatán. This stability is surprising, particularly when we consider that no real apparatus of state or military forces of any significance existed at the time. The Spanish Crown, whether by accident or by design, established a system of control that would effectively channel, dissolve, or repress all discontent and protest. This contrasts with the constant civil wars and peasant rebellions of the first century of independence (Katz 1988).

Even the documents the Indians presented before the authorities reinforce this consensual image of colonial order. Almost invariably, the Indians would describe themselves as poor, ignorant wards in need of the paternal and benevolent protection of the authorities. Particularly venerated were figures such as the bishops and viceroys, who represented divine or human majesty.

Yet from an early stage, more skeptical visions would emerge, painting for us the image of a society of voiceless unrest hidden behind an apparent calm, in which violent disturbances and uprisings would be frequent. Diego Medrano, a parish priest trained in the harsh life along the northern frontier, noted, "The motives and causes of these rebellions can be reduced to a generality which pertains to them all. Of course, there are certain peculiarities which influence particular cases and render the hostilities more bitter. Nonetheless, the causes of the rebellion can be found in the instability and inconsistency of the Indian temperament, their thievish and innately cruel nature, and in their great hatred of Spaniards" (Naylor and Polzer 1986, 448). Certainly, such a view may be a result of the particular region in question, where raids by the "barbarian" Indians and uprisings of those subjugated by the colonial order were as violent as they were endemic. Yet even in the center of the viceroyalty, where the Pax Hispanica ostensibly reigned, it is worth noting how, over time, opinion among the clergy, officials, and settlers shifted toward pessimism. In 1681, Juan Rodríguez Calvo, a parish priest from Michoacán, reported to his bishop, "The Indians are highly proud and disobedient, and on the outside they show a false humility, pettiness and submission with their superiors, all the while they have their vices and Pharisaic customs. They are cruel and vengeful, harboring their hatred and resentment even until death. They are terrible liars, inclined to theft, fraud and deception" (Carrillo Cázarez 1993, 339). The king's officials were even more forthright, and their views increasingly skeptical. For example, the visitor-general of the Spanish Crown, José de Gálvez, who went to San Luis Potosí, Guanajuato, and Michoacán to punish a series of uprisings in 1767, informed Viceroy Carlos Francisco de Croix, the *marqués de Croix*, that "among them—the Indians—one [found] not only wicked and cunning men, but also those that [were] generally given to evil, even though they [were] born with lesser qualities than rational people given to good" (Gálvez 1990, 53). Manuel de Flon, *intendente* of Puebla, painted for Viceroy Marquina a disastrous picture of licentiousness, insubordination, and arrogance among the indigenous peoples within his jurisdiction, resulting in the ruination of their agriculture and disordered government:[2]

> From what I have seen, by asking for lands to add to their villages to the detriment of the owners; by managing to irritate them and the officials, forcing them to incur improper legal processes, journeys and expenses with their trivial and unfair appeals; by keeping what was lent to them; abandoning their sowing; and ultimately by not obeying what they are ordered to do, confident in their stupidity and destitution with which they are regarded, it would appear that they do not aspire to anything more than regaining the very kingdom that

cost the Spanish monarchy so many pains and efforts. In conclusion, your Excellency, the behavior of the Indians is nothing in my view but a veiled uprising. (Flon to the Marquina, January 8, 1802, Archivo General de la Nación, Mexico City, *Criminal*, vol. 333: 4)

If we carry out an exercise in reinterpretation, following the example of Ranajit Guha (Guha 1988), it may be possible to suggest that there was a continuous "low-intensity" resistance among the Indians of the center of the viceroyalty, which at times shifted almost imperceptibly toward a "rebellion" never actually experienced as such. Of course, without more information, it is always risky to adopt the views of those with an interest in describing indigenous peoples in the worst possible terms. Although it may appear paradoxical, historians studying radicalism and protest run the risk of giving more credibility to offenders than to victims. Such a theme has a long and complex historiographic evolution after Mexican independence. Those writers who sought to construct a patriotic consciousness dedicated themselves to undermining as best they could the image of the *siesta colonial*, even though this would make Hernán Cortés one of the forerunners of independence (González Obregón 1952). At a time when the building blocks of national identity were either dubious or an object of controversy, it was tempting to construct that identity as a discourse of "contrast," a historical secular opposition to foreign rule. This perspective gained even greater momentum after the revolution of 1910, with the consolidation of the modern-day Mexican state. In this sense, the pre-Hispanic period became a sort of lost "golden age," and the colony an American version of the Middle Ages, an age of ignorance, backwardness, and oppression. The best-known example of this was the anthology of stories about indigenous rebellions by Vicente Casarrubias, published in its thousands by the government for educational purposes in a *Biblioteca Enciclopédica Popular* (Casarrubias 1945). This publication, and others, contributed to an image of colonial society in which only the threat of punishment would maintain a semblance of order. From this perspective, the history of Mexico would become a long struggle for independence, democracy, and public freedom. Figures as varied as Cuauhtémoc, Miguel Hidalgo, Benito Juárez, Francisco I. Madero, and Emiliano Zapata would become national heroes on the altar of the homeland.

More recently, interest in social and ethnohistory has allowed for studies to be developed that return to indigenous peoples their role as the

protagonists of historical development (see Reina 1987–88). In methodological terms, we see an emphasis on the need for a less obvious reading
of the literature, recovery of oral memory, and focus on a long-term vision
seeking out continuities between the ethnic conflicts of the past and those
of the present (Barabas 1986). The most notable conclusion drawn from
such a train of thought was expressed by anthropologist and historian
Guillermo Bonfil Batalla: "The recent history of Mexico, that of the last
five hundred years, is the story of permanent confrontation between those
attempting to direct the country toward the path of Western civilization
and those, rooted in Mesoamerican ways of life, who resist" (Bonfil Batalla
1996, xv).

Such an interpretation has helped call into question the hegemony and
inevitability of the nation-state, in which many contemporary social movements coexist. The notion that the Indians never accepted Spanish rule is
a common view, and sees them maintaining a continual defense of their
identity and collective resources. This can be seen, for example, in the recent formation of the Consejo Mexicano 500 años de Resistencia Indígena,
Negra y Popular (Mexican 500 Years of Indigenous, Black, and Popular
Resistance Council) or in discussions surrounding the various constitutional modalities of ethnic autonomy. Across Mexico (and Latin America
as a whole), such discussions are not just academic, but entail significant,
wider social and political consequences.

Yet these protests and uprisings were not permanent, nor were they
equally spread across all territories covered by New Spain. Within a single
region, it was entirely possible to find one village with a tradition of
protest, while its neighbors preferred to adapt to the new order of things,
paying their tributes on time, devotedly attending Mass and obeying the
king's officials. We do not have to delve too deeply into the source material
before we realize that reactions among the native population to the conquista varied greatly. Whether villages would choose to adjust to or resist
colonial rule was influenced by the groups' prior experience, forms of community organization, the interests of the leaders, the presence or absence
of institutional means to express discontent, the actual chances of success
of any act of resistance, and, of course, other factors that depended largely
on circumstances at the time.

It would be a mistake to project our contemporary ideas of free will and
the individual onto such a corporative society. The majority of indigenous
peoples lived in villages organized like "republics" of Indians, each with

their own governor, *alcaldes* (magistrates), and *alguaciles* (constables). These "officials of the republic" administered the land, water, community work, exercised local justice, and could issue fines or sentence offenders to a flogging for their crimes. Often, whether individuals would participate in (or abstain from) a rebellion would be decided by the community authorities. If necessary, participation would be obligatory, under threat of punishment. Although it is almost a contradiction in terms, under such conditions joining an uprising could actually constitute an act of conformity.

Yet it is clear that numerous aspects of European cultural and spiritual fabric held the interest of indigenous peoples, and although it would be reductionist to do so, one might easily write a history of the "five hundred years of indigenous integration into the Western world." Many of the cultural characteristics we distinguish as "Indian" today in respect to Western modernity were in fact adoptions or reappropriations of the practices or institutions that were common in sixteenth-century Castilla and Extremadura. Indeed, language, one of the most powerful cultural characteristics, suggests a strong and progressive Spanish influence (Lockhart 1999, 378–468). The anthropologist George Foster (1962) explored these themes a number of years ago, but his trail was not taken up by others, except through sporadic allusions and isolated works.

Colonial rule also provoked responses that would not fit so easily into such a romanticized vision of the past, despite their epic side. Many Indians did not view themselves as *conquered*, but as *conquerors*, and we see this not only in the well-known case of the Tlaxcalteca—important allies of the Spanish in the final battle of Tenochtitlán—but across other indigenous peoples. The legend of the founding of the city of Querétaro is attributed, for example, to two Otomí *caciques* and conquistadors— captains Fernando de Tapia and Nicolás de San Luis Montañez—who with the miraculous help of Saint James and his fiery holy cross brought the "barbarian gentiles" to the true faith and obedience to the Catholic king (Gruzinski 1985, 33–46). Some Indian groups of New Spain rewrote their history, representing theirs as another of the "nations" that would be integrated into the heterogeneous mosaic of the Spanish Empire. This reconstruction of the past attempted to show the colonial powers that their relationship with the natives could be unequal, but that it also meant the recognition of a space of rights and particular privileges. This strategy continued, to a certain degree at least, until the last decades of the viceroyalty.

The king's officials, however, especially on a local level, did not see things that way, and often acted arbitrarily and with complete indifference to the rights and historical merits of the natives. However, when the Indian communities were sufficiently persistent, they managed to ensure that the viceroy or the court would grant them protections, rewards of lands, titles, and even coats of arms (Kellogg 1995).

Various authors have revisited this "consensual" imaginary of the colonial Indians, translating it into terms of social analysis. In this sense, the occasional outbreak of violence could be interpreted, as William Taylor has suggested, as a regulatory mechanism allowing authorities to correct certain situations that could otherwise lead to greater and more serious crises (Taylor 1987, 248, 249). Marcelo Carmagnani, in his study of the Tehuantepec Rebellion of 1660, which prompted acts as serious as the murder of the *alcalde mayor* (chief magistrate) and other Spanish settlers, maintains that at the end of the day, the rebellion generated "a new equilibrium between Indian and Spanish society" and "a reformulation of the pre-existing colonial pact" (Carmagnani 1992, 22). It was also thought that at the end of the eighteenth century the authoritarian modernity the monarchs of the Bourbon dynasty claimed to introduce had broken with these ancient agreements and was one of the deciding factors in the final crisis of the viceroyalty (Hamnett 1992).

At times, it would appear easy to view the negotiating or adaptive attitudes of the indigenous groups as opportunistic, or to refer to them in terms implying moral judgment, such as "collaborationists." But it may be that these "conquistador Indians" and "loyal vassals" sought to manipulate the hierarchical principles of colonial order for their own benefit. In the round, it can be said that they practiced a combination of tactical resistance and strategic adjustment. Which leads us, inevitably, to a discussion of precisely what is understood by the term "resistance."

In the Beginning Was the Name

As John Gledhill points out in his introduction to this book, rebellion has gained the sympathy and interest of many contemporary authors. The attraction is evident: rebellions generate much documentary information, they bring to light in an explicit way the conflicts that normally remain obscured from view, and they oblige their key protagonists to define their interests, alliances, and hatreds. While economic and demographic cycles do not attract many readers, the great social upheavals of the past

lend themselves well to the notion of a "good story" and its corresponding moral lessons. Although history, sociology, and anthropology usually
tend to be considered sciences (or at least sciences "in a certain sense"),
in practice, academic discourse is not so far removed from the traditional
approaches that sought, above all, such moral lessons. Behind many works
(including, no doubt, some of my own) lies a more or less explicit narrative that contemplates native peasant societies through a nostalgic lens,
while at the same time calling upon us to condemn the processes that have
shaped Western modernity.

This interest in important events of the past, and, in particular, those
that appear to have contemporary resonances, has not disappeared. Hardly
a year goes by, for example, without an important work, or numerous
articles and theses, being published on the rebellions in Chiapas (Viqueira
2005). Other regions and groups, by contrast, do not have past or present
traditions of sufficiently open and violent protest to merit a similar quantity of column inches, as Guillermo de la Peña notes in chapter eleven.

Yet the spectacular nature of uprisings sometimes leaves in shadow
other reactions that were, in fact, much more common. For some time,
historians and anthropologists have focused increasingly on the hidden
or daily modalities of indigenous mobilization: brief local riots, discreet
disobedience of the orders of the viceroys or *oidores* (judges), clandestine
religious traditions, or even the skillful subversion of the institutions and
legal appeals that the empire itself granted the Indians. We see the paro-
dying ceremonies of Carnival (Bricker 1989), the implicit argument behind
certain ritual dances (Taylor 1994), and indeed all that James Scott—whose
influence in this sphere is quite evident—called the "infrapolitics of the
oppressed" or "the arts of hidden resistance" (J. C. Scott 1985).

Jan de Vos, recognizing the variety of responses to the colonial situation, grouped them together under three categories: open resistance,
veiled resistance, and negotiated resistance (Vos 1994), or, as Mario Ruz
more poetically put it: the "combative," the "everyday," and the "sacred"
faces of resistance (Ruz 1992). This broadening of the definition allows us
to go beyond the simple dialectic of rebellion and submission. We can thus
approach the question with a fresh perspective on the history of groups
that do not have such a tradition of open protest, allowing us to seek out
elements of social activism within the interstices and undercurrents of the
sources. Yet the term "resistance" is now so broad that its methodological utility for research purposes is no longer certain. Terms that attempt

to cover everything often elucidate very little, or simply shroud a concept in a comfortable and nebulous vagueness. In this sense, "resistance" is no longer a noun but an adjective, a simple rhetorical device.

Even from this broader and more diverse perspective, we need to ask whose attitudes and behaviors are habitually classified as resistance. The variety of protagonists involved in episodes of unrest and acts of violence in New Spain was great: laborers from the haciendas, the urban masses, artisans, and even the descendants of the conquistadors themselves. Such situations are viewed collectively as conspiracies, rebellions, or social movements; strangely, resistance is only spoken of when the protagonists happen to be indigenous (or, more recently, black slaves).

This brings us to the term "resistance" itself. Giving a name is in itself an act of creation: by assigning a name, a conceptual entity once immersed in the amorphous chaos of the past suddenly becomes identified. This supposes, however, that the term that has been named has something relevant for us, something that separates it from the rest. To name is to define, and any definition implies exclusion.

The concept of resistance is of relatively modern usage; previously, we would speak of indigenous "uprisings" or "rebellions," and from a historiographic perspective it may prove interesting to track its origin and evolution. I will not devote myself here to reviewing the various definitions of resistance; suffice it to say that there is, in other contexts, a bacterial or viral resistance to medication, a resistance to heat or electricity, and the resistance mounted by an armed force in the face of attack. This conquered armed force will resort to any action against the occupation or invasion of the country, against an enemy superior in number or arms. The classic example is the Résistance in France and other European nations to Nazi occupation during the Second World War. This may even be traced back to indigenous history, given that it started to appear in ethnological literature in the middle of the century. So defined, it has a romantic ring to it, recalling those who risked their lives to defend their principles, their families, and their land against a superior power. It might also be traced to other no less prestigious origins. Since the end of the nineteenth century, the anarchist imaginary and discourse abounded in "societies of resistance," "pockets of resistance," and calls for worker or "popular" resistance.

Whatever its provenance, our discussion of resistance may lead us to the notion that the Indians never accepted Spanish rule. At most, their adjustment to the colonial order would have been perfunctory, in the face of a reality that they could not openly oppose, with no relinquishing of rebel sentiments. Unlike concepts with greater descriptive neutrality (violent disturbances or *tumultos*, rebellions, and strikes), resistance implies a priori an intention. Such a train of thought leads us toward an altogether more slippery notion: the motivation behind the human behavior that we witness. However much we trust our ability to rigorously reconstruct events of the past, no two ostensibly identical or simultaneous events ever share the same roots or the same meaning.

Studies of contemporary formal legal proceedings reveal an equally ambiguous perspective. Judges and *fiscales* (prosecutors) would record in their minutes and documents their preconceived ideas about the causes of indigenous unrest. Frequently, then, researchers are faced with suspiciously identical statements from witnesses and those accused of crimes, statements following an almost parallel narrative pattern. The prosecutors tended to accentuate the seriousness of the acts and the intentions behind the crimes, while the defendants, as one would expect, tried to apologize and denied their intentions were subversive.

Indeed, even to refer to reactions to the conquista "in general" is nonsense, for attitudes and behaviors at the time were as heterogeneous as the indigenous peoples themselves. I will, therefore, refer specifically to the particular situations of Indian groups in the center of the New Spanish viceroyalty: these were regions of early and intensive colonization, where the presence of the king's officials was close, and where the most well-known and celebrated episodes of the evangelization took place. Conditions within the missionary north and in the Mayan area of New Spain should be considered in their own right.

Rituals of Defiance

Words can tell us much, but their message often remains ambiguous, while episodes of collective violence, by complete contrast, often appear straightforward in their intentionality. Nevertheless, ascertaining what is behind an outbreak of collective violence is not a simple matter. Some manifestations of violence seemed to lack planning or reason, and appeared, above all, to give expression to contained emotions. In some sense, then, we see how the recorded insults, the stoning of buildings and the sacking of homes belonging to certain community figures, might represent the concrete manifestation of desires and hatreds that were often hidden beneath the surface. Even in cases where there were concrete reasons behind the violence, doubt still remained as to whether the actions taken actually reflected the feelings of the masses or simply those elements who claimed to speak for them. Such elements—the caciques, the governors, and Indian fiscales of the church—were frequently figures with some knowledge of the political system and who may have had ideas that were not necessarily shared by the majority of their followers.

We might also focus our attention on those acts and concrete manifestations of behavior that were not premeditated, but which emerged without previous planning. William Taylor, in his pioneering work on violent village disturbances, focused on the material expressions of behavior as an indirect means for understanding the ideas, prejudices, and hatreds of the participants (Taylor 1987, 208-9). Here, I want to refer to a group of expressions we might consider as ritual forms of defiance.

Although it is almost universally accepted that episodes of "instinctive collective violence" are a common feature in violent disturbances or revolutions, we do not witness this here. While some acts are indeed often instinctive—when a person is suddenly surprised or threatened—this is not the case with collective expressions of violence, which tend to demonstrate a certain level of coordination and deliberation.

Another expression in common parlance is that of "mindless violence." Beyond the obvious fact that any human action requires a certain rational capacity, we see how acts of violence within society and throughout a specific period in time do not appear randomly or spontaneously. On the contrary, they are as unique to each cultural context as language, art, or sport. There is a grammar of collective violence, yet we may only catch a glimpse of it in its externalized form—its "vocalization"—in the stonings, insults, and attacks.

This vocalizing metaphor, although it might appear strange, works well here because social violence implies forms of communication. There is not necessarily anything new in this perspective; Crane Brinton pointed out decades ago how, paradoxically, there must be shared cultural elements between protagonists in order for a prolonged and violent conflict, war, or revolution even to exist. Certain conventions always regulate the initiation of hostilities, implicit limits that must not be exceeded, and elements that signal the protagonists' victory or defeat (Brinton 1938).

Indeed, the violence we see during disturbances and rebellions goes beyond mere resentment or indignation against someone perceived as an enemy, and beyond aggression against immediate objectives with "rational" or pragmatic aims. Such violence is rich in symbolism that does not have an immediate function or utility, but that communicates certain concepts or messages. When the Spanish reconquered New Mexico in 1693, after the Pueblo Indian rebellion, they found in a church: "the holy corporals covered in excrement, two chalices inside a pouch covered in manure, the shape of a crucifix cut with lashes, the figure of Christ covered in excrement where the holy altar stone [lay] on the main altar, and a statue of the blessed Saint Francis, its arms cut off with an axe" (González de la Vara 1992). At the very least, several shared concepts emerge here that would not be so resonant for a non-Catholic audience: the importance of the corporal (the cloths on which the chalice and the host are placed after consecration), the chalices (to receive the wine that is the blood of Christ), the association of excrement and manure with desecration, and the value of benediction, given by the saint through his arms.

This contrasts with other situations where the symbolism required a translation. In 1639, when the Bacalar Maya, taking refuge in the mountains, "returned to the vomit of their idolatry and abominations of their ancestors," the missionaries who went to get them found "shapes like statues of men dressed as Spaniards all over the path" (López de Cogolludo 1957, I:644). Their guides had to explain to them "that the rebels had closed the path so that the Spaniards could not pass, and that their path was guarded by their idols, and they would hold and enchant any Spaniard wishing to pass through" (644).

At times, the symbolism was connected to something more complex, repetitive, and predictable, where everything was more than just the sum of its parts. We are talking specifically here about "ritual," and in the case of violent disturbances and rebellions, we are referring broadly to "rituals of defiance."

The notion of defiance as a behavior is not new for specialists in animal behavior. The fight for dominance has a ritualized component—the declaration of hostilities, the intimidation of the opponent, and the show of aggression. The outbreak of violence can be avoided, and also concluded, when one of the sides accepts its inferiority. We are not generally talking about fights to the death, in this context.

In human societies we witness similar behaviors, some so highly formalized that they end up losing their original meaning. Conflict adopts specific, indirect, symbolic, or vicarious forms, of which sport is the most routine (even though, as has been seen more and more often, it can often lead to more direct forms of violence). Although this may appear the preserve of complex societies, this is not always the case. Brother Vicente of Santa María, in his *Relación histórica de la colonia del Nuevo Santander* (Historical Report of the Colony of New Santander), told of the conflict between two indigenous groups of the arid region of northern Mexico— whose communities were little more than isolated *rancherías* (hamlets) and lacked anything similar to a state or ruling class—using terms not uncommon to the ritualized wars of medieval times:

> When mutually and without surprise two or three nations declare war, they signal the day and field of battle . . . They take to the attack when the case is heard and the confrontation is focused more on shouting and a desire to destroy themselves than to achieve an outcome. Their withdrawal is at the very moment when one of the champions turns his back on the enemy, and as he goes, attempting to save himself, the others keep on following him. Every one of the warring nations withdraws, filling the air with clamors of joy, indicating both satisfaction and victory. (Santa María 1973, 126)

These are the various components of violence already described: defiance, the intimidation of the opponent, a conflict based on rules seeking to minimize human losses, and conventions signaling the victory of some and defeat of others. These are the components of ritualized violence seen in the rebellions and violent disturbances at the center of New Spain.

Defiance Sounds the Return of the Chichimeca

Rebellions and violent disturbances tend to be noisy, even at the risk of alerting the fighters' opponents or even the forces of order. This is not to say that the villages and cities of the past were usually silent. Provincial "stillness" is more urban myth than rural reality. Daily life was marked by a range of different sounds—people talking as they walked the streets, the murmur of *novenas* (prayers) emerging from the home of a deceased family member, the creaking of carts as they rolled across the paving stones, the shouts of drinkers in the bar, and the monotonous tap-tap of textile looms. This was the harmonious and reassuring buzz of daily life.

The authorities reserved the right to break this silence of whispers and vague echoes through the town crier who made known the latest regulations, the beat of the drum that signaled public punishments, and toll of the bells announcing the death of some important figure. The maintenance of "sound order," if we might call it so, was jealously guarded by the authorities. Inebriated individuals were tolerated until they became "rowdy," marital quarrels were overlooked until they reached scandalous levels, and public or private parties and the music that went along with them required prior permission.

As a result, violent disturbances and protests were usually accompanied by the spirited violation of this auditory harmony—discordant shouts, "strong words" (i.e., insults), sardonic verses (or words "offensive to chaste ears," as they were known), drums, and fireworks (aside from the other works already cited, see Castro Gutiérrez 1996 and 2003). Troublemakers would also frequently seize the church towers to toll the bells—as they do today at the Metropolitan Cathedral in Mexico City during serious political crises.

At times, the shouting would become a threatening wail. In the villages of the bishopric of Michoacán (a battle front in the sixteenth century), rioters would howl "like savages," or unexpectedly appear half-naked and covered in body paint. The meaning of this quasi-Carnivalesque behavior is often obscured from us, but the symbolism was clear to witnesses at the time. The reference was to the "Chichimeca," a group of seminomadic indigenous peoples who lived in the north of modern-day Mexico (the Guachichiles, Pames, Zacatecos, Guamares, those known as the "Striped Ones," the "Raw Food Eaters," and others). The Chichimeca were at first indifferent to the presence and movements of the Spaniards, but in the mid-sixteenth century started attacking colonizers, Spanish settlers, black slaves, and "peaceful" Indians alike. For forty years they led what would be known as the "Chichimeca war," and made daring raids even into the larger villages. In the long run, the Crown was forced to renounce its failed strategy of military subjugation and effectively "purchase" peace, by giving the Chichimeca land, subsidies, and exemptions from tributes. This was a political move that allowed the border to be consolidated and, with time, the peaceful integration of the ancient warriors (P. Powell 1977).

The long and bloody conflict left a deep footprint in the collective imaginary of Indian communities. Those from Michoacán, for example, reinterpreted the dance of the *moros y cristianos* (which recalls the battles of the Spanish *Reconquista* between the eighth century and the fifteenth) and turned it into a dance of "loyal Indians against the Chichimeca" (Ciudad Real 1976, 81–82). It is not surprising, then, that the leaders of the rebellions would imagine the close presence of the Chichimeca hidden along the outskirts of their villages, or that those leaders would say they had sent the Chichimeca letters calling them to action. In the disturbances of 1767 in Venado (north of San Luis Potosí) the rumor went around that the rebels had summoned the "striped Chichimeca." When the rebels' neighbors from Hedionda came to join them, many arrived *embijados*, or covered in body paint. In Real de Guadalcázar, one of the leaders was referred to as a Chichimeca, but was in fact an Indian seen *empelotado* (naked) and embijado during the unrest. In Guanajuato, an indigenous mulatto citizen from León was accused of going out in public with his face striped and blackened, shouting, "and in every way similar to the ways and customs of the *Mecos*" (Castro Gutiérrez 1996). Indeed, Lorenzo Arroyo, one of the rebel leaders from Michoacán better known as *El Meco* (the "wild one"), habitually went naked and painted in order to reinforce his image.

Nakedness among the rebel Indians was important and deserves further comment. The establishment of colonial rule brought with it a campaign to change the Indians' body image. In effect, religious figures suspected (with good reason, perhaps) that many forms of clothing, body painting, headdresses, and tattoos had religious meaning. Those religious figures were also disgusted by the custom among many indigenous groups, especially those in particularly hot climates, of seminakedness, and were shocked at the public display of male and female genitalia. For these reasons, church officials introduced, with variable success, a type of headdress in the form of the typical indigenous style of hair known as the *balcarrota* (seen, for example, in the representations of Saint Juan Diego in paintings of the Virgin of Guadalupe) and different variations of Spanish peasant dress. The subjugated Indian, the good Christian and obedient subject of the king, was seen as the man whose hair was short and dress decent. Defiance of the established order turned the natives into the image of the rebel: naked, defiant, implacable, and armed once more with bow and arrow. Hence the imaginary Chichimeca would have their rowdy and sonorous reemergence in a society from which they had been wiped out decades earlier.

Rebellion as a Ritual of Possession

The visual horizon of the cities and villas of the time was a series of concentric circles containing the suburbs of Indians on the margins, the neighborhoods and improvised huts of the poor mestizos and mulattos, and the streets and central blocks where the homes of merchants, clerical canons, and large land and mine owners were found.[3] The nexus, of course, was the *plaza mayor*, the town or royal square. From there rose the buildings of authority: the main church or cathedral, the buildings of the town hall, the public jail, and, of course, the pillory, where criminals were flogged or executed. These points of reference were deliberately utilized for religious ceremonies (in particular, Corpus Christi) or civil ceremonies (royal proclamations, celebrations of the birth of royal children, and announcements of peace with other kingdoms). Viceregal orders were also proclaimed and posted there.

In the eighteenth century, these architectural symbols would take on an even greater sense of magnificence. The urban modernization of the Bourbon period would drive the poor, the "indecent," the "badly dressed," the beggars, and the street vendors toward the suburbs (Sánchez de Tagle 2000). Violent disturbances were, in this sense, a human river that came from the margins to flood the center. It did not matter where it came from; the plaza mayor was almost always the destination. There, people would go around the four sides of the square shouting, sometimes throwing stones at homes and buildings, or storming the royal houses. Such acts demonstrated a surprising similarity to the ceremonies of land possession under Spanish law, ceremonies in which the landowner would go along his boundaries, challenging anyone who was opposed to them to present themselves in public, pulling down branches and moving stones as he did so (Seed 1995). What we see, then, is the subversion of a judicial ritual that, at the time, was already well known.

For a time, the persecuted and the marginalized would occupy public spaces and seize the symbols of power, despite the ephemeral nature of their action. Sometimes this appropriation would be literal. In Tehuantepec in 1660, the Indians took the king's standards from the government buildings and moved them to the Indians' town hall (Carmagnani 1992). The feeling of euphoria that came as a result was like a collective intoxication, and has led Natalia Silva Prada to make comparisons between these disturbances and Carnival (Silva Prada 2007, 416–18). Perhaps the references made by judges and fiscales to the *borracheras* (drunkenness) of the rebels were not so far off the mark, although the source of their intoxication in this case was power, not alcohol.

The rebels tended to focus their attack on particular architectural elements, such as the pillory and the public jail. The pillory (a pole in the plaza mayor) was where offenders were publicly shamed or flogged, and was a symbol of authority, distinguishing between what was seen as acceptable and what was clearly forbidden. Debate continues as to whether it represented an oppressive (as we tend to see it today) or protective element. The pillory as a protective force is not so inconceivable, when one considers that it was a visible reminder that justice was done. But the view of the urban masses in this regard leaves no room for doubt: frequently the pillories were either broken or burned, as occurred in San Luis Potosí in 1767. It is not so strange, then, that when sentencing those behind such acts of disturbance, judges ordered the pillories to be rebuilt, but this time in stone.

The fact that the public jail was also frequently stormed, is, in this sense, revealing. Sometimes there was a specific reason behind it: either to free those imprisoned because of their involvement in the unrest, or because of the wider claims that spurred the rioters on. But in other cases, the jail itself was the target, in which case those who were there for specific crimes, such as domestic violence, cohabitation, theft, or fights, were also freed. In a sense, the rioters called into question the legitimacy of justice, and the idea of prison attacks began to take root. We see, for example, how one of Miguel Hidalgo's first acts in 1810 was to free the prisoners of his parish of Dolores, and the same occurred in violent disturbances in other villages and cities (Van Young 1992).

Rethinking Resistance: Words and Actions

This review of the rituals of violence—although not exhaustive—allows some conclusions to be drawn. On the one hand, it seems clear that behind the day-to-day reality of colonial life and the declarations of loyalty and reverence before the judges and viceroys, there ran an undercurrent of indignation and irritation.

The Indians had many reasons to take offense. The elite and indigenous institutions could argue that they were not in fact the *conquered*, but the *conquerors*, and that their merits rendered them privileged vassals. For the majority of natives, however, this was of only relative comfort. The colonial order was, in large measure, focused on appropriating their work, their money, their production, and their consciences. Daily experience would provide them with ample evidence of humiliation and subjugation. They were also largely destitute and sometimes struggled to keep their families and pay their tributes and ecclesiastical contributions. They were also the main recipients—with or without reason—of repressive action by the judges and courts.

Yet the Indian population seems to have generally accepted society such as it was, even though this may have been more out of resignation than active support. There was no nostalgia for the time of the ancient Mexican rulers, who with the passing of time seemed to become more and more remote. There was no alternative organized religion—like Candomblé in Brazil, discussed in chapter seven of this book—to draw together their hopes and dreams for a better life. Their existence was hard, subject to arbitrary action and violence. Yet they seem to have concluded that this was how life was and would always be.

Nonetheless, indigenous groups did not view themselves as a defenseless and passive mass, nor did they act as such. Frequently, they successfully defended what they saw as their rights: their own local government, land, water, and past limitations set on tribute charges and forced labor. They would come before the judges again and again, appealing to their status as minors and insisting on the protection that, according to the law, the judges had to give them. Indeed, they would become quite skilled litigants, as one *corregidor* (a Spanish official in charge of a district) pointed out when he stated that "there [were] among these noisy Indian peoples, friends of innovation, inquiry and knowledge, taking on the Spanish ways and becoming, many of them, good notaries and readers" (Acuña 1987, 305). It may be that they were practicing a primitive version of "compliant defiance" several centuries before Matthew Gutmann (chapter fifteen) would find and define this behavior among the inhabitants of the outlying areas of Mexico City.

While institutional appeals remained open and Indians were offered a reasonable chance that their complaints were being dealt with, they would not risk an uprising. When this ceased to be the case, episodes of violence would erupt, revealing the hidden undercurrent that existed beneath resignation and daily negotiation. For several hours the Indians would own the town, seize the plaza mayor, and destroy the symbols of a justice that they saw as foreign. In their minds, at least, they were ancient warriors once more, parading their manliness, their nakedness, and their bravery in front of their terrified Spanish neighbors.

It is not easy to name such attitudes and behaviors. At times, those of us who specialize in social analysis tend to intellectualize the past, to think that men and women who lived centuries ago always had ideas about themselves and the world that were clear, organized, and systematic. The reality, almost certainly, was much more confusing, ambiguous, and contradictory.

Within the episodes of collective violence I have addressed, there is a combination of ethnic conflict characteristic of colonial society, a harsh daily negotiation to meet the demands of work, material resources, and the necessary obedience that Indians would show, as well as an underlying hostility toward institutions and figures representing authority. We might refer to all of this as resistance, but ultimately this gives an incomplete and simplified reflection of a very complex reality. Adjustment and resistance were complementary attitudes, and without a joined-up study of these, the survival of indigenous groups from the colonial age to today cannot truly be understood.

Notes

Translated by Sarah Maitland

1 All quotations from Spanish-language sources have been translated into English specifically for this chapter.
2 The intendente was a regional governor position created during the eighteenth-century Bourbon reforms.
3 Royally chartered municipalities with lesser privileges than cities.

CHAPTER THREE

Indian Resistances to the Rebellion of 1712 in Chiapas

JUAN PEDRO VIQUEIRA

One of the most frequent criticisms of studies of popular resistance is that they often present society as being divided into two largely homogeneous and clearly differentiated sectors whose interests are radically opposed: the elite and the dominated. The former seek to increase their control over and exploitation of the latter, who consistently resist these efforts. This notion of popular resistance appears to be a poor substitute for the Marxist theory of class struggle, just as unacceptable but much less coherent. As well as oversimplifying the social situations studied, reifying social categories in analysis, and implicitly suggesting the existence of objective interests, such an approach ignores the possibility that alliances can be formed between sectors of different social classes and results in a political Manicheism: the elite class is the personification of evil, whereas all acts of resistance by the subordinate classes are good. In this chapter, I want to show, through a specific historical analysis, the enormous diversity of plans, designs, and actions that can be found among the "popular" or "subaltern" classes.

The argument will logically be more convincing if a historical situation is chosen in which the society in question was highly polarized. The Indian uprising staged in Chiapas in 1712 fulfills this condition (Martínez Peláez, n.d., 124–67; Klein 1970; Bricker 1989, 111–40; Gosner 1992; Ximénez 1999, IV:221–84). A small minority of Spanish (just 2 percent of the total population) held all the important political and religious posts and monopolized large and medium-sized trade in the *alcaldía mayor* (province) of Chiapas. A large body of exploited Indians (92 percent) lived by farming the land and by working as porters in the transport of merchandise. Mestizo, mulatto, and black people accounted for just 6 percent of the population. Chiapas thus had a social structure in which it seems possible to distinguish very clearly between the powerful and the oppressed classes. The uprising made the existing polarization even more acute, as the authorities interpreted it as an Indian revolt against Spanish rule. However, even in such an extreme case as this, the behavior of the "subordinate classes" was far from being homogeneous. In the very heart of the rebellious region, there were Indians who either opposed the uprising itself or opposed certain decisions made by its leaders.

To Rebel: A Choice

The participation by a large proportion of the indigenous population in the uprising was not the inevitable consequence of objective conditions of oppression, but of a choice based on an interpretation of the situation at the time, a decision made in the light of a plan for establishing a new social order, one seen as more fair, but possible to implement. There are two types of situations in which we have an acute awareness of our own freedom: when we actively plan an action and when we find ourselves forced to make a decision and are unsure of what to do.

The uprising was by no means a spontaneous outbreak, but the result of concerted action. From the beginning, the Spanish authorities suspected that the chain of events that triggered the rebellion resulted from the maneuvers of a small group of Indians. A key protagonist in this "conspiracy" was Gerónimo Saraos. Saraos enjoyed great authority. For many years, he was a *fiscal*—the main assistant of the *cura doctrinero*, or parish priest—in Bachajón. He was also one of the very few Indians who were fluent in Spanish. However, following a dispute with the new cura doctrinero, he was forced to go into exile in Cancuc, where he had several friends: Agustín López, the *sacristán* (another parish officer); Gabriel Sánchez; Sebastián García, a former *regidor* (councilman) and brother of the priest's *mayordomo* (steward); and Miguel Gómez, also a former regidor (Viqueira 2007).

These five friends must have grumbled on many occasions about the abuses being perpetrated by the Spanish. In Los Zendales, the Indians complained about excessive amounts of tribute, which for the past thirty years they had had to pay almost exclusively in money instead of in corn, beans, and chilies. This forced men to leave their villages for weeks at a time to work as laborers in haciendas, as porters on the road to Tabasco, or as laborers on cocoa plantations in the Río Tulijá valley, in order to obtain the necessary cash. In years of bad harvests—and recently there had been several—the sum to be paid doubled or even trebled (on the situation prior to the uprising, see Viqueira 1995).

Conflicts among the Spanish had also increased in recent years. As a result, the *alcalde mayor* (Spanish regional governor) of Chiapas had been removed from office and, although he was later reinstated, died just a few months later. The responsibility for maintaining order then fell to the two deputy alcaldes of Ciudad Real who were opposed to one another and lacked any real authority.

In addition, since 1709, the provinces of Coronas y Chinampas and Guardianía de Huitiupán had been shaken by extraordinary events: Preachers foretold the end of the world. Statues of saints were seen to sweat, and the Virgin Mary manifested herself in the village of Santa Marta. A large number of Indians, including the wife of Gabriel Sánchez, Magdalena Díaz, went on a pilgrimage to worship that image of the Virgin. To put a stop to the cult, the bishop confiscated the statue of the Virgin using trickery, and made the Indians return to their villages.

Saraos and his friends decided that these signs pointed to the end of the era of Spanish dominion over Indians. Someone who was able to communicate with the gods was needed to lead the way. The daughter of the sacristán, María López, a young Indian fourteen years old, recently married, and well known throughout the town for her religious devotion, proved just the person they needed. At a meeting together in her presence, the five friends discussed how to attract the divine forces to their cause of electing a new king and establishing a new law according to their own ways, so that they could escape from the endless suffering imposed on them by the *caxlanes*, the name given by the indigenous population to the Spaniards.

Two months later, María began to preach that the Virgin Mary had appeared to her and demanded that an *ermita*, a chapel, be built in her honor. The cura doctrinero, Fray Simón de Lara, opposed this "vile deceit," but the Indians expelled him from Cancuc. Saraos supported the miracle of the apparition of the Virgin with all his authority, not only in Cancuc, but also in other regional towns and villages. He sent letters to Oxchuc and Bachajón, inviting the indigenous populations there to come to see the Virgin. Following the success of this first move, Saraos sent similar summonses to the towns and villages in Los Zendales, Guardianía de Huitiupán, Coronas y Chinampas, and Los Llanos, and to the Zoque communities. By the beginning of August, a large gathering of Indians congregated around the chapel in Cancuc. María López—now known as María de la Candelaria—proclaimed that the Virgin had told her that the king of Spain had died: the time had come in which those favored by the Mother of God would be the Indians, and all of the Spanish must be annihilated, even the clergy.

Although some Indians supported the miracle of the Virgin of Cancuc decisively in the hope of ending Spanish rule, others were undecided about whether or not to join the rebellion. On August 16, Domingo López, the *alcalde* (mayor) of Los Plátanos, received a letter from Cancuc containing an invitation to come and worship the Virgin, and to bring with him the town's statues, processional crosses, and *varas*, or staffs of authority. The alcalde understood very well that this was a summons to rebel against the Spanish. He was not convinced that this was a good idea, but since his fellow council members and a large majority of the townsfolk were enthusiastic about the visit to Cancuc, he finally agreed to accept the invitation.

On his way home, he met a small-scale Spanish merchant with whom he was acquainted, Juan de Figueroa. This trader was upset because since his arrival in the town nobody had taken care of him, and he had not managed to get anything to eat. Domingo López calmed his friend down and invited him to lunch at his home. Throughout the meal, the merchant observed that the alcalde was worried and unhappy, and eventually asked him why. Domingo López told him about the invitation. The merchant convinced him that the authorities would crush the rebellion in the end, and that the price for taking part in it would be very high. The alcalde was no longer in any doubt. He called a messenger and ordered him to overtake the envoys sent to Cancuc with the reply from the *cabildo* (the municipal council) and make them return. This is how Los Plátanos, a town occupying a strategic position between the rebel region and that of the Zoque communities, came to stay out of the rebellion.[1]

The greatest Indian opponents of the uprising were the governors. Their motives are not difficult to ascertain: occupying the highest level of local political power and enjoying great prestige, they owed their posts to the Spanish authorities. In fact, the rebellion was only able to spread because the alcaldes mayores in Chiapas had neglected to appoint governors in Los Zendales, Coronas y Chinampas, and Guardianía de Huitiupán, which therefore lacked authorities loyal to the Spanish regime. As soon as the contingents summoned by Cancuc crossed the borders of these three districts, the governors made sure that all who seemed prepared to join the fray were kept in line.

In Los Llanos province, the governor of Escuintenango, Aquespala, Coneta, and Comalapa worked zealously for the Spanish throughout the uprising.[2] In Chiapa de Indios, when the Spanish authorities sought help to rescue their troops based in Huixtán, the governor and the *principales* (high-ranking Indians, or elders), who had "always been a faithful and very fine people," persuaded initially reluctant Indians to enlist.[3] In Jitotol, despite the fact that the indigenous villagers fled on discovering that the soldiers of the Virgin had attacked the nearby town of Simojovel, the governor made sure that no communication was established between the Zoques and the rebel region.[4]

In Tabasco, the alcalde mayor ordered the governors to intercept all calls to arms from Cancuc. The governor of Tapijulapa, Don Diego de Torres, also played an important role in containing the uprising. A few days before the battle of Huixtán, the invitation to visit the Virgin of Cancuc came to Amatán, a neighboring town in Tabasco. The people of Amatán, unsure of what to do, decided to ask Diego. He advised them "not to allow themselves to be deceived by the rebels, who [were] vile Indians possessed by the Devil" and told them that he would defend them.[5] The governor then sent the letter from Cancuc to Fray Fernando Calderón, the Franciscan friar in charge of the parish that included Amatán, Tapijulapa, Oxolotán and Puxcatán, advising him to come as quickly as possible to put the minds of the Amatán Indians to rest. However, some two weeks later, another rebel summons came to Amatán, this time in a much more threatening context. It was brought by two Indians from Guardianía de Huitiupán, who told the townspeople that Asunción Huitiupán had been forced to rejoin the uprising by the soldiers of the Virgin and had attacked Simojovel, killing many of its inhabitants. Fray Calderón was in town that day and managed to have the two messengers imprisoned. However, when he wanted to send them to Tapijulapa, the Amatán Indians refused, fearing that such an action would provoke a violent incursion by the rebels. As his arguments were not succeeding in making the *amatecos* change their minds, the friar called on the governor to come. Accompanied by several soldiers, Don Diego convinced the Amatán Indians to move en masse to Tapijulapa, where he could protect them from attack by the soldiers from Cancuc.[6]

The governors were not the only Indians in important offices who opposed the rebellion. Initially, many fiscales tried to convince people not to pay homage to the Virgin of Cancuc, but they had much less success in this respect than the governors. The main assistants of the parish priests in Indian towns and villages, the fiscales, were able to read and write in their native languages, and in a few exceptional cases could also speak Spanish. The curas doctrineros usually had sufficient confidence in these assistants to entrust them—unofficially—with the tasks of teaching the catechism to children and recording births, marriages, and deaths in the parish registers.

Several fiscales strove to discredit the miracle of Cancuc: two from Ox-chuc, one from Tenango, another from Petalcingo, two from Tumbalá, an-other two from Tila, and one from Los Moyos.[7] Even in Cancuc itself, one of the fiscales—Domingo Pérez—opposed the heretical cult, passing infor-mation on what was happening in his pueblo to the Spanish authorities up to the very day when the uprising was declared.[8] The majority of these fiscales paid for their loyalty to the church with their lives: the rebels took them as prisoners to Cancuc, where they were whipped and then hanged. Only one of the fiscales from Tila, after being severely flogged, managed to escape and took refuge in Tabasco. The fiscal from Los Moyos gave in when threatened by the rebels, and as a result saved his own life.[9]

Some other fiscales wisely opted to keep a low profile at first. After the battle of Huixtán, an Indian from Chenalhó, Sebastián Gómez, arrived in Cancuc claiming that he had ascended to heaven where he had spoken to the Holy Trinity, the Virgin Mary, and Saint Peter, and been granted the au-thority to appoint new bishops and priests. Quickly, all of the Indians who could read and write were summoned to be ordained by Sebastián Gómez de la Gloria—as he had come to be known—and by María de la Candelaria. Since, save for a few rare exceptions, the only literate Indians were the fis-cales, this summons was a clear attempt to involve them in the uprising by offering them an extremely prestigious office. Almost all heeded the call—perhaps partly through fear, but also probably because they began to believe that victory over the Spanish was possible. After being ordained, they returned to their towns and villages, where they prayed the rosary, celebrated Mass, consecrated the bread and the wine, baptized children, performed marriage ceremonies, heard confession, and gave extreme unc-tion. In their sermons they preached that the Virgin had appeared in Can-cuc to proclaim that the Indians would take the place of the Spanish, and that the Spanish had become the new Jews because they refused to believe in the apparition of the Virgin. The Indians, on the other hand, had become the true Christians (Viqueira 2002, 201–58).

Some of the more important priests were not content with preaching sermons, saying mass, administering the holy sacraments, and leading religious processions. Instead, they began to commit the same abuses as the Spanish priests. The most authoritarian seems to have been the brother of Sebastián Gómez, Domingo, who held the office of *vicario superior*, or high priest. When Sebastián Gómez de la Gloria returned to Las Coronas y Chinampas, he sent his brother to Cancuc to keep the priests under control. However, Domingo began to abuse his position with such despotism that he came to be hated by all the people of Cancuc, who eventually had him whipped and hanged.[10] In spite of this example, other priests did not learn their lesson. Even Gerónimo Saraos got carried away with the office of bishop. He set off to visit the towns and villages of Los Zendales, performing baptisms and marriages and celebrating Masses. In exchange for these services, he charged exorbitant fees and demanded that people give him a ration of fish. In response to mounting complaints, Nicolás Vázquez—at that time the main captain of the soldiers of the Virgin—took Saraos prisoner, with the permission of María de la Candelaria, along with Lucas Pérez, who was accused of similar abuses, and ordered them to be taken to Cancuc. There they were stripped of all their worldly possessions and brutally flogged (Viqueira 2007, 84–89).

Although the bulk of the *justicias* (native cabildo officeholders) from Los Zendales went to Cancuc when summoned, some refused. In some cases, this was because the Indians that they represented did not want to join the rebellion. In others, it was because Spanish inhabitants of the towns and villages persuaded them not to believe in the Cancuc miracle. Opposition on the part of justicias cannot be explained as a defense of positions and privileges. The posts of alcaldes and regidores were renewed every year, which meant that in medium-sized towns and villages, the vast majority of adult men held one of these offices at some point in their lives.

When the soldiers of the Virgin finally occupied their villages, almost all renounced their initial position and joined the rebels. They were allowed to keep their offices, from which position they cooperated diligently with the ringleaders of the revolt. For those who remained loyal to the king of Spain, there was no mercy. Sebastián Pérez, for example, a notary on the cabildo of Chilón, was brought to Cancuc, was subjected to four hundred lashes, and had his feet burned, which caused him to become *"impedido,"* or "incapacitated."[11]

It was only in Huitiupán that the justicias, supported by the fiscal, directly disagreed with the opinions of the majority of the population. Although they tried to persuade their fellow villagers not to go to Cancuc, only a few stayed with them in the village, mostly because they were ill. Following the battle of Huixtán, the large majority of the people of Huitiupán chose to escape from Cancuc and distance themselves from the insurgent movement, acknowledging their mistake to the justicias and to their cura doctrinero. But a few days later, the soldiers of the Virgin occupied Huitiupán, killed the priest, and forced the village's inhabitants to take part in the bloody attack against the neighboring town of Simojovel, whose inhabitants had refused to participate in the uprising. The justicias paid dearly for their initial opposition to the rebellion: the followers of María de la Candelaria killed the two alcaldes, two of the regidores, two *alguaciles mayors* (other council officials), the community mayordomo, and one of the fiscales.[12]

It was not only Indians who held a religious or political office who rejected the rebel movement, but also various ordinary indigenous people. We know of at least two cases in Huitiupán. Marcos López, an Indian from Tuxtla who had settled and married in Huitiupán, apparently feared that the rebels would see him as a *ladino* (culturally and linguistically hispanicized) infiltrator, and he therefore decided to leave the village along with his wife and children. Another inhabitant of Huitiupán, Juan de Montoya, accompanied this family in their flight. Following the insurgents' defeat, their loyalty to the Crown was rewarded: the alcalde mayor of Tabasco appointed them alcaldes in Huitiupán.[13]

Not all of the Indians who took refuge in Tabasco opposed the uprising. Some had to escape because they belonged to rebel factions opposed to the leadership of María de la Candelaria. As is common in revolutions, there was no lack of violent conflicts among the rebels themselves. The most notorious case was that of Magdalena Díaz. According to some sources, it was this elderly Indian woman, the wife of Gabriel Sánchez, who came up with the "idea" of an apparition of the Virgin in Cancuc, after going to see the Virgin of Santa Marta. In the beginning, she appeared in public alongside María de la Candelaria, but felt sidelined by the growing leadership of the younger woman. Travelling to Yajalón, she set up a cult centered on herself, causing a schism in the rebel movement. Eventually, the troops of María de la Candelaria occupied Yajalón and returned her to Cancuc by force, where she was executed.[14] Her closest collaborator, Juan Gutiérrez, a native of Tila, managed to escape from the soldiers of the Virgin and sought refuge in Tabasco. There, he claimed that he had fled out of fear of the rebels, who had "committed all sorts of atrocious murders of people who speak Spanish, even if they [were] Indian, because they claim[ed] that they [were] giving advice to the Spanish, and they [were] killing any ladinos in cold blood, and it [was] for this reason that he fled with his wife and children."[15]

As little was known about what was happening in the rebel-controlled region, at first the alcalde mayor of Tabasco took Gutiérrez at his word. However, when Cancuc was taken, several prisoners and witnesses mentioned his name. Tried and found guilty, among other crimes, of having been a "dissident anti-papist arch-heretic," Gutiérrez was hanged in Tacotalpa, the capital of Tabasco.[16]

There were also some Indians who, because they did not find themselves forced to take sides, withdrew to their *milpas* (corn fields) and simply waited for the storm to abate before returning to their villages.[17] Others deserted the rebel region for purely personal or emotional reasons, as in the case of Magdalena Hernández, a young Indian woman from Chamula married to an Indian from Mitontic, Andrés Jiménez. The rebellion had separated Magdalena from her blood relatives: while Chamula remained under Spanish control, her husband sympathized with the uprising and became a spy for the cause. When troops from Ciudad Real attempted a raid on Coronas y Chinampas, Andrés Jiménez warned his comrades of their arrival. Seeing her chance, Magdalena Hernández fled to Chamula, in spite of her husband's having threatened her with death if she dared to leave the milpa. When she had to explain herself to the Spanish soldiers who captured her, instead of professing any heroic act of loyalty to the Crown, she simply declared that she had run away from Mitontic "for love of her mother and father who were in Chamula."[18]

Other dissidents contributed to undermining the revolt without openly opposing the uprising. One Indian from Cancuc, for example, went in secret to some Indians from Chamula who had been seized for carrying a letter from Pedro Gutiérrez, the alcalde mayor of Chiapas, to the leaders of the rebellion, officially warning them to lay down their arms in exchange for their pardon. He told them that they were going to be hanged and helped them to escape. He accompanied them to the gates of the pueblo, telling them not to be afraid and that "God would look after them."[19]

Other Indians disobeyed orders of rebel leaders because they felt compassion for the victims of the violence that went hand in hand with the revolution, especially for the ladina women of the region. The vast majority of these women—who were Spanish, *mestiza*, or *mulata*,—had been born and raised in Los Zendales. Belonging to a small group of ladinos who had been settling in the province since the middle of the seventeenth century, these women had always been integrated into the world of the Indians and were very familiar with their languages and customs. But at the same time, their families represented a foreign element. Their menfolk—and perhaps even the women themselves—had had to find a niche for themselves, often resorting to violence, protected by the power of the alcaldes mayores and the merchants, who used them as local intermediaries. Their fathers and husbands were not especially rich—had they been, they would not have settled permanently in the area—and their mediocre fortunes depended almost entirely on what they could procure from the Indians, through buying and selling products, or contracting Indian labor. They constantly sought to distinguish themselves from the Indians, whom they treated as people of lower quality.

When the invitations began to arrive from Cancuc to go to see the Virgin, the *alcaldes ordinarios* in Ciudad Real ordered one of the inhabitants of Chilón, Captain Pedro Ordóñez, to gather together in his town the entire population of Spanish, mestizo, black, and mulatto men from the region. Ordóñez managed to assemble around forty badly armed men and waited for further instructions from Ciudad Real. On August 12, however, the soldiers of the Virgin attacked Chilón. After an initial confrontation, the ladinos, who had taken refuge in the town monastery, seeing that their forces were insufficient, agreed to surrender their weapons in exchange for the rebels' sparing their lives. However, the rebels broke their promise and killed almost all the men, beating them to death or throwing them from the highest part of the monastery.[20]

Two days later, on August 14, the soldiers of the Virgin moved on to Ocosingo. On this occasion, the ladino men, knowing what had happened in Chilón, made no attempt to resist. Almost all fled the village, leaving their wives and children behind. When the soldiers of the Virgin arrived in the village, they killed all the children, around forty in number.[21] The rebels then beat the women and locked them up in the jail. The following day, the women were forced to set out for Cancuc, along with the few ladino men who had remained in the village. On the way, the rebels executed all of the men and any women too weak to move quickly enough. Five or six days later, almost all of the ladina women from Chilón, after being stripped of their possessions and jewelry, were bound and forced to march to Cancuc under threat of the whip.[22]

On arrival in Cancuc, the women were taken to the chapel of the Virgin. Their rosaries were taken off them, placed behind the sleeping mat, and then returned to them, having been "blessed." They were forced to make an offering and take part in a strange religious ceremony. As nobody in Cancuc bothered to feed them, several women managed to gain permission to return to their towns and villages in search of provisions. There, they were forced to work as *molenderas* (corn grinders)—traditionally the work of Indian women—in the service of the local rebel leaders, to make it very clear that the social order, which had previously favored them, had been reversed.

A few weeks later, these ladinas were called back to Cancuc, where they were informed that María de la Candelaria had ordered them to dress like Indian women and wear their hair loose, so that they could no longer be distinguished. During their second stay in Cancuc, they were constantly made to attend masses led by the Indian priests and María de la Candelaria, and they were punished with a lashing if they refused. To complete their integration into the new society, the spokesperson for the Virgin ordered that they were to marry Indian men. Many refused to comply, but were stripped naked, tied to a chair, and whipped until their resistance crumbled. Others, seeing what fate awaited them if they attempted to resist, obeyed without a word.

After Spanish troops eventually liberated these women, the president of the *Audiencia* (Royal Court of Justice) in Guatemala, Toribio de Cosío, listened to their testimonies about their experiences during the uprising. Although he did not question them specifically on this point, many of the women bore witness to the compassionate gestures, solidarity, and valiant support that, in the midst of the horror that they were suffering, they had received from certain Indians. In their testimonies appear the actions of individuals who did not succumb to the frenzy of collective violence: the rebel captain from Chilón, who, in exchange for two pesos, allowed Antonia López, a mestiza, to stay in the town, defying orders from Cancuc and consequently saving her from a forced marriage; the Indian woman from Cancuc who hid Agueda de Estrada in her home when the Spanish troops attacked Cancuc, so that the rebels could not exact revenge on her for their defeat; the Indian woman from Sivacá who rescued María Vázquez when the soldiers of the Virgin were taking her, injured, as a prisoner to Cancuc, after having murdered her three young children, and who gave her shelter in her house, fed her, and nursed her back to health; and last but not least, the ambiguous case of José López—the only one mentioned by his name—an Indian from Tumbalá, who intervened in favor of Gerónima Domínguez, a *parda* (woman of mixed Spanish and African descent) from Ocosingo who was one of the servants of the cura, so that she would not be murdered, as had her mother and brothers. At first he aroused the anger of the ringleaders, who were about to kill him, but shortly afterwards not only managed to earn their pardon, but persuaded a priest to marry him to Gerónima.

Such were the striking contrasts indelibly etched in the memories of the women who experienced them. However, the women were urged to forget those memories by those who heard their tales and compiled their accounts, in order to convey to future generations, without any sort of nuance or moral ambiguity, the only truth judged worthy of historical endurance: that the rebellion in Cancuc had been a merciless all-out war of every Indian against every Spaniard and ladino.

Toward the end of October, reinforcements from Guatemala arrived in Ciudad Real, with the president of the Audiencia himself at their head. With more men and more weapons, the Spanish launched their final campaign against the rebels. On November 21, Toribio de Cosío's men entered Cancuc, after ousting the soldiers of the Virgin from trenches they had dug at the entrance to the town. Yet although this was the last armed confrontation of the uprising, the Spanish encountered serious difficulties in restoring normality to the region: every time the king's troops approached a town or village, its indigenous population would flee and hide in the mountains.

Shortly after the taking of Cancuc, Toribio de Cosío wrote communiqués to the Indians, advising them to give themselves up and to present themselves to him in Cancuc, in return for which he would pardon them (see also Castro Gutiérrez, chapter two). The alcalde mayor of Tabasco did the same when he advanced into Chiapas. In order to dispatch these communiqués, it was necessary to find Indians familiar with the region and willing to deliver them. These Indians were chosen from among those who had been taken prisoner or who lived in the towns and villages that had surrendered. It is likely that those chosen as messengers, thinking that the revolution had failed, had shown themselves willing to aid the Spanish in bringing peace to the region without causing new armed conflicts, as the death toll had been high among the indigenous population. However, apart from the first envoys sent by the alcalde mayor of Tabasco, who succeeded in returning safely, all of the others paid with their lives for accepting this charge from the Spanish. The rebels executed them and left their bodies in the forest to be devoured by wild animals.[23]

One case that had a particular impact on the Spanish authorities was that of a woman from Chilón, Dominica Gómez, who was in Cancuc when the pueblo succumbed to the assault by the troops from Guatemala. Dominica Gómez offered of her own volition to bear the communiqué from the president of the Audiencia to her community. She overcame the initial skepticism of the Spanish—this did not seem like a task that a woman could perform adequately—by explaining that her husband was a principal, and that he would surely succeed in convincing the Indians from Chilón to return to obedience to the Castilian Crown. Dominica Gómez must have been a skilled negotiator, because, unlike the rest of the messengers, she managed to exact a promise from Toribio de Cosío that, if she succeeded in her mission, her entire family would be exempt from paying tributes. Her husband managed to persuade the Indians allied with him to lay down their arms and to report to Toribio de Cosío to receive instructions. However, while her husband, Agustín Jiménez, along with an alcalde, a regidor, and various other principales, was in Cancuc, the indigenous faction that had refused to surrender attacked the homes of their neighbors who had betrayed the cause of the rebellion and killed three residents, among them Dominica Gómez.[24]

Other Indians who immediately offered to collaborate with the Spanish were the alcaldes from Cancuc. Their offer did not seem in any way suspicious to Toribio de Cosío, given that it was the authorities from Ciudad Real who had initially granted them this office a couple weeks before the start of the uprising, after imprisoning the former justicias, whom they believed to be involved in the false miracle of the Virgin of Cancuc. The new alcaldes had kept the authorities in Ciudad Real informed about what was happening in Cancuc up to the very moment of the outbreak of the rebellion. What does not seem to have been understood by the president of the Audiencia is that throughout the uprising, these justicias had remained in their posts, at the service of María de la Candelaria and her followers. Be this as it may, during the entire time that the troops from Guatemala stayed in Cancuc, the two alcaldes displayed proof of their loyalty, and in return for this the president of the Audiencia confirmed them in their office for another year.[25] Their ability to change their allegiance in order to be always on the side of the powerful seems largely to have worked in their favor. However, one of them proved too clever for his own good. When the Spanish began the search for María de la Candelaria—who had managed to flee with her father, husband, brother, and daughter-in-law after the battle of Cancuc—Domingo Pérez secretly tried to sabotage their efforts. It was even said that he had come across the father of the *indiezuela*, the little Indian girl, but that he let him go free, an act that Domingo Pérez vehemently denied. However, around the middle of 1713, he advised an Indian who was suspected of knowing the whereabouts of María de la Candelaria to say nothing, even under torture.[26] His scheming came to the attention of the alcalde mayor of Chiapas, who judged him and found him guilty, although it is not known what punishment he was given.

In all of the towns and villages that the Spanish troops were occupying, the captains found some Indians who would help them to find fugitives hiding in the mountains or who would carry the message to them that the president of the Audiencia would pardon all those who returned to their homes voluntarily. Once a town had recovered the majority of its inhabitants, the Spanish official in charge of pacifying the region distributed the posts of governor, alcalde, and regidore among these loyal collaborators. However, in return for this, the official ordered them to denounce all those who had actively participated in the revolt, whether as ringleaders or as simple soldiers. For although the Spanish authorities had a reasonably accurate idea of who the main ringleaders of the uprising had been, they remained ignorant of almost all of the local leaders, and even more so of the ordinary soldiers. To prevent the accused from fleeing once more to the mountains, the authorities carried out their investigations in secret, and let us not forget that they had offered a general pardon to all those who gave themselves up voluntarily. Once the authorities had compiled their list of supposed culprits, they called a meeting of all the town residents, under the pretext of carrying out a census of tribute payers, and took them prisoner by surprise.[27] The punishments meted out were particularly severe. Although, in cases of mutiny or rebellion, the Spanish authorities normally only punished the main leaders, on this occasion nearly

100 prisoners were sentenced to death, and many more were flogged and banished from their towns.

The authorities trusted the claims of their informants and collaborators that they had not been involved in the uprising, and also that they had told the truth in denouncing the guilty parties. However it is quite probable that these two assumptions were not always correct. It is by no means impossible that a large number of these helpful Indian individuals had changed sides only after the victories won by the troops from Guatemala and that, after gaining the trust of the Spanish military commanders, they had taken advantage of the opportunity to dispose of their enemies within their communities, by passing them off as dangerous subversives.

Civil wars and revolutions are generally opportune moments for settling scores between neighbors under the guise of political and ideological purging. In fact, during the uprising of 1712, there were at least two cases of this type, which were especially dramatic because they involved deadly encounters between husbands and wives. In the first, Diego Guzmán Malenchi, an Indian from Tumbalá, besought the ringleaders of the rebellion to kill his wife, Potenciana Alvarez, a parda, with whom he was certainly not on good terms. The execution was carried out extremely viciously: the woman was tied to a stake, flogged, and eventually killed.[28] Another similar case is that of María Hernández, an Indian woman from Tila, who "consented" that her husband be killed by her lover, Juan Vázquez, an important rebel captain who participated in the battles of Ocosingo, Huixtán, Simojovel, Oxchuc, and Cancuc.[29]

With this in mind, it is not impossible that during the pacification led by the Spanish troops in Los Zendales there were new scores to settle, this time under the pretext of denouncing the rebel leaders to the Spanish authorities. This is something that was suspected, for example, by the lawyer who defended the stepmother of María de la Candelaria, Nicolasa Gómez. The Spanish forces had captured her two weeks after the battle of Cancuc. During her trial, Nicolasa protested that she had had nothing to do with the miracle of the Virgin of Cancuc. In spite of this, the alcalde of Cancuc, Domingo Pérez—whose double-dealing is already known to us—declared that it was she who had advised María de la Candelaria. The fiscales and various principales of the pueblo supported this declaration by the alcalde. However, the defense lawyer, Don Tomás de Mora, cast doubt on their words, saying: "The witnesses who have testified against the defendant in this case desire to make her appear guilty because they have endeavored to save themselves from the crimes that they themselves have committed, which are flagrant and widely known."[30] However, in spite of this plausible allegation by the lawyer, María de la Candelaria's stepmother was condemned to death.

One month later, the same lawyer would argue once again that the only proof that existed against two other accused parties—Sebastián Gómez and Juan Ortés of Tila—were statements by two witnesses who may have been "driven by a certain passion or hatred."[31] One of these witnesses was the uncle of Juan Ortés. This defense was also in vain: the two accused parties were shot as criminals and their bodies quartered. Parts of their corpses were displayed in various places along the road from Yajalón to Tila.

*   *   *

With this collection of brief stories of Indians who in one way or another opposed the rebellion of 1712, who disagreed with the means used by its leaders, or who, in retrospect, declared themselves opposed to the uprising in order to gain favor with the Spanish, I have aimed to show how, even in an extremely polarized situation, the members of the popular classes opt to follow different, and even conflicting, paths. The diversity of thoughts, attitudes, and actions within any social group is a fact that cannot be denied without seriously distorting the reality in question.

For this reason, when we investigate resistance, we cannot ignore the fact that, in one way or another, members of the lower classes always argue, struggle, and fight among themselves over their objectives, the means to be employed to achieve them, and the potential consequences of any planned collective action. To attempt to silence the doubts, differences, and rivalries that were present among individuals leads to a situation whereby they are presented as objects motivated by supposed objective interests, rather than as social beings capable of questioning the meanings of their actions and making different decisions depending on their personal values. Furthermore, those belonging to the "popular classes" are not necessarily justified in their actions simply because they are victims of social inequality. There is no shortage of examples of people from among the masses who have been involved in the persecution or lynching of ethnic or religious minorities, who have joined fundamentalist or extreme right-wing movements, who have endorsed dictatorial regimes, or who have resorted to fear in order to exterminate their enemies or even their allies.

For all of these reasons, I believe that we should not idealize popular struggles simply because they are popular. Condemning the hard living conditions suffered by the lower classes does not provide us with a motive for justifying all of their actions, and it is impossible to do this without contradicting ourselves as a result of the diversity of the political affiliations within this population group. Both their ends and their means, therefore, must be subjected to a close critical scrutiny. As Alan Knight argues in the concluding essay in this book, it is not, in any case, the historian's place to judge: little is achieved by condemning or absolving the dead. The historian's task should be that of understanding, and helping others to understand, situations and realities in the past, not elevating bronze heroes or denouncing villains (Bloch 1997, 156–59). However, as Mikhail Bakhtin rightly points out, every principle, every human action, speaks to us, questions our vision of the world and our values, and compels us to take sides, even if we only do so secretly in our own private thoughts (Bajtín 1989, 294–323). History is always written from the perspective of our own present concerns. It is a question of accepting our values such as they are, and not passing them off as laws of history, objective necessities, or causes of the oppressed to produce a convenient evacuation of politics — that is, debates around the ends, means, and consequences of collective action — in the name of "popular resistance."

Notes

Translated by Sarah Magee

1 Archivo General de Indias (AGI), Guatemala, 296, exp. 9, ff. 32v–34.
2 AGI, Guatemala, 294, exp. 23, ff. 20v–25.
3 Ibid., ff. 28–30v.
4 Ibid., 296, exp. 9, ff. 65–66.
5 Ibid., 293, exp. 12, ff. 23v–26.
6 Ibid., 293, exp. 11, ff. 188–96v.
7 Ibid., 293, exp. 12, ff. 203–20v; and 296, exp. 9, ff. 25v–27v.
8 Ibid., 293, exp. 12, ff. 17v–18v.
9 Ibid., 293, exp. 12, ff. 115–16.
10 Ibid., 293, exp. 10, ff. 37v–39.
11 Ibid., 295, exp. 7, ff. 5–6v.

12 Ibid., 296, exp. 9, ff. 62v–86v; and 293, exp. 11, ff. 112v–30v.

13 Ibid., 296, exp. 12, ff. 40–44v and 161v–62v.

14 Ibid., 296, exp. 11, ff. 148–63v.

15 Ibid., 296, exp. 12, ff. 44v–47v.

16 Ibid., 294, exp. 23, ff. 633v–637.

17 Ibid., 296, exp. 9, ff. 36–38.

18 Ibid., 296, ff. 263v–65.

19 Ibid., 296, ff. 137–41.

20 Ibid., 293, exp. 12, ff. 15v–21v.

21 Ibid., 295, exp. 6, ff. 45–48v.

22 The description of the misfortunes of the ladina women is based on their own testimonies found in AGI, Guatemala, 293, exp. 12, ff. 203–10v; 295, exp. 6, ff. 1v–64; and in "Sublevación de los indios tzendales: Año 1713," *Boletín del Archivo General de la Nación* 19, no. 4 (1948): 497–535.

23 Ibid., 293, exp. 11, ff. 130v–33v; exp. 12, ff. 194–95 and 333–335v; and 294, exp. 23, ff. 283v–84v and 391–391v.

24 Ibid., 293, exp. 11, ff. 188v–89v; and 295, exp. 7, ff. 2–3.

25 Ibid., 294, exp. 23, ff. 220–20v and 302v–4; and 296, exp. 9, ff. 27v–30.

26 Ibid., 294, exp. 23, ff. 714v–17v.

27 Ibid., 293, exp. 12, ff. 226v–27v and 275–76.

28 Ibid., 293, exp. 12, ff. 253–63.

29 Ibid., 293, exp. 12, ff. 404–20.

30 Ibid., 295, exp. 6, ff. 116v–17.

31 Ibid., 295, exp. 7, ff. 202–3 and 212–15.

CHAPTER FOUR

The "Commander of All Forests" against the "Jacobins" of Brazil

The Cabanada, 1832–1835

MARCUS J. M. DE CARVALHO

From 1832 to 1835, peasants, Indians, runaway slaves, and a handful of landlords in the frontier of the provinces of Pernambuco and Alagoas rebelled, demanding the return of Pedro I, who had left the throne of Brazil on April 7, 1831. Although the rebellion was crushed, its most important leader fled into the forests, where he founded a community with hundreds of followers. They resisted the encroachments of the landed aristocracy until their leader's arrest in 1850. *Cabanos* were those who lived in *cabanas*, or forest huts. Sources also refer to them as "gente das matas," people of the forests. After the rebellion's defeat, resistance continued for years. Rebellions as such are seldom the result of spontaneous, immediate reaction against ruling elites or the state apparatus. Rather, they are usually preceded by several acts of resistance. Collective action requires some kind of consciousness. That takes time to build up, even if it is a utopian consciousness, as in the case of the Cabanos, who fought for the return of the Brazilian emperor. Addressing some of the issues Alan Knight raises in his conclusion to this book, this chapter illustrates an arc of resistance, from the start of a collective consciousness to open rebellion, and then returns to resistance. Moreover, the Cabanada and its aftermath help us to understand how these subalterns turned clientelistic networks to their advantage during the process of state formation in Brazil. One of the side effects of rebellions can be the construction of strong bonds among people of different backgrounds and personal interests. Rebellions also forge leaders who would never gain authority in more peaceful times and result in the production of reams of documents about these rebels, traitors, or bandits, that is to say these subalterns, that would not exist were it not for the threat to state hegemony. This chapter will also examine the role of personal bonds in resistance and rebellion as well as the trail of documents such events leave behind. This chapter begins with an examination of events leading up to the Cabanada.

The Fall of Pedro I and the Rebellion of the "People of the Forests"

The abdication of Pedro I had a considerable impact in Brazil. Unable to control the Parliament, Pedro I left for Portugal, leaving behind his five-year-old son, who would become Pedro II in 1840. With a child in charge, liberals in Pernambuco felt more confident than at any time since the secessionist 1824 rebellion.[1] After the abdication, the regency at Rio de Janeiro removed from office the governors of several provinces and scores of army officers and state officials. On April 14, 1832, army officers, recently discharged from their posts, led a three-day barracks uprising, known as the Abrilada, in the capital city of Recife. Plantation owners, who supported the Abrilada, armed their dependents and other people who lived under their jurisdiction under the promise of further compensation. But those armed bands ran out of control after the elite rebels gave up the fight; this was the Cabanada. For Manuel Correia de Andrade (1965) and Dirceu Lindoso (1983), the Abrilada triggered the Cabanada, because of the mobilization of armed bands in the interior who rebelled when government troops were sent to disarm them. The restoration of Pedro I was the professed motivation of both the Abrilada and Cabanada rebels, but the restoration of Pedro I had different meanings for the participants (M. C. Andrade 1965, 34–38; Quintas 1985, 201–2).

The Abrilada involved different interests and class positions. As one "liberal" paper stated, there were men who had participated in the liberal rebellion of 1824 who, by 1831, sided with the absolutists and restorationists. Uniting this ideologically disparate group were the jobs and privileges they lost with the abdication.[2] The Abrilada also found support among Portuguese clerks and artisans, victimized by increased nativism in Recife after the downfall of Pedro. Poor Brazilians felt as if independence had been incomplete, for Portuguese immigrants occupied most posts in the urban retail trade. This unrest also reached the army, because Portuguese soldiers and officers advanced more rapidly in their careers and several of the key commanding posts were still in their hands. Prior to the Abrilada, in November 1831, Brazilian-born lower-rank officers had led an uprising with the support of an urban crowd from Recife, demanding that poor Portuguese immigrants be expelled. Instead, in the following months, the regency diminished the size of the army. Scores were dismissed without compensation and left without prospects on the streets of Recife.[3] Those former soldiers also supported the Abrilada of 1832. One of the rebel officers, for example, had been a major in Pernambuco's corps of black freedmen.[4]

The Abrilada also attracted army officers, including Portuguese-born captains and majors; although the army had played an important role in the events leading to the abdication, as soon as Pedro had sailed, the civilian-led regency curtailed officers' privileges, such as their right to be tried by military courts (Werneck Sodré 1965, 120). In Pernambuco, officers also resented that they had not been invited to join the higher ranks of the recently created Municipal Guard in charge of police work in the province.[5] It was commanded by civilians, but all army officers were compelled to enlist or lose their wages.[6]

The Abrilada was doomed, however, when the rebels failed to seize the major fortresses of Recife. The remaining two hundred rebels fled to the countryside, finding protection among sympathetic landowners, who were also disgruntled by the regency's policies. These restorationist landowners had been captains and sergeants major of the colonial Ordenanças (local militia).[7] They had lost part of their prestige due to the reforms of 1827–31 that created the position of justice of the peace and the national guard, which would perform most of the tasks of former captains and sergeants major. One of these was Captain Major Torres Galindo, a plantation owner who had lost the elections in 1829 for the local justice of the peace, but maintained his armed retinue, arresting and releasing people at will, as if he were still in office.[8]

After the fall of Pedro I, new provincial governors and judges were appointed throughout Brazil. They dared to confront local power bosses loyal to Pedro I, including Torres Galindo, who was already circulating restorationist manifestos in Vitória in February 1832.[9] Galindo went further, distributing weapons and ammunition and mobilizing his personal retinue and ranchers throughout his area of influence, where many people had helped the imperial troops during the rebellion of 1824.[10] One of his allies was Antônio Timóteo de Andrade, a modest rancher in the district of Panelas, who also had helped to crush the rebellion of 1824. He was a lowerranking reserve officer, a subordinate of Captain Major Torres Galindo, who would become a major Cabano leader. Moreover, according to a state official, he was black ("negro").[11] After he was killed in combat, his brother took his place. Together they encouraged rebellion among the Indians and peasants around the district of Panelas (M. C. Andrade 1965, 49; Callado 1981, 136, 181).[12]

On the frontier between Pernambuco and Alagoas, there were also planters who supported the Abrilada because of previous strong ties to the emperor: those who helped the army quell the liberal rebellion in 1824 had received benefits from the Crown such as land grants. Sergeant Major Manoel Affonso de Mello received a medal for his bravery then, fighting against the republicans.[13] According to his local enemies, Mello had been compensated by the emperor; nevertheless, he also seized land and property from the republicans of 1824.[14] Lieutenant Colonel João Batista de Araújo also assembled troops near the frontier of Pernambuco and Alagoas in 1824, receiving a medal for his efforts. After the abdication, he was dismissed from his commanding post.[15] Mello and Araújo were also in contact with the Indians of Jacuípe, who had fought against the rebels of 1824 and feared for their safety after the fall of Pedro I. In 1832, they mobilized hundreds of men.[16] Despite a failed attempt to seize the government of Pernambuco in Recife, the Abrilada had a greater impact in the hinterland because of the broad support Pedro I had there in 1824. All those who had benefited from the campaign in 1824 were mobilized by the Abrilada leaders, including the Indians of the Jacuípe River Valley and many nonelite ranchers, such as the "negro" Timóteo.

After the Abrilada in Recife, a thousand well-armed men were sent to the interior to arrest Galindo, Mello, Araújo, Timóteo, and the remaining Abrilada leaders. This army was commanded by Captain Carapeba, who had previously been sentenced to death for his participation in the rebellion of 1824 and had been in hiding until the abdication. The new Comandante das Armas of Pernambuco, Major José Joaquim da Silva Santiago, was also a republican from 1824. In 1832, Santiago sent Carapeba to fight against his local enemies, for Santiago's family had lands near the frontier between Pernambuco and Alagoas.[17] The troops sent from Recife made a difference: by late 1832, most of the remaining leaders of the Abrilada had been arrested or killed.

Thus, by late 1832, there was not much left of a restorationist rebellion led by army officers and landowners. Armed Indians, peasants, and slaves, however, roamed the forests between Alagoas and Pernambuco. Their continued uprising became known as the Cabanada. Its principal leader was Vicente de Paula, the son of a priest, although little is known about the father. Vicente de Paula's manifestos stated that the Cabanada were fighting to restore Pedro I. But even after Pedro died in Portugal in September 1834 and the army employed a scorched-earth policy, they continued to fight.

In summary, the sequence of events is as follows: first, the government troops attacked Torres Galindo in Vitória and Manoel Affonso de Mello and João Batista de Araújo on the frontier between Pernambuco and Alagoas (M. C. Andrade 1965, 48).[18] However, Araújo, Mello, and Galindo soon moved to Panelas, where they joined Timóteo and found a more defensible position.[19] In September they were already moving through the jungle and hills from Panelas to Jacuípe and Água Preta, where they could hide and later return in their sorties southwest of the forests, in the plantation areas of Rio Formoso and Porto Calvo.[20] In October, the force sent from Recife went to Jacuípe in order to draft the Indians who refused to cooperate with conscription, a perfect excuse to evict them. Soon the Indians, too, rose in rebellion. By mid-1835, thanks in part to the negotiations of the bishop and several priests, as well as a promised amnesty to rebels (except for Vicente de Paula and runaway slaves who joined the rebellion), many of the Cabanos finally gave up the fight. By November, Araújo, Mello, and Galindo had been arrested and most of the landowners surrendered. That is when the reports to the Comando das Armas started to mention constant attacks of "savages" and "bandits" against their headquarters.

At that point, de Paula became infamous, not only for his expertise as a commander, but also for "stealing" slaves from the *engenhos* (plantations) in the vicinity of the forests. There is no evidence that he ever sold any of the so-called stolen slaves who fought with him. Had he done that, he would have become a rich man. According to those who fought against him, his most faithful battalion was formed of slave runaways and stolen slaves, categories extremely difficult to differentiate. Scores of slaves fled to join the Cabanos: they chose to be stolen from their masters, causing de Paula's few landowner allies considerable discomfort. Serafim Soares, possibly the last landowner to surrender, told the commander of the government troops that he did not like Vicente de Paula's leadership, because "he had never enjoyed the company of blacks."[21] After the defeat of the Cabanada, although de Paula continued to steal slaves, according to Frei Messina, a friar who met him in 1842, he was a very poor man, but well respected and obeyed. He lived in Riachão do Mato, a village he founded after he fled from government troops in 1835.[22]

Clientelism, Eviction, and Politics

The Cabanada cannot be understood without reference to existing clientelistic networks. Clientelism is not a given, but a relationship in which all participants have their own motivations. Obeisance has a price. Peasants, squatters, landless workers, and Indians used these networks as a strategy to gain access to land, or to keep the land they already had. The reforms from 1827 through 1831, which created the post of justice of the peace and the national guard, help us to understand the range of clientelism. For the liberals in Brazil, the justice of the peace and the national guard were important counterweights to the excessive power of the Crown. At the local level, however, the power of the justice of the peace was practically unlimited; they could do almost anything within their territorial jurisdictions (Flory 1981, 66). The national guard, meanwhile, grew to function as the personal retinues of local landowners.

Holding one of these positions could augment local authority, but it was very important to be allied to the provincial power interests. For example, as long as João Batista de Araújo had connections with the governor of Alagoas, his enemies among the Pernambucan elite could not touch him; when Pernambucan authorities tried to arrest him he crossed the border into Alagoas, another jurisdiction. However, as soon as the regency named another governor, troops were sent against him from both Pernambuco and Alagoas. The case of Torres Galindo is similar: as a powerful landlord, he could still act with the authority of a captain major, despite losing the elections for the justice of the peace and the formal disappearance of his former post. But as soon as his enemies rose to power, much stronger forces from Recife were sent against him.

There is no reason to believe that the Cabano leaders escaped these clientelistic networks. Vicente de Paula had been a sergeant in the Ordenanças. He may have been a subordinate of Ordenanças captain Antônio Timóteo—the man who convinced him to rebel. As for Timóteo, he was brought into the insurrection by Torres Galindo, a former captain major, the highest office in the Ordenanças hierarchy. Later, de Paula would sign his manifestos and correspondence as "General" of the Cabanos, but he referred to his troops as "Ordenanças," thus maintaining the colonial reserve army hierarchy throughout the rebellion.[23] His becoming a self-proclaimed general is part of the dynamics of clientelism. The relationship between the client and the patron is unequal, but this imbalance may shift in favor of the client, who may become a political boss himself. Such was the case for Vicente de Paula. At the end of the Cabanada, although he had never been an officer in the Ordenanças, he was the de facto general of the "people of the forests." In 1833–34, military commanders said that he led 600 men, but Vicente claimed in 1833 that he commanded over 3,550 men.[24] His enemies often called him a "caudilho," a military strongman whose power rested on violence, yet the Cabanos understood local and national politics in their own terms, which were not about who would succeed Pedro I but about the loss of their land and relative autonomy, and they were able to state that through de Paula's manifestos.

Indians were also involved in clientelistic networks. Throughout the colonial era, they had been employed to fight against the enemies of Pernambuco's landed aristocracy, such as the Dutch invaders and Palmares maroons.[25] According to the governor of Pernambuco in 1827, although extremely poor, Indians had participated in the political events of the previous years, fighting for different contending factions (Pereira da Costa 1983, 238–39). Local authorities expected the Indians to always fight for them; however, Indians chose their allies and enemies according to their own interests whenever they could.[26] By fighting on the side of the crown in 1824, for instance, the Jacuípe Indians were able to keep their land and the surrounding forests safe from the expansion of nearby plantations.[27] They also received weapons and payment, however small that payment may have been. In 1832, their clientelistic networks led them to ally with local power bosses such as Araújo, Mello, and Timóteo.[28] The Jacuípe Indians were on the same side they had been before: they fought for Pedro I. The only difference was that those who had been defeated in 1824 were now in power. In 1832, the Indians of Jacuípe refused to cooperate with the force sent to arrest Araújo, Mello, and Timóteo. When the government decided to draft all of them between the ages of eighteen and twenty-five, they rose in rebellion and became known as the most "ferocious" Cabanos.[29]

Most troops that fought the Cabanos were commanded by landowners

who seized the opportunity to evict the rural poor. In spite of constant re-
quests, no significant number of national guardsmen from distant plantations fought the Cabanos. Landlords who could not expand their holdings in the area had no incentive to send their retainers to the fight. In
fact, the Provincial Assembly of Pernambuco correctly observed that, in
April 1835, one of the major reasons for the war was actually the presence
of troops.[30] Not all Cabanos were evicted peasants, but a large number
of them were expelled from their land by the invading army from Recife
that had the support of local planters. These same planters led the local
national guardsmen, financed by state funds and who made up the majority of troops deployed against the Cabanos. They amounted to 1,240
men in the Jacuípe River Valley, in September 1832.[31] The following year,
a full battalion of incarcerated army soldiers were pardoned in order to
fight against the Cabanos. Army troops from Rio de Janeiro and Ceará also
came in. By June 1833, roughly eight hundred army troops were fighting
against the Cabanos, but the private retinues of landlords, including the
national guard, had increased to more than three thousand men.[32]

These were extremely unreliable soldiers who often deserted, taking
their weapons with them: clients disobeyed when the risks became too
high. In some cases, they deserted not to their homes, but to the Cabanos.
Drafted very near the area of the rebellion, the "guardas nacionais" were
reluctant to fight against the rural poor, among whom the guards might
have found themselves had they not been drafted. By late 1832, landlords
complained that troops were becoming increasingly difficult to muster.
Those who were fighting against the Cabanos were demanding the same
wage the governor of Pernambuco was paying to the Municipal Guard of
Recife.[33]

It was not only clientelism and the draft that prompted rebellion, but
also eviction: Brazilian legislation did not grant any protection to those
who lived on public lands. Many peasants may also have lost their lands
to increasing sugar production and been pushed into the forests, where
they joined the rebellion. Sugar plantations occupied most of the land near
the coast and in the valleys along major rivers. By the late 1820s, it was
only on the frontier of Pernambuco and Alagoas that plantations could
still advance. In fact, in 1829, a member of the Council of Government of
Pernambuco, arguing for European immigration, suggested that the only
area that still had fertile lands available for cash crops was in the Jacuípe
Valley.[34] Incidentally, this council member, Manoel Zeferino dos Santos,

would become governor of Pernambuco in October 1832, exactly when the Cabanada was becoming most intense. It is worth mentioning that both his family and that of Colonel Santiago, his commander of arms, owned land fought over during the Cabanada.[35]

The Indians not only feared eviction, but forced labor. Landlords saw them as cheap manpower, especially after treaties signed with England stipulated that the Atlantic slave trade should cease by the late 1820s. In 1829, the governor of Pernambuco, Thomaz Garcia de Almeida, wrote that the best solution for the coming scarcity of labor would be to replace slaves with Indians.[36] He repeated the same argument in his inaugural address the following year.[37] After the abdication, Governor Francisco de Carvalho Paes de Andrade, a leader of the liberal faction, reiterated the proposal.[38] Neither governor indicated how they intended to employ the Indians, but according to Abbey Luís Ferreira Portugal, also a member of Pernambuco's provincial council in 1830, Indians needed protection. In several instances they were forced to work as if they were slaves.[39]

In the early 1830s, subsistence farmers lived amid the forests of the Água Preta district. But after the Cabanada, the sugar industry invaded those lands. In 1846, Pernambuco's governor decided to make the town of Água Preta, on the forests' northern limit, head of a separate county. Although some of the greatest battles of the Cabanada were fought nearby, once the Cabanos were crushed, plantations expanded. In 1846, the governor recalled that many people, former Cabanos, were still "savages," in his words.[40] By that same year, the historian Peter Eisenberg (1974, 242) counted at least forty-four engenhos there. Some of the area's major planters, including Feliciano Joaquim dos Santos, José Antonio Correia Pessoa de Mello, his nephew Pedro Ivo Veloso da Silveira, and Luís Beltrão Mavignier, had commanded troops against the Cabanos. The clans of Manoel Zeferino dos Santos, governor of the province after November 1832, and of the commander of arms, Colonel José da Silva Santiago, also owned engenhos in the area. They did not get along well, to the point that each asked the regency at Rio de Janeiro to fire the other. The governor complained that the commander of arms was using the Cabanada as an excuse to attack and plunder an engenho belonging to his family.[41] Their families were among the planters mentioned in Eisenberg's study. For them, the Cabanada was an opportunity to expand their holdings.

Throughout the rebellion, the Cabanos tried to conquer the site in the Jacuípe River Valley where government troops established their headquar-

ters. They also attacked the villages of Barra Grande and Porto Calvo, but
their major target was the Jacuípe-based headquarters: they seized and
subsequently lost that position several times during the war, always returning to take it back.[42] It seems, therefore, that the Cabanos were not
just raiding engenhos, but attempting to conquer sites nearer the coast
and outside the forests. Although the forests offered them protection, in
some instances they acted as if they had been pushed there by the first incursions of the "Jacobin" troops, as Vicente de Paula referred to the enemy
in 1832. The troops pushed the Cabanos into the forests, hoping to starve
them, but the Cabanos soon learned to live on a diet of lizards and mush-
rooms.[43]

The strategy of the Cabanos was clear: they attempted to conquer the
lands on the fringes of the coastal plantations; when that failed, they hid
in the forests and hills further west.[44] By late 1832 few of the Cabano landowners, such as "Colonel Barrinhos" (Manoel Joaquim de Barros) and
"Major Vicentinho" (Vicente Ferreira de Santana), were still commanding
troops and most had lost land. But leadership was not about their economic situation. The major Cabano leader, de Paula, had been a poor man
and remained a poor man. It is fair to assume that landowners who supported him did so because of local political rivalries, but most Cabanos
were defending themselves against the draft and eviction. The restorationist ideology fit their struggle, for the Jacobins were trying to seize their
lands.

Still the authorities were not capable of winning a clear victory. In March
1834, changing their strategy, they put four thousand troops around an
area stretching from Porto Calvo to Sirinhaém, on the coast, and roughly
sixty kilometers inland to Água Preta. They spread proclamations ordering the people to settle elsewhere, or otherwise be treated as Cabanos.
Those who gave up their weapons were pardoned. Hundreds of starving
women and children were "pardoned," but left unattended. The government troops then shot at anyone remaining on site and destroyed all food
crops, as if wishing to clear the land of human inhabitants in order to seize
it.[45] Even so, in May 1834, the Cabanos were still able (for the last time) to
seize the Jacuípe Arraial.[46]

By January 1835, 862 men, in addition to an uncounted number of
women and children, had given up the fight and presented themselves
at Água Preta.[47] Many, however, did not. By May 1835, the commander of
the government troops could still claim that he had taken 1,072 prisoners

and killed 2,326 since June 1834, in addition to an uncounted number of Cabanos who died of hunger and illness in the forest.[48] The remaining Indians of Jacuípe, along with 398 others, gave up the fight in April 1835.[49] Several priests were already in the area trying to convince the "people of the forest" to surrender, for Pedro I had died. In March, the bishop of Pernambuco arrived in the conflict area and preached to the people who came out of the forests.[50] Four thousand réis were paid to those who gave up their guns, a paltry sum according to the commander of the government troops, but alluring nonetheless for Cabanos who were ill or suffering from malnutrition.[51] In June, Barrinhos, João Timóteo, Serafim Soares, and other Cabano leaders surrendered with their troops, totaling another 1,021 men.[52] Although amnesty had been offered to Vicente de Paula in 1834, he chose not to surrender. His only two conditions, freedom for the slaves who followed his lead and permission for his followers to keep their weapons, had been rejected.[53] When he fled into the forests of Alagoas with his runaway-slave troops, the authorities estimated that he led only 50 to 150 men. Thereafter, the state authorities sought to capture or kill him.[54] The nearby plantations could expand without problems.

The Motivations of the Cabanos

The Cabanada involved landowners, peasants, slave runaways and Indians. As the involvement of landowners dwindled, however, that of subalterns increased. Thus, the Cabanos were basically poor people. Moreover, to argue that they were involved in a broader clientelistic network is not to deny their ability to make choices based on their own interests. Rather it means that the rural poor's affiliation with different elite factions was a necessary condition for access to land in Pernambuco. Throughout the rebellion, government authorities emphasized that the Cabanos did not rebel for ideology, but to steal cattle, horses, and food.[55] But for the people of the forest, stealing from their enemies was likely to have been considered a legitimate activity, particularly in the light of their eviction from their own lands. Pillaging was not the limit of the Cabanos' political ideas, however. In their manifestos, they stated that they were fighting for the restoration of Pedro I to the Brazilian throne. In the historical literature, there has been disagreement about how to interpret this demand. Why were they fighting for the sake of an emperor who had done nothing to improve their lot?

As John Gledhill argues in the introduction to this book, the literature on resistance has tended to ignore "'popular movements' that appeared to be reactionary by traditional Left standards" (9). Maybe that explains why it was so difficult to get to grips with the Cabanos' stated purpose to restore Pedro I to the Brazilian throne. For Manuel Correia de Andrade, the Cabanada was sui generis, because while peasants, Indians, and escaped slaves made up its cadres, its professed aims were reactionary. He suggests that this scenario is paradoxical because the Cabanos had no chance of upward mobility while elites were failing to maintain the balance of power among themselves. Once the rebellion started, the fear of retaliation and the strong leadership of Vicente de Paula kept the Cabanos fighting (M. C. Andrade 1965, 197–212). For Dirceu Lindoso, the apparent contradiction between the cadres of the rebellion and their stated purposes was not real; rather it resulted from the ideological nature of the sources left by those who quashed the insurrection. Its restorationist discourse disguised the real intent of the Cabanada, which, according to Lindoso, was abolitionist and anti-latifundium. He suggests that this apparent contradiction was resolved in practice, because, after the rebellion, the few remaining Cabanos created an "alternative space," a community that was out of the reach of the state, where they revived Indian traditions mixed with African ones (Lindoso 1983, 80–81).

In his manifestos and letters, de Paula made very clear his restorationist intent and opposition to the Jacobins, who, for him, were against the king and the cross. Under the leadership of the "Comandante" or "General" of all forests or, even more pompous, the Comandante Geral do Imperial Exército de Sua Majestade Imperial Dom Pedro I (General Commander of the Imperial Force of his Imperial Majesty Pedro I), the Cabanos fought so bravely that there is no reason to suggest that de Paula lied to hide his true intentions from his enemies.[56] Rather, one must seek the meaning of Pedro I's restoration to the Cabanos. In fact, Pedro's return had different meanings for those who participated in the Abrilada and those who participated in the Cabanada.

The Abrilada rebels fought to keep the jobs, prerogatives, and privileges they had had during the reign of Pedro I. The main Cabano leader, Vicente de Paula, on the other hand, identified the "jacobinos" as the men who had brought havoc to the area where he lived by, for instance, burning peasant homes.[57] The men who seized power after the fall of Pedro I benefited from the reforms of 1827–31, which created the justice of the peace and the national guard. Thereafter, the law was in their hands. Long-standing local political arrangements were broken after the fall of Pedro I. Even the army had almost been eliminated as the ultimate source of authority against seigneurial justice. Even the forests were no longer protected, as they had been since colonial times, when the woods were a royal monopoly for naval construction (Lindoso 1983, 99–101). Following an old argument of Barrington Moore Jr. (1966, 21), one can say that the emperor, the authority of last resort against the encroachments of the landed aristocracy, had been eliminated. However minimal that protection could be, the old times—when the common forests still had some legal protection, when the rural poor were not being pushed into these forests, when peasants had to obey a few captains major instead of scores of justices of the peace—seemed to have been better. Until the fall of Pedro I, the Indians' cooperation with the Crown in 1824 had been advantageous to them. Thereafter, they faced draft and eviction from the Jacuípe valley.

The evidence indicates that, far from withdrawing from society, the Cabanos actually were actively involved in politics, making alliances with planters in the countryside and merchants in town, who sent them ammunition. After the rebellion, de Paula played an important role from the forests in Alagoas politics, as M. C. Andrade (1965) and Lindoso (1983) have demonstrated. Local power bosses sought his support in their political quarrels because of his strong following of battle-hardened men. Most of the time, however, he was referred to by state and local authorities as a bandit, a slave thief. Authorities knew where he lived—Frei Messina had been in Riachão do Mato in 1842—but they were unable to arrest or kill him.

Slaves, however, still fled to join de Paula in Riachão do Mato. There is no indication that those "stolen" slaves were resold, something that could easily have been done in Pernambuco, if de Paula had chosen to do it. Vicente de Paula remained a poor man until his eventual arrest in 1850. Slave runaways were probably assimilated into the community as people of lower status, not chattel. They could probably climb the hierarchy, for de Paula's enemies considered the battalion of black men as his best troops. Frei Messina's description of Riachão do Mato portrays a peaceful, disciplined, and large peasant population who obeyed their leader. Nevertheless, Vicente de Paula was not a maroon leader: he led peasants and Indians, in addition to stolen slaves.

It is significant to note that government sources frequently referred to him with contempt not only as a bandit but also as a caudilho, in recognition of his local power. In the early 1840s, Vicente de Paula had command over a multiethnic population that may have exceeded a thousand people. As such, he was a unique caudilho, well acquainted with local and national politics, or at least as well acquainted as most landowners. In 1848 he had a chance to legalize his situation through allegiance with the conservative party leaders, against the Praieira Rebellion.[58] Instead, he used the opportunity to attack engenhos, steal cattle, and take slaves with him (Mello Rego 1899, 76).[59]

Sources usually refer to his followers as the "people of the forest," an imprecise term for a mélange of runaway slaves, Indians, and free and freed men and women. Due to the extreme violence employed against the Cabanos, it is difficult to say whether all of them were originally forest dwellers. It is perfectly possible that many were pushed into the forests by the troops that hunted them. One way or another, although they did not attack Jacuípe, Porto Calvo, or Barra Grande again, they were able to keep their way of life and their lands in the province of Alagoas. The area where Cabanos had lived in Pernambuco, however, started to be conquered by the plantation complex soon after the rebellion was crushed. In the late 1850s the railroad was cutting through the jungle, from Recife to Água Preta, and by the turn of the century the plantation economy had reached that district. As the hills to the west were not appropriate for larger plantations, today one can still see part of the forests where the "gente das matas" dwelled.

It would be romantic to portray Riachão do Mato as a utopia, as Lindoso suggests it was. It is likely that the coexistence of Indians, runaway slaves, and free peasants was problematic: the Cabanos certainly had their own politics. Yet although documentary information is scarce, Frei Messina, who visited Riachão do Mato in 1842, described a community that included blacks and Indians, living in peace. They were fervently Catholic, according to Messina, but on their own terms. For example, they easily divorced. Vicente de Paula may have approached Eric Hobsbawm's social-bandit model (Hobsbawm 1981, 9–11, 58, 131–42), in the sense that he was a thief in the eyes of the landed aristocracy but a hero in Riachão do Mato. That does not mean, however, that their movement was prepolitical, as it has been portrayed by Hobsbawm in his studies about social bandits; rather the contrary. The Cabanos understood local and national politics through their own framework and interpretation. The attack on their lands occurred after the fall of the emperor. The Jacobins were obviously their enemies. Their political engagement was clear and simple: they wished to restore the previous situation. The return of Pedro I had a specific meaning, which led them to action. They fought for it, made alliances for it, but were defeated.

It is also important to notice that Vicente de Paula did not seek total isolation from society at large. He tried to find a modus vivendi with the state, as usually happens with enduring, long-term resistance movements (see Knight, conclusion). This aim is most clearly demonstrated by the fact that in 1841, to the surprise of state authorities, de Paula, attempting assimilation into the formal hierarchy of the state, sought a commanding post in the national guard.[60] He was rejected as an outlaw. Indeed, in spite of his request, he continued to steal slaves so that, in 1845, the Pernambucan government offered one million réis for his capture: the greatest price put on a head in that province in the first half of the nineteenth century. If a slave arrested or killed him, he should be freed and receive that reward, deducting his own value from that amount.[61] Nobody ever received the prize. Likely plenty of people, even former allies, were interested. The problem was that, as Vicente de Paula had become a powerful boss, a caudilho himself, it was not easy to capture or kill him.

His request to become an officer of the national guard also suggests that his perception of the Brazilian national state may have changed. In 1840, Pedro II, the son of Pedro I, became king: the Jacobins had been defeated in the political arena. The regency had fallen. The Crown had been restored. Although Vicente de Paula's request for a post in the national guard had been denied, the elites sought his military help in settling their political quarrels. In 1844, he invaded the capital of Alagoas with four hundred cavalry, swinging the balance of power toward one of the local factions. Again, in 1848, when landowners in Pernambuco started yet another war between themselves (the Praieira Rebellion), both factions sought his support, writing deferential letters to a man they had consistently called a thief.[62] Moreover, each party later alleged how dishonest the other had been in calling on such a "bandit" (M. C. Andrade 1965, 193–95; Pessoa de Mello 1978, 123–24; Mello Rego 1899, 34; Figueira de Mello 1978, 128). De Paula remained a "thief of slaves" until he was entrapped and arrested in 1850. He had been invited to a meeting to discuss amnesty. His willingness to attend the meeting perhaps indicates that the Cabano leader had finally accepted the rules of the political game. The Brazilian state had become stronger, hegemonic. Betrayed but alive after eleven years on the prison island of Fernando de Noronha (where he led a rebellion of prisoners in 1853), he was finally released in 1861, and vanished into the interior of Pernambuco and Alagoas.[63] He was then a seventy-year-old man (Mello Rego 1899, 212).

*   *   *

The Cabanada was fought in the plantation frontier. For centuries, forest populations posed a problem for plantation owners, unless they were absorbed as a labor force or at least as dependent allies. After independence, the imperial state had to fight against a republican rebellion in Pernambuco in 1824. The army sent from Rio de Janeiro landed between the provinces of Pernambuco and Alagoas, where Indians and the poor population at large were mobilized to fight against the rebels. Those who cooperated with the Crown were compensated through clientelistic mechanisms, which helped them keep their lands beyond the reach of the losing faction of the local elites. After the abdication in 1831, some of the elite remnants of the rebellion in 1824 seized control of the state repressive apparatus and took the opportunity to expand their holdings. Ranchers, peasants, and Indians who had helped the imperial army in the struggle against the rebels of 1824 now faced draft and eviction. In 1832, the people of the forests rebelled. Vicente de Paula's manifestos demonstrate deep resentment against the Jacobins, who had invaded the lands of rural people and burned their houses and food crops. Defeated in 1835, the surviving Cabanos fled deep into the forests of Alagoas, where they could protect themselves. The Cabanada shows that, sometimes, the same subalterns who help state authorities fight other subalterns and disgruntled elite members may also become rebels themselves. Clientelism is a relationship. Sometimes clients disobey and the weak become powerful. The defeat of a rebellion, however, may not mean the end of the story. Resistance may resurface. Led by Vicente de Paula, the surviving Cabanos founded a town, where they resumed their resistance against the landed aristocracy, harboring runaway slaves, and stealing cattle and other property until the final arrest of their leader and the construction of the railroad, which finally conquered the forests.

Notes

1 In 1823, after Pedro I closed the Brazilian Constituent Assembly, a group of federalist liberals seized the government of Pernambuco. The liberals declared independence, forming the Confederação do Equador, which was not supported by all of the landed aristocracy. Pedro I blockaded Pernambuco's harbor and landed an army on the frontier between Pernambuco and Alagoas, crushing the rebellion. Pedro's allies were granted noble status, among other benefits from the crown (Cabral de Mello 2004).

2 *Diário de Pernambuco* (Recife), June 7, 1831. Accessed on microfilm in the Laboratório de Pesquisa e Ensino of the Federal University of Pernambuco (LAPEH) in Recife.

3 "Correspondência Oficial," April 17, 1832, in *Diário de Pernambuco* (Recife), April 26, 1832. ANRJ (Arquivo Nacional, Rio de Janeiro), Ministério do Exército, IG1 270, April 17, 1832.

4 ANRJ, Ministério do Exército, IG1 270, April 17, 1832.

5 APEJE (Arquivo Público de Pernambuco, Jordão Emerenciano), Atas do Conselho de Governo 2, January 11, 1832, January 18, 1832.

6 *Ordem do Dia* of February 9, 1832 in *Diário de Pernambuco* (Recife), February 16, 1832.

7 All healthy men from the age of fourteen to sixty-five were enrolled in the Corpos de Ordenanças to be summoned when needed.

8 APEJE, Atas do Conselho de Governo de Pernambuco 2, March 30, 1830; Juízes Ordinários 2, April 20, 1830. *Diário de Pernambuco* (Recife), May 13, 1831; *Diário de Pernambuco* (Recife), July 6, 1831.

9 APEJE, Ofícios do Governo 34, February 29, 1832, April 9, 1832.

10 APEJE, Ofícios do Governo 34, February 27, 1832.

11 ANRJ, Ministério da Justiça, IJ1 694, September 24, 1832.

12 BNRJ (Biblioteca Nacional, Rio de Janeiro), Seção de Manuscritos, I-32, 11, 2, August 13, 1832, September 14, 1832, September 28, 1832.

13 *Publicações do Arquivo Nacional* (Rio de Janeiro), 1931, 22:344–49.

14 APEJE, Correspondência da Corte 32, March 14, 1831.

15 *Publicações do Arquivo Nacional* (Rio de Janeiro), 1931, 22:344–49.

16 "Correspondência Oficial," June 2, 1831 in *Diário de Pernambuco* (Recife), July 2, 1831; ibid., July 12, 1831, August 4, 1831; ANRJ, Ministério do Império, IJJ9 280, June 20, 1831; APEJE, Presidentes de Província 8, May 2, 1832.

17 APEJE, Presidentes de Província 8, July 5, 1832; ANRJ, Ministério do Exército, IG1 270, April 19, 1832, April 20, 1832, IG1 May 5, 1832; *Diário de Pernambuco* (Recife), May 4, 1832; ANRJ, Ministério do Exército, IG1 270, April 19, 1832, November 22, 1832; APEJE, Atas do Conselho de Governo 2, August 7, 1832.

18 BNRJ, I-32, 11, 2, May 9, 1832.

19 BNRJ, Seção de Manuscritos, I-32, 11, 2, September 14, 1832.

20 ANRJ, Ministério da Justiça, IJ1 694, September 17, 1832.

21 ANRJ, Ministério da Guerra, IG1 94, May 24, 1835.

22 IAHGPE (Instituto Arqueológico, Histórico e Geográfico Pernambucano, Recife), Estante A, Gaveta 16, November 26, 1842.

23 See, for example: ANRJ, Ministério do Exército, IG1, Portarias of September 1, 1833 and November 20, 1832.

24 BNRJ, I-32, 11, 2, October 8, 1833.

25 Palmares encompassed the area where the Cabanos would live (Freitas 1990).

26 When on the winning side, they could keep their lands and benefit from their involvement. The Indians of Barreiros district, for example, fought against the Cabanos to their own advantage (Carvalho 1996).

27 *Publicações do Arquivo Nacional* (Rio de Janeiro), 1931, 22:344–49.

28 APEJE, Presidentes de Província 8, August 27, 1832, September 4, 1832, October 24, 1832; ANRJ, Ministério da Justiça, IJ1 694, August 29, 1832, November 3, 1832; BNRJ, I-32, 11, 2, September 11, 1832, September 14, 1832.

29 ANRJ, Ministério da Justiça, IJ1 694, November 3, 1832; Ministério do Exército, IG1 94, April 4, 1835.

30 ANRJ, Ministério do Exército, IG1 94, April 30, 1835.

31 APEJE, Presidentes de Província 8, September 19, 1832. In addition to that corps, there were also several garrisons throughout the counties of Rio Formoso and Água Preta. ANRJ, Ministério do Exército, IG1 65, December 10, 1832, December 19, 1832.

32 ANRJ, Ministério do Exército, IG1 65, February 25, 1833, April 15, 1833, May 15, 1833, August 25, 1833, August 31, 1833; BNRJ, I-32, 11, 2, "Proclamação" of March 16, 1834, February 1, 1834.

33 APEJE, Correspondência da Corte December 3, 1831; Atas do Conselho de Governo 2, April 26, 1832; ANRJ, Ministério do Exército, IG1 65, May 29, 1832, December 10, 1832.

34 "Parecer," in APEJE, Atas do Conselho de Governo de Pernambuco 2, August 11, 1829.

35 ANRJ, Ministério do Exército, IG1 65, May 25, 1833; *Diário de Pernambuco* (Recife), October 13, 1832.

36 "Relatório a Assembléia Provincial," December 1, 1829, in *O Cruzeiro* (Recife), 167: December 1829.

37 IAHGPE, Estante A, Gaveta 12, "Relatório a Assembléia Provincial," December 1, 1830.

38 "Relatório a Assembléia Provincial," December 1, 1831, in *Diário de Pernambuco* (Recife), December 5, 1831.

39 APEJE, Atas do Conselho de Governo de Pernambuco 2, April 1, 1830.

40 APEJE, R 7–1, Ministério da Justiça, April 15, 1846.

41 ANRJ, Ministério da Guerra, IG-1 270, July 13, 1833, July 25, 1833; IG-1 65, February 27, 1833, May 15, 1833, May 25, 1833, June 12, 1833, July 27, 1833.

42 BNRJ, Seção de Manuscritos, I-32, 11, 2, December 13, 1832, March 3, 1834 and March 21, 1834.

43 BNRJ, I-32, 11, 2, September 28, 1832, January 15, 1834; ANRJ, Ministério do Exército, IG1, May 1, 1834, May 24, 1834.

44 See, for example: BNRJ, Seção de Manuscritos, I-3, 2, September 11, 1832, November 5, 1832, January 17, 1833, April 21, 1833, May 31, 1833, June 17, 1833, August 26, 1833, August 31, 1833, December 28, 1833, January 12, 1834, February 21, 1834.

45 ANRJ, Ministério da Guerra, IG1 270, May 7, 1834; IG1 94, May 24, 1834.

46 Ibid., 94, May 18, 1834.

47 Ibid., 270, May 7, 1835; IG1 94, May 24, 1834, January 5, 1835.

48 Ibid., 65, May 19, 1835; IG1 94.

49 Ibid., 94, April 3, 1835, April 13, 1835, April 24, 1835, May 15, 1835.

50 Ibid., 94, April 4, 1834; IG1 270, July 31, 1835.

51 Ibid., 94, April 24, 1835.

52 Ibid., 270, June 11, 1835.

53 Ibid., 94, April 4, 1835.

54 Ibid., 270, June 22, 1835; IG1 94, August 11, 1835, October 20, 1835.

55 *O Harmonizador* (Recife), March 12, 1832; *Diário da Administração de Pernambuco* (Recife), April 12, 1833.

56 See letter of Vicente de Paula in ANRJ, Ministério da Guerra, IG1 94, September 1, 1833.

57 BNRJ, Seção de Manuscritos, I-32, 11, 2, August 10, 1833.

58 The liberals fell from power in 1837. In 1844, they returned to preside over the cabinet under Pedro II, who was crowned in 1840. The praieiros were a local branch of the liberal party. When they lost the government in 1848, they rebelled. Some of the men involved in the Praieira were veterans of the Confederação do Equador in 1824.

59 See also APEJE, "Relatório do Presidente da Província Honório Hermeto Carneiro Leão à Assembléia Provincial," May 18, 1850.

60 APEJE, Polícia Civil 4, October 30, 1841, October 14, 1841, November 29, 1842.

61 APEJE, R 1–2, Reservados, August 28, 1845.

62 See documents in *Autos do Inquérito da Revolução Praieira (1849)* (1979), Brasília: Senado Federal, pp. 40, 313; APEJE, Ofícios Reservados, R 18–5, February 11, 1849.

63 APEJE, Seção de Impressos, "Relatório do Presidente José Bento da Cunha Figueredo a Assembléia Provincial em 1854."

CHAPTER FIVE

A "Great Arch" Descending

Manumission Rates, Subaltern Social Mobility, and the Identities of Enslaved, Freeborn, and Freed Blacks in Southeastern Brazil, 1791–1888

ROBERT W. SLENES

In April 1848, a plan for slave rebellion centered on Vassouras, in the Paraíba Valley, Rio de Janeiro's coffee-plantation hinterland, was discovered and quelled. The sources on the conspiracy reveal that it was linked to a political-religious movement similar to the community "cults of affliction" for healing social ills and for "governance" documented in the old Kingdom of Kongo region, a major provider of slaves for Brazil's southeast (Rio de Janeiro, São Paulo, Minas Gerais, and Espírito Santo). These sources also suggest that the planned rebellion had a considerable impact later that year on debates in the Brazilian parliament over the suppression of the Atlantic slave trade, which still flourished, although outlawed since 1831. In short, the definitive abolition of this commerce by parliament in 1850—almost passed in 1848—may have reflected internal slave pressure, predicated on African values, not just the threat of British intervention.[1]

My research on this subject throws light on the formation of slave identity in the plantations of Rio de Janeiro and São Paulo from circa 1791, when export agriculture and bonded labor acquired new vigor in the Southeast, to abolition in 1888. My results point to a slave consciousness, formed from a common experience and culture, which was radically opposed to that of the masters (Slenes 2007a, 2007b). This argument, consistent with recent research on slave rebellion in southeastern Brazil, counters other work that emphasizes slave strategies of assimilation and the absence of a unified identity in the *senzala* (slave quarters), reflecting significant possibilities of "black" (black and mulatto) social mobility into and within free society.[2] To define what is at stake, therefore, I begin by outlining present debates regarding the frequency of manumission, the degree of social mobility among freeborn and freed blacks (groups subject to legal distinctions during most of the period studied), and the construction of patterns of social race over the long term, which are closely linked to discussions about slave (and black) identity formation.

Taking the long view, studies on Brazilian slavery have moved through the same paradigms as those on American bonded labor, clearly responding to changes in the north, but always within the crucible of local debates (Slenes 1999, chapter one). Gilberto Freyre, in his classic *Casa grande e senzala* (1980), developed arguments similar to those of the American historian Ulrich B. Phillips (1929, 1966) about the patriarchal nature of slavery and the close relations between masters and slaves, but he did so in a way that gave his work recurrent appeal among his compatriots.[3] Using, as Phillips had not, a nonracist idiom that valued African culture, he stressed as an explanation of the Brazilian case (in contrast to the American, with its legacy of lynching) the supposedly innate openness of the Luso-Brazilian character, libido, and church to non-European "Others," even while recounting stories of masters' cruelty toward their slaves.[4] The "São Paulo School of Sociology" (Florestan Fernandes 1966 especially) reacted to what it saw as Freyre's apologetics for Portuguese colonialism and the planter class; taking its cue from E. Franklin Frazier (1939) and other American opponents of Phillips, it portrayed slavery as so harsh and bondspeople's institutions, particularly their familes, so broken by slavery, that blacks were no more than anomic victims, incapable of effectively challenging the slave regime or achieving social mobility after emancipation.

Contesting the São Paulo school, João Reis (2003), Silvia Lara (1988), Sidney Chalhoub (1990), and others found decidedly nonanomic bondspeople in the archives who made life difficult for slave owners and authorities, sometimes in rebellion, more often in subtle, yet subversive ways. In doing so, these historians were influenced by researchers such as Sidney Mintz and Richard Price (1992), Eugene Genovese (1974), and Herbert Gutman (1976), as well as by Brazilianists who anticipated or accompanied the new scholarship in the United States directed against Frazier's legacy (Dean 1976; Slenes 1976; Schwartz 1985; Stein 1985). Above all, they applied the insights of Gutman's "mentor," the historian of the English working class E. P. Thompson (1968; 1974; 1978b). The "rebellious" culture of Thompson's eighteenth-century "plebeians," hidden behind outward deference toward "patricians," had particular resonance for Brazilian scholars at that historiographical moment and in the context of apparent working-class passivity under Brazil's recent military dictatorship (Lara 1995; Chalhoub and Silva 2009). For one following this literature, James Scott's *Domination and the Arts of Resistance* (1990)—important for the reflections in this book—seemed like a valuable systematization of the lessons from Thompson and from the paradigm shift in slave studies in the 1970s.

Yet, Scott's "summing up" came at a time when slave studies were moving beyond uncovering "day-to-day" and "hidden" resistance and moving toward exploring the complexities that the full recognition of working people's "agency" poses for studying their behavior and social identity. In Brazil, these complexities are nowhere more apparent than in the extensive new bibliography on the slave family. It is now clear that, contrary to the opinion of Fernandes, there was a strong presence of nuclear, extended, and intergenerational slave families on southeastern plantations. But if this shows that slaves "resisted" a dehumanization previously believed to be inherent in New World slavery, what is its deeper meaning? Was a slave community with substantially homogeneous African roots thereby strengthened, such that bondspeople acquired a deeper will to confound their masters, even as kin ties made them more vulnerable and less voluntaristic? (Slenes 1999; confrontation was discouraged, but the disposition to "resist" was heightened). Or were owners thereby more able to impose their rule on quarters that were divided ethnically and avid for the "peace" bestowed by new kinship ties? (On resistance pacified, see Florentino and Góes 1997.) Or did the family, given high manumission rates for creoles (blacks born in Brazil) and access to land for freeborn and freed blacks, encourage Brazilian-born slaves to aim at working their (and their loved ones') way out of bondage, while distancing themselves from African co-workers? (On resistance deflected towards amoral familism and group infighting, see Mattos 1998.) Explicit in all these formulations are questions that go beyond slaves' immediate intentions, to probe the context in which they, their masters, and others took considered action. Just as historians of free workers are asking why "class consciousness" occurred in some cases but not in others, so too are historians of slaves raising queries about the configuration of antipathies, alliances, and social identities in and outside the senzala, rather than taking it for granted that bondspeople simply resisted.

The issues of manumission and of the fate of *libertos* (former slaves) have become central to research in this area. Many historians now portray the Brazilian slave system as peculiarly open to upward mobility—the movement of bondspeople out of slavery and of freeborn and freed blacks into the ranks of small landholders and even of small slave owners—and thus also characterized by competitive tensions within the senzala. This proposition about manumission and mobility sometimes takes the form of a neo-Freyrean argument (relatively static, largely culturalist, but recognizing the oppressive nature of slavery), with bonded workers, however, joining masters as agents (Paiva 2001; Góes 2003, 2007; Florentino 2007). This formulation is facilitated by Freyre's (1980) characterization in 1933 of Brazilian slavery as violent, even while integrative, and also by his willingness to admit, if not emphasize, that bondspeople had cultural resources of their own permitting self-interested action.[5] It also builds on recent work that repudiates the São Paulo school's characterization of Freyre as simply an ideologue of the elite who hoodwinked readers with his "myth of racial democracy." To have resonance, it is argued, a "myth" must be in tune with "principles [widely] considered fundamental to the making of the social order" (Fry 2005, 164). For many neo-Freyreans, substantial manumission and mobility under slavery, whether expressing slave-owner sensibilities or a more diffuse national culture, are precisely what established the dominant social chords that (to their ears) still echo long after the death of forced labor. The argument has implications for contemporary social policy; some of the scholars who thus position themselves regarding slave society have spoken out against so-called race-based affirmative action in university admissions as something that would replace historical Brazilian harmonics with dissonant tones from America (see, for instance, Florentino 2007 and Góes 2007.)

On the other hand, the argument from manumission and mobility has resulted in decidedly non-Freyrean studies, particularly by Hebe Mattos (1998, 2000, 2008): non-Freyrean in the sense of focusing on changing social conditions and struggles over time as the determinants of "political" outcomes and cultural patterns. This work is both support and challenge to my own research. Mattos proposes something akin to a "great arch" explanation for the configuration of social race in Brazil from the colonial period to the early twentieth century. In *The Great Arch: English State Formation as Cultural Revolution* (1985), P. Corrigan and D. Sayer—taking their inspiration and metaphor from E. P. Thompson (1978a, 257)—characterize the "bourgeois revolution" in England as a long-term social and cultural transformation, not dateable to a particular political upheaval. Arising from continual conflict and negotiation among diverse social groups, this "state"—characterized in brief by the inclusive, polysemic ideal of "English liberties"—achieved consent by distributing rewards to a broad spectrum of power contenders. While Mattos does not frame her study with reference to Corrigan's and Sayer's work, her argument regarding slavery and the formation of social race in Brazil bears similarities to it. Yet, her great arch has a pronounced downward movement. (In my use of the metaphor I stress the arch's shape, not just its span.) Thus, a polysemic name for its ideal, "racial democracy" ("ethnic democracy," in Freyre's words), when finally used with some frequency in the 1940s, referred to a curve that no longer "soared" as it did at independence (in the free sector of Brazil's slave society) and that would continue descending in the decades that followed.

With her focus on Brazil's southeast, Mattos argues that slavery and notions of race were molded, up to circa 1830–50, by three conditions that were strikingly different from those prevailing in the United States. First, there was the continual introduction of large numbers of enslaved Africans. Second, there was the high manumission rate among creoles and even among partially acculturated Africans, reflecting slave owners' policies of dominion. Masters favored bondspeople who demonstrated strategies of accommodation and assimilation, even rewarding them within slavery, in part to divide the senzala politically. Third, there was the existence of abundant territory, such that freeborn and freed blacks had significant possibilities of access to land (as valued clients of large landowners, if not as proprietors themselves) and even to slaves. (On urban Rio, see also Faria 1998 and Frank 2004.) This was in a society—like the American South—where a substantial minority of households had bondspeople and most masters were small slave owners (Schwartz 1982). The result of the combined agency of all groups within this context was the formation, by the late eighteenth century, of a relatively large population of freeborn and freed blacks in which many effectively held land and a politically significant percentage owned slaves (Luna and Costa 1980, 1982; Klein and Paiva 1996; Barickman 1999; Libby and Paiva 2000; Luna and Klein 2003).

Increasingly, then, bondspeople, even Africans, could imagine themselves or their children approaching or entering freedom and then moving upward; thus, there was no general formation of a "slave identity," nor even of a black identity that embraced Africans and their descendants of various hues, whether freeborn, libertos, or enslaved. Indeed, there frequently was tension in the senzala between creoles and Africans.

Reflecting political realities in the broader society, continues Mattos, the constitution of 1824, which defined voting rights, did not create racial barriers to citizenship, in contrast to most of the states in the American union. A growing population, however, combined with expanding plantation agriculture and higher land prices, made "negotiated" squatting or independent farming increasingly difficult for freeborn blacks and former slaves in the decades following independence. Then, too, higher slave prices toward the end of the African trade and particularly after its suppression limited libertos' access to bonded labor (see Frank 2004). They also reduced slaves' chances of purchasing freedom. Furthermore, after 1850, many creole slaves, particularly those brought from other parts of Brazil through the internal slave trade, suffered restricted access to rewards from slave owners, in effect taking the place of the previously discriminated Africans (see also Slenes 2004).[6]

The geographic mobility conferred on former slaves by abolition and by subsequent labor competition among elites provided immediate benefits to libertos, particularly in Rio. Yet, the policies of the republican state (since 1889) and Brazil's severely unequal development during the twentieth century further exacerbated black-white social disparities (Andrews 1991, 1992; Teles 2004; Rios and Mattos 2005; Gomes and Cunha 2007). Nevertheless, despite (or because of) the clear downward movement in Brazil's great arch from circa 1830, blacks in the postabolition period, many still remembering a time when their position in free society was more favorable, actively pressed for the creation of a nonracialized society. In doing so, they anticipated, and in some ways even influenced, Freyre's formulation in 1933, but with their own goals in mind (Mattos 1998; on the role of blacks in articulating a positive image of a mixed-race identity for Rio and Brazil in the 1920s, see T. Gomes 2004). The result, one might say, was not myth but a contested field of discourse (a common battleground) about past and future.

It will be clear by now that the argument I wish to advance about slave mobility and identity formation in the plantation context, particularly from 1791–1850, is fundamentally different from that of Mattos. Yet, in the end, it strengthens her notion of a great arch, even while suggesting revisions to it. I approach my subject from the vantage point of a new paradigm in research on slavery, one developed concomitantly in Brazil and the United States from insights by historians of Africa into the processes of cultural continuity and change in that continent and the diaspora (see, among others, Craemer, Vansina, and Fox 1976; R. F. Thompson 1981, 1984; and Thornton 1988, 1991, 1998a). João Reis (1986, more emphatically in the expanded 2003 edition), Mary Karasch (1987), Mariza Soares (2000), and I (Slenes 2000, 1999, 2007b) have all stressed the ability of the enslaved (in Africa, the Middle Passage, and Brazil) to make active use of their cultural heritage—in some cases to negotiate their entry and acceptance into a new creole society, in others to reaffirm or invent their continuity with the past, often together with companions of different origins.[7] On the plantations of the southeast, I believe it was largely the latter, the firm assertion of roots in Africa, which took place as a result of the circumstances that bondspeople confronted. A common experience, perceived as harshly oppressive, induced plantation slaves (like the rank-and-file *Cabanos* discussed in Marcus de Carvalho's essay in this book) to move toward an identity based on "class." As a result, they highlighted certain shared cultural characteristics, and even "domesticated" (reinterpreted in their own terms; see John Monteiro's chapter in this book) cultural elements of European origin, as markers of this new identity (Barth 1969), in a process that combined class- and ethnogenesis.

Dale Tomich (2004) has called the increased vigor of the slave trade and slavery in Brazil and Cuba, after the fall of plantation production and the retraction of the market for people in Saint Domingue (since 1791) and in the British Caribbean (following the end there of the transatlantic human commerce in 1808), the "second slavery." It is possible that Brazilian manumission rates at the onset of this transition increased (if, indeed, they moved inversely to a downward trend in real slave prices), but recent research suggests that, if they did, they subsequently declined. Manolo Florentino (2005, 341–42) notes that in the city of Rio slave prices rose much more between 1825 and 1835 than slave rental rates and concludes that bondspeople increasingly had to hire themselves out for more hours to buy their freedom. Work by Douglas Libby and Afonso Graça Filho (2003), documenting a steep decline in the presence of freed people in São

José d'El Rey in southern Minas Gerais between 1795 and the 1830s, raises the possibility that this change began earlier and was more general.

Whatever the case, recent demographic studies suggest that, from the point of view of slaves in the southeast, there were two polar experiences in bondage, existing before this second slavery but perhaps made more divergent by it. On the one hand, small properties abounded, with significant proportions of creoles among adults (people aged fifteen or more). On the other hand, there were also large properties, with a highly Africanized, "newly recruited" labor force.[8] In the former, manumission seems to have been much more common. One indicator of this comes from later official population statistics and data on freedoms from 1872 to 1875, available for nearly all Brazil. These provide fairly accurate yet lower-limit estimates for manumission rates (Slenes 1976, 486–94). In the province of Rio de Janeiro, the annual rate from these data was more than twice as high in "non-plantation" as in "plantation" counties: 5.4 versus 2.5 per 1,000 (compare the estimate for all the American South of only 0.45 per 1,000 annually in 1850; Fogel and Engerman 1974, 1:150).[9] It is likely that this difference reflects contrasts in *average* holding size—and thus underestimates the real divergence between rates in small and large properties.

Indeed, recent studies of manumission in wills and inheritance proceedings, which have linked individual freedoms to slave evaluation lists for various places and times in the southeast, suggest larger contrasts. Seven regional and temporal analyses of owners who freed slaves in wills show that small holders released far more people this way, proportionally, than large ones.[10] (Manumitting testators owning one to twenty slaves freed from 21.7 percent to 41.7 percent of their bondspeople, whereas those with forty-one slaves or more freed from 1.8 percent to 6.8 percent.) Equally importantly, four analyses that calculate the percentage of bondspeople freed in the wills of all deceased owners, dying testate or intestate, reach similar, if less extreme, conclusions. In the plantation county of Campinas, western São Paulo, at the height of the second slavery (1836–45), the death of "small owners" (those having one to twenty slaves) resulted in the manumission by will or during probate of 6.5 percent of the bondspeople possessed by these deceased. This was twice the 3.3 percent released at death by "large owners" (with 41–100 slaves) and over six times the 1.0 percent freed by "very large owners" (with over 100).[11] These figures, multiplied by two (estate divisions of slave master and mistress), approximate "generational" rates; assuming twenty years per generation (an underestimate), we obtain upper-limit annual manumission rates of, respectively, 6.1, 3.2, and 1.0 per 1,000.

More microhistorical research is needed on manumission, particularly work that also links bondspeople freed at baptism, and by "writs of freedom" (cartas de liberdade) registered in notarial books, to lists of slaves in censuses and inheritance proceedings. (Data from Campinas [Ferraz 2010] suggest that the registered *cartas* and the manumissions in wills are only slightly overlapping sets of about the same size.) Still, one study that does this for baptismal manumissions shows that small owners freed far more infants, in proportion to the number of slaves they owned at death, than large holders. And the only study that does such linkage with both baptisms and writs of freedom (as well as with manumission in wills) similarly finds that large owners freed few slaves through baptism or cartas, indeed, fewer than they did on their deaths.[12] This research is suggestive since the "social logic"—to be discussed later—that I believe led small owners to show more "largesse" than grander ones when manumitting in wills, should also have caused them to be more favorable to other types of freedom. Thus, I suspect from the data currently available that the manumission rate in large properties was generally higher than that in all the post-1830 American South, where owners' rights to free their workers were usually restricted by law; yet, the door to freedom in such properties probably was not open wide enough, even for creoles, to have a significant "outward-turning" effect on slave identity. Indeed, for the slaves themselves, surely the more relevant measure of deprivation was the experience of bondspeople in small properties, which must have made the large holdings seem like closed systems offering little chance of freedom.

To be sure, the plantation environment was a complex one, providing possibilities for significantly improving one's lot *within* slavery (Slenes 1976, chapter ten; Góes 2003). Thus, I do not argue that slaves turned their backs on the freeborn and freed sector, nor that competitive tensions in the senzala were absent. Yet, the new manumission studies suggest that incentives within plantation slavery did not lead to a broad channel toward freedom, but to a bottleneck, whose restricted rewards would not have been sufficient to turn individual tensions into group animosities— unless, that is, there were other strong reasons for division in the quarters. It becomes imperative therefore to examine the similarities and differences in the cultural traditions that Africans in Brazil's southeast brought with them.

Of the new Africans brought to southeastern Brazil, about 93 percent between 1790 and 1811 and 75 percent between 1811 and 1850 came from western Central Africa (the area from Gabon to northern Namibia, from the Atlantic to the Great Lakes).[13] This is important, for it is now clear—thanks especially to historian Jan Vansina's work—that the region is a single "culture area" (Craemer, Vansina, and Fox 1976; Vansina 1989, 1990, 2002, 2004). It is bound together not only by its Bantu linguistic heritage, but also by its peoples' "common view of the universe" (for instance, a special reverence for the spirits of the "first comers" to one's territory [Klieman 2003]) and their "common political ideology," the latter including "assumptions about roles, statuses, symbols, values and . . . the very notion of legitimate authority" (Vansina 1989, 341). Then, too, Bantuphone peoples in eastern Central Africa (responsible for about 18 percent of the enslaved sent to Brazil's southeast between 1811 and 1850) tend to share broadly similar cosmological assumptions with those in the western Central region regarding the etiology of disease and misfortune. Thus, both groups frequently seek therapy (to restore "health") in cults of affliction (Janzen 1982, 1992; Van Dijk, Reis, and Spierenburg 2000).

In addition to these broad commonalities, one may also identify specific traditions that especially configured the encounters between Central Africans in the New World. Even in the mid-nineteenth century, when the "slaving frontier" extended deep into the continent, a substantial proportion of forced migrants to the Americas from western Central Africa were drawn from closely related societies in the "Atlantic zone," polities on or relatively near the coast, largely transformed into "slave societies" and slave exporters by their strategic position as suppliers of the Atlantic trade (Miller 1988, chapter five; Slenes 2002, 2007a, 2007b). Thus, the Ovimbundu (in the Benguela highlands), the Mbundu (in Luanda's hinterland), the Kongo (in the lower Zaire basin and northern Angola), and neighboring groups inland accounted for a large core group in the senzala.[14] The proportion from the "old" Atlantic zone (the area of the three groups mentioned) seems to have been particularly great among bondspeople leaving from "Congo North" (the mouth of the Congo and Zaire River and points up the coast) and from Benguela, because of continual raiding and warfare in the respective immediate hinterland (Thornton 1997; Candido 2006).[15]

The case of Congo North is particularly important, because it accounted for more than 40 percent of bondspeople who entered southeastern Brazil from western Central Africa between 1811 and 1850 (more than from Benguela or from Luanda and its associated ports). Probably half of these were from (but not necessarily native to) the Kongo culture area in the lower Zaire basin (Koelle, 1963, cited by Curtin 1969, 256, 295–96; Thornton 1997).

The slave trade provoked intense cultural exchanges within Africa. Even persons from the far interior shipped directly to Brazil usually learned one of the commercial pidgin languages (based on Kikongo, Kimbundu, or Umbundu, respectively the tongues of the Kongo, Mbundu, and Ovimbundu) on their way to the coast. Others who spent some time as slaves in the coastal societies before being sold into the transatlantic trade must have acquired further notions of the languages and cultures of these areas. Still others who were born of slave women bought from the interior would have been fully "fluent" in Kongo, Mbundu, or Ovimbundu culture, yet also would have had some knowledge of their mothers' traditions (and thus could have served as go-betweens for newly arrived people from the African interior, both in their home societies and in the Brazilian senzala). Finally, if Joseph Miller's model is correct, the influx of slaves from the broader Atlantic zone (if not from farther afield) into the Kongo and Mbundu areas was so large that it probably had a cumulative cultural impact on the very coastal societies to which the newcomers were accommodating themselves.

Central Africans moved further toward the formation of a common culture in the Middle Passage, as they discovered affinities in vocabulary and cosmology across their closely related languages (Slenes 2000). Similarly, after they arrived in Brazil they continued to draw upon common elements of a widespread Atlantic-zone tradition (indeed, a western-central African tradition) that, in the closed plantation context, could easily have supplied identity markers for the senzala. I focus here on the belief in tutelary territorial spirits. The Kongo and Mbundu have long attributed to these spirits virtually the same characteristics (Slenes 2002, 2007b; Thornton 2002) and similar notions are widely diffused among other groups (Boulanger 1974, 60–63; Klieman 2003). I document that these beliefs crossed the Atlantic, in a study of three black religious movements (Slenes 2007b): the *Cabula* in northern Espírito Santo, recorded in 1900; a religious practice with antislavery overtones in São Roque, western São Paulo, documented in 1854; and the slave cult conspiracy of 1848 in Vassouras.

The ritual vocabularies of the Brazilian movements are clearly of western Central African origin, showing a strong resonance with Kimbundu and Kikongo (the Cabula and the 1848 lexicons) or clearly originating in Kikongo (the São Roque wordlist). Furthermore, the morphology of their rituals is similar to the well-documented community cults of affliction in the Kongo, variously named Bakhimba, Ndembo, or, more commonly, Kimpasi. In Brazil, as among the Kongo, the cults included both men and women among their initiates and priests and were characterized by ritual death and rebirth through possession by named spirits. In the case of the Kongo, these were local territorial genii. It is likely that the Brazilian movements also cultivated local spirits (not those of their adepts' origins), since this was the common practice among migrant groups in Central Africa. For the Kongolese (indeed, for many other Bantu groups), such local genii were responsible for the well-being or misfortune of people within their "jurisdiction," irrespective of lineage or origin, and thus needed to be properly propitiated. Especially powerful in these genii's ranks were the spirits of the most ancient inhabitants of the land (Klieman 2003). In Brazil, this would have meant the "first-comers" among Brazilian Indians. Thus, it probably is not a coincidence that the subsequent Macumba and Umbanda religions, clearly derived from the earlier Brazilian cult tradition, given their ritual vocabulary, confer special powers on *Caboclo Velho* (old Indian of the forest) spirits.

The discovery of Kimpasi-like cults in southeastern Brazil confirms the argument that a large core group of people from the Central African Atlantic zone, with a particularly strong Kongo and "near-Kongo" component after 1810 (I include here Mbundu), formed the cultural matrix of the senzala on the plantations of Brazil's southeast, one that could attract and accommodate other Bantuphone migrants, including the "Moçambiques." Indeed, the strong similarities between the three Brazilian cults and the fact that they were far flung within the southeast mean that essentially the same religious tradition was spread everywhere in the region's senzalas.

This religious tradition was also a political one. The bibliography on Central African community cults of affliction presents them not just as manifestations of spiritual concerns but as institutions of "governance." Specifically in the case of the Kongo, "in regions where strong chiefships or external government existed, the [Kimpasi, or 'sacred medicine'] cults could cross-cut these mutually-exclusive polities." In areas "where such forms of centralized government were absent, the cult elite could take over many governmental functions" (Janzen and MacGaffey 1974, 96).

In addition to being a response to severe community crisis, the cults of affliction provided a way for power holders to justify their stewardship (Janzen and MacGaffey 1974, 96–97; Janzen 1982). Yet, there is another side to this story, as attested by the discomfiture that Kimpasi movements in the middle and late seventeenth century caused the Kongo political elite (Hilton 1985, 197–98) and by the role these cults played as cradle to the "Antonian" movement's intervention (1704–6) in a struggle for succession to the Kongolese throne (Thornton 1998b; Slenes 2008). In short, Kimpasi also could mobilize discontent to hold the "stewardship" of those in power to account. Given the character of these cults in Central Africa, one may conclude from their presence in Brazil that slaves drew upon their past, not just to create new norms and consecrate their lives in the new environment, but also to put in place their own political institutions, aimed at mediating conflicts among themselves and diagnosing the broader causes of affliction.

I turn now to the plan for rebellion in 1848 in Vassouras (Slenes 2006, 2007b). The conspiracy was formulated at the apogee of British pressure on Brazil to abolish the slave trade. Its discovery mobilized government authorities at the highest level. The "president" (governor) of Rio province sent to the provincial legislature a dossier of documents for evaluation from local authorities. The committee assigned to that task expressed no doubt in its secret report about the connection between English pressure and the slaves' movement. One may discount the authors' paranoia about direct action by secret British agents, but accept as plausible their identification of other vectors of revolution: traveling hawkers who brought goods to the plantations and "free" Africans, liberated from slave ships intercepted by the British, who had been put by the government into the custody of employers in the interior under conditions akin to slavery. Such people brought the news of contention between Britain and Brazil to the senzala and may have helped spread the conviction that it was time to "seize the day."

If the cult of 1848 was a Kimpasi-like society, then the history of the Brazilian abolition of slavery may have to be rewritten. In a speech to Parliament in 1852, no less a figure than Eusébio de Queiroz, the minister who presided over the passage of the law of 1850 ending the slave trade, attributed great political significance to this conspiracy. In his evaluation, "public opinion" at the end of the 1840s had turned against this commerce; yet, it was necessary that "signs of a grave nature . . . [in] Vassouras [and other places] produc[e] a terror that [was] salutary, because it provided the opportunity for that opinion, contrary to the traffic, to develop further and make itself felt."[16] Indeed, Parliament, meeting in secret sessions, almost approved a bill in late 1848 that was very close to that passed in 1850.

For subsequent years, the evidence suggests that the African (or African-creole) pressure of Kimpasi-like movements continued to have a significant political impact. Maria Helena Machado (1994, chapter three) has shown that slave revolts in São Paulo in 1882–83 were led by charismatic "sorcerers," men who, as had the Kikongo-speaking leader of the cult of 1854 that I analyzed, organized secret societies, used divining mirrors and figurines of Saint Anthony in their rituals (the saint himself probably reinterpreted within a Central African matrix, as had occurred before in the Kongo), and promised to make rebelling slaves invincible.[17] These thinly documented movements, when put in the context of the "thickly described" Kimpasi-like groups of 1848, 1854, and 1900, offer strong circumstantial evidence that Kongo, near-Kongo, or Atlantic zone community cults of affliction were still active in the 1880s as key institutions underlying slave resistance.

If plantation slaves in the nineteenth-century Southeast turned "inward," drawing upon a common Central African culture in delimiting their identities, one would expect to find evidence of this in the sociology of slave revolts. The documentation available on the movements of 1848 and the 1880s does not permit a study of the social profiles of those involved. The sources on three other conspiracies and revolts, however—one in a county in southern Minas, the others in Vassouras and Campinas, and all in the 1830s—have permitted such analysis. In none of these cases were significant divisions found among Africans, between Africans and creoles, or between different occupational groups (M. F. Andrade 1998–99; F. Gomes 2006, chapter three; Pirola forthcoming). The southeast would appear to be strikingly different from Bahia, where ethnic divisions, particularly between Africans and creoles, have consistently been found.

If mobility out of large slaveholdings was rather limited, and if bondspeople in the nineteenth-century plantation context tended to form an identity in radical opposition to that of their masters, then clearly one part of Mattos's great-arch explanation can no longer be accepted. Yet, the over-all movement of the curve she projects is confirmed by my research, even if some important adjustments must be made to it. I limit myself here to two comments. First, restricted mobility out of the nineteenth-century plantation senzala should be considered together with the reduction of opportunities for the free poor. The reduction of opportunities was prob-ably more severe than even Mattos postulated, given recent studies show-ing the sometimes high proportion of blacks among small slave owners before the mid-nineteenth century. São José d'El Rey in 1795 may not have been unusual among small-holding areas in Minas at that time; 44 percent of its owners holding one to five slaves were freeborn or freed blacks (Libby and Paiva 2000), something that surely discouraged a polarization of iden-tities into "Afro-descendant" and "white" categories. Rising slave and land prices, however, in combination with more rapid growth in the free popu-lation than in the slave population, particularly after 1850, could only have meant that freeborn and freed blacks—indeed, the free poor in general— were increasingly deprived of a crucial opportunity for mobility that the slave system had made available to them. The combination of restricted mobility for slaves and freeborn blacks and libertos may have led many in all three groups toward closer association, both in culture and in identity formation. Significantly, the São Roque cult of 1854 attracted "free" people, perhaps particularly the freed. Likewise, the episodes of 1848 and 1854 were led by a liberto. Then, too, the *jongos*, black challenge songs of slave origin in the Paraíba Valley and central western São Paulo, still contained complex metaphors of recognizable Central African (particularly Kongo) origin in the mid-twentieth century, which links them to the Macumba and Umbanda religions of that time, as well as to the nineteenth-century cults of affliction (Slenes 2007a). It is difficult to imagine how this could have occurred if slaves and free blacks had not already felt affinities with each other before abolition. It may well be that the danger presented to the elite by the conspiracy of 1848 went beyond the limits of the senzala to in-clude an increasingly significant proportion of the free poor. In any case, I suspect that by the end of the slavery period there was (in the planta-tion areas) more of a shared sense of an oppositional black consciousness drawn with African markers—a common African Brazilian identity—than had been present at independence.

My second comment is on the arch's apogee at the end of the eigh-teenth century. There is no question that overall manumission rates in

Brazil were high, from an early date; after all, at least three-fourths of Brazil's black population (blacks and mulattos) in 1872 were freeborn or freed, compared to 6 percent in the U.S. South in 1860 (Graham 1999, 31). If rates were "low" in large plantation properties, then this means that they were very high indeed in small holdings, which abounded in the Brazilian slave system in the colonial period and even in the nineteenth century. Libby's and Paiva's study (2000) of São José d'El Rey in southern Minas in 1795 — based on a census that systematically indicates the social status, enslaved, freeborn, or freed, of everyone included — may provide a window into Brazil's small slaveholding sector at precisely the high point of the arch's curve.

The freed in this parish formed an extraordinarily high percentage of the "ever-enslaved" (slaves plus freed) of both sexes and all origins in the higher age groups: 24 percent of forty-year-olds and 36 percent of sixty-year-olds.[18] Among ever-enslaved creoles, these figures were, respectively, 56 and 70 percent (or 62 and 77 percent for creole women). For African-born women they were, respectively, 17 and 52 percent. While some will rightly object that one cannot leap directly from these data to conclusions about people's chances for manumission during their life course (conceivably many of the freed were in-migrants to the parish or wrongly classified freeborn blacks), these percentages are nonetheless consistent with the predictions of the models I developed to analyze manumission over time in a closed cohort initially aged ten (Slenes 1976, 489–94) — that is, if one uses not the "national" annual manumission rate from 1872–75 (6 per 1,000), but a figure (12 per 1,000) close to the levels prevailing in the provinces with the highest rates.[19] While this does not prove that the data for São José portray the experience of a closed age cohort from birth (or from arrival in Brazil at around the age of ten or older), it does indicate that such a result would be historically plausible. In any case, even if the correct percentages for freed people among the survivors of initial cohorts reaching ages forty and sixty were half of those indicated here (thus corresponding to the predictions of my models using a 6 per 1,000 manumission rate), they would still point to the same conclusion: that slaves in small holdings, particularly the Brazilian-born, had significant, realistic hopes of getting themselves or at least some members of their families (especially women) out of bondage by the time the beneficiaries reached forty. Surely, identity strategies in such a context, where assimilative projects were not quixotic, would have been very different from those in large properties.

A key question that remains is why smaller holdings were more "friendly" to freedom. One possible answer is that greater contact between masters and slaves in this context, combined with less cultural distance between the two poles, there being proportionally fewer Africans present (Márcio de Sousa Soares 2009, 92), was more conducive to the development of patron-client ties and thus to manumission. This, however, is an argument that emphasizes workers' negotiations for masters' favors without attention to the two sides' relative powers of persuasion. An alternative answer may have to do with the vulnerability of "peasants" transformed into first-time small slave-owners, an important subset of small proprietors before 1830 or 1850. These people were surely at a disadvantage in the struggle to obtain workers' "consent," particularly in a society where a rigid color line had not emerged to socialize the cost of slave control. Lacking such "wages of whiteness" to track down runaways, small owners also faced a situation in which only a few fugitives could break them. One thinks here of the unmarried West African (Mina) freedwomen, active in petty commerce in Rio de Janeiro and São João del Rei (Minas Gerais) before 1830, who manumitted most of their slaves, largely also West African females, in cartas and wills (Faria 1007).

In sum, high manumission rates in small holdings could (partly) be the result of "favor" forced; many small owners may have obtained their workers' reluctant consent (to stay on and indeed "work") only by convincing them that the chance of freedom later, for themselves or family members, outweighed the potential, not negligible costs (Chalhoub 2010) of trying to escape from the system. Still, in terms of day-to-day politics, the "hidden transcripts" of both sides in this context—"hidden transcript" is James Scott's term (1990) for what subalterns and superalterns say about each other privately to their peers—would surely have been more ambiguous, less deeply antagonistic, than in situations of highly polarized power and limited worker horizons.

The complex interlinking of the many Brazilian "slaveries" and "slave societies" suggested in this essay, particularly with respect to the processes of identity formation inside and outside the senzala, is still speculative. This is an interim report that tries to fit work in progress into a broader picture. Yet, I believe my analysis has considerable interest, for it offers a potential solution to seemingly intractable debates in Brazilian historiography. It may also provide a way to reconcile the divergent existing images of Brazil's construction of social race. If the hypothesis, here revised, of Brazil's great arch holds up under scrutiny, then clearly the country once offered considerable hope (relative to other New World slave societies) for a nonracialized conception and practice of citizenship. Moreover, the long experience of tough, yet necessarily subtle, face-to-face bargaining by slaves in small holdings with superalterns who were not radically different in power, color, or caste (in stark contrast to the relations between plantation slaves and their owners or between bonded workers in small properties and their "master-race" overlords in the United States) may well lie at the origin of a culture of interpersonal politics on the field of "race" still marked (especially to foreigners' eyes) more by "cordiality" than confrontation, despite the steep descent of the arch over the last two centuries.[20] The approach taken here may make it possible to perceive what truly is at stake—what has already been lost and what may yet be lost—if that descent is not reversed.

Notes

1 On British pressure, particularly its increase in 1848, see Bethell (1970, 291–92).

2 "Black" is a translation of the Portuguese *negro*, as it is used increasingly in Brazil to encompass the census categories of *preto* and *pardo* ("black" and "brown"). I translate *pardo* as "mulatto," but the term in the nineteenth century also included many phenotypical *pretos*, freeborn or freed, who had distanced themselves socially from slavery.

3 See Slenes (1999, 62, note 54), for a comparison of passages from Freyre and Phillips.

4 Freyre became more conservative over time, increasingly stressing social harmony in Brazil's slave society (compare Freyre 1971).

5 Freyre (1980, 65, note 55, added in 1946) sides with Melville Herskovits against Frazier (albeit confusing their identities), recognizing the African values of slave families.

6 On increasing public and private discrimination against blacks during the century, see Spitzer (1989), Graham (1999), Grinberg (2002), Chalhoub (2010).

7 The polarization (African cultural continuity versus creolization) expressed by Lovejoy (1997) and Price (2003) is not helpful.

8 In São Paulo province, 1829, the adult African to creole ratio was 302:100 in holdings with over forty people, compared to 165:100 in holdings with ten people or less (calculated from data in Luna and Klein 2003 and in a personal communication from Herbert Klein).

9 Calculated from *matrícula* (registration) data from 1872–75 on slave population

and manumission for Rio's counties (Directoria Geral de Estatística, *Relatórios* [1877, 1878], citations in Slenes 1976, 707).

10 On Rio das Velhas mining-farming *comarca* (region), Minas, from 1720–84, see Paiva (2001, 175); on Campos, a Rio plantation county, from 1735–1807 and 1807–30, see Márcio de Sousa Soares (2009, 91–92); on mixed farming in Porto Feliz, São Paulo, from 1788–1878, see Guedes (2008, 192); on Campinas, from 1836–45 and 1860–71, see Ferraz (2010, 131–32); on coffee-producing Juiz de Fora, Minas, and slave owners in three nineteenth-century families, see Freire (2009, 321).

11 On Rio das Mortes comarca, southern Minas, from 1716–89, see Paiva (2001, 176); on Juiz de Fora, the same families and period, see Freire (2009, 323); on Campinas, from 1835–46 and 1860–71, see Ferraz (2010, 131–32). Salles (2008, 291, 307, note 26) gives similar data for Vassouras, 1836–88, regarding people freed during inheritance, not in wills.

12 On São João del Rei, Minas Gerais, from 1750–1850, see C. Silva (2004, 151); on Juiz de Fora, same families and period, see Freire (2009, 310).

13 For data on the slave trade, see Florentino (1997, 222–23, 228–29, 234) for 1790–1831; Karasch (1987, 12–15, appendix A) for 1831–50 (including Africans transshipped from Brazil's northeast).

14 These are modern "umbrella" names for, in each case, peoples with closely related languages and cultures but probably (during the slave trade) without a common identity.

15 According to Candido, the great majority of slaves from Benguela were natives of groups later denominated "Ovimbundu."

16 Eusébio de Queiroz Coutinho Mattoso Camara, speech to Chamber of Deputies, July 16, 1852, reproduced in Malheiro (1976, 2:210).

17 On Saint Anthony, see the work of Slenes (2008).

18 My calculations, here and following, are derived from data in Libby and Paiva (2000, 106, 110, 114).

19 In my models with a 12 per 1,000 manumission rate, 13 to 33 percent of survivors from an original slave cohort aged ten would be free when they were forty years old, and 29.4 to 52 percent would be free when they were sixty; that is, double my calculations based on a 6:1,000 manumission rate (Slenes 1976, 491).

20 See Fry (2005, 167–78).

PART TWO

Resisting through Religion and for Religion

This section, taking up Ortner's point that "casualness about religion" was a significant defect of the classic resistance literature (1995, 181), foregrounds religious belief within discussion of different forms of resistance. As these chapters demonstrate, shared religious belief, symbols, and practices created deep social and cultural rootedness within communities, which could justify and inspire resistance in diverse circumstances. The chapters on Brazil highlight the need to understand how religions maintain their social bases and adjust to challenges, while also indicating how, as discourses of religious resistance were appropriated into structures of political power, the sites and meanings of religious resistance shifted. The chapters on Mexico argue that nonviolent, civil strategies of resistance, be they formally organized, spontaneous, group, or personal, were fundamental to the successful thwarting of state attempts to contain religion within the realm of private belief and cloistered practice.

Patricia Pessar's analysis of republican-era backlands millenarian movements in Brazil once again explains rebellion as a response to the breaking of established social pacts, highlighting not only the political changes and the growing capitalist transformation of the backlands, but also the efforts of the Catholic Church's ultramontane faction to "strip rural inhabitants of the symbols, identities, and practices that had been sustained over the centuries in folk Catholicism" (125). Millenarian ideas began as a technology of colonial rule, so these movements responded to a hegemonic crisis triggered by elites' abandonment of earlier ideologies by throwing these ideas back in their faces in an effort to restore the moral foundations of economic and spiritual security. The irony deepens after millenarianism, which began as part of a hegemonic project and then became subversive, is reappropriated in modern times by the state, the media, and the Catholic Church. Yet Pessar argues that this coming full circle does not entirely eliminate the subversive element. Although what provided "a culturally appropriate toolkit for problem-solving thought and agency" (141) in the 1800s and early 1900s appealed to a narrower segment of rural society by the 1930s, and despite the fact that the specifically religious dimensions of the movements are even less significant today, these militant traditions, since their meaning derived from the hegemonic crisis of another era, continue to inspire contemporary forms of social activism.

Luis Nicolau Parés's examination of the Afro-Brazilian religion Candomblé closely complements Pessar's discussion by arguing that Candomblé practitioners, to the extent to which they employ any explicit concept of resistance at all, focus on "conserving" what they have rather than struggling for something they do not have. Although both Candomblé studies and Candomblé politics are marked by confrontations between purist "Afro-centric" and "syncretic" positions, Candomblé's cosmology reproduces ideas about ancestrality and tradition that seem central to African religious systems.

Historically, Candomblé has simultaneously acted as a space of subversive dissidence and as a vehicle for the negotiation of new spaces in the wider social order. It achieved elite recognition, under politically conservative regimes, in the 1930s and again in the 1970s, but recognition focused on "elite *terreiros*" (temples) that emphasized the purity of Yoruba traditions, as opposed to the syncretic Candomblé houses accused of commercialized charlatanism. Black activists influenced by Pan-Africanism in the United States drove further "re-Africanization" in the 1980s. Although Parés argues that state recognition of Candomblé should not be seen as simply a top-down process, the benefits offered in the 1990s, including the registration of some terreiros as national cultural heritage sites, still concentrated on elite terreiros, while the tutelage of Candomblé by the state, NGOs, and black activists deepened the appropriation of the religion's symbols to promote tourism and build political clienteles. Parés therefore concludes that we are more likely to find "the nourishing ground for future challenges to today's authorities" in the apparently apolitical practices of less respectable religious traditions in terreiros frequented only by poorer Bahians (163).

Jean Meyer's discussion of Catholic resistance to the Mexican postrevolutionary state's measures against the church from the mid-1920s onwards continues this theme, stressing the church's social rootedness as the key to understanding its durability and adaptability. His contribution takes the form of a *mea culpa* for past sins of analytical omission resulting from his focus on the regions that produced the militant forms of resistance that he terms *Widerstand*, some of which became foci of further violence in the 1930s. Pacific, civic, and "sociological" forms of resistance, or *Resistenz*, were the rule rather than the exception in Mexico's five northern and four southern states between 1926 and 1929. *Resistenz* also occurred in states where armed conflict was intense (as Patience Schell's chapter demonstrates), and Meyer shows that marginal pockets of *Widerstand* can be found even in states such as Oaxaca, but the latter was characterized by a general absence of violent conflict or serious interference with Catholic devotions or education, thanks to a far from unique process of compromise among civil, military, and ecclesiastical authorities. Meyer's preliminary comparative reflections on these less studied experiences of religious conflict uncover some intriguing paradoxes for further investigation, such as why some apparently "reasonable men" failed to prevent armed conflicts while military commanders who did not appear particularly "soft" in one context proved so in another, but his evidence clearly suggests the need to recognize how a weak central government was constrained by the subterranean forces of popular piety and the equally silent tendency of local elites to outwardly respect, but not implement, orders from above.

Patience Schell's chapter on the Union of Mexican Catholic Ladies (UDCM) continues the theme of taking the motivational force of religious beliefs seriously, but adds a gendered dimension to the discussion. The "ladies" who are the chief protagonists of Schell's study did not seek radical changes in gender roles or the class differentiation reflected in their own self-image as decorous women who "counseled peaceful protest . . . while servants in the street attacked police and firefighters" (190). Yet even if class, along with the projection of respectable images of motherhood and women's "natural roles," offered these women a measure of protection, Schell shows that these socially conservative, middle-class women did take substantial risks, could suffer serious consequences as a result, and were seen by their opponents as directly challenging power structures. In this sense, she argues, they deserve inclusion in studies of resistance. Furthermore, in their desires to "serve for something," these unlikely rebels, resisting religious persecution and sexually provocative dress styles alike, also acted against their gendered marginalization from the political sphere. In this respect, their actions did contribute to social change, and here Schell explores some interesting parallels between Mexico and Brazil. UDCM resistance was, it seems, a little too successful from the standpoint of the church hierarchy, which reimposed clerical control by making this lay organization part of Catholic Action in 1929.

CHAPTER SIX

Millenarianism, Hegemony, and Resistance in Brazil

PATRICIA R. PESSAR

Most studies of millenarianism in Brazil and elsewhere predate the emergence of resistance studies. As such, many of the concerns and methodological debates central to resistance studies went unaddressed. Most research produced from the 1950s through the 1970s reductively attributed millenarian (and related charismatic) movements to *external* changes imposed on subordinated populations: isolating the triggers for millenarian movements became the highest priority. These triggers included colonial contact and gradual domination, changes in state rule promoting centralization and homogenization, and profound transformations in relations of production. One group of scholars maintained that these external processes produced anomie among "pre-modern" or "backward" populations. Millenarian movements were viewed as potential antidotes for this social "affliction" (Queiroz 1965). Another group, who held more teleological conceptions of history, understood millenarian movements to be a stage through which less advanced peoples might travel on their inevitable journey to cultural and political rationality and modernity (Worsley 1957; Hobsbawm 1959; Jarvie 1964). Both schools thought millenarian activity was somehow extruded from the societal firmament as "less-developed" peoples became overwhelmed by those "more developed."

Commencing in the late 1970s, critics countered that an imperial, subject-object model of history informed the theories that privileged colonization, acculturation, and modernization as principal agents for millenarian movements (Fabian 1979; Pessar 1982). Johannes Fabian noted, "All too often these studies suggest, in the end, that charismatic leaders and their followers may *think* and *say* that they assemble to bring about

the millennium, cargo, or universal brotherhood, while 'in reality' they react to oppression and cultural contamination. What drives them, in other
words, happens *to* them, behind their backs, . . . as objects of causation. . . .
Causal explanations in this vein necessarily 'victimize' (make objects of)
religious enthusiasts and are therefore incapable of *understanding* movements" (1979, 13–14). This new school insisted on a central role for culture,
and more specifically religious discourse, within analyses of millenarian
and other charismatic movements. Scholars probed how problem-solving
thoughts and actions were mediated by messianic leaders, prophets, and
their followers through cultural categories and root metaphors, like the
millennium (Janzen 1979). Significantly, a growing number of scholars
ceased to produce narratives about us, civilization, and modernity while
purporting to speak about "the 'savage'—the other" (Fabian 1979, 14).
This new literature revealed that many religious enthusiasts did indeed
assemble in pursuit of the millennium, cargo, or universal brotherhood.
They did so because these key metaphors were understood as numinous
resources for reflecting on new forms of subordination and oppression
and for regaining lost power (D. T. Monteiro 1974; Murão 1974; Janzen 1979;
Pessar 1981). A serious engagement with "native" epistemologies and practices, therefore, created important analytical room for culturally "thick"
studies of the subjectivities, motivations, accommodations, and struggles
of oppressed people engaged in social change and social movements. This
literature represented a bold challenge to two common representations of
native and "peasant" millenarianists. The first cast them as prepolitical objects of history and (to use today's terminology) situated them in a wholly
different subject position from fully political actors (Worsley 1957; Hobsbawm 1959). Contrastively, the second type of representation insisted that
millenarian enthusiasts were wholly motivated by class interests and religious discourses were mere masks (Fáco 1963; Moniz 1978).

   Advances in the study of millenarianism were carried further with the
advent of resistance studies (Brown and Fernández 1991). This new scholarship opened additional space for the critical study of culture and power
and of popular practices associated with religion (Comaroff and Comaroff
1991). Yet, as John Gledhill notes in his introduction to this book, the debates around subaltern resistance raise further questions about the possible meanings of "socially progressive" politics. This chapter follows in
the tradition of those who seek to widen the analytical boundaries around
the concept of resistance. This broadening allows for both the inclusion of

alternate subjectivities, cultural forms, and social spaces that foster challenges to elite appropriation and domination (Miceli 1984) and also the acknowledgement that resistance can encompass conservation and defiant resilience in ways that complicate teleological notions of socially progressive politics.

What Luis Nicolau Parés (chapter seven) argues for Bahian Candomblé is equally apt for backlands millenarianism. The type of resistance these subcultures entail connote "the idea of not losing what one has rather than winning what one does not have." In this type of resistance, the intergenerational transference of culture tends to be conservative rather than transformative. Backlands millenarian movements were motivated, in part, by country folks' resistance in the mid-nineteenth century to punitive actions taken by Catholic Church officials. These authorities attempted to strip rural inhabitants of the symbols, identities, and practices that had been sustained over the centuries in folk Catholicism. Backlands millenarianism, as a subculture of resistance, emerged out of this unequal struggle. The movements treated in this study are Canudos (Bahia state, 1867–97), Contestado (Santa Catarina state, 1844–1912), Juazeiro (Ceará state, 1870–present), and Santa Brígida (Bahia state, 1938–present).

If one were to follow James Scott's (1990) pioneering work on millenarianism as a reservoir of subaltern hidden transcripts, there might be a temptation to focus on millenarianism as a specific subculture of resistance rather than on the broader configurations of power and cultural productions in which millenarianism is embedded and has been transformed. In this chapter, millenarianism is envisioned as a constituent element of Brazilian popular and dominant cultures, with both cultures being understood as mutually constituted (Hall 1981). I argue that from colonial times to the present, millenarian identities, subjectivities, meanings, and practices have been fostered and reworked through unequal struggles, accommodations, and appropriations between elite and subaltern actors. Consequently, "the millennium" has been a key metaphor both in discourses of rule and in a backlands subculture of resistance.

Brazilian Millenarianism as Elite Discourse

Millenarianism originated in Portugal as a foundational state narrative and technology of colonial rule (Myscofski 1988; T. M. Cohen 1998). Antônio Vieira, one of the earliest Jesuit leaders in Brazil, sermonized:

> The Portuguese reign was founded on July 25, 1139, when King
> Afonso I Henriques conquered the Moors. . . . God had said to the
> King at the dawn of this victory: 'I want you and your descendants
> to establish my kingdom . . . All the kings are of God, but the other
> kings are God's produced by men: *the king of Portugal is of God and
> created by God, and thus more rightly His.'* . . . The history of Portugal
> is truly a sacred history, a history of salvation. . . . The Portuguese are
> the angels of God sent to the pagans who have long awaited them
> (Isaiah 18:2–7). Soldiers and missionaries are united in a glorious
> mission. . . . For this mission, the union between the spiritual and
> temporal powers is necessary. (Hoornaert 1974, 35, emphasis added)

Central symbols in this early colonial text are the messiah (the founding
king of Portugal having been fathered by God, not man), a "new" land
transformed into God's promised Heaven on Earth, and millenarian enthusiasts (the Portuguese colonial soldiers and missionaries "united in
a glorious mission"). Sixteenth-century "Messianic warriors" like Jesuits
Vieira, Manuel da Nóbrega, and José de Anchieta (Hoornaert 1974, 32) laid
the foundation for the belief—or at the very least the assertion—that in
Brazil terrestrial authority was sanctified by God and the human actions
of the colonizers were wholly providential (P. Oliveira 1985).

Early Jesuit and Capuchin missions were also explicitly eschatological.
Instructors simplified Christian doctrine to "the singular but dramatic
issues of salvation and damnation" (Myscofski 1991, 84). Missionaries
also introduced elaborate penitential practices, like self-flagellation, and
proclaimed the imminent day of judgment. These teachings were further
elaborated and disseminated by lay religious figures like the thaumaturge
Francisco Mendonca Mar. He is said to have undergone conversion upon
hearing Vieira preach. Shortly afterward, Mar dedicated himself to spreading the Jesuit's message by traveling on foot across the Rio São Francisco
region of the Brazilian northeast (Levine 1992, 274). It is this region where
the subaltern strand of millenarianism featured in this chapter was to
grow and flourish.

As the colonial period progressed, elite leaders benefited from ecclesiastical teachings and monarchical or patrimonial rituals of rule into which
millenarianism was embedded (P. Oliveira 1985; de Groot 1996; Schultz
2001). In Brazil (as elsewhere) the attempt to construct hegemony represented an attempt to lessen the need for coercion and force directed against

subordinated populations. It did not result in "a shared ideology but a common material and meaningful framework for living through, talking about, and acting upon social orders characterized by domination" (Roseberry 1994, 361). For most of the colonial period, officials of the monarchy and the church generally collaborated to create discourses and rituals intended to construct subjects who came to view hierarchy, order, and paternalistic authority as divinely preordained and socially inviolate (Otten 1994; de Groot 1996). Their rituals of rule included royal coronations, processions of lay religious brotherhoods (de Groot 1996), sermons delivered on sugar estates (Hoornaert 1974; Freyre 1980), and humble backlanders' petitions to favored saints (Zaluar 1973). To up the ante, church fathers in concert with secular rulers added the promise of salvation for those who obeyed these precepts, and eternal damnation for those who refused (Cuoto 1873).

The Deterioration of State-Church Relations

As the colonial period drew to a close in the 1800s, there was a dramatic decline in these symbolic displays and institutional demonstrations of unity and shared mission between the state and the church. Brazilian liberals — including emperor *and mason* Pedro II (1840–89) — came to reject as retrograde and superstitious ideas about the sacred origins of the state and its divine predestination. Exemplifying this secularizing trend, Pedro II returned in 1872 from a trip to the "enlightened" capitals of Europe and abolished the practice of the royal hand kiss — a remnant of Portuguese absolutism viewed as analogous to the kissing of the pope's foot or hand (de Groot 1996).

Although the emperor's personal interest in religion waned, he could not avoid nasty entanglements with ultramontane officials of the Vatican and the Brazilian church. In 1864 Pope Pius IX had promulgated the "Syllabus of Errors" denouncing national churches, masonry, and the dominance of civil law over canonical law. Six years later, the First Vatican Council declared papal infallibility and ordered the institutional centralization of all churches under the authority of the Universal Church in the papacy. These measures had two highly significant impacts on Brazil (Bruneau 1974). First, government officials came to attribute even the mildest assertion of church independence to the pernicious influence of ultramontanism and, thus, saw it as a threat to national sovereignty. Second, a small group of Brazilian clergy encouraged by Rome proceeded to assert their autonomy from the secularizing Brazilian state (Bruneau 1974; Mainwaring 1986). Their efforts to expel masons from lay religious brotherhoods and their refusal to obey subsequent state rulings outlawing their actions led to the brief imprisonment of several influential bishops. "Never," observes religious historian C. G. de Groot, "had the chasm between the will of the imperial state—and thus the 'sacred and inviolable' emperor—and the will of God been so visible" (1996, 61).

Zealous ultramontane clergy responded to threats to their power by attempting to reform and shore up the Brazilian church, discipline parishioners, and tie them far closer to clerics than to their popular religious leaders. Thus, what had begun as a contest between elites of a secularizing state and a centralizing church transmogrified into a struggle between reformist clergy and rural folk.

Ultramontanism and "the Folk"

In the late imperial and early republican eras, foot soldiers of a centralizing Roman Catholic Church joined in a mission to discipline parishioners to regard the church as the exemplary, moral foundation for all social life. In this spirit, ultramontane clerics set out to root out "folk" Catholicism by separating "the sacred from the profane, the religious from the festive, and the spiritual from the social" (Azzi 1977, 11). Local religious practices introduced centuries earlier by colonial missionaries and endorsed by them as vehicles for divine protection were now branded as "abominable superstitious practice" (de Groot 1996, 84). In this repressive climate, visiting missionaries imposed penalties on those who dared to engage in popular religious practices, like the dance of São Gonçalo (de Groot 1996). The Pope also prohibited the public singing of popular hymns (*benditos*) in Portuguese ("em língua vulgar") rather than in the sacred language of Latin (Hoornaert 1997, 43). Equally if not more distressing were orders from the Vatican and reformist priests to abandon time-honored devotions to Mary and other saints and to replace these with a singular, "orthodox" devotion to Christ as embodied in the "Heart of Jesus" and "Christ the King." That many backlanders did not take kindly to these disciplining reforms is reflected in the fact that most of the leaders of the messianic movements discussed here railed against Christ the King, with some even likening the saint to the Antichrist, and thus saw him as a sign of the impending apocalypse (Pessar 2004).

As proponents of a Romanizing church gained sway, they insisted that religious ceremonies be physically removed from secular settings. And in this reformist spirit, bishops ordered the destruction of makeshift chapels, which one denounced as having been erected by devotees without ecclesiastical authorization or consecration. "These are not chapels," he wrote dismissively, "these are little cottages or huts." It is hardly surprising, then, that a Capuchin friar sent to monitor the millenarian community of Canudos in 1895 reported in horror that its leader's home was called and treated as a religious sanctuary (Hoornaert 1997).

Church leaders also proscribed pilgrimages and resettlement to the new pilgrimage center that grew around the messianic figure Padre Cícero. Pilgrimages to Juazeiro were officially prohibited in 1894 by the bishop of Ceará. This followed his earlier decision to terminate all religious functions in the chapel of Juazeiro where Padre Cícero had preached and a great miracle attributed to him had been performed. The "dispossessed" responded by decorating their home altars with photographs of Padre Cícero and by wearing rosaries with medals coined in Europe that bore effigies of the messianic leader. As Ralph Della Cava states, "While these practices, too, were condemned [by church authorities] as 'gross superstition,' they were in reality acts of defiance" (1970, 63).

Finally, as ultramontane priests staked claims to exclusive rights both to mediate between humanity and the supernatural and to oversee their parishioners' pursuit of salvation, they sought to eliminate popular lay competitors like thaumaturges, healers, and spiritists. Those select priests whom the popular classes dared to elevate for their profound spirituality and miraculous powers were also severely censured by their superiors. That church reformers had patchy success in these related projects is well illustrated by the careers of Padre Cícero and the popular missionary Padre José Antônio Maria de Ibiapina (1807–83) (Della Cava 1970).

Padre Ibiapina: Scapegoat of the Church and Hero to the Poor

Although ultramontane reformers labored to eradicate discourses and practices of mystical enchantment in the countryside (D. T. Monteiro 1974), they by no means represented a unified church (Della Cava 1970; Hoornaert 1997). Other clergy members, like Ibiapina, could and did sometimes work at cross-purposes. Padre Ibiapina did so inadvertently when his good works, counsel, and healing encouraged common folk to venerate him as a living saint (Hoornaert 1981). For example, after having provided advice to an ailing woman who was subsequently cured, the missionary was hailed by the folk as a "miracle worker." Much to the chagrin of church officials, backlanders erected an unauthorized chapel over the site where the woman was cured; moreover, pilgrimages became commonplace to both this and other sites where cures attributed to Ibiapina had been performed. Soon a series of articles appeared in a regional newspaper that enthusiastically publicized the missionary's "miraculous" cures. Five months later (in July 1869) the bishop of the state of Ceará ordered all of Ibiapina's missionary work in the interior to cease (Della Cava 1970).

This censure conformed to the church's now firm commitment to scientific medicine. As clerics came to see it, when science regulated humanity's dealings with the body, the church could regulate humanity's dealings with the soul. As one priest stated, "The doctor and the priest are the creatures chosen by God to alleviate the suffering of their fellow-men, and both have the same 'secret of the confessional': the doctor for things that concern the body, the priest for things that concern the soul" (de Groot 1996, 89).

Unfortunately, official medicine was not available for the majority of the Brazilian population (Costa 1985). Rural healers like Padre Ibiapina and the messianic leaders of Contestado, Juazeiro, and Santa Brígida continued to attract large and devoted followings (Vinhas de Queiroz 1966; Slater 1986; Pessar 2004). This occurred even though the state and the church had joined forces—with the state criminalizing folk healing in 1890 and the bishops of northern Brazil issuing their Collective Pastoral Letter of 1915 against spiritism (de Groot 1996). Indeed, Pedro Batista's several imprisonments in the early 1940s for folk healing only served to enhance his popular appeal. An early follower of Batista wrote in a chapbook:

> In the city of Águas Belas
> His suffering was great.
> Eleven months of prison . . .
> High-ranking authorities
> Ordered him to cease curing
> And giving counsel
> So that the people would leave him.
> He responded thusly:
> It is for this that I have come;
> No one can hinder me.

It is an order from the Eternal Father
I am destined to complete. . . .
With Jesus they did the same;
I too will persevere (Oliviera n.d., 9)

Not only was Padre Ibiapina disciplined for encouraging folk healing, but he was also censured for creating a lay order of nuns at a time when Rome had ordered the abolition of all lay orders in Brazil. Church officials charged that, without permission from Rome or any Brazilian bishop, Ibiapina had proceeded to found twenty-two charity houses and to require their *beatas*, the most devoted among their members, to wear the habit and make a profession of vows just as if their calling and religious congregation had been canonically approved. In 1872 Ibiapina was forced to relinquish control of the charity houses. Apparently, before he left northeastern Brazil he delivered an apocalyptic warning that as long as one charity house survived, God would do no harm to his people (Della Cava 1970).

Despite ecclesiastic censure, and with Ibiapina's warning likely in mind, the millenarianists of Canudos, Juazeiro, and Santa Brígida established their own charity houses and lay order of beatas (Della Cava 1970; Levine 1992; Pessar 2004). Maria das Dores, herself a beata, created both religious institutions in Santa Brígida some three-quarters of a century after Padre Ibiapina had delivered his prophetic warning. She had earlier helped to keep the folk Catholic traditions practiced in charity houses alive in her home community of Água Branca, Alagoas, and in Juazeiro. Despite repeated threats of excommunication by local priests and the frequent need to hide her activities, Maria das Dores remained dedicated to the study and perpetuation of the principal novenas, prayers, hymns, and penitential acts called *a antiga lei* (the old law). The faithful used this reverential term to distinguish the old law, which included a constellation of Luso-Brazilian practices introduced by early missionaries and still supported by populist clergy like Padre Ibiapina, from (in their view) a far less efficacious, Romanized liturgy and set of mandates.

Comments by contemporaries of Maria das Dores underscore the fact that they and she considered many of these traditional practices to be transgressive and best maintained in secrecy. According to a priest stationed in the 1990s in Água Branca, das Dores "had her own prayers. Their religion was based on the structure of the Catholic Church, but deep down they had their secrets, which the priests did not know. This caused a certain conflict over power." Luis Nicolau Parés's discussion in chapter seven of secrecy and its role among subalterns in preserving alternative and diversified identities in the face of disciplining, centralizing forces is pertinent to the efforts of Maria das Dores. Another commentator, schooled in the antiga lei by Maria das Dores, noted of Santa Brígida's early years, "We prayed locked in a house. I think [Maria das Dores] was afraid of the police or something; she had no official documents." It should be added that if das Dores and her acolytes were afraid, so too was the priest who visited the community occasionally during the 1940s and 1950s. He thought it necessary to travel there with an armed guard—a "conflict over power," indeed.

The Creation of Backlands Millenarian Movements and a Subculture of Resistance

Despite concerted attacks, many backlanders refused to abandon core elements of folk Catholicism. They called upon this system of symbols to interpret and redress the ravages the rural poor experienced during the late 1800s and early 1900s. Backlanders found themselves deep in the clutches of state and ecclesiastical centralization, escalating rural violence, natural disasters (e.g., devastating droughts and epidemics), and an economy increasingly controlled by an agrarian bourgeoisie whose members reneged on time-honored patronage pacts. In an environment that inspired apocalyptic fears, many concluded that their immediate well-being and ultimate salvation had been irrevocably compromised by elite members of a secularizing state bent on desanctifying its authority, a modernizing church committed to eradicating popular religious practices, and a new brand of patrons in the pursuit of individual wealth and bourgeois trappings. In these unsettling times, messianic leaders inverted millennial tropes and hurled them against the elite descendants of those who had earlier evoked these same symbols to legitimate conquest and promote subaltern compliance.

João Maria and José Maria (Contestado), Antônio Conselheiro, and Padre Cícero not only confirmed backlanders' fears and anger. They also celebrated folk Catholic beliefs and practices as alternative and efficacious vehicles to reestablish material security and to ensure personal salvation on the imminent day of judgment (Della Cava 1970; D. T. Monteiro 1974; Murão 1974; Diacon 1991; Otten 1994; Hoornaert 1997). The messianic leaders furnished their followers with counterhegemonic identities (e.g., *romeiros* [pilgrims] and beatos), institutions (outlawed penitential societies and religious brotherhoods), discourses (popular notions of the apocalypse and of heaven on earth), and practices (the antiga lei; illegal spiritual curing rites; the redistribution of charity among the poor; collective forms of labor; and the repudiation of modern and expensive commodities like fancy clothing and makeup). The leaders also assumed the role of ideal patrons. They did so by redistributing the charity they received and by providing poor followers with land and trades (Vinhas de Queiroz 1966; Hoornaert 1997; Slater 1986).

Consistent with the overall, multivocal nature of symbols and the specific invitation to reversal and retribution contained in apocalyptic and millennial tropes, the millenarianists of Canudos, Contestado, and Juazeiro proceeded to brand as "satanic" the laws of the newly founded Republic. High on the millenarianists' list of horrors were the Republic's enactments of compulsory civil marriage and the secularization of cemeteries. Significantly, the romeiros of Canudos and Contestado did not place their hopes for themselves and the nation in the reinstatement of the mason Pedro II. Rather, as the verses reproduced below illustrate, they anticipated the return of a more "traditional" Portuguese monarch, Dom Sebastian. He had perished centuries earlier in the Crusades and had long become the object of messianic expectations in Portugal and Brazil (Hermann 2004).

> Dom Pedro the Second set forth
> For Lisbon he was bound
> And so the monarchy came to an end
> And Brazil was left aground!
> Backed by the law
> Those evil ones abound,
> We keep the law of God,
> They keep the law of the hound! [Satan] . . .
> The Anti-Christ was born
> That he might govern Brazil,
> But here is our Counselor
> To save us from this ill!
> Dom Sebastian, our King
> His visit we're awaitin'
> And woe to that poor sinner then
> Who is under the law of Satan!   (Da Cunha 1944, 63–62)

Padre Cícero, too, fostered hopes of reversal and retribution by prophesying in the early 1900s: "The people will turn against the rich, and they will kill and overthrow the nobility and the powerful" (Otten 1994, 68).

My interpretation of Canudos, Contestado, and Juazeiro is inspired by those scholars who generally subscribe to Marxist understandings of political economy while seeking to decenter notions of power and struggle. In doing so, a claim is staked for culture as a strategic site for contestation between dominant and popular classes (e.g., Bourdieu 1977; Williams 1977; Foucault 1978). Ultramontane reforms, republicanism, and heightened capitalist development promoted an ideological crisis in Brazil. At stake were those meanings about power, order, responsibility, and destiny, which for centuries had permitted subaltern and elite alike to live through, talk about, and act upon a social order based on domination (Roseberry 1994). In these ideologically and socially chaotic times, elite actors who sought to advance new hegemonic projects demonstrated far less tolerance than they often had in the past or would show in the future for alternative, popular discourses and practices (Pessar 1982; Levine 1992; Hoornaert 1997). Consequently, the holy cities of Canudos and Contestado were obliterated by the Brazilian military while pilgrimages to Juazeiro were prohibited by church leaders who also defrocked Padre Cícero.

Symbols That Are Good to Think On

Claude Lévi-Strauss (1967) tells us that myths are good to think on. Certainly in Brazil the narrative of an apocalypse, the millennium, the messiah, and the Antichrist have provided a rich vocabulary for both the powerful and the subaltern to assess their times, to reflect on their place, and to imagine their futures. Precisely because millenarianism affords such a powerful and widely shared language, I have sought in my work to widen the circle of actors and institutions conventionally included in studies of millenarianism. In addition to the millenarianists, politicians, and clergy routinely featured, other significant players in the social production of millenarianism, such as scholars, journalists, artists, filmmakers, and curators, merit inclusion (Pessar 2004).

It is my contention that many members of the intelligentsia have been drawn to actual episodes of millenarianism for more than the simple desire to document them faithfully. These social commentators have used the context of millenarianism and its rich vocabulary to advance claims about, and to help forge, the Brazilian people and nation. A striking example is Euclides da Cunha. At the turn of the twentieth century, his *Os Sertões* told a bourgeois tale about national destiny in which reason would come to triumph over religion. It was an epic about the fashioning of a people — a triumph of eugenics in which the weaker races would either be subsumed by their lighter-skinned compatriots or totally disappear. It was also a tale about place, one in which a modern Brazil would cast off the shackles of the backward Northeast and rise up along the nation's urban coastal rim and in the commercial, central south. It did not take long for *Os Sertões* to be recognized in elite circles as a national treasure, "the Bible of Brazilian nationality" (Levine 1992, 18).

Due to the significance millenarianism has long enjoyed within the national imaginary, scholars have been able to use it as a springboard into larger national debates. For example, professor of legal and forensic medicine Raimundo Nina Rodrigues (1897) appropriated the case of Antônio Conselheiro and Canudos to advance several claims about the nation and its citizenry. Pointing to the "fanatics" of Canudos, he decried the degenerative effects of miscegenation for the nation and insisted that the backlanders' underdeveloped minds rendered them incapable of understanding republicanism — a more abstract form of governance than the previous monarchy (Levine 1992; Villa 1997). Studies of millenarianism have also contributed to a larger national dialogue over the ability of the tropics to support a modern people and nation, and the role of certain regions and their populations in building, claiming, and governing such a nation. Adopting a "two Brazils" model, many scholars generally viewed the backlands and its millenarian enthusiasts as obstacles to national development and centralization (Queiroz 1965; Montenegro 1973). Others who similarly embraced the two-Brazils construct disagreed and concluded that rural folk embodied a progressive, communitarian spirit; and as such, backlanders like Conselheiro and his followers were vanguards of a Brazilian socialist utopia (Fáco 1963; Moniz 1978). Finally, for Brazilians who confronted years of censorship and authoritarian rule and ultimately emerged from their grip, millenarian movements have provided a context to probe the contours and the promise of popular political struggle for a more democratic nation (Arruda 1993; Moura 2000). As one author expresses it, "The messiah of Brazil is the Brazilian people" (Chacon 1990, 16).

Millenarianism, Hegemony, and Resistance

An engagement with Brazilian millenarianism over the centuries cautions against any sweeping and totalizing narrative of millenarianism as either the property of the oppressed or as "reaction," "protest," "accommodation," and so forth. Surely for the elite Portuguese colonizers and missionaries there was no trace of resistance and protest in the millenarian symbols so central to their statecraft. In their writings on the hegemonic process, Philip Corrigan, Harvie Ramsay, and Derek Sayer (1980, 17–19) assert that rituals of rule, along with their constituent "categories of moral absolutism," make possible a way of discussing political priorities, which render unsayable much of what is lived as political problems. It is true that for Brazil's subaltern peoples millenarian discourse became what Ranajit Guha (1983) calls a "borrowed language," one that induces the subordinated to "speak in the language of [their] enemy" (75). It is equally the case, however, that millenarianism, and Catholicism more generally, harbored potentially subversive elements. These included the former's invitation to symbolic inversion and the latter's notions of resentment and retribution. I would, therefore, amend the claims of Corrigan, Ramsay, and Sayer and propose that elite rituals and other such hegemonic ventures intended to impose domination and forge popular consent frequently displace the "publicly unsayable" into forms of popular culture, including Scott's hidden transcripts. These popular forms await historical conjunctures, like the end of the nineteenth century in Brazil, when the unsayable can, and must, be openly voiced and put into practice.

My research reveals that once a subculture of millenarian resistance is consolidated (as it was in late 1800s Brazil), new movements are no longer dependent on the same degree of uncertainty, resentment, and upheaval that occasioned their predecessors. Moreover, through a process I call intertextuality, older movements can inspire and guide later ones. The agents for this recreation are sometimes devotees who feel socially subordinated or spiritually dissatisfied with processes of routinization within their millenarian communities (Pessar 1991, 2004). These observations help to account for the fact that rural millenarian movements like the one created by Pedro Batista occurred well into the 1900s, at a time when at least one scholar had consigned such popular mobilizations to the dustbin of history (Pang 1981).

The Juazeiro and Santa Brígida movements nicely illustrate the process of intertextuality. Prior to his death, Padre Cícero is held to have prophesized his rapid return. This promise is commemorated in the following bendito:

> In the year of '34
> He told us
> My children, I am going on a journey
> My Father in the sky has told me.
>
> I am going, but I will return.
> Follow my commandments
> With faith recite your rosaries
> So you will be able to recognize me.

When Pedro Batista appeared in the Northeast a few years later, devotees of Padre Cícero carefully evaluated Batista's words, performances, and actions against those of their previous leader. For his part, Batista adopted most of the *mandamentos* (commandments) his predecessor had issued. When Batista's romeiros later settled in Santa Brígida, Juazeiro served as a symbolic, architectural, and organizational model. Indeed, the holy city was commonly referred to as "the new Juazeiro." Several decades later, in 1971, five years after Batista's death, the poorest strata of his romeiros attempted to authenticate and install a new messiah, whom they referred to as *O Velho* (the old one). According to these millenarian enthusiasts, "Padre Cícero is the Father, Pedro Batista is the Son, and the Velho is the Holy Ghost." Following that tenet of resistance studies that calls for the placement of acts of resistance within dynamic configurations of power, it should be noted that the Velho's career as a messiah proved unsuccessful. One of his many disadvantages was the presence of a military dictatorship whose guardians were less than receptive to popular subaltern leaders. Local military officials threatened to imprison O Velho as an impostor, because of his and his followers' claims that he was Pedro Batista. Moreover, at the time of the dictatorship when votes were basically insignificant, the Velho and his supporters could not play the same electoral card that Batista had employed so successfully in the mid-1940s.

As I have argued in detail elsewhere (Pessar 2004), we are well served in complicating conventional understandings of millenarianism by blurring the temporal and spatial divides erected by social scientists and historians around individual movements. Employing the concept of intertexuality,

I recommend a charting of the travels of millenarian discourses, social memories, and practices among movements, as well as a consideration of the ways elite perceptions and management of older movements influence the fates of newer ones. Intertexuality is an analytical concept I would recommend not only for the study of popular social movements, but also for collective acts of resistance more broadly.

The Subculture of Backlands Millenarianism in Twenty-First-Century Brazil

Having reviewed the long and winding history of Brazilian millenarianism, I turn now to the present and pose several questions. How are yesterday's millenarian mobilizations remembered today? Is resistance central to these social memories and, if so, resistance against which registers of power? And finally, are those alternative subjectivities, cultural forms, and social spaces, which long fostered challenges to elite domination, still viable in light of moves by the church and state to appropriate and domesticate the histories of millenarian struggles and the identities and cultural products of contemporary millenarian subjects?

Although the leaders and followers of the four backlands movements considered here found little or no grounds upon which to negotiate with elite church officials, "negotiation" is the very word that several contemporary priests use to characterize their appreciation for, and relations with, millenarian enthusiasts and practitioners of folk Catholicism (Steil 1996; Barreto 1998). These clergy characterize negotiation as a process in which rural folk infuse religious sites with their own popular beliefs and unorthodox practices, and in which church leaders attempt to incorporate some of these into institutional orthodoxy and reject others as unacceptable superstition.[1] According to Santa Brígida's Padre de Lima: "One has to adapt to the history and conditions of the place where one lives. It's no use hitting your head against a brick wall. You have to work to take down the walls. You have to bring the people, especially the older people with you. We must also adapt to their ways. They are not the only ones who should adapt to us." One is left to ask whether the walls Padre de Lima speaks of dismantling consist of the identities, orientations, and practices, like those associated with backlands millenarianism, that have aided rural subjects to sustain oppositional identities, motivations, agencies, and communities. It often seems that way within today's Santa Brígida and Juazeiro. There church pews fill with children and their parents singing uplifting hymns about love and community. Cast aside are their grandparents' *benditos* about sin, salvation, divine retribution, and the apocalypse.

The current welcoming stance of church authorities toward select features of folk Catholicism needs to be placed in the context of ever-increasing numbers of Brazilians turning to Evangelical Protestantism. Perceiving their virtually undisputed position as spiritual defenders of the nation's morality and faith challenged (Birman and Pereira Leite 2000), Catholic Church officials seek ways to retain their members and to infuse their rituals and theology with excitement and passion. In this new historical conjuncture, certain clerics have come to reclaim popular, charismatic leaders like Antônio Conselheiro, Padre Cícero, and Pedro Batista. Moreover, in the wake of liberation theology, Conselheiro has been recast by some as a humble defender of economic and social justice. Largely forgotten in this revisionism is Conselheiro as religious rebel: a popular *beato* whom a Bahian archbishop had advised state authorities in 1880 to incarcerate in the state mental hospital as a religious fanatic (Levine 1992).

For their part, amidst fears of mass culture and globalization, representatives of the state and media look to identify and to appropriate the "primordial" and "authentic" within Brazilian society and culture. In this environment, contemporary millenarian subjects (in Juazeiro and Santa Brígida) and past millenarian struggles (in Canudos and Contestado) have been recently reconstituted as objects of "national patrimony," "cultural rescue," and tourism. In this elite project, the alterity of millenarian subjects and sites has been simplified and appropriated. Yesterday's subaltern backlanders have become us, the nation.

In government-funded media productions and tourist initiatives, there is either an erasure or defanging of the central role in subaltern consciousness and resistance that folk Catholicism assumed, and continues to play, in backlands millenarian communities. In the case of Santa Brígida, for example, filmmakers uncritically attach the term "folklore" to cultural products and practices that older *romeiros* revere as belonging to the *antiga lei*. Left unstated are the facts that many of these forms had been proscribed by the church and were passed on surreptitiously by defiant *beatas* like Maria das Dores. Filmmakers also gloss over the fact that many of the performers of folklore are far less (if at all) motivated by concerns for preserving authentic Brazilian culture than by expressing religious faith and devotion. One is reminded here of Candido da Costa e Silva's criticism that in dominant scholarship on folklore the "folk" have yet to be given an adequate opportunity to express their own beliefs and motivations (Costa e Silva 1982).

For their part, most of the descendents of original millenarianists in the communities of Contestado, Canudos, Juazeiro, and Santa Brígida have been willing to market their only scarce and suddenly coveted resources: local cultures, religious performances, and millennial histories. Moreover, local politicians in these four millenarian communities have eyed each other for tips on how to gain state and federal funding and how best to attract the media and tourist dollars. In Santa Brígida, only a handful of elderly individuals have adamantly refused to cooperate in projects of cultural rescue and tourism. Foremost among these are members of the Men's Penitent Society, who have made it clear that their prayers are intended solely for a divine audience.[2]

These latest developments in backlands millenarianism occasion a pressing question: do elite appropriations of past millenarian struggles and popular cultures alongside backlanders' overall compliance signify a coming full circle? Has that brand of subaltern millenarianism long practiced by Brazilian backlanders been leached of its potential as a discourse and practice of alterity and resistance? Does it once again conform to the interests of the dominant classes—albeit, now repackaged in a more commodified form?

Surely none of the messianic figures featured in this study could have imagined that their lives and popular mobilizations would become cultural fodder for urban Brazilians nostalgic for an authentic rural past; neither could they have foreseen that their struggles and religious convictions and practices would be commemorated in state-supported folkloric events, museums, and theme parks.[3] (Yes, there is a Padre Cícero theme park!) Similarly, it would have been well beyond the ken of those backlanders persecuted by church and state officials for their devotion to Padre Cícero to envision that during the presidential election in 1998 Fernando Henríque Cardoso and Luíz Inácio da Silva (Lula) would launch their respective political campaigns in northeast Brazil beneath a statue of Padre Cícero in Juazeiro. And those who fell at Contestado would have scarcely imagined that a century later an official Mass entitled "Popular Celebration for the Martyrs of Canudos" would be celebrated annually on the grounds of the bloody battle (Pinho 1997, 181).[4] Having noted these trends, it is also the case that traces of backlands millenarian resistance do remain alive and inspirational within certain subaltern circles. For example, contemporary agrarian rebels of the Movimento Sem Terra evoke the struggles of the fallen at Canudos and Contestado (Moura 2000).

There is, nonetheless, real reason to question whether the brand of folk Catholicism treated in this study will remain a source and inspiration for struggles among Brazil's subaltern youth. Youthful Brazilians in their roles as students, viewers of television and film, and parishioners have been exposed to revisionist narratives of late nineteenth- and early twentieth-century millenarian leaders in which folk religion has been greatly downplayed. It is perhaps inevitable, then, that in the testimonies, songs, poems, and commemorative dramas composed by young people in towns like Canudos and Santa Brígida the spiritual and supernatural qualities of past millenarian leaders are minimized or wholly absent. Instead we find heroes praised for their commitments to social justice and for their organizational talents. A popular young poet resident in Canudos writes about Conselheiro:

> What longing for Antônio . . .
> Antônio persecuted
> Antônio defender of the oppressed people.
> What longing for Antônio
> Antônio of truth
> Antônio of equality (Pinho 1997, 193)

For her part, a fifteen-year-old romeira in Santa Brígida recently lamented never having met Pedro Batista and added: "I know he was a very great man who fought for the poor people and gave them land. My teacher said that we should be proud to live in Santa Brígida and should always remember that Pedro Batista was a poor backlander who was not afraid to defend his people. . . . The older people talk about his miracles, but I don't know about that stuff."

Some parting thoughts on the future of backlands millenarianism as a subculture of resistance are necessary.[5] In the 1800s and early 1900s, this constellation of identities, meanings, and practices afforded a culturally appropriate toolkit for problem-solving thought and agency. Its symbols and discursive structure invited rural subjects to negate their problematic conditions and search within relevant cultural categories for logical and moral alternatives. In the face of elite attacks on folk Catholicism and its constituent millenarian elements, many backlanders defiantly refused to lose what they had for the unlikely promise of becoming benefactors of a purportedly improved repertoire of cultural, spiritual, and material resources. By the time Pedro Batista began to attract his followers in the late 1930s, there was a relatively reduced geography in northeastern Brazil— what I liken to a folk Catholic Bible belt—from which to attract followers. This geography consisted of towns and villages underserved by the clergy, in which institutions like the Men's Penitential Society and charity houses were maintained clandestinely and pilgrimages were taken to Juazeiro despite strong ecclesiastical opposition.

Over the course of the twentieth century, newer generations of backlanders have been exposed to, and come to imagine themselves more fully as subjects within, a centralized state and nation, a market economy, and a modern Catholic Church. The hegemonic crises of nineteenth- and early twentieth-century Brazil are long past. Indeed, the successes of elite projects have fostered a counterdialectic among millenarian enthusiasts. It has found a figure like Maria das Dores choosing to outlaw certain folk Catholic practices and institutions in Santa Brígida that are considered too *fina* (powerfully numinous) to be perpetuated by younger generations (Pessar 2004). I see similar signs of resignation and forfeiture in the decision reached in 1988 by the few surviving beatas of Padre Cícero. These elderly women elected to deliver into the hands of academics, who were assembled in Juazeiro for a symposium, the holy and previously sequestered altar clothes of their leader (Paz 1998). The bloodstained clothes were held by devoted romeiros as indisputable evidence that a miracle had occurred in Juazeiro when the host being administered to a young beata by the priest turned into the blood of Christ. Despite initial orders to surrender the clothes to the bishop of Ceará and threats of excommunication should they refuse, the beatas remained defiant and secretive. With no new recruits to safeguard their treasure and, one suspects, still-lingering suspicions about the church, the elderly beatas presented the long-sequestered clothes to apparently more trusted guardians—academics attending a symposium.

To reiterate, I trust that select elements of backlands millenarianism will continue to inspire and "authenticate" resistance by subaltern Brazilians. The invitation to invert the terms of domination is unlikely to lose its attraction. Yet, as the case of the landless movement illustrates, class identity (or those tied to race and ethnicity) and appeals to collective human, not divine, agency will most likely characterize those who recall past millenarian struggles. There is little reason to believe in the mass appeal for contemporary resisters of identities and subjectivities like romeiros, beatos, and santos. The same holds for such practices as the construction of holy cities and the performance of penitential rituals in anticipation of divine intercession to correct injustices and invert axes of power.

Notes

1 See Carlos Alberto Steil (1996) for a discussion of the negotiations between pilgrims and the priests assigned to the Bahian pilgrimage site of Bom Jesus da Lapa.

2 See Campos (2004) for an ethnographic study of Os Aves de Jesus, a penitential group of mendicants and devotees of Padre Cícero who live in Juazeiro and await the day of judgement.

3 See Boaventura (1997) for a study of the history and goals of the Canudos state park.

4 This instance illustrates the analytical "fuzziness" within certain acts that demonstrate elite appropriation of the popular but are, nonetheless, advanced by a more politically progressive segment within an elite institution.

5 For studies of O Vale do Amanhecer, a large millenarian movement active today in the capital city of Brasília that draws upon a very different symbolic repertoire, see Holston (1999).

CHAPTER SEVEN

Where Does Resistance Hide in Contemporary Candomblé?

LUIS NICOLAU PARÉS

Candomblé is the name given to Afro-Brazilian religions whose development is particularly associated with the state of Bahia. Originating in values and ritual practices brought to Brazil by African slaves, Candomblé emerged as a religious institution during the nineteenth century.[1] Historically discriminated against, often persecuted, it nonetheless persisted with such tenacious vitality that in the 1930s it began to be valorized by the intelligentsia as a cultural asset in the Brazilian nationalist project. Perceived as a potent source of symbolic capital, Candomblé has, since the 1970s, increasingly attracted the interest of the state, black activists, tourists, and, more recently, NGOs. While Candomblé's past seems to fit Foucault's contention that "where there is power there is also resistance" (1978, 95–96), its present seems to confirm Lila Abu-Lughod's reverse dictum: "Where there is resistance, there is power" (1990, 42).

Candomblé—a religion with a history of secrecy and concealment—is consequently now overexposed in the public sphere and its signs are appropriated, disputed, and resignified by a plurality of actors with divergent political agendas. In this "field of forces," social actors from black movements who have secured key positions within the state apparatus have lobbied successfully for public policies for the preservation and promotion of Candomblé. This chapter therefore asks how the concept of resistance applies to a religious institution whose most emblematic temples seem to have fallen under the embrace of the state's official protection.

Patricia Pessar and Ilka Boaventura Leite (chapter six and chapter twelve) raise a similar question: How can movements historically associated with resistance retain their oppositional thrust when millenarian communities are marketed as centers of religious and historical tourism and *quilombos* acquire a juridical status that transforms them into legal right and state policy. All these cases invite us to examine the shifting meanings of the concept of resistance in Brazil, where the state still aspires to play an important role in the mediation, promotion, and tutelage of social movements. Indeed, the state should not be reduced to a monolithic, exclusive representation of the dominant, nor its recognition of Candomblé to a simple top-down movement. The present-day situation is the result of a complex system of alliances and a long history of negotiation.

The Concept of Resistance in Afro-Brazilian Religious Studies

From the late 1970s onward, under the influence of authors such as Eugene Genovese and E. P. Thompson, Brazilian studies of the history of slavery have been responsible for spreading the concept of resistance into Afro-Brazilian religious studies. Candomblé, identified since the early twentieth-century studies of Nina Rodrigues as the classic example of the persistence of African traditions in the New World, began to be described as an emblem of black resistance to white domination, demonstrating the ability of subaltern groups to articulate counterhegemonic discourses or alternative spaces of identity within social structures of inequality. Conceptual polarities such as assimilation and resistance, and negotiation and conflict, became the new theoretical paradigm framing interaction between masters and slaves or, more generally, between whites and blacks, the latter now being portrayed as historical subjects with political agency. Resistance was associated both with revolts and with a wide range of nonviolent forms of behavior encoded in daily social relationships.

In a pioneering work originally published in 1960, Roger Bastide had, however, already envisaged Candomblé, together with Afro-Catholicism, as a "class subculture" that demanded study from a sociological perspective that considered "relations between blacks and whites in a dualist social structure, relations of exploitation and domination on the one hand, *and of resistance and struggle on the other*," as well as from a cultural perspective that examined "the relations between this class subculture and white civilization" (Bastide 1986, 162–63, emphasis added). Hence, for Bastide (1986, 754), and this is a critical idea for my subsequent reflections, religious resistance was closely tied to racial and economic (class) struggles.

Crystallizing around the resistance-assimilation paradigm, two antagonistic theoretical ways of conceiving Afro-Brazilian religion emerged. One continued to represent Candomblé as a traditional set of practices originating in a primordial African past, transplanted into the New World and tenaciously preserved through the generations. The other, critiquing this as essentialist traditionalism with an obsession for "Africanisms," portrayed Candomblé as a modern institution emerging from the Brazilian creative hybrid reconfiguration of a variety of "cultural fragments"—of African, but also of European and American, origin.

Debate between scholars who stress African continuities in the New World and those who highlight discontinuities has been recurrent throughout Afro-American studies. Africa-centered scholars tend to emphasize the idea of "cultural resistance" and sympathize with black cultural nationalism, while America-centered or "creolist" scholars highlight processes of "cultural synthesis" and have sometimes been accused of Eurocentrism because of an alleged assimilationist bias. Although simplistic, this dichotomy demonstrates that observers' political and ideological sensibilities often determine their intellectual positioning in debates (Trouillot 1988; Price 2003, 7–8). One theme that exemplifies these theoretical and ideological antagonisms is Afro-Catholic "syncretism," the cultural process by which Catholic saints were linked to African deities. Creolists tend to present Afro-Catholic syncretism as evidence of the creative, harmonious hybridism of Afro-American cultures. "Afrocentrics" tend to sustain the "camouflage" theory: the use of Catholic saints' iconography was only a surface strategy to hide the worship of African gods from the master's repressive control. Thus, what seemed to be accommodation was in fact veiled resistance, and, as Bastide (1986) argued, apparent acculturation could hide counteracculturation movements. The creolist position seems to support Gramsci's (1971) ideas about how hegemonic ideology is internalized by subaltern groups, promoting consent to rule. The Afrocentric camouflage theory seems to support Scott's (1990) ideas about "hidden transcripts"— occult subversive discourses and gestures of defiance running in parallel to apparent conformity to public transcripts and the official ideology.

The camouflage theory has lately been questioned in the light of recorded historical situations in which Afro-descendants continued to worship Catholic saints together with African gods despite the absence of any coercive force. In Andrew Apter's view, the Catholicism of Candomblé "was the religion of the masters, revised, transformed, and appropriated by slaves to harness its power within their universes of discourse" (2004, 178). The ritual mimesis of dominant Catholicism would be an embodied way of critically apprehending and controlling the master's spiritual universe. Yet one might suggest that Afro-Catholicism usually involved the juxtaposition of complementary efficacious resources, excluding neither strategic camouflage nor sincere devotion as possibilities. This reveals the analytical importance of recognizing the heterogeneity of positions within subaltern groups and that attitudes of assimilation and resistance are not necessarily mutually exclusive, but can be ambiguously interwoven in paradoxical symbiosis. By creating spaces of negotiation, processes of creolization would also allow for challenges to the dominant order.

While the concept of resistance has been widely applied to Candomblé by intellectuals, politicians, and black activists, its use among insiders is rare. Those who do use it tend to be devotees who have appropriated the external discourse or former intellectuals who have been initiated. Furthermore, the meaning of the word resistance, as it is employed in the everyday speech of Candomblé practitioners, generally aligns with the Afrocentric "continuity" position in the academic debate.

The term may imply, metaphorically, the notion of reaction to a force, but it does not overtly connote the idea of protest or rebellious dissidence. Mãe Stella, high priestess of one of the most influential *terreiros* (temples) in Salvador, once declared: "Candomblé's resistance, from the 1930s until the end of the 1970s, was the result of the high-priestesses who went to Rio de Janeiro to talk to president Getúlio Vargas demanding freedom for the cult. This was obtained, but discrimination persisted" (Joaquim 2001, 28–29). Although historical evidence for this presidential interview is lacking, resistance is here portrayed as negotiation and organized political action against discrimination, not as oppositional conflict.[2] When an initiated black activist declared in 2007 that "black women in Candomblé have been resisting for centuries and we are still here to resist whether they like it or not," this conveyed a sense of durability, survival, and defiant resilience. Speaking of a Candomblé ceremony celebrated on May 13 (the anniversary of abolition), another high priestess declared: "This date is marked by our resistance and our power in preserving our culture."[3] The argument by José Maurício Arruti (2004) for quilombo communities, discussed by Leite in chapter twelve, is equally valid for Candomblé terreiros: they both were "resistant because one way or the other they lasted until today."

Referring to temporal continuity from the past to the present, this notion of resistance evokes the idea of not losing what one has, rather than winning what one does not have, the conservation of something rather than its transformation. Conservation relies on intergenerational cultural transfers in which individuals reproduce the values and practices of their predecessors. Anchored in the past, rather than projected to the future, this ideology of resistance is conservative, rather than progressive or revolutionary. One could even postulate it is reinforced by the logic of African religious systems, since they are often oriented towards the past, be it in the form of ancestral cults or through ritual practices that reiterate cyclical return to origins. African cosmologies contrast with Christianity's teleological view of history and orientation toward the future, salvation, and life after death (Peel 2000, 171–72). To a certain extent, Candomblé's cosmology feeds a notion of resistance closely interwoven with the semantics of ancestrality and tradition, evoking primordial origins in Africa.

The State's "Culturization" of Religion

Because resistance defines itself in relation to domination, we must understand the different configurations of power that have historically conditioned the practices of Candomblé and their consequences. To a great extent, the idea of Afro-Brazilian religion as a form of cultural resistance stems from its association with slavery. In chapter five, Robert Slenes shows, for example, how "cults of affliction" of western Central African origin underpinned actions against slavery in southern Brazil. The power asymmetries imposed by a racialized slave society and the hegemonic position of Iberian Catholicism placed African religious practices in a structurally marginal space that could be used for the organization of rebellious protest. This was also the case in Bahia, particularly in the first half of the nineteenth century, where some slave revolts were initiated in candomblés (Reis 2003).

Yet Candomblé cannot be reduced merely to a space of subversive dissidence; it should also be understood as a space of negotiation. John Monteiro (chapter one) notes how colonial indigenous people "forged their own space" by adopting European symbols and discourses, and we have already seen how Afro-Catholic syncretism suggests similar processes among the black population. Candomblé practitioners have always demonstrated pragmatism, tactically adapting to varying elite attitudes that ranged from repression to selective tolerance. Hence both concealment and interaction with the wider social order have been inescapable factors in Candomblé's historical formation.[4]

Despite these recurrent simultaneous dynamics of seclusion and negotiation, the long history of Candomblé has been portrayed as a transition from a past of black ethnic exclusivity and reclusive invisibility to a present of social inclusiveness and public visibility. The beginning of this critical shift coincided with a new configuration of power relations: the transition from the Old Republic to the Estado Novo in the 1930s, whose modernist project to forge a new Brazilian national identity based itself on the ideology of *mestiçagem*, or harmonious cultural and racial mixture. Different forms of black popular culture—samba, carnival, and last but not least, Candomblé—began to be acclaimed as national cultural heritage. Scholarly recognition of Candomblé was initiated with the celebration, in January 1937, of the second Afro-Brazilian Congress in Salvador. Yet this carefully structured visibility of Candomblé—a process that Paul Johnson (2002, 79) succinctly describes as a transition "from tumor to trophy"— was very selective, affecting only temples belonging to the Nagô "nation." Since the late nineteenth century, these *orisha*-worshipping congregations had established their reputation as guardians of an "authentic" African tradition of Yoruba origin, as opposed to the increasing numbers of "mixed" and "syncretized" houses that worshipped mostly Brazilian deities known as *caboclos* (Parés 2005).

Beatriz Góis Dantas (1987, 1988) argued that the intellectual construction of the Nagô tradition "as a true religion, in contrast with Bantu magic/sorcery" disguised a subtle form of domination. On the one hand, the promotion of Nagô ritual "purity" concealed an attempt to "cleanse" Afro-Brazilian religion of its most "dangerous" aspects, such as "black magic" and homosexual priesthood, thereby ostracizing significant numbers of practitioners. On the other hand, the stress on African purity "exoticized" the Nagô temples, reducing them to "cultural ghettoes" and depriving their social actors of real inclusion in Brazilian national civil society. Dantas was subsequently criticized (Silveira 1988; Ferretti 1995; Serra 1995) for overemphasizing the role played by intellectuals and for undervaluing the agency of practitioners in their competition for prestige and ritual legitimacy. Yet although the inner dynamic of Candomblé cannot be reduced to the influence of external factors, the curiosity of intellectuals and the circulation of their texts and images in the public sphere created a new kind of social visibility for Afro-Brazilian religion that affected old practices of concealment and discretion, forcing new strategies of negotiation. However, only a minority of terreiros—the very ones whose prestige had already been established (along with a few others led by charismatic priests)—benefited from the new relationships with the public powers. The process came to consolidate the centrality of what I shall call the elite terreiros, usually referred to as "traditional" by Candomblé people.

Throughout the 1940s, 1950s, and 1960s, artists and intellectuals, whether locals such as Jorge Amado, Dorival Cayimi, and Vivaldo da Costa Lima, or foreigners such as Pierre Verger, Roger Bastide, and the painter Carybé, continued to disseminate images of Candomblé. At the same time, famous high priestesses, such as Mãe Senhora from the Axé Opô Afonjá or Mãe Menininha from the Gantois, cultivated liaisons with influential celebrities, receiving and initiating famous artists, writers, and pop stars, as well as politicians. Yet although politicians, looking for votes or seeking clients, had customarily flirted with Candomblé, the 1970s ushered in a new phase in the growth of "public" Candomblé and the marketing of religion as culture (Sansi 2007).[5] In March 1975, Antonio Carlos Magalhães opened the doors of the Bahian governor's palace to dozens of Candomblé women who came to thank him for his support for Afro-Brazilian religion (Santos 2005, 145). In January 1976, his successor, Roberto Santos, signed a decree ending the requirement that Candomblé practitioners obtain police permission to celebrate their religious activities.[6] These symbolic gestures marked a new relationship between the state and Candomblé.

The political establishment now put black culture to work in shaping an image of Bahia that would appeal to the national and international tourism market. Recycling the representations of black culture projected since the 1940s by the above-mentioned artists, institutions like Bahiatursa (the official tourism agency, founded in 1972) began to promote Salvador as a mystical city and Candomblé as a tourist attraction and an exotic spectacle.

Since then, Candomblé has become a trademark of Bahia, a diacritical mark of Bahia's regional identity (*baianidade*) (Pinto 2001; V. Silva 2001; Johnson 2002; Santos 2005; Van de Port 2005). Candomblé was publicized as a true religion, not a sect, and Bahiatursa contributed to this transition through an ambivalent discourse. Although its pamphlets and magazines used stylized images of Candomblé to stimulate foreign appetites for the exotic, they also advised tourists on proper behavior during religious ceremonies, allegedly defending the terreiros against exploitation by unscrupulous tourism agencies. Public authorities assumed the roles of promoters and regulators of the social legitimacy and authenticity of Candomblé, evoking the familiar paternalism of politicians in the past (Santos 2005, 155).

We should not forget that this was the era of dictatorship and the government of Antonio Carlos Magalhães (ACM), the "strongman" of Bahia. It is not surprising that the increasing visibility of Candomblé in the 1970s coincided with a period of conservative political power, just as happened in the 1930s during the Estado Novo. The alliances between some sectors of the elite and Candomblé corresponded to a populist policy intended to gratify the dispossessed with symbolic gestures, but they also disguised the elite's secret dependency on (and fear of) black spiritual power. Even if Afro-Brazilian religion and politics operate according to different logics, what is produced in the religious field (symbolic capital) can be converted into what is currency in the political field (political capital) (Bourdieu 1984; Selka 2008, 101, 104). Indeed, from the practitioners' point of view the personal accumulation of *axé* (life force, vital energy), on which Candomblé is based, can easily be equated with or transformed into social or political power.

The state's tutelage of Candomblé was only an aspect of a wider process of the commodification of black culture, in which ethnic elements were used to promote the regional identity of baianidade and tourism. This "production of identities" involved institutional redefinitions, the reconfiguration of the intellectual panorama, and the creation of new models of cultural policymaking (Agier 1992). State initiatives included the foundation of the Afro-Brazilian Museum in 1974 (Santos 2005, 113), sponsorship of Afro-Brazilian cultural groups (carnival *blocos* [groups], *capoeira*, *baianas do acarajé* [street sellers of fried bean cakes], etc.), and the use of public space for the display of imagery representing the orishas (Sansi 2007). These external dynamics had profound effects within the religious community. The old inner conflict between the Africanized houses and the syncretized ones was reproduced under new capitalistic terms, opposing the altruistic religious vocation of the former against the material and commercial interest of the latter. Tourists emerged as new actors, who, as exponents of capitalistic consumerism, were promoting the greed of religious entrepreneurs accused of charlatanism, professionalism, and "umbandization."[7]

The perception of tourism as a potential source of income was thus not an exclusive prerogative of the state. The condemnation by Candomblé practitioners of the dangers of tourism started in the early 1970s and persists today. In 1974, for instance, during the foundation of the Confederação Baiana de Cultos Afro-Brasileiros (Bahian Federation of Afro-Brazilian Cults), its president Antonio Monteiro stated that "Candomblé could not be transposed into carnival feasts, transformed into folklore or industrialized in the name of progress" (Santos 2005, 131). In 1983, the five high priestesses of the best-known terreiros in Salvador signed a public document denouncing the use of Candomblé for "tourist propaganda" and "folkloric exploitation" (Consorte 1999, 71).

The Candomblé community has not traditionally aligned itself with any particular political project: the temples have always pragmatically used the resources and possibilities available at each particular moment. The state's attempt to coopt Candomblé was successful insofar as some temples accepted the official embrace, often in expectation of material benefits, but resistive forces, as demonstrated by the reaction against tourism, persisted. The old dilemma between visibility and invisibility reemerged. At a time of increasing external interference and public exposure, orthodox voices loudly warned against risks of profanation and transgression of secrecy. This reaction may also be interpreted as an attempt by the traditional houses to maintain their centrality in the face of the advances of "modernity."

Candomblé, the Black Movements and Re-Africanization

Influenced by the U.S. civil rights movement, black nationalism, African independence movements, and reggae, a significant growth of black political organizing occurred in the early 1970s. Yet, at that time, the black leadership did not readily identify Candomblé as a space of resistance, since it was negatively perceived as an expression of syncretism, assimilation, and alienation. Resistance was a political concept applied to a racialized class struggle. As Jonatas da Silva put it, "There was not yet a clear comprehension of the role of culture in politics" (Santos 2005, 164–65).

The end of dictatorship and the modest emergence of a black middle class with access to higher education marked, in the early 1980s, the crystallization of the black movement as a political force and an influential minority. Its leadership then began to recognize Candomblé's potential in furnishing cultural symbols for political action. "Afro-Brazilian civilization," until then the object of anthropological study, became a matter of political discussion, with black intellectuals claiming the right to be subjects and agents of their own self-representations. The search for racially defined ethnicity found in Candomblé an emblem of African identity, a rich source of cultural referents and dignified icons to guarantee the necessary unity for achieving the political goals of black empowerment and social equality.

In sync with U.S. Pan-Africanist ideology, Brazilian black activists fought against white hegemony and racial discrimination, while the more radical promoted ideas of political and cultural separatism. In this ideological context, an antisyncretism movement emerged in both the U.S. Santeria traditions and in Brazilian Candomblé (Palmié 1995), arguing the need to separate African deities and Catholic saints, whose blending was perceived as the legacy of white acculturation and the period of slavery.

In Brazil these ideas were voiced during the second Conference of the Tradition of Orisha Culture, held in 1983 in Salvador, which brought together members of the priesthood from both Africa and the diaspora. As suggested by the conference's title, Candomblé depicted itself not just as religion, but also as the ultimate expression of Afro-Brazilian culture and tradition (Sansi 2007). It was during this event that Bahia's most important high priestesses not only signed the above-mentioned denunciation of tourism, but also demanded the removal of Catholic imagery from terreiros, thus becoming the most visible advocates of what came to be known as the "re-Africanization" movement (see V. Silva 1995, 269; Consorte 1999).

This "act of decolonization" against Catholicism is an indication of the relative autonomy of Afro-Brazilian discourse and practice, calling into question Dantas's hypothesis that the construction of Nagô purity was a machination of the white elites. Instead, the re-Africanization process could be interpreted as a counteracculturation movement (similar to messianic or fundamentalist movements praising a return to the origins) occurring when cultural transformation is advanced enough to impede any pure and simple recreation of the original culture. Counteracculturation,

far from being the return to the origins that it would like to be, is just another type of cultural change. It does not regenerate the old but creates the
new. As Bastide (1996, 78) suggested, the discourse of continuity between
African and Afro-Brazilian religious traditions results from an ideology of
compensation that places value on roots in the past to counterbalance real
discontinuity. Although support for the antisyncretism movement was not
unanimous within Candomblé, signaling Candomblé's lack of internal cohesion, it expressed the political mobilization of a significant part of its
leadership in defense of a black identity and a project of social justice that
challenged the current configuration of power relations.

What is worth retaining for our argument is the existence of two independent groups, namely the state (or some elite politicians in alliance with
intellectuals) and the black movements (or antiracist activists), both appropriating Candomblé's signs to promote different collective identities,
one regional (baianidade), the other ethnic (négritude). Both the regional-
ist and the radical discourses emerge from the same source, the recognition of Brazil's African roots, but they are voiced from opposite ideological positions. At an early stage, both identities may have overlapped when
black cultural groups such as Ilê Aiyê or Olodum, coopted by state funding,
depicted themselves as representatives of baianidade, too (Pinho 2004,
230). As suggested by Patricia Pessar, in relation to other Brazilian subaltern cultural producers, these groups had to face "the dilemma of appreciating inclusion and the ability to profit monetarily from elite embrace,
yet struggle to hold onto those forms of alternative subjectivities, cultural
forms, and social spaces that foster challenges to elite domination" (2004,
223). Nevertheless, the embrace of Candomblé by both government officials and black activists (together with the scant material benefits it may
have brought) affected a very limited number of religious congregations,
namely the elite terreiros.

The "Politicization" of Culture in the 1990s

If the growing exposure of Candomblé in the public sphere during the
1970s and 1980s could be portrayed as a form of culturization of religion,
the 1990s saw a process of the politicization of culture and therefore the
politicization of religion. The process was framed within the international
agenda of neoliberal multiculturalism and promotion of the so-called

politics of difference. The recognition of cultural rights of minorities and the search for cultural identity became fundamental tools for political mobilization, resulting in new processes of ethnogenesis (de la Peña, chapter eleven). This trend was globally followed by the increasing "ethnicization" of black identity.

In Brazil, the 1990s saw the consolidation of the black movement's political strategy of "capturing the state," its members assuming positions within the state apparatus, particularly through the Palmares Cultural Foundation, a department of the Ministry of Culture founded in 1988 with the goal of promoting cultural and social policies for the black population. The Palmares Foundation gave institutional voice to ideas of preserving and memorializing black culture, as well as to a discourse on historical reparation. In this context and as part of the wider agenda of antiracist policies, the promotion of Candomblé's symbols as identifiers of blackness gained renewed strength.

Via the Palmares Foundation, black intellectuals and politicians began to promote a new expanded concept of quilombo that went beyond its historical meanings to include any community that self-identified as black and claimed ownership of the land it occupied. This wider concept of quilombo (examined in depth by Leite in chapter twelve) became emblematic of black movements' political force and emerged as a metaphor for a broad notion of resistance that included the many strategies a group can use to perpetuate itself in a particular space, often struggling against the capitalistic greed of the market (i.e., landowners, real estate speculation). The semantic inclusiveness of the quilombo concept was designed to encompass urban black communities too, most significantly Candomblé terreiros. From this perspective, religious congregations—now categorized as "black territories"—could be incorporated into quilombo politics and join the territorial demands of the black subaltern population (Chiozzini 2005).

Yet, the most politically effective governmental initiative in relation to Candomblé was probably the policy of *tombamento* (listing) undertaken by the National Historical and Artistic Heritage Institute, by which a few terreiros were officially registered as national cultural heritage sites. After much discussion, this process was inaugurated in 1984 with the tombamento of the Ilê Axé Iyá Nassô Oká, purportedly the first candomblé in Brazil (Serra 2005). This case established a legal precedent for a policy that, from 1999 to 2005, declared national "black monuments" four houses in

Salvador (Bahia) and one in São Luis (Maranhão). The federal policy was replicated by the state of Bahia's own Cultural and Artistic Heritage Institute, which, from 2004 to 2006, listed eight other houses. These tombamentos crystallized the preexisting hierarchy of prestige within Candomblé, strengthening the position of the elite terreiros, while stimulating a competitive dynamic among an increasing number of other houses aspiring to recognition.

The intervention of public powers has continued. One of the most recent examples was a survey of the terreiros in the state capital, the outcome of a collaboration between several municipal and federal governmental agencies, the university, and Candomblé associations (Santos 2007).[8] One of its goals was to provide data to guide public policies, such as the regulation of the rather chaotic occupation of land by the terreiros. The project also intended "to include the *terreiros* in the tourist itinerary of the city," in a future partnership with Bahiatursa.[9] Therefore, the project furthered the continued marketing of Candomblé as one of the city's cultural commodities.

Other municipal initiatives have been implemented, such as a health service program delivered to the black population through the terreiros, and a subvention program intended to renovate the physical infrastructure of some fifty temples.[10] Given the general poverty of Candomblé houses, the latter program, which affects less than 5 percent of the temples in the city, is bound to exacerbate competition and has already caused discord due to suspicions of preferential treatment for some. Although a recent leftist turn in Bahian politics speaks of replacing the populist strategies of ACM's "Carlismo" with public policies of social equality, one cannot ignore the political potential of religion in mobilizing the black popular classes.

Paralleling state interventions, a number of NGOs, hoping to reach a wider religious community, have become increasingly involved with Candomblé. Whether they originate within or outside the terreiros, these NGOs emerge as new mediators between the religious domain and the secular world of politics. Entities such as KOINONIA and ACBANTU have been active in stimulating networks of terreiros, encouraging the communities to form civil associations in order to access state benefits.[11] Yet despite these efforts, a mere 0.4 percent of the terreiros claim to receive funds from municipal or federal government programs.[12] Although the figure may be slightly underreported, in light of such numbers all the choreographed discourse on the official preoccupation with Candomblé sounds rather like hollow rhetoric, even if the recent convergence of initiatives involving civil society, the state, and black movements may be expressed in other nonmaterial ways, such as the so-called movement against religious intolerance.

If, in the 1980s, the "enemies" of Candomblé were Catholicism (in the view of the antisyncretic re-Africanization movement), Umbanda, and tourism, by the late 1990s neo-Pentecostal churches emerged as the new, galvanizing enemy. There have been numerous incidents revealing the aggressive attitude of these churches against Candomblé (Sansi 2001; Johnson 2002, 158; V. Silva 2007). Yet the episode that ignited the Candomblé community was the death by heart attack, in January 1999, of a Candomblé high priestess, after she saw her picture used to illustrate an article on charlatanism in the newsletter of the Universal Church of the Kingdom of God. Her daughter, with legal assistance from KOINONIA, initiated a long judicial process against the church, which, after successive favorable results for the plaintiff, is now awaiting adjudication by Brazil's supreme court.[13]

Over the years, the case generated great political mobilization with demonstrations, seminars, and commemorative events in various governmental institutions. The campaign against religious intolerance thus added force to the alliance between the black movements, political parties, state agencies, NGOs, and the Candomblé community. In a religious institution known for the independence and competitive dynamics of its constituent parts, this campaign was an important step forward, because a significant number of terreiros were able to coordinate efforts for political action against a common opponent. In that sense, the movement against religious intolerance expresses an increasing political awareness within Candomblé. Yet although reflexive collective political action blends well with talk of resistance, once government agencies are also involved, something seems to be awry.

A preliminary conclusion that can be drawn is that in the last decade black movements and NGOs have had an impact on public policies in relation to Candomblé, at federal, state, and municipal levels, as reflected in tombamento processes, subvention programs, and campaigns against religious intolerance. These changes signal a rearrangement of the forces operating in the religious field where the state, NGOs, and black activists become the main advocates and protectors of Candomblé. Although these agents intend to strengthen cultural preservation and social equality, Afro-Brazilian temples continue to be marketed as the ultimate authentic site for tourists, their symbols increasingly re-mediated for consumerism and political purposes. As a notable example of the latter in Bahia, the identification of Candomblé as a black territory aims to fortify the fight against social and racial discrimination.

The strength of the discourse of négritude within Candomblé is due in part to the growing number of young black activists and intellectuals associated with political parties who become initiated, thus blurring the boundaries between internal and external social actors. Yet the racial diacritic is not gratuitous. In Salvador, most Candomblé initiates are non-white (90.7 percent) with low levels of formal education (67.8 percent with primary education or less).[14] This means that Candomblé continues to be, to a great extent, a religion of poor black people with low levels of literacy. In that sense, Candomblé can effectively operate as an endorsement of a black ethnic identity.

This ethnicization of Candomblé nevertheless constitutes itself in opposition to its simultaneous universalization. Particularly in the southern cities of the country, the religion has become open to anyone regardless of color, gender, or social class and a majority of priests are intellectualized, white, middle-class males who follow re-Africanized modes of ritual (Prandi 1991; V. Silva 1995; Lepine 2005). Increasingly dominated by text-based knowledge and individualized forms of belief and practice, Johnson calls this new trend "Protestant Candomblé" (2002, 169). Hence, the stress on Candomblé's blackness cannot avoid a Bahian regional character, reproducing the situation of previous decades, where négritude defined itself in metonymic contiguity with baianidade.

These circumstances have generated complex paradoxes. On the one hand, some sectors opposed to black-movement racial policies criticize the government for sponsoring Candomblé as the authentic religion of Afro-descendants, discriminating against other religions, namely Evangelical churches. On the other hand, these churches are recruiting their devotees among the poorest sections of the black population, many of them ex-Candomblé practitioners, so that it is more and more difficult to ignore the "blackness" of Evangelical churches too.[15] The end result is that precisely when Candomblé is gaining the state's official recognition as an emblem of black identity, its black grassroots are being stolen by Pentecostal evangelism (Sansi 2007). Hence, today the real dominant force

Candomblé has to resist is not the state, but the wealthy Evangelical movements that are also increasingly operating in the political field.

Where Does Resistance Hide?

Given Candomblé's power dynamics over the last four decades, the question is: How do participants respond to and engage with these politicized representations of their religion? Despite increasing political awareness and even mobilization (as in the campaign against religious intolerance), political ambivalence still remains a common option. Candomblé practitioners resort to cordiality and politeness in public, while in private they behave according to their personal motivation and ritual obligations: the spiritual religious logic usually speaks louder than human political slogans. One might contend that throughout the history of Candomblé there has always been a small number of individuals and groups who were very aware of their political agency and leadership, from the Nagô houses emerging at the end of the nineteenth century to the growing number of militants today that assume an ethnic-political stand as Candomblé devotees. However, remembering the inner diversity within subaltern groups, one might equally contend that most practitioners still have little consciousness of the political dimension of their religious practices and could thus be characterized as cases of an apparent lack of resistance in the face of domination.

Because resistance must involve consciousness, intentionality, and deliberate effort by the social actors involved, one is forced to limit resistance to a very small number of temples. Indeed, those more politically self-aware and prone to using the discourse of resistance are the dozen or so traditional terreiros that have been systematically used to construct and market the public image of Candomblé. It is their political engagement that to a great extent determines their elite status, yet, paradoxically, they are the ones more fully coopted by state cultural policies, most visited by famous people, and, lately, even portrayed in fashion magazines. Hence, by some standards they would appear to be the ones that have undergone a greater degree of accommodation.

And yet, how representative of the whole institution are these elite houses and the public discourses produced by priests, politicians, militants, and intellectuals on them? Their persuasive discursive practices operate mainly at the symbolic level and affect the institution's inner prestige dynamics, but they have little effect on the life and ritual activities of most practitioners. So where does the silent majority stand? What is the perception from below? Does the Gramscian dynamic of hegemonic ideology reproduce within the subaltern group as well? Do most congregations only aspire to reproduce the values of the traditional Nagô-Ketu houses? The trend imposed by them is more or less followed by the rest, and yet among the invisible majority there is perhaps still space for both religious and political heterodoxy. It may be among this silent majority that the really resistive "hidden transcripts" persist.

Although there are no clear criteria to differentiate one group from the other, it may be analytically helpful to distinguish (as I have suggested throughout this chapter) between the elite terreiros and the rest. Alternatively, we might think in terms of two poles with a wide continuum in between: at one end the socially visible terreiros, politically active and in close proximity to public powers, at the other the terreiros with no media or social visibility, "apolitical" and peripheral in the discourse of public authorities. My argument is that differential positioning in this continuum involves different relationships with the establishment and that therefore one might talk of different kinds of resistance.

The elite terreiros have developed a sophisticated negotiation strategy that one could characterize as concealment through revelation or, in Annette Weiner's terms, "keeping-while-giving" (1992). Concurrently, the nonelite terreiros would have preserved alternative discourses of dissidence through embodied ritual practices with no overt political intentionality. These are not mutually exclusive possibilities: both can merge or overlap depending on circumstances.

One example of keeping while giving can be identified in the Axé Opô Afonjá, one of the most prestigious terreiros. Realizing that public hyperexposure threatens to undermine the "authenticity" of Candomblé, the Afonjá leadership decided to substantially increase their own activities of dissemination and self-representation. In 1980, the terreiro opened within its walls a museum and in 1986 a primary school with a pioneering pedagogical program based on Afro-Brazilian civilization. Senior members of the terreiro have also published books, videos, and an internet site to divulge the aspects of the religion they see fit (Castillo 2008). Yet within all this controlled publicity, the idea of secretism—"the promotion of the reputation of possessing secrets" (Johnson 2002, 166)—is systematically reiterated.

What lies behind secretism could be viewed, using Weiner's (1992) terminology, as the crucial "inalienable possession," the control of which allows one to preserve a differentiated identity.[16] Some religious values and practices — not only objects, as discussed by Weiner — have to be kept out of circulation, to be protected and hidden from the other, whether academics, tourists, white people, or contemporary religious experts. This defensive attitude is no longer the result of persecution, as in the past, nor of any internal imperative to use the secret to regulate the religious hierarchy, but a response to the need to preserve some of Candomblé's distinctive signs against external appropriation in order to maintain authority and identity.

The phenomenon is apparent in the struggle against Pentecostal churches, accused of copying and reproducing Candomblé's characteristic ritual practices, such as possession, cleansing, exorcism, and drum playing. It can also be perceived in the attitude of young black activists who, after undergoing initiation, take on fundamentalist positions in advocating secretism and oppose any form of ethnographic publication on Candomblé as intrusive colonialism. But it also surfaces from within the institution, in the veiled disdain by the Bahian priesthood for initiates from the south of the country who are perceived either as "aspiring to the wholesale reproduction of [Bahian] identity" or, alternatively, as undermining "traditional" Bahian religious authority by means of their re-Africanized practices and symbols (Harrison 1999, 244–45).

In all cases, the subtext to these attitudes is the existence of a "deep knowledge" (Apter 1992) that has to be preserved against outsiders at the risk of losing something subjectively felt as essential. One could interpret this paradoxical underwriting of the esoteric through the public rhetoric of secretism in terms of Scott's notion of the "hidden transcript." Although it only obliquely constitutes a subversive discourse, this concealment through partial revelation would be one of Candomblé's most elaborated forms of reauthentication, of preserving a differentiated radical alterity even when yielding to processes of partial accommodation.

Let us now examine the other extreme of our analytical polarity. In his critique of "agency" Gutmann (chapter fifteen) underscores the need to look at "compliance" and "apathy" in order to understand the responsibility the "politically unsuccessful" bear for their misery. Despite his stress on activism, rebellion, and intentional forms of opposition, he finally concedes that "the uninvolved and uninformed are never quite so, and that visions of better worlds can also be the stuff of daily life for those who seem to shun public politics" (321). It is in these "'apolitical' and 'apathetic' interstices" that one might explore unintentional forms of defiance (321).

The official public discourse on Candomblé—elaborated by the hegemonic religious leadership, the state, black movements, and other interlocutors—reinforces a beneficent side of the institution that perpetuates the status quo and the ideological interests of its manufacturers. It is a magnificent, spectacular display of choreographed images and sounds, white dresses, colorful beads, and the flashy costumes of the orishas dancing in public ceremonies. Yet, behind this ceremonial facade and the rhetoric of African and Bahian identities lurks a complex universe of muted practices: initiation rituals, sacrificial blood, and, most especially, healing and witchcraft services to satisfy the needs of clients, often based on capitalistic exchange and the priests' self-interest. This contrast between the visible and the invisible, between ideology and practice, evokes the old moral antagonism established in the 1930s (if not earlier) between "positive" collective religious worship and "negative" individualistic witchcraft.

A whole range of practices remain unspoken in the public discourse on Candomblé, but do these covert activities constitute a form of resistance? Is the occult economy of blood sacrificial offerings a subversive contestation of the logic of capitalism or just an extension of it? Embodied ritual practices do not constitute recognizable conscious political action (though sacrifices can be offered to win an election or defeat a political enemy). Jim Wafer (1991, 57–58) suggests that the re-Africanized terreiros that claim to preserve purity are trying to emulate the hegemonic notion of an "official religion" and are thereby losing their oppositional force. For him, the truly alternative cultural field of contestation to the ideology of the dominant classes operates in the caboclo and Exu worship that the elite terreiros try to dismiss and negate (while also practicing).[17] The lack of respectability of these deities, their "sexual provocation, slang, obscenities, *cachaça*, cigars, etc." and their potential association with violence, disorder, and ultimately witchcraft, constitute the effective radical transgression of established values (Lapassade and Luz 1972). Not surprisingly this is the main battlefield where Evangelical churches are fighting Candomblé.

As observed by John Comaroff and Jean Comaroff (1992, 259) in the context of colonization and enslavement, resistance has often consisted of producing certain kinds of historical consciousness, rather than outward protest. This historical consciousness expresses itself via circulating ideological discourses, but it can also be encoded in embodied attitudes and gestures, in dance, music, and in signifying ritual practices with no overt political intentionality. In the midst of persistent inequality, Candomblé continues to produce empowering narratives, and the silent majority's tenacious practices, though grounded in specifically religious logic, continue to produce the basic symbolic capital used by different social actors (both insiders and outsiders) for political purposes. The kind of tacit resistance inscribed in religious behavior, regardless of individual or collective political self-awareness, may be identified with what Marshall Sahlins (2002, 56) calls "the resistance of culture." This apparently "non-resistive" majority, alien to ideologies and partisan interests, trying to solve the "times of difficult experience" with the aid of the gods and through the tenacious reactivation of their religious knowledge, may constitute the nourishing ground for future challenges to today's authorities, whether external or internal to Candomblé.

Notes

1 *Terreiros* (Candomblé congregations) worship a series of spiritual entities often associated with forces of nature, who receive periodic ritual offerings in their shrines and "possess" selected initiated devotees during drumming-dancing public ceremonies.

2 Space limitations do not allow me to discuss how gender affects resistance in Candomblé, but predominantly female leadership may have contributed to its negotiated rather than conflictive nature.

3 *A Tarde*, May 14, 2008, 11.

4 For detailed analyses, see the work of Harding (2000), Reis (2001), and Parés (2006).

5 For the nineteenth century, see *O Alabama* (September 23, 1864, 1–2; September 26, 1868, 4). For the twentieth century, see the work of Maggie (1992).

6 Decree n. 25.095, January 15, 1976.

7 Umbanda is a Brazilian mediumistic religion emerging in the 1930s in Rio de Janeiro and spreading throughout Brazil. It draws elements from a plurality of sources (Candomblé, Kardecist Spiritism, Caboclo cults, Catholicism, and Asian esoteric traditions) and is perceived as a "syncretic mixture" from the perspective of "orthodox" Candomblé (see Ortiz 1991).

8 The preliminary results of the research identified 1,152 terreiros in the metropolitan area of Salvador (Santos 2007).

9   SEHAB, "Cresce número de terreiros de candomblé em Salvador," May 8, 2007, at http://www.salvador.ba.gov.br/, accessed April 29, 2009.

10 *A Tarde*, May 11, 2007, 8.

11 See "Programas: Egbe—Territórios Negros," at http://www.koinonia.org.br/, accessed April 29, 2009.

12 *A Tarde*, May 11, 2007, 8. Based on the above-mentioned survey of the terreiros of Salvador.

13 *Fala Egbé* Informativo, no. 7, year 3, August 2005.

14 *A Tarde*, May 12, 2007, 14. These data, from the survey of the terreiros of Salvador, relate to the leadership of the congregations. The racial classification resulted from self-identification of the interviewees.

15 "Movimento Negro se aproxima dos evangélicos," *O Cronista*, n. 1, June 2007: 5.

16 For the applicability of the concept to processes of ethnic identity, see the work of Harrison (1999).

17 Exu represents the dynamic principle that animates everything, is the messenger between gods and humans, and is also a morally ambiguous trickster. Demonized by Catholicism, in a wider religious context (Candomblé, Umbanda, Pentecostalism), Exu is associated with disorder and evildoing.

CHAPTER EIGHT

Catholic Resistances in Revolutionary Mexico during the Religious Conflict

JEAN MEYER

Humanity does not live by bread alone, or by the word of God. Above all else, we live by society. Like any movement established on an extensive popular base, the Christian churches are aware of this. Not only do they promise an auspicious tomorrow in another life, but by their very existence they provide something immediate, emerging from the depths of their powerful history. They offer structures for meeting, training, and action. They ask, receive, and give. In a country like Mexico, religion belongs to the people's culture and it shapes the people; for many it provides a guarantee of mental survival, dignity, and hope against all odds. It can constitute an element of both ethnic and national identity and a form of patriotism. In a world of misery and suffering, it is both comfort for the afflicted and luxury for the poor: the church as collective property, the festival as an embodiment of the community. The Catholic Church was able to adapt to secularization because it preserved its popular base, never sacrificing its "secular egalitarianism" to elitism, whether intellectual, mystical, or reformatory.

Since the Age of Enlightenment, throughout the process of "disenchantment of the world" (Max Weber), generation after generation has wanted to privatize religion and strip it of its importance and its social roots. These efforts have been particularly visible on a political level and even more so in church-state relations. Obliged to face up to this new reality, the Catholic Church fought for some 150 years, using defensive rearguard tactics in an apparent state of desperation. Despite its political defeats, however, it showed a surprising capacity to assimilate change and engender innovations through two forms of resistance to be discussed below: *Widerstand* and *Resistenz*.

Although I have periodically returned to the subject of the Cristero Rebellion, I have recently highlighted my own "sin of omission." In my original work on the Cristero Rebellion, I studied the secular conflict between the church and the state from 1926 to 1929, in which spontaneous uprisings, in response to the drastic anticlerical measures of President Plutarco Elías Calles, turned into a war, known as the Cristero Rebellion. The war lasted until June 1929, when both "majesties" arrived at a modus vivendi, known as the *arreglos*, which allowed public worship to be reinstated and brought an immediate end to the war. I should have extended my work further to include those Catholics who did not take up arms. I did, however, attempt a study of anticlericalism (Meyer 1993a) and armed *agraristas* (including both Catholic and non-Catholic peasants) against the Cristeros.[1] Nevertheless, when it came to those regions of the country, the north and the southeast, that did not participate in the insurgency, I contented myself with my own vague pseudopsychological affirmations; such as José Vasconcelos's classic affirmation that the north of Mexico is *pocho* (overly affected by U.S. culture and Yankee Protestantism), that Mexico ends in the Tehuantepec Isthmus, and that the southeast has never been truly evangelized (1957a, 779–82).

A group of young historians from Chihuahua courteously opened my eyes by informing me of the results of their research. I had to make my mea culpa (Meyer 1993b) and rectify this: the absence of Chihuahua and the north, in general, was not due to the fact that they were not Catholic areas, as I had asserted hastily, but to the existence of a modern Catholicism, organized into associations mobilized for civic battle, capable of infiltrating congress and the local government with revolutionary representatives who were also Catholic and thus able to make an agreement with the local bishop for the discreet nonenforcement of the Calles law, which implemented the anticlerical restrictions of the constitution of 1917. This situation explains why Chihuahua, despite having a powerful armed movement in place and supported by old *Villistas* (supporters of Pancho Villa), did not rise up during the Cristero Rebellion. Following the pact agreed to with the governor, the bishop prohibited armed combat, threatening combatants with excommunication. Similar events took place in Sonora, Coahuila, San Luis, and Nuevo León.

I made the same mistake regarding Veracruz, Tabasco, and Chiapas (Ríos 2002) and had to make the same mea culpa, with particular reference to the second Cristero uprising of the 1930s and the spectacular popular mobilization that led to the reopening of the churches. Too preoccupied by my Cristeros, I had lost sight of entire regions of the country and large sections of society: the inhabitants of Mexico City and the numerous Catholics opposed to violence and capable, in the 1930s, of achieving important victories. It was the shortsightedness of the investigator who gets too close to his subject. In more recent research (Meyer 2007), using archives in Oaxaca that had been closed in the 1960s, I have addressed these other societal responses. Thus, this other face of the religious conflict will be the subject of this chapter, focusing on Oaxaca and, to a lesser extent, Chihuahua.

Two Resistances

The historian Martín Broszat, with the help of the German language, offers a key understanding of the concept of resistance: the distinction between Widerstand, political resistance that eventually leads to the taking up of arms and Resistenz, a medical-biological concept, describing the defenses used by an organism to obtain immunity. The concept of Resistenz does not appear in my work on the Cristero Rebellion, for the simple reason that I examined armed conflict; therefore the five states of the north and the four states of the southeast do not appear. This does not mean that the religious conflict did not affect the periphery, nor that the Catholics of these regions did not defend their churches and the Catholic Church as an institution with significant success, but that they did it in the form of Resistenz, without resorting to the great armed conflict that was seen in the Altiplano, the Bajío, and the west. While pacifist, civic, and sociological resistance (Resistenz) characterized the rest of the country, it was also present in the zone of military resistance, given that Catholic opinion on the armed conflict was divided. In the military zone of the Cristero Rebellion, there were many in favor of peaceful resistance and firmly opposed to the armed struggle (Hijar Ornelas 1999, 9).

Some General Considerations

The decision to support armed struggle (Widerstand) or peaceful resistance (Resistenz) is not a choice that can be made freely and completely voluntarily. The circumstances are decisive: a conciliatory local government opens itself to Resistenz and thus can avoid Widerstand. Moreover, the locations in which an armed uprising develops are contingent upon people's having the desire and capacity to rebel. Participation in the Cristero uprising did not depend only on geographical, historical, and social factors, but also on psychological factors. Federal general Cristobál Rodríguez explained to me that "the same fanaticism" reigned everywhere and that despite this, "the perfidious efforts of the clergy" did not obtain the same results everywhere. One can deduce from this "the warrior character of those from Jalisco and the submissive character of those from Querétaro." As I do not have the means to perform a psychological geography of Mexico, I refer the reader to José Vasconcelos: "The leaders of the revolution knew too well that to recruit they had to go to the north, the south and the coasts but it was useless to try recruiting in the Mesa Central (Hidalgo, Puebla, the Federal District, Mexico . . .) because men from this region, in the majority, were not made to be soldiers . . . where the people eat less and drink more" (Vasconcelos 1957b, 891). Physical geography certainly plays its part (who would have thought it a good idea to venture into the mountains on the outskirts of Celaya?) but to a lesser extent than one may think: the Altos de Jalisco, the uplands of the state of Jalisco, which has become a symbol of the Cristero Rebellion, does not easily lend itself to guerrilla warfare, unlike the mountains of Durango. Surrounded by a belt of plains and valleys, these gently undulating plateaus with the occasional rugged slope are incredibly open and easily accessible thanks to the railway lines that run the length of three of their four sides and the roads that cross them. Yet these high plains, densely covered by numerous towns and hamlets, revealed themselves to be particularly unyielding. Likewise, on the plains of the state of Zacatecas, the Cristeros could say: "I know that from now on we are going to win running," because it was impossible to fight for more than fifteen minutes in one place without running the risk of being parted or surrounded. Thus, sociogeographic determinism cannot explain everything, as we shall see when we venture to the north and southeast of Cristero Mexico to the domain of Resistenz resistance.

Oaxaca as a Paradigm

The state of Oaxaca responded to the suspension of public worship in 1926 by prohibiting worship and the administration of sacraments in private and with the temporary closure of churches to allow the state to carry out an inventory of their contents, a move that had caused riots in some other parts of the country. In light of the discussion about how the circumstances are decisive for Resistenz versus Widerstand, what happened in Oaxaca? Before we answer this question, we will first introduce the main protagonists, the state governor, Genaro Vásquez, and the man in charge of the archdiocese, Carlos Gracida. On November 8, 1925, thirty-three-year-old Genaro Vásquez (1890–1967) was named interim governor, a post that he would occupy during the three years of religious conflict, without ever holding the elections stipulated in the local constitution.[2] His able and prudent government was characterized by moderate agrarianism and a significant effort in the field of education: in the governor's official documents in the state archives, one can read the two mottos he chose: "Roads and Schools" and "Although the Indian is wrong, we have to admit he is right." He developed the educational "cultural missions" inaugurated by José Vasconcelos when he was minister of education and personally attended to the diverse aspects of governance (Iturribarría 1955, 425). A loyal supporter of President Calles, he was appreciated as such by the president. He maintained an intense correspondence with Calles during these years, curiously without ever broaching the subject of religion.

Vásquez's lack of enthusiasm for anticlericalism never damaged his career. Toward the end of 1928, Genaro Vásquez ended his governance of the state to become a national senator. Shortly thereafter, he became secretary general of the Partido Nacional Revolucionario, founded in 1929, and continued to have a brilliant career. He became, for example, founder of the Department of Indigenous Affairs, minister of the supreme court, attorney general of the republic at the time of President Lázaro Cárdenas, and organizer of the first Inter-American Indigenous Congress. Brought up Catholic, he maintained his friendships with many Oaxacan priests, in particular with Canon Agustín Espinosa and Canon Carlos Gracida. Canon Gracida described Vásquez as "a young Oaxacan, a lawyer and good friend of Father Agustín Espinosa." The good relationship between Canon Gracida and the lawyer-governor Vásquez would be of vital importance during the Cristero Rebellion. Moreover, Canon Espinosa would become Carlos Gracida's right hand when he administered the archdiocese from 1926 to 1929.[3]

Canon Carlos Gracida (1867–1948)

Born in Oaxaca, Gracida was ordained to the priesthood at the age of twenty-three and by the age of twenty-eight he founded and became principal of the Catholic College of the Holy Ghost. In 1910 he became archdeacon of the same. In 1915, he assumed the post of vicar-general, and in 1918 became governor of the prelacy. Between 1915 and 1920, he had to lead the church under a series of governor-generals who supported the general and president Venustiano Carranza and viewed the clergy with great suspicion; in 1917, Gracida even spent time in prison. Seeking to prevent *Carrancista* hostility from escalating into open persecution of the church, as it had done in other states, from 1918 to 1920 he succeeded in negotiating the return of confiscated churches and ecclesiastical goods. Generals, governors, even President Carranza himself, attributed the return of these goods and buildings to Gracida. Highly regarded by the elites before the revolution (1910–17), he was regarded with the same esteem by the new revolutionary elite. Just as he had been matchmaker for the former, so he became for the latter; in 1922 he performed the marriage of the daughter of General Elizondo, who, according to Gracida, "got on very well with [the church] and was much loved and highly regarded by all" (Esparza 2004; Meyer 2007).

At the beginning of 1926, the government of Oaxaca, like all other states, received instructions from the Secretaría de Gobernación (Federal Ministry of the Interior) to apply article 130 of the constitution published on January 18 in the *Diario Oficial de la Federación*.[4] Article 130 nationalized church property, prohibited public worship, and required priests to register with the government in order to practice. Thus began the crisis. After careful consideration, the prelacy indicated to all parish priests that municipal mayors were obliged to apply Article 130 and that in order to do so it was necessary to "submit the list of ten people in charge of the church with their addresses . . . one list for each church" and also a list of the priests for each church. The clergy in Oaxaca complied and in July the vicar-general submitted a list of all priests with copies of their birth certificates. The only incident recorded in the episcopal archives between February and July 1926 was the protest of Seminary Rector Andrés Corrales, who wrote to the governor to inform him that there was no primary school hidden on seminary grounds, which would have violated constitutional Article 3, mandating lay primary education.[5]

Nonetheless, the hierarchy began preparing people for the worst. On March 2 Archbishop José Othón Núñez y Zárate summoned all priests in the city to discuss "important matters." On April 24 he ordered that "tomorrow the Collective Letter from the Mexican Episcopate dated April 21 will be read in all masses."[6] On June 14 the prelacy made public the letter from Pius XI to the archbishop of Mexico expressing his support for the Mexican faithful during such trying times. In Oaxaca, as in Puebla and many other parts of the country, Archbishop Núñez opted for legal, juridical defense through lobbying the government with moderate demands. The Liga Nacional de Defensa de las Libertades Religiosas, a militant Catholic organization almost nonexistent in Oaxaca, characterized him as "astonishingly lukewarm" if not a "traitor."[7] Archbishop Núñez never failed to promote "prudence" or "patience," words that we find throughout his correspondence.[8] Thus, before the suspension of public worship in response to the implementation of Article 130, which became known as the Calles Law, he agreed to submit the list of the ten laymen in charge of the churches with the list of their priests, as decreed by the state, a decision that not all bishops made.

At midnight on July 31, 1926, in Oaxaca, as in the rest of the republic, public worship was suspended. The subsequent handing over of the churches and their inventories of goods to the committees of ten inhabitants was carried out without major incident. Still, there was an attempted rebellion in Tlaxiaco, aggravated by the execution of Rafael Acevedo and his son Vicente on August 6 at the hands of soldiers (for the crime of distributing Catholic propaganda), and another in Oaxaca City, in the church of the Siete Príncipes, quickly controlled by Canon Gracida. The isolation of many parishes in a mountainous state that was as vast as its territories were secluded explains how various parish priests, like Francisco Castellanos from Candelaria Loxicha, were surprised by the suspension and questioned the validity of the news, wondering whether it was merely attempted provocation.[9]

The day following the suspension, petitions flooded in from local authorities begging priests and archbishops to celebrate once more "the holy sacrifice of mass in the parochial church." Priests wrote to request that the prelacy "lift the order of suspension of worship . . . which would cause joy to be reborn in the hearts of these poor parishioners."[10] Another priest wrote to the vicar-general: "I hope you are able to resolve the 'Strike.' As we are so removed, we find ourselves as if in limbo, unable to answer a multitude of questions as to when this will be resolved."[11]

During August and September, the handover of the churches and their inventories continued to be carried out by the priests without violence or resistance. At most, a priest may have refused to sign the necessary documents, but it is clear that they all oversaw the inventory, thus complying with the government's wishes, something that was not done in every diocese. In the State Judicial Archives, which I reviewed district by district, there was nothing about the religious conflict, no grievance mentioned between church and state or in relation to any priest in particular. All the inventories can be found in the Oaxaca Government Archives, parish by parish, church by church, as can the lists of the ten inhabitants in charge of each church. The same information was recorded in 1927 and 1928, as was the handing back of the churches to the priests in the summer of 1929, after the signing of the arreglos, yet again with another inventory. The lists are interminable.[12]

The result: not a single attempt at resistance, not even passive resistance by clergy or the faithful, and no government violence, with the sole exception of the case of the "martyrs of Tlaxiaco," noted above. This calm explains why the religious situation in Oaxaca at the end of 1926 was singular when compared to the regions that would soon become the backdrop to the Cristero Rebellion. Moreover, the priests carried out their pastoral role without any difficulties (which went against federal instructions); thus Father Ramón J. Calderón, priest of Teposcolula, reported on October 26 that he had baptized 112 infants, married twenty-one couples, and attended to various infirm parishioners. Another priest recorded the gross earnings of the trimester, the parish chapter assembled as usual, the prelacy functioned as normal, and even the rector of the seminary had reopened the premises and had no problems.[13]

Moreover, the state government did not have anything to report. It informed the federal government periodically about the successful application of the Calles Law and acknowledged receipt from the municipal presidents "of the statistical charts containing the data relative to the church in their area." At times, a note like the following was added: "It is recommended, on behalf of the State Governor, that the department be informed as soon as possible if the priest Francisco Vidrio, noted in the above mentioned chart, has complied with all the legal requirements." If the priest had complied, he was left in peace.[14] The Oaxaca state government only indicated that two cases were important. One was that of "young Mario Cervantes, student of the Instituto de Ciencias y Artes del Estado [who] has been hostile to the institutions that govern us, by haranguing the believers and religious associations in subversive discourse inside this city's church of San José; acts in which he was surprised yesterday." His offence took place on October 8, 1926. The other notable case was that of "the youth Alejandro Ruiz, pupil of the Mixed Normal School for teachers of the state, in receipt of a government grant [who] also took part in propaganda activities of this nature . . . against the efficacy of the precepts contained in Article 130 of the Constitution." Both pupils were expelled to avoid the "danger of contaminating the other pupils with their negative tendencies" and as "the example[s] of improper conduct."[15] The measure was published in the *Periódico Oficial del Estado*.

Nevertheless, there was an element of Widerstand in Oaxaca. Oaxaca participated very little in the Cristero Rebellion. The official information is not always clear and refers generally to "bandits," "wrongdoers," "armed persons," and "rebels" without any more precision. Hence I prefer not to comment on the activities of such people on the Isthmus between Tehuantepec and Juchitán and in the southeast, at the border of Guerrero, because it has not been possible to determine their motivation. Despite the enormous amount of material about the period in the state archives, there is certainly no abundance of information relating to the "rebellion" or "revolution" of Catholics; in fact it is severely lacking. A huge amount of research has been carried out, almost in vain, as it has not produced much more information than that which has already been published in *La Cristiada* (Meyer 2005). It should be made clear that there were only two Cristero focal points in the state of Oaxaca, of which only one was in the archdiocese. The regions are Huajuápam in the northwest, which is the headquarters of the diocese of the same name, and La Montaña, the region of Miahuatlán-Juquila, in the southwest. Both regions are mountainous and isolated from the center. They are linked by the Tlaxiaco region, another Catholic focal point, but of a more passive resistance.

In his government report for the year 1928, the governor indicated:

The religious question had not been of any importance previously, however in recent months fanatical Catholic activities have been noticed. This is brought to light by the activities of the priest Eugenio Martínez, who, leading a group of armed individuals, made incursions into La Mixteca through Huajuápam; also, the open seditious propaganda of the priest Epigmenio Hernández in the regions of Pochutla, Jamiltepec and Juquila accompanied by an engineer by the name of Arnulfo Viveros, amongst others. In order to counteract the effort of those who wish to incite a state of disorder, perhaps in connection with other fanatical groups from other federative entities, the leadership of military operations and this very government have already dictated the measures to be taken and hope that in a short time all danger will be averted. Conversely, priests Miguel Guillermo Hernández and Maximino Amador approached the government, requesting authorization to "carry out their ministry" in Juchitán and Pochutla: this was granted to them (*Informe de Gobierno*).[16]

It is impossible to obtain exact figures; however, if one considers that no group would have contained more than ninety men and that they generally operated in groups of twenty to forty, there could have been at most four hundred rebels in La Mixteca (without counting those who were mentioned but unidentified). In Michoacán, in stark contrast, even in 1929, the Cristeros were counted in their thousands. In not representing a military threat, these rebels spared Oaxaca from the horrors of war and the vicious circle of uprising, repression, and more uprisings that was all too familiar to other regions of the country. This same fact allowed the governor to maintain his conciliatory political stance and the church to impart its spiritual and sacramental services, so that the vast majority of Catholics practiced peaceful and tranquil Resistenz: visiting churches, practicing religion, supporting the clergy, and making petitions and pilgrimages.

The Modus Vivendi between the Government and the Church of Oaxaca

Just as there is a lack of information regarding Catholic combatants, there is an abundance of documentation to demonstrate the almost normal functioning of the Catholic Church. This makes it possible to expose indirectly the existence of a gentleman's agreement between both majesties, an unspoken pact that two or three documents suddenly shed light on. In the ecclesiastical archives, there are three noticeable thematic absences: the government is never criticized, the Liga Nacional de Defensa de las Libertades Religiosas is never mentioned, nor are any references made to Catholics who took up arms. In contrast, it is remarkable how many documents the municipal authorities sent to the episcopacy, using a tone of absolute respect, regarding matters such as the celebration of religious festivals, payment of tithes, and petition of priests. It must be remembered that Oaxaca, exceptionally, had five hundred municipalities, thus allowing the church to benefit from an extraordinary network of complicity.

From March 1926, Archbishop Núñez y Zárate coordinated the defense of the church's interests in a firm but prudent way, always searching for contacts and dialogue with the local government, "bringing together the intellectuals and using them to make up two commissions, one named the executive commission and the other investigatory; the executive commission was responsible for making representations before the government and the courts; the other was concerned with researching what should be done in each case." When the government requested the list of priests and the ten laymen responsible for each church, the archbishop decided to comply with the requirement.[17]

Upon the suspension of public worship, he gave explicit instructions that the inventory and handover should not be an incentive for confrontation. A circular outlined the new terms for masses:

> His Excellency the Prelate has deemed it fit to dictate the following rules which should be adhered to for the celebration of Holy Mass, during the suspension of worship in churches. The resident or non-resident priests,
>
> First—Must never perform two masses in the same day.
>
> Second—Each must have a fixed abode and within it a provisional oratory for the celebration, with the approval of the Vicar.
>
> Third—Only in exceptional cases, with extenuating circumstances and the authority of the Vicar himself, may they celebrate Mass in dwellings other than those already approved.
>
> Fourth—The non-resident priests will celebrate in one of the dwellings approved for celebration and, only if it is agreed by the Vicar, will they be able to celebrate in their own residence.[18]

These guidelines were, in fact, illegal. After the church suspended public worship in response to the Calles Law, the federal government prohibited the celebration of Mass or administration of sacraments in private dwell-ings. In many parts of the country, the assiduous application of this pro-hibition pushed the church underground: various priests and lay people lost their lives for violating it (Meyer 2005, 1:49).[19] This was not the case in Oaxaca. Moreover, having a list of all dwellings approved for the cele-bration of Mass in the episcopal offices would have been criminal impru-dence if the local government had had any will to enforce the prohibition.

In Oaxaca, the church did not disavow legal responses to the conflict and entrusted its civic resistance (Resistenz) to the laity. Not only did the church maintain priests in their parishes (with very few exceptions), it aided the development of all aspects of spiritual, sacramental, and cul-tural life, something that was made possible thanks to the existence of a network of lay organizations known as *cofradías*, *hermandades*, and *mayor-domías*. It was only possible to maintain a priestly presence throughout the state because the government allowed it; in other states, authorities, believing that priests promoted and led rebellion, forced the clergy to move to the capital or main cities. Perhaps a strong Catholic insurgence in Oaxaca would have provoked the same reaction; just as the Huajuápam uprising provoked the expulsion of the bishop, his cathedral chapter, and priests.

After the suspension of public worship, the military authorities in Oaxaca followed the same course as Governor Genaro Vásquez, seem-ingly appeasing the federal government without disturbing the church. On May 26, 1927, on the instructions of the federal government, General Matías Ramos, in charge of military operations, published a circular with the following instructions: "The President of the Republic has ordered the 'reconcentration' of all parish priests in the capital due to the sedi-tious activities that the priest Benito Vásquez has been developing in Mix-tepec, [due to] others' activities in Cuilapam, Tepelmeme, Silacayoapan and [to the] similar efforts of those who reside in the rest of the State."[20] Word spread among priests that "there [was] government regulation that any priest who enter[ed] the City [of Oaxaca] [would] not be allowed to leave."[21] Yet not only did the general postpone the date set from June 25 to August 10, but instead of "reconcentration" he ordered residential as-signment (as was done throughout the Cristero zone). As he explained to the vicar-general: "I have superior orders to have all the priests here, but I think that those from outside the city could have a better life in their towns and for that reason I have left them alone; but as they are already on [government] lists, if a rebel uprising occurs here, then I will send for them all."[22] The vicar commented to his superior: "The general, convinced that the clergy does not encourage uprising and that ordering concentration could provoke it, has opted just for the priests to present themselves."[23] The general's gamble paid off and the civil government of Oaxaca won with him; a serious uprising never emerged thanks to the presence of clergy who attended to the spiritual needs of the faithful.

Allied with their clergy, protecting and pressuring their priests, with the tolerance of state authorities and the active participation of the numerous and dispersed Oaxacan local authorities, the Catholic community lived intensely in these years. The anticlerical minority in the state attributed the great religious resurgence to the terrible and continuous earthquakes that punished Oaxaca, but they did not take into account the role of powerful lay organizations, both traditional and modern, or the fact that the clergy had to delegate so much work to the laity, such as handing over administration of the churches, the celebration of many religious acts and the distribution of the Eucharist. A paradoxical result of the religious conflict was the promotion of the laity, such as the organization of Catholic women discussed by Patience Schell (chapter nine). Popular, lay, communal Catholicism revealed itself to be a powerful factor within resistance (Resistenz), leaving Catholics safeguarded against anticlerical propaganda. Reports paint consistent pictures of full churches on Sundays, festival days, and for the Rosary.

In Comparison: The Case of Chihuahua, 1926–1927

In the case of Chihuahua, one particular and decisive factor must be taken into account: the attitude of one bishop who, while in a unique political situation, had both prestige and moral authority. The bishop of Chihuahua, Antonio Guízar y Valencia, like many of his colleagues, was opposed to armed action and anticipated the instructions given by Papal Nuncio Fumasoni Biondi to Tabasco's Bishop Pascual Díaz on December 12, 1927: "The bishops should not only abstain from supporting armed action but they should remain outside of and above any political party."[24] From 1926, months before the first uprisings, Guízar y Valencia had witnessed the organizational success of the Liga with trepidation; for this reason he opposed Liga actions, like the Catholic boycott of goods and services begun in July, as well as its propaganda, even before armed conflict was mentioned. Moreover, like his colleagues Archbishops Pedro Vera y Zuria in Puebla and Martín Tritschler in Mérida, he came to a discreet arrangement with the local government so that the Calles Law implemented in July 1926 did not affect his diocese.

The state of Chihuahua was Catholic and also had the revolutionary tradition of the *Maderistas*[25] and Villistas. An example of this tradition was the brave young Catholic journalist Silvestre Terrazas, who was anti-Porfirian, a brilliant representative of social Catholicism, a Maderista and later an important part of the local Villistas. In June 1925, when the recently founded Liga had 36,395 members, 4,000 of them were from Chihuahua. In 1926, the state had thirty-five centers and seventy-two sections of the Liga (Meyer 1993b). Various municipal presidents were Liga members and various deputies were Catholic.

Moreover, in Chihuahua, "Governor Enríquez and General Jesús Agustín Castro had the good sense to have known how to interpret the will of the people and the rare tenacity to comply with it and adhere to it." Curiously, the person writing this on March 26, showing an unusual display of sympathy toward the government in his "Memorial dirigido al Señor Presidente de la República," was none other than the bishop of Tacámbaro, the ardent Leopoldo Lara y Torres, soon to become a militant member of the armed struggle.[26]

In September 1926, the regional leaders of the Liga met in Mexico to discuss everything except the war that had begun that summer. At the end of the conference, the delegate from Chihuahua requested a private audience with Rafael Ceniceros y Villareal, Liga president, and informed him that the time had come to take up arms. He claimed to control eight hundred men. Ceniceros replied that he agreed but that they must wait. After the first spontaneous uprisings of August and September, the Liga called for armed conflict in November and December of 1926 and passed instructions down to the local leadership for a general and national uprising to begin on January 1, 1927, to be supported by a revolutionary army that was to come in from the United States. René Capistrán Garza, the Liga representative in the United States, announced that Ciudad Juárez would be taken on January 1. Ciudad Juárez was never attacked, no army crossed the border, and in Chihuahua nobody moved. Why not?

In Jalisco, when the popular Archbishop Francisco Orozco y Jiménez had heard the beating of war drums, he categorically refused to allow the Unión Popular (the western equivalent of the Liga) to participate in the war. In doing so, he managed to avoid many uprisings in the autumn of 1926. In December, however, the call of the Liga, with its great promises, was too tempting. Archbishop Orozco y Jiménez, who judged the Liga's attempted uprising as criminal and disastrous, found himself leading a clandestine existence to avoid imprisonment or exile. I have not found a single document or testimony that identifies whether at that particular time he condemned or tolerated the uprising.

In Chihuahua, Bishop Guízar y Valencia made his views clear in the autumn of 1926 and in January 1927. He had supported the Liga as a movement of civic struggle, until September 1926. When the Liga turned to armed uprising, he did not merely renounce his support but condemned its actions and prohibited Catholics from associating with it. In Chihuahua, the Liga was so well established and organized that its national directors, lost in the enthusiastic dreams of inexperience, were already imagining themselves forming a provisional government in Ciudad Juárez. Guízar y Valencia was extremely alarmed when he heard about the planned uprising, and not only wrote secular and pastoral letters against armed resistance but sent explicit instructions to suspend any preparations. Moreover, he convened the state leadership of the Liga and strictly prohibited any participation in an armed movement. Bishop Guízar y Valencia insisted that the defense of their rights and those of the church had to be carried out legally, while maintaining respect for state authorities. He demonstrated to them that the de facto tolerance exercised by the state government was the product of the patience and discretion of the church and also due to the influence of Catholics in the government. Those who tried to argue against him were overruled and threatened with excommunication (Meyer 1993b). In January 1927, when the Liga-orchestrated Cristero uprising swept through west central Mexico, Bishop Guízar y Valencia went even further, renewing his prohibition and openly condemning the *ligueros* as rebels. According to rumors, an uprising was being planned in Camargo in collaboration with old Villistas, but the threat of excommunication proved effective (Ríos 2002).

*   *   *

The religious conflict of 1926–38 and the great, armed, Catholic uprising that came to be known as the Cristero Rebellion are two very separate issues. The Cristero Rebellion was resistance in the form of Widerstand, and as such formed an intrinsic part of the conduct of Catholics when faced with the government of President Calles, but it was not everything. There was also another form of resistance, the nonviolent Resistenz. The anticlerical offensive of the 1920s that became antireligious in the 1930s had a national dimension and was continuous; thus it was present in all regions of the country, provoking resistance in various forms, everywhere. Yet because armed conflict is more visible and spectacular, we have underestimated the power of popular piety in this resistance. In Oaxaca, Resistenz was almost general and permanent while Widerstand remained marginal in quantity and peripheral in quality; the people's identification with the Catholic Church as both an institution and a faith remained impressive. Moreover, there were very few cases of unrest prompted by this "popular religiosity." I found no more than two. The first, of minor importance, occurred in 1926 in the town of Itundujia (Tlaxiaco), before the suspension of public worship, but already during the tense anticipation of a catastrophe: "An Indian woman who didn't even speak Spanish said that God had spoken to her saying that they should worship a stone in the countryside . . . and now there are great pilgrimages from towns even very far away who travel to see the miracle."[27] Edward Wright-Rios studied apparitions in a cave in Ixpantepec (Juquila) from November 1928 until 1934.[28] They were initially accepted by the priest and then later discredited.

Yet was the success of Resistenz in Oaxaca unique? In order to answer this question, it would be necessary to study all the states, all the dioceses in which there were no significant Catholic uprisings, such as Chihuahua, Sonora, Chiapas, and Campeche, and then carry out a detailed comparison between the regions of Widerstand and those of Resistenz. Thus in the state of Oaxaca, the existence of the Cristero focal point of Huajuápam could lead to interesting parallels with that in the Altos de Jalisco. The region remained a "deviant case," embracing right-wing *sinarquismo*[29] and then the militancy of the Partido Acción Nacional. In 1962 there was a harshly repressed and little-known "Cristero" uprising in the region. The neighboring state of Puebla appeared to have practiced Resistenz similar to that in Oaxaca, and one is tempted to compare the moderation of Governor Claudio Tirado with that of his colleague Genaro Vásquez and similarly compare the moderation of the archbishop of Puebla, Monsenior Vera y Zuria, with that of his colleague José Othón Núñez y Zárate.

This leads us once again to the question of personalities and the main players on history's stage. How should we consider this factor? In 1926, Jalisco had an interim governor, Silvino Barba González, a man of goodwill who tried to open President Calles's eyes to the danger of frustrating and destroying the hopes of the Catholic people of Jalisco. At the same time, the archbishop of Guadalajara, Francisco Orozco y Jiménez, was struggling to convince his colleagues not to suspend worship and, after July 31, 1926, to prevent the uprising of his faithful. Both men failed, and in Jalisco the path of Widerstand prevailed. But unlike Oaxaca, Jalisco had already known pure Jacobean revolutionaries between 1914 and 1924; its Catholics had already organized themselves and grown accustomed to the conditions of war during these harsh struggles.

In the case of the army, as well, the personalities of the leaders are certainly important; however, generals who were humane and respectful of the lives of civilians and even enemy fighters, generals like Manuel Ávila Camacho or Lázaro Cárdenas, in Jalisco and Michoacán, could not avoid the great war that assaulted the west. Before taking leadership of military operations in Oaxaca in 1928, as a conciliatory figure, General Espinosa y Córdoba made war in Michoacán. Claudio Fox, Espinosa y Córdoba's replacement in Oaxaca after his accidental death, was not previously well known for being lenient, but in Oaxaca he was just that. Could it be that soldiers conduct themselves prudently when not under attack? Why was their anticlericalism, at least that of a few, so visible in the Cristero zone, yet never manifested in Oaxaca?

It is necessary, then, to return to the question of specificity. Did the fact of governing a state with an indigenous majority living in a multitude of small, strongly structured communities, as in Oaxaca and Chiapas, weigh heavily on a governor's conduct? How did Genaro Vásquez manage to be a perfect *Callista*, on excellent terms with Calles himself, and at the same time the man of the modus vivendi with the local church? Could it be a continuation of Oaxacan sovereignty and also a consequence of his theory "Although the Indian is wrong, we have to admit he is right"? Substitute the word "Catholic" for "Indian" and it becomes clear.

Many local authorities had the same attitude as Genaro Vásquez and did not follow, or only half adhered to, the official orders. "Let the Indian be right" means wisely recognizing the strength of the silent resistance of the people and the local elite; it is also being aware of the state's weakness. The silence of President Calles about these matters in his correspondence with the loyal Genaro Vásquez adds evidence to these conjectures. It was impossible to do anything; such was the state of affairs. Was this recognition wisdom or impotence? Impotence can be a form of wisdom, and it allowed, on a national level, first the arreglos of 1929, then progressively their application during the presidency of Lázaro Cárdenas from 1935 to 1938. When there is no great, armed uprising, but rather widespread, peaceful resistance the state does not dare to demand that its instructions be adhered to; it stops before resorting to violence.

And if religion was not the objective, the motive, the cause of resistance, but resistance itself? Resistance to what? This, I certainly don't know. The "disenchantment of the world," to take Max Weber's phrase, desired by a few leaders of the time? What is certain is that resistance in its two forms, Widerstand and Resistenz, contributed to the reenchantment of Mexico.

Notes

Chapter translated by Tara Plunkett

1 Beneficiaries of the government's land reform program.
2 Fideicomiso archivos Plutarco Elías Calles y Fernando Torreblanca, Archivo Joaquín Amaro, exp. 302, leg. 20/41; exp.306, leg.48/66; exp.227, leg.88/98.
3 Archivo Histórico Arzobispado Oaxaca (hereafter AHAO), Correspondencia, January 28, 1920.
4 Publication in this official government newspaper was the final step to creating a new law.
5 AHAO, Diocesano/Gobierno/Mandatos 1920–1940 and Correspondence, March 4, 1926.
6 AHAO, Correspondencia.
7 Founded in 1925 to defend the Catholic religion and eventually seeking to lead the rebellion, the Liga united the leadership of the Knights of Columbus, the Union of Mexican Catholic Ladies, the Catholic Association of Mexican Youth, the National Confederation of Labor, and the National Parents' Union.
8 AHAO, Correspondencia, anonymous to Vicente Medina, January 20, 1928; "Prudence," found in AHAO, Correspondencia, March 15, August 7, September 24, 1926, and AHAO, Fondo Diocesano, Gobierno, 1926–29.
9 AHAO, Correspondencia, August 7, 1926.
10 AHAO, Correspondencia, August 2 and August 7, 1926.
11 Ibid., September 2, 1926, Fr. S. Ramírez in Cacahuatepec to Canon Agustín Espinosa, diocesan chancellor.
12 Archivo General del Poder Ejecutivo del Estado de Oaxaca (hereafter AGEPEO), Fondo Revolución, Ramo Asuntos Eclesiásticos, districts of Ocotlán, Tehuantepec, Etla, Juquila, Villa Alta, in July and August 1926; July, August, and September 1929.
13 AHAO, Correspondencia, Actas de Cabildo, 1926.

14 AGEPEO, Fondo Revolución, Ramo Asuntos Eclesiásticos, Ocotlán district, 1926 (November 26, Head of the State Department to the municipal president of Magdalena Ocotlán).

15 *Periódico Oficial*, October 9, 1926, 484–85.

16 *Informe de Gobierno presentado por el H. Gobernador* (Tipografía del Estado de Oaxaca, 1928).

17 AHAO, Correspondencia, March 15, 1926.

18 AHAO, Diocesano/Gobierno/Parroquias 1925–29, September 24, 1926.

19 Eighty priests were shot and murdered during the conflict.

20 AHAO, Diocesano/Gobierno, circular of General Ramos, May 26, 1927.

21 AHAO, Correspondencia, Fr. Antonio Valencia to Canon Espinosa, July 3, 1927.

22 Ibid., C. Gracida to Mons. Núñez, August 6, 1927.

23 Ibid., Diocesano/Gobierno, C. Gracida to A. Espinosa, July 20, 1928.

24 Archivo Histórico del Arzobispado de México, Conflicto Religioso, Obispos, Pascual Díaz.

25 Supporters of Francisco Madero, president from 1911 to 1913, who instigated the uprising against Porfirio Díaz in 1910 that precipitated the Revolution.

26 "Memorial dirigido al Señor Presidente de la República," March 16, 1926 (Meyer 2005, 2: 247, footnote 51).

27 AHAO, Fondo Diocesano, Gobierno, Correspondence, Fr. Castro to Canon Agustín Espinosa, May 8, 1926.

28 AHAO, Correspondence, priest of Juquila, A. Canseco, January 16, 1929.

29 A conservative, nationalist movement seeking to "restore" a Catholic social order to Mexico.

CHAPTER NINE

Gender, Resistance, and Mexico's Church-State Conflict

PATIENCE A. SCHELL

A black-and-white photograph froze the moment in 1925 when the general council of the Unión de Damas Católicas Mexicanas (UDCM) met in Mexico City. Even in a color photograph, it would have seemed a dour gathering. Eight women and one man stare forcefully at the camera. The middle-aged man in clerical garb is Father Leopoldo Icaza. The women who surround him are also middle-aged (or older) and frumpy. Their black dresses looked old-fashioned in 1925. No bobbed hair peeks out from under hats. These decent women had buns securely pinned in place. Everything about this photograph projects an image of social privilege, bourgeois respectability, and conformity. What can these people tell us about resistance? But in May 1925 UDCM members played a pivotal role in the church-state conflict that would soon become open rebellion in some parts of Mexico (see Meyer, chapter eight). By summer 1926, volunteer work in the UDCM meant defiance of the totalizing revolutionary project: violating the constitution, protesting in the streets, and organizing clandestine worship and education. These women were at the forefront of everyday resistance to postrevolutionary anticlericalism.

This chapter has two goals: first, through discussion of Catholic women's challenges to state anticlericalism, to enrich our view of resistance through a wider understanding of marginality and relationships of power; second, to situate Catholic women's organizing at the heart of politics and day-to-day resistance in the church-state conflict. Focus on the conflict has tended to be on the Cristero Rebellion or on the negotiations between the church hierarchy and government. The historiography has often infantilized Catholic women, assuming that their activities resulted from some false consciousness meticulously managed by the clergy (Quirk 1973; O'Dogherty 1991, 129–53). This focus has created a view of the conflict and Catholic responses that sidelines or denies women's participation, while also ignoring the response of Catholics who were peaceful in their protests.

Before turning to the church-state conflict, I will address the theoretical terrain of resistance and what I believe to be its limitations. Discussion of resistance often begins with James C. Scott, whose work has already been discussed in the introduction. Critics of Scott's work and the subsequent literature his approach inspired have challenged Scott's disavowal of organized or legal resistance as a route to political change. Concerned with material interests, Scott risks making peasants and their motivations appear one-dimensional (Gutmann 1993, 75, 78), ignoring the myriad forms of possible marginalization and the multiple identities to which actors have access at any one time. As the Subaltern Studies Group recognized in the early 1980s, subordination takes many forms, including those of race, age, gender, and class. Moreover, subalternity itself is a relative category, not fixed, and depends upon circumstances (Coronil 1994, 649; Mallon 1994, 1494, 1511). This more nuanced approach demonstrates that individuals live within stages of "compounded powerlessness" (Ortner 1995, 184), which are themselves relative and unstable.

This chapter seeks to question and expand our notions of what constitutes resistance by presenting a case of resistance to religious oppression. As Sherry Ortner argues (1995, 180–82, 190), resistance discussions have not yet addressed religious belief from an ethnographically thick perspective. In chapter six, Patricia Pessar argues that social scientists do not always take religious beliefs and spiritual motivations seriously, even when addressing religious movements like millenarianism. Yet as Daniel H. Levine and Scott Mainwaring argue, "Religion is clearly a powerful motivating force. . . . Religious ideas inspire and legitimate action while religious structures simultaneously produce enduring social bonds that make collective endeavors possible. . . . Religion provides enormous political energies, which change expectations, challenge accepted notions of the legitimate, and refocus action on new areas and issues of conflict" (1989, 208–9).

Numerous examples demonstrate how religion has fostered conflict resolution and created spaces of resistance. In Northern Ireland, the site of a complicated social and political conflict cloaked in religion, clergy and religious groups actively worked for the peace process, through informal diplomacy, carrying messages, arranging meetings, and working with various political groups (McCartney 1999). According to Jonathan Powell (2008), the historic settlement in Northern Ireland owes a debt of gratitude to the persistent endeavors of Catholic and other clergy. In Latin America and Spain, the Catholic Church and its clergy have sometimes stood on the side of dictators, but at other moments lay people and elements within the hierarchy have condemned economic and political injustice, as well as political violence. Numerous civil peace associations have arisen out of parish groups in the Basque Country (Funes Rivas 1998, 39). In Chile, in 1973, Cardinal Raul Silva founded the Comité de Cooperación para la Paz en Chile (Committee of Cooperation for Peace in Chile), providing legal and social aid to victims of the Pinochet dictatorship and their relatives. The Catholic organization survived, in part, because the church's moral authority was too powerful for the military regime to confront (Lowden 1996). Historical examples, too, are plentiful. Religion gave its moral force to abolition movements in the United Kingdom and the United States. Later on, the U.S. civil rights movement drew on traditionally black church networks and the "social gospel" Protestant tradition (Eyerman and Jamison 1991, 128; Davis 2006, 231–67). In the case discussed here, religion became the source of marginality (being Catholic under an anticlerical state), while fostering the courage to resist, overtly and covertly, a government considered unjust.

The historical actors discussed below were marginalized not only as Catholics, but also as women. Yet gender offers another rich conceptual approach not adequately taken up in the resistance literature. A gender-aware focus could enhance many discussions of resistance as gender is "a primary field within which or by means of which power is articulated" (J. W. Scott 1986, 1069). Gendered resistance need not be confined to gender inequality, but can target other forms of subordination. In the United States and Britain, but not Brazil, abolition movements fed into feminist organizations and demands for suffrage; but the fact that the women involved in Brazil's abolition movement did not challenge patriarchy does not undermine the essential role that these women played in the campaign (Kittleson 2005, 99–100; Davis 2006, 231–67). Moreover, essentialist assumptions about women as apolitical queens of the hearth could be a strategic advantage for overt resistance. Students of protest movements in the 1970s and 1980s have noted that throughout Latin America a shared concern with "the rights of motherhood" prompted cross-class alliances that justified women's political action. The military regimes' own understandings of power could not allow them to see these women as a threat (Eckstein 1989, 26). In this book, Margarita Zárate (chapter ten) discusses the practical difficulties faced by mothers in Michoacán who participated in land seizures, attended meetings, and demonstrated. Despite the difficulties, motherhood proved a profound motivation to struggle for land: mothers fought for their children and in defense of their families.

Several important points arise here. First, involvement in a resistance movement does not necessitate challenging all forms of power relations. Thus, women could use gendered discourses that limited the female sphere to tackle another form of marginality. Second, the political activism of these women does not "naturally" follow one particular line of development. Third, we must take seriously the subjectivity of historical and contemporary actors. In the case discussed here, these Catholic women saw themselves as battling religious persecution, as Christian martyrs had done millennia before. They demanded recognition of their civil rights and religious freedoms, practicing civil disobedience and other forms of resistance until their demands were met. From the perspective of the postrevolutionary state, the actions of defiant Catholics, pacific and military, were a "rebellion" and deserved to be treated as an attempt to undermine the state. On both sides of the conflict, historical actors recognized resistance.

Origins and Development of the UDCM

Founded in Mexico City (1912), the Unión de Damas Católicas Mexicanas quickly began organizing activities to educate, moralize, and entertain the poor and working class. Amid the daily hardships of civil war, members gathered medicines to combat epidemics, while protesting against the anticlerical extravagances of various revolutionary factions. In the early 1920s, new leadership encouraged greater educational and social work. Part of the lively civil society that characterized the 1920s, the UDCM continued to challenge government anticlericalism overtly and implicitly, by strengthening Catholic social action.

Membership grew rapidly. In 1925 the UDCM had 22,885 members, nearly double that of 1924. Membership tended to be highest around the capital and in Catholic strongholds. In 1925, Mexico City's regional center had 1,768 members while Puebla had 825; Guadalajara had 828 and

San Luis Potosí had 1,600.[1] In 1924, the largest regional centers, in terms of dependent local centers, were Jalisco (with twenty-seven local centers), Mexico City (with fourteen), and Puebla and Zamora (each with ten).[2] Financial contributions from regional and local centers to the national organization also indicate regional disparities and strengths; in 1924, Monterrey's centers contributed over 172.60 pesos, while Mexico's regional center offered 95 pesos. San Luis Potosí contributed 35 and Querétaro almost 30, while Guadalajara's regional center offered 20.[3]

Membership was open to all women, married and single, and fees depended upon the ability to pay; unfortunately, records do not differentiate among types of members.[4] Yet some of the members were clearly made uncomfortable by undifferentiated class mixing, and the organization had a reputation for being elitist. In Mexico City, at least, women teachers (educated but earning little) actively participated in the organization, while UDCM activities, such as night schools and unions, were extremely popular with working-class women.[5] Margarita Gómez González, for example, learned to read at a UDCM school in Guadalajara along with other "servants." A domestic worker active in Catholic social action in Guadalajara, she later worked with the Cristeros (Vaca 2006, 104–6).

The membership of married women begs the question of who UDCM husbands were and how they reacted to their wives' political activism and charitable work. Records consulted to date, however, do not provide definitive answers. In Minas Gerais, Brazil, the Apostolado da Oração (an international lay group focused on evangelization), which encouraged women's religious activism, helped members take a stand against husbands who opposed their volunteer work (Van den Hoogen 1990, 182). The same may well have been true for Mexico. But husbands were not always an issue. Dolores Palomar Arias and Margarita Gómez, both activists from Guadalajara, did not have to answer to any husbands regarding their work. Palomar was a widow and Gómez never married (Fregoso Centeno 2006, 55–56; Vaca 2006, 98–99). As a widow, mother, and good sister, Palomar had already fulfilled her female duties; even if her family did not support all of her overt and covert Catholic work, they had few grounds on which to chastise her (Fregoso Centeno 2006, 57).

Sources do not specify reasons for women's involvement in the UDCM, although genuine religious belief was undoubtedly one motivation. But national secretary Clara Arce offers us another clue, when she assured national president Elena Lascurain de Silva that she only wanted to "serve for something."[6] Serving for something appeared to be an intrinsic part of the appeal of the UDCM. In a reflection on the various roles of the UDCM, an unknown author wrote, "There are many people who think that they are not capable of anything, and it is perhaps [because] they don't know themselves well." If they knew themselves better, "they would [have] recognize[d] that God [had] given them some gifts [to share] in greater abundance than [were given] to other people . . . Those gifts [were] talent, prestige, experience, social relations, friendship, money, etc."[7] The UDCM, and the Catholic Church more generally, not only offered women the opportunity for social activism in civil society, but also encouraged women to take up important responsibilities. While the postrevolutionary government had no interest yet in women's political or civil activism, and women made few legal gains in the new constitution, the Catholic Church encouraged women's activism. Although in Bahia, the Liga Católica das Senhoras Brasileiras never had the success of the UDCM, a new identity was still emerging for Catholic women there. "Whether they participated in public charitable activities or remained in the home as housewives shaping the characters of their children, the new ideology cast these roles in the vocabulary of public militancy" (Borges 1992, 180). In Mexico, this same militancy can also be seen in how women depicted their maternal role. One dama wrote, "When the country calls [our sons] to struggle for liberty and religion, they have to be turned over not only healthy and virile but also conscious of their duties as Catholics and citizens who know how to defend their rights, give their lives for their highest ideals, and not for the convenience of a miserable salary, nor to defend petty ambitions, finally, who know how to die without vacillation FOR GOD AND FOR COUNTRY."[8]

Confronting the State

In February 1926, the implementation of constitutional Article 3, restricting religious primary education, proved a breaking point for church and state. Constitutional restrictions included the prohibition of religious primary education, the church's holding real estate, and public displays of religiosity. Until recently the historiography has focused on the armed conflict that broke out in the summer of 1926, but violence was the minority response. Nonviolent responses included legal action and lobbying, a boycott of goods and services, public demonstrations (including the continued use of churches), and day-to-day violations of the law, amid an atmosphere of fear, uncertainty, and insecurity. Catholic government employees found that their jobs were at risk. All Catholic educational institutions, even those not prohibited constitutionally, faced arbitrary closure. Continued Catholic social activities meant the threat of incarceration.[9] The events discussed below unfolded in an atmosphere of religious persecution and despair.

Moreover, there was a strong gendered element to the government's anticlericalism. Restrictions on Catholic public and private life threatened the education of children, undermining Mexican women's primary responsibility. In response, women used their gendered responsibilities to justify political action, while the government argued that they were not proper women. President Plutarco Elías Calles referred to UDCM leaders as "ladies who leave their husbands at home while they organize processions of female servants" (Calles quoted in Quirk 1973, 172–73). Unable to see beyond his own gendered framework of power, Calles could not recognize women either as political actors or as a viable threat.

The "processions of servants" that Calles dismissed were often spontaneous street demonstrations against the implementation of the constitution. A protest in Mexico City offers an interesting example of how cross-class cooperation existed, without disturbing class hierarchy. The Sagrada Familia Church, newly built in the middle-class Colonia Roma, was closed in February 1926 for government inventory, in line with the new regulations. Domestic servants, unable to attend their weekly Lenten exercises, spread the news; in response, three thousand protestors crowded the streets, ranging from other domestic servants to the wife of *El Universal* newspaper's editor. UDCM accounts highlight class differences: elite women counseled peaceful protest and calmly marched to the responsible government ministry while servants in the street attacked police and firefighters. Perhaps respectable ladies threw rocks, too. But if they had done so on a significant scale, it would have undermined their claim to moral authority based on their gender and social position. Barbara Weinstein discusses how, during the 1932 Constitutionalist Revolution in São Paulo, middle-class and elite women's appearance in the streets highlighted the extraordinary new politics of the time (2006, 32). Likewise, in Mexico, elite and middle-class women in the street, where honor and virtue were potentially threatened, proved the extent of public anger. In the aftermath, UDCM leaders were outraged that any women, regardless of class, would have been subject to government violence as the protestors were.

Class mediated gender in terms of the depictions of women's behavior, but gender mattered more than class in UDCM perceptions of an affront. The UDCM called on Catholics to drape homes and businesses in black as a public symbol of morning after the government's violent response to women demonstrators (Schell 2003, 182–83).

Protests went beyond the symbolic, seeking to hurt the national economy and undermine government programs. One such attempt was the boycott declared by Catholic lay organizations, including the UDCM. The 1926 boycott included all nonessential consumables, a refusal to pay utility bills, and abstention from sending children to state schools.[10] Having received the hierarchy's approval for the boycott, the UDCM told its regional and local committees exactly what was expected of them. UDCM centers were instructed not to reduce their work and, even if the police closed their offices, as had already happened to the Knights of Columbus, to find alternative meeting spaces. UDCM offices and UDCM-sponsored institutions (like a hospital in Zacatecas) were in fact closed; goods were confiscated and damas taken in by the police (Bernasconi Giannetto 1999, xxix–xxx).

Yet there was no need to remind UDCM members to redouble their work; the organization redoubled efforts and adapted to emerging needs. Thanks to regulations from July 1926, priests were not allowed to officiate without registering with the government, to perform religious acts outside of churches, or to participate in any political activity. Those priests who were found not to have registered were subject to imprisonment or a fine of 500 pesos (Quirk 1973, 168). Jean Meyer estimates that 3,390 priests left their rural parishes, many of them moving into the cities (Meyer 1976, 72, 75). But in the city they had neither work nor home. In Mexico City, UDCM members took on the role of caring for these men who had previously cared for others' spiritual needs. When the bishop of Huejutla, José Manrique y Zárate, was imprisoned in Mexico City, UDCM members visited him and helped ease his situation as much as possible. When two other bishops were imprisoned, it was UDCM protests that helped to free them. Those bishops who fled into exile from Mexico City counted on the UDCM to make arrangements and see them off.

For priests, the situation was equally bad or worse. Many were virtually destitute: 352 priests were initially imprisoned in Mexico City and then living in internal exile, many without friends, funds, or employment. UDCM members petitioned for their freedom and, when it was granted, found them places to live. Money for those forced abroad, medicine for the sick, and burials for those priests who died were all arranged. Knowing the importance of celebrating mass, both for the emotional well-being of these priests but also for believing Catholics, the UDCM found an estimated 65,300 homes in which to hold clandestine masses, especially for poor Catholics.[11] In July 1927, addressing the priesthood, Mexico's hierarchy singled out the UDCM for praise: "The heroic ladies, who, with exquisite charity, have received you, have taken you from prison and have found you guarantors and asylum."[12] From exile in the United States, these bishops also assured the UDCM that their work was terribly important. "[It is] in great part thanks to [the damas] that the bishops have maintained with honor and with glory the decorum of the Church in a very unequal struggle against the power of darkness."[13]

As their financial situation continued to be precarious, the exiled bishops asked the UDCM to increase its fundraising efforts. The request indicates the importance that the UDCM's day-to-day work had in the battle against the Mexican State.

> You, generous souls, charitable daughters of the Church . . . do not abandon your priests and prelates, your afflicted Mother Church when they are most in need . . . when the exiled Bishops, whose diocesan sources of incomes are destroyed, are feeling poverty the most, when so many less instructed souls abandon the [front] lines of those who work for their faith . . . Abandoning us in this moment, we say sincerely, would be for our hearts a mortal blow . . . but one that would flood us with bitterness to see ourselves in the middle of poverty without the good daughters, who from the beginning have been at our side helping and sustaining us.[14]

In this plea, the exiled bishops showed how much they had grown to count on the UDCM for moral courage and hope. Interestingly, the bishops depicted the church as a mother to this group of women who used maternity to justify public activities. The situation temporarily reversed the hierarchy of dependency: the clergy depended on women, including but not limited to UDCM members (Fregoso Centeno 2006, 56), for their survival. UDCM support assured the exiled bishops that they were not alone.

Not only priests and bishops, but Catholic laypeople were imprisoned at different points in the conflict. National president Lascurain de Silva herself was summoned before the police.[15] The Mexico City regional center, responding to the arrest of two damas and eighty other people, organized a committee to address the needs of religious prisoners. Committee members visited them in prison, bringing them food and warm clothing. The committee noted that at one point it was feeding so many prisoners that it had to use a milk wagon for deliveries. For prisoners being taken to the infamous Islas Marías prison, the committee provided money and coats. On Christmas and New Year's the damas gave all prisoners, regardless of why they were incarcerated, food. One delivery to the penitentiary included 400 clothing bundles, 800 sandwiches, and oranges. In total, from 1926 to 1928 more than 6,800 imprisoned people had received help from the damas and 10,333 meals were delivered. Not only feeding and clothing the prisoners, the damas also sought the release of the prisoners of conscience. But it was not only people at risk from the police. One zealous police officer imprisoned sanctified communion wafers: the damas managed to secure the wafers' release.[16]

The UDCM not only founded new committees, but also adapted the work of old committees. The original purpose of the Mexico City "Wardrobe Section for the Poor" was to clothe poor babies born in the general hospital, but the section also gave clothing to "people from the highest class, [who] due to the current circumstances [found] themselves now in a very bad situation."[17] In the period 1926–28, the section had given away 1,480 articles of clothing donated for "respectable people" and 6,794 articles sewn by section members. More than ten thousand other articles were given to the hospital. The section of "Perpetual Aid," which was supposed to help the "shameful poor" financially and spiritually, had increased the number of families helped from 73 in 1926 to 119 in 1928.[18] The catechism section also adapted, seeking to make up for the lack of (legal) Catholic teaching in schools by opening more catechism centers for poor and rich children alike. By 1928, in Mexico City there were seventy-two catechism centers in private homes, churches and *vecindades* (tenements), with 4,000 children attending.[19] In Guadalajara as well, clandestine catechism continued (Fregoso Centeno 2006, 55).

In an address read out at a primary school in Mexico City, one student explained the value of Catholic education: "We are all children of poor families, but in their poverty [there is] the consolation of the holy fear of God. [Our parents] cannot give us riches, as fortune has never smiled on them; they want the best inheritance that parents can give to their children to come to us: a religious education. [As] well we know, it is not lack of money that causes unhappiness in families or nations, but the [lack of]

knowledge of Christian responsibilities: the only [knowledge] that dignifies and exalts family and country."[20] Lascurain de Silva was one of the
audience members hearing this student describe faith as the most valuable, indeed the only, legacy poor parents could leave their children. For
this anonymous child or teenager, faith offered consolation, dignity, and
a belief that God was present. In attacking Catholicism, Calles and his
government undermined this student's dignity and community. Precisely
seeking to undermine this community, in February 1926, the federal government had prohibited religious participation in primary education,
based on constitutional Article 3. Until then, the government, unable to
offer places to all of Mexico's children, had turned a blind eye to Catholic
primary schools on the grounds that any education was better than none.

"Compliant Defiance"

While using legal routes to protest, and seeking an amendment to Article 3,
Catholics voiced their defiance by removing their children from state primary school (also in support of the boycott). In Guadalajara, for example,
it was reported that 22,000 students out of 25,000 school-age children
ceased attending primary school (Schell 2003, 185). Catholic schools
that complied with Article 3, not being near a church, not having a religious person in charge, and not having a religious name, could continue
to operate under the Secretaría de Educación Pública (Ministry of Public
Education, the SEP). This understanding of the regulation allowed space
for superficial compliance and covert resistance. Classes in church history and religion continued, taught outside of official hours or in a nearby
church. Children were told not to carry religious textbooks with them. Crucifixes were hidden when inspectors came to visit schools nominally under
lay authority (Schell 2003, 187).

Thus, the UDCM, along with other Catholic groups and individuals,
sought to circumvent the offending legislation. In their 1928 report, the
Mexico City regional center admitted that circumventing Article 3 was
their policy.[21] Although the UDCM had its own schools, its help was available to all Catholic schools. For example, the UDCM found trustworthy lay
people to teach or nominally take charge of a school.[22] Lascurain de Silva
became the principal of the Colegio Gratuito de San Felipe de Jesús, in
Mexico City, incorporated into the SEP as school number 232. As I have argued elsewhere, because Lascurain de Silva was frequently mentioned on

the front pages of the capital's broadsheets, this transfer of power would have fooled no one, but did obey the letter of the law. School 232's seventy students now received religious education at a nearby church.[23] Moreover, the UDCM and the SEP both presided over end-of-year examinations in the autumn of 1926 (Schell 2003, 187). In this case, a cozy relationship with the SEP school inspector helped operations continue. When inspector Toribio Velasco resigned, he hoped that he had become a friend to director Lascurain de Silva, and he assured her that he bid her goodbye with genuine feeling and not just social convention.[24]

Regulations were ignored for a variety of reasons, including personal relationships. Inspectors may have had personal ties to some schools. Additionally, as inspectors were always responsible for the same schools, personal ties could develop. Religious belief may have played a role, as well. Considering the shortage of SEP schools, inspectors may have looked the other way to keep children in education. Finally, there were too few inspectors to police schools adequately. In another case, an SEP inspector found a crucifix hanging on the wall during his inspection. Rather than closing the school, as the law demanded, the inspector warned the headmistress, who had previous notice of his visit, not to repeat the violation.

Clearly, the implementation of Article 3 depended on grassroots decisions. It also depended on support at the highest levels, which was not consistent. One Catholic school received notification that they could offer catechism at the school, in violation of Article 3, outside of regular hours; an inspector would only visit during the school day.[25] The minister of public education, José Manuel Puig Casauranc, informed the Unión de Colegios Católicos Mexicanos (Union of Mexican Catholic Schools), an association protecting the interests of Catholic education, that he would not enforce the prohibition on the display of crucifixes in primary schools, because the crucifix was not just a Catholic symbol but a universal, moral one; yet he decided not to inform Calles about his decision until the country's situation "normalized."[26]

Gendering Resistance

Faced with so much need, UDCM members were reminded that they had a responsibility to help other members and these women's families. Everyone was to subscribe to *La dama católica*, the UDCM magazine, which would serve as the principal means of communication. Because the resolution of the conflict was ultimately in God's hands, members were urged to pray. Finally, "it [was] especially hoped that women [would] maintain modesty in their dress as an external manifestation of their religiosity."[27]

Historically, ideals of women in Mexico had maintained that their virtue held up the family's honor. Here external manifestations of virtue took on a political and religious meaning, too. In 1920s Mexico, hemlines and sleeves had risen, undergarments were less constricting, and fabrics were light: Mexican women had begun to dress like flappers. Condemnations of these international fashions came from both Mexican clergy and the Vatican. So a modestly dressed woman, flouting fashion, demonstrated her virtue and Catholicism. During Lent of 1926, the young women involved in a prayer group helped devise a vow for women to dress "decently." Pledge cards were distributed around Mexico City to encourage more participation.[28] In Guadalajara, the Cruzada Feminina por la Libertad (Feminine Crusade for Liberty) also used clothing to protest; they dressed in mourning, sought to enforce the boycott in stores, sought to convince car owners to return their license plates to the government, and tried to convince parents to withdraw their children from government schools (Fernández Aceves 2000, 157).

Dress was just one means women used to live out their protest. In 1925, a group of women from Mixcoac, outside Mexico City, wrote to the archbishop explaining how they would express their anger at the seizure by government-supported schismatics of La Soledad Church in Mexico City. "We promise always to confess to Christ, showing ourselves in word and deed obedient to our Pastors and the Church's teachings, not attending shows that offend Christian morality, nor wearing fashion that sullies the virtue that should be the principal adornment of all Catholic women, ensuring that immoral publications do not enter our homes, and working so that our sons, husbands, and brothers take communion and make their lives that of practicing Christians."[29] The women understood that how they lived was itself a form of resistance that reinforced their authority, as women, over morals and the domestic sphere.

Other letters indicate the depth of anger about government anticlerical policies and women's determination to resist. Members of the UDCM in San Andres Tuxtla, Veracruz, promised Archbishop Mora y del Río that they were "prepared to take [this protest] to martyrdom, before permitting [their] churches and religion to be snatched."[30] The members of the regional center of Tehuantepec, in Oaxaca, presented themselves as "fervent apostolic and Roman Catholics" and hoped that La Soledad Church would "soon be restored to [their] true and legitimate religion, thus ending the criminal attempt that [they] protest[ed] against, as it [affected their] rights and beliefs." The women ended their letter, adding that they had already protested to Calles directly.[31]

Before the revolution, a sense of common purpose and community had been fostered through a decade of Catholic social activism. In the anticlerical climate of the revolution and afterwards, that collective purpose shifted toward defending Catholic social and religious life through any means available, as the letters cited above make clear. The concept of "oppositional consciousness" helps explain Catholic mobilization and the position taken by these women. "Oppositional consciousness . . . is an empowering mental state that prepares members of an oppressed group to act to undermine, reform, or overthrow a system of human domination. It is usually fueled by righteous anger over injustices done to the group and prompted by personal indignities and harms suffered through one's group membership. At a minimum, oppositional consciousness includes the four elements of identifying with members of a subordinate group, identifying injustices done to that group, opposing those injustices, and seeing the group as having a shared interest in ending or diminishing those injustices" (Mansbridge 2001, 4–5). Additionally, oppositional consciousness recognizes the "need for collective action to redress the perceived injustices or to overthrow the system of domination" (241). Responding to government policy, Catholics shared that righteous anger over perceived injustices and recognized the need for collective action.

Tactics of Resistance and the Renewal of Church Authority

Although religious worship was suspended and some churches seized, collective action continued in churches; the Basilica of the Virgin of Guadalupe, Mexico's religious heart, remained the focus. In mid-September 1926, the UDCM organized a pilgrimage to the Basilica, bringing spokeswomen from each center to show a national presence.[32] In late October, with the approval of the Pope, the Basilica hosted a ceremony to consecrate Mexico to Christ the King, to which Lascurain de Silva was invited.[33] Another pilgrimage to the Basilica in November 1926 was to support the Unión de Colegios Católicos Mexicanos. Part of the point was to ask the Virgin for a "cure to the difficulties that afflict the country and new blessings for Catholic Schools." Anticipated numbers were large enough that special trains were arranged to transport the children.[34] Public demonstrations of this sort fall within a broader understanding of overt tactics of resistance. By filling the churches, by processing and singing, Catholics continued to demonstrate their defiance. Prayer itself could also be an overt or covert weapon of resistance. Public prayer clearly makes a provocative statement, as bodily displays of defiance always do. Yet private prayer, in the home, could also be a strategy of resistance. Prayer as a communal act, for example, in the family home, could build and strengthen decisions to protest. Individual private prayer could provide a source of solace and a space for reflection. In all cases, prayer could fortify an individual and group to face the difficulties of maintaining the church under an anticlerical government.

These public events, private moments, and subversive activities coexisted with continued lobbying for constitutional amendments and with personal attempts to sway political leaders. The UDCM used whatever tactics were at its disposal to push for a satisfying resolution to the conflict; it also collaborated with the hierarchy in these efforts. The bishop of San Luis Potosí, Miguel de la Mora, wrote to Lascurain de Silva, on August 28, 1928, informing her that negotiations for a peaceful solution to the religious conflict could begin. He wanted "a small group of prudent, honorable, and discreet Catholic ladies of pure intentions" to begin this discussion. Because of their gender, women were invited to the highest level of private negotiations.[35]

Notions of Mexican femininity and assumptions regarding women's nature offered a strategy for use in these and other delicate negotiations. For instance, in 1929, the UDCM appealed to the president's wife, Cármen G. de Portes Gil, to use her influence to stop the deportation of women to the Islas Marías penal colony and to deliver a letter to her husband with the same request. For these convicted women, their punishment was double: being imprisoned on a remote island but also being categorized as and incarcerated with hardened criminals. A threat of sexual violence was implicit. The UDCM assumed that gender values women shared would transcend political or religious disagreements. Suggesting that Portes Gil was a responsible patriarch, the women hoped he would concede this "generous and magnanimous gesture." A delegation of "respectable ladies" delivered this letter to Mrs. Portes Gil. The enclosed letter to the president used similar rhetorical techniques, focusing on the hardship that "weak and

delicate" women would undergo in a prison for the most difficult criminals. Writing in the "name of the Mexican woman," the UDCM sought
to "knock on the door of his heart." Although asked in person to intercede, Mrs. Portes Gil refused to receive the letter for her husband.[36] UDCM
records suggest that, as in the case of the Sagrada Familia, class mitigated
gender in terms of how these convicted women were treated. The protections of gender were limited: only the poorest had been accused of rebellion.[37] Once the government realized that women were also capable of
sedition and "rebellion," they suffered repression and arrest just like men.
But clearly class continued to mediate the state's response.

Despite collaboration with the hierarchy, the conflict also forced the
UDCM into greater independence at all levels. The implications of the conflict were profoundly local, but Catholic responses were much more powerful when Catholics were united. This tension is reflected in the changes to
the organization's regulations, sought at some point in 1926, to provide
greater autonomy to local and regional centers.[38] Nonetheless, it was not
easy for the centers to function in the repressive atmosphere. In 1928, Paz
Gómez Linares reported that fourteen of Mexico City's local centers had
suspended work, as their members were "dispersed and persecuted."[39]

While the new regulations gave greater scope for autonomy, they paradoxically increased central control. The centers were reminded that the
UDCM professed "full and constant submission to the directions coming
from the Holy See." It also appears that there had been territorial conflicts
among Catholic social groups. UDCM members were reminded that "under
no circumstances, should either the Centers or the members obstruct any
activity of other institutions that [had] the healthy goal of working for the
betterment of society."[40] The central committee was also concerned that
the regional and local centers were not always collaborating sufficiently or
working for the same goals.[41] In addition, the various levels did not respect
their financial responsibility for the organization as a whole; local centers
were reminded that they must pay their "federal charge" to the national
organization.[42] While Catholics needed to present a united front to challenge the government successfully, within the UDCM, centers acted and
organized without national authorization, while also competing for local
power among other Catholic groups.[43]

The *arreglos* that ended the Cristero Rebellion, and the creation of
Catholic Action in 1929, sought to reassert the clergy's authority. The
changes to the UDCM were largely cosmetic, as far as members were con

cerned. Lascurain de Silva and Clara Arce wrote to Archbishop Pascual Díaz that the UDCM, "with light modifications that in no way alter its nature and ends, rather only a few details in its organic structure that are required in order to be one of the four fundamental organizations of MEXICAN CATHOLIC ACTION, now [became] the UNION FEMININA CATOLICA MEXICANA."[44] But the whole point of the change *was* to alter the nature and ends of the independent lay organizations, firmly subordinating them to clerical control. Their resistance had been too successful.

* * *

This chapter has addressed the UDCM and its peaceful defiance of the government's anticlerical project, seeking to open up discussions of resistance, power, and social change. Any nuanced theory of resistance requires the ethnographic thickness advocated by Ortner. That understanding of the wider context, of individual and community worldviews, and of multiple subjectivities must include serious consideration of religious belief. As a source of community cohesion that fosters the courage to resist overtly and covertly, religion has been a factor in resistance movements across place and historical period. I have analyzed a religious movement that was, in certain aspects, socially conservative and, as far as we know, populated mainly by middle-class Mexican women—yet, if resistance is taken as conscious, collective actions that directly challenge power structures, then the activities of the UDCM, hiding priests, organizing street protests, ignoring education restrictions, petitioning congress, and praying for religious liberty, have to be resistance.

In the case of the UDCM, we have seen how religion and gender created marginality while offering the means to challenge that marginality. Gender roles, although acting as a supporting structure to systems of domination, can also crack that same edifice and threaten structural integrity. UDCM grassroots resistance, defined as apolitical, reinforced gendered understandings of women's natural role: women were caretakers and the conflict created whole new categories of people in need of care, including the priests themselves. Moreover, assumptions that women were not part of a world of violence offered some protection to women that men did not have in the same situation. This protection that gender afforded has been recognized in other women's social and activist movements, such as the Madres de Plaza de Mayo (Navarro 1989, 257).

Just as the UDCM never sought to change gender roles, it did not seek to alter class structures. A formally cross-class organization, the UDCM never questioned class inequalities, either in the wider society or within the organization itself. The UDCM had no problem with disparities of wealth, as long as the poorest were able to earn a fair wage. Moreover, we see in reports how essentialist assumptions about class created a discourse in which, during street demonstrations, elite women stood decorously while domestic servants threw missiles at firefighters. Thus class was inseparable from gender.

The UDCM resisted what it considered to be a fundamental threat to its moral core. The battle fought in Mexico was for souls — and it was a clash of worldviews. The secular anticlerical state sought to undermine the most deeply held beliefs of these Catholic women and threatened their "God-given" responsibilities, of the spiritual realm and child-rearing. But members of the UDCM, like religious women elsewhere, used their religiosity to leverage positions of authority and to resist the anticlericalism of the postrevolutionary state.

Notes

Thanks to "Rethinking Histories of Resistance" workshop participants and to Stuart Durkin for their helpful comments. Earlier versions of this paper were also presented at the Guadalajara Gender Studies Seminar (Universidad de Guadalajara and CIESAS-Occidente), at the Manchester Centre for Latin American and Caribbean Studies Seminar Series, and at the ESSHC Conference (Lisbon), at which questions and comments from the audiences were most useful.

1 "Informe de la Secretaría General," *La dama católica* (January 12, 1925): 10–11.
2 "Informe de la Secretaría," n.d., Archivo Histórico de la Unión Feminina Católica Mexicana, Universidad Iberoamericana (hereafter AHUFCM) 4/23/8.
3 Goribar, "Informe de la tesorería," from October 1, 1923, to September 30, 1924, AHUFCM 4/23/12–13.
4 "Naturaleza y fin de la unión," 6, n.d. (1926 folder), AHUFCM 2/11/822.
5 "Extension de la Unión de Damas Católicas," 3, n.d., AHUFCM 6/34.
6 Arce to Lascurain, March 27, 1926, AHUFCM 2/11/655.
7 "Naturaleza y fin de la unión," 4, n.d. (1926 folder), AHUFCM 2/11/822.
8 "De la sublime . . . misión de las madres . . . ," n.d. (1926 folder), AHUFCM 2/11/769.
9 Lascurian to Calles, February 24, 1926, AHUFCM 2/11/635.
10 LNDLR and UDCM to Episcopal Committee, July 7, 1926, AHUFCM 2/11/792.
11 Gómez, "Informe de los trabajos llevados a cabo por el Centro Regional de

México de la U.D.C.M. de agosto de 1926 a diciembre de 1928," 2–3, 4, Archvio Histórico del Arzobispado de México Pascual Díaz (hereafter AHAM PD) 60/2. It is not clear how this figure was calculated.

12 "Exhortación del Sub Comité Episcopal . . . ," June 1927, AHAM Mora y del Río (hereafter MyR) 72/10.

13 Episcopal Committee to "providing committee," July 22, 1927, AHUFCM 2/12/884.

14 Ibid.

15 Juzgado Primero Numerario de Distrito to Lascurain, July 24, 1926, AHUFCM 2/11/807.

16 Gómez, "Informe," 3, AHAM PD 60/2. A full description is in May 29, 1927, AHUFCM 2/12/874.

17 Gómez, "Informe," 5.

18 Ibid.

19 Ibid., 7.

20 Anonymous, n.d., 1926, AHUFCM 2/12/859.

21 Gómez, "Informe," 5, AHAM PD 60/2.

22 Ibid.

23 Report, March 10, 1926, AHUFCM 2/11/641 and SEP statistics April 10, May 1, June 1, July 1, 1927, AHUFCM 2/12/870, 872, 876, 879.

24 Toribio to principal, February 28, 1828 [*sic*], AHUFCM 2/13/905.

25 Sylva to Lascurain, May 1, 1926, AHUFCM 2/11/690.

26 "Resumen de la contestación . . ." October 16, 1926, AHUFCM 2/11/756.

27 Lascurain to all centers, July 14, 1926, AHUFCM 2/11/799.

28 "Acción: Por la modestia cristiana," *Acción y Fe* (April 1926): 155–57.

29 Córcoles de Sanches et al. to Mora y del Río, March 19, 1925, AHAM MyR 84/3. UDCM letters of loyalty came in from all parts of the country including Mérida (March 10, 1925), Aguascalientes (March 6, 1925), and Querétaro (March 6, 1925). Residents of Coatepec, Veracruz, wrote to the pope, and included three pages of signatures (March 7, 1925) while residents of Minatitlán, in Oaxaca, wrote to the Pope in Latin (n.d.).

30 E. de Solana and Solana de Carrión to Mora y del Río, March 4, 1925, AHAM MyR 84/3.

31 Salinas vda. de Romero and Ortiz Moreno to Mora y del Río, February 28, 1925, AHAM MyR 84/3.

32 Circular 7, September 13, 1926, AHUFCM 2/11/800.

33 LNDLR executive committee to Lascurain, October 29, 1926, AHUFCM 2/11/793.

34 Unión de Colegios Católicos Mexicanos, November 10, 1926, AHUFCM 2/11/754.

35 De la Mora to Lascurain, August 28, 1928, AHUFCM 2/13/922.

36 UDCM to Cármen G. de Portes Gil and Portes Gil, all April 27, 1929, AHUFCM 2/14/946–48.

37 Arce to G. Bendini, May 20, 1929, AHUFCM 2/14/952.

38 "Proyecto de reglamento para agencias . . . ," AHUFCM 2/11/818.

39 Gómez, "Informe," 8, AHAM PD 60/2.

40 Regulations, 2, AHUFCM 2/11/819.

41 Ibid., 4.

42 Ibid., 15.

43 See Arce to Lascurain, February 4, 1926, AHUFCM 2/11/622.

44 Lascurain and Arce to Díaz, March 7, 1930, AHUFCM 2/15/974.

PART THREE

Rethinking Resistance in a Changing World

Extending the discussion begun by Patricia Pessar and Luis Nicolau Parés, these chapters offer further reflections on the way states have come to accommodate some kinds of "politics of difference," and on the emergence not only of "new actors" among the subaltern groups in society, but also of new mediators between those groups and the state. Echoing the concerns of the chapters in the first section regarding essentialist assumptions about undifferentiated subaltern groups, these chapters carefully disaggregate subaltern groups. Several even question where to place resistance itself, recognizing that the fiercest conflicts often rage within communities and that the concept of "compliant defiance" can provide a more ethnographically "thick" framework to understand not only everyday resistance and organized protest, but also apathy and resignation. These chapters also address how understandings of history, ethnicity, and culture, while being recognized as unstable, positional, and relational, feed into identity and provide powerful inspiration, justification, and opportunities for resistance.

Margarita Zárate analyzes the case of the Unión de Comuneros "Emiliano Zapata" (UCEZ), an independent rural movement that emerged in western Mexico in the 1970s. Although "peasant" social movements were still the principal protagonists at this time, the UCEZ anticipated the cultural politics of the Zapatista Army of National Liberation in Chiapas by promoting the idea that people who saw themselves as mestizo *campesinos* should reidentify with their indigenous ancestry. Zárate uses ethnographic material from a study of three socially diverse UCEZ communities to argue that it is difficult to draw a definitive line between instrumental motivations and other kinds of motivations in subaltern politics. Taking up James Scott's insight that "the struggle to define the present is a struggle to define the past," she explores the political work done by UCEZ's counterhegemonic constructions of history while emphasizing the ambivalence that persists within the UCEZ "bases" as a consequence of past experiences. She shows how issues of gender and popular religiosity complicated the UCEZ's secular community-building projects, just as they complicated the projects of radical agrarian reformers in the 1920s and 1930s. She links her argument to later chapters by exploring the movement's struggle to achieve public legitimacy and the ambiguous relationships established with political parties and state authorities by a militant movement obliged to resort to the law to achieve its agrarian goals.

Guillermo de la Peña analyzes recent processes of ethnogenesis in the Sierra of Manantlán, also in western Mexico. Local indigenous identity is shaped by their acute sense of being victims of dispossession and racist aggression by mestizos, yet, ironically, this led part of the community of Ayotitlán to abandon efforts to recover lost lands as communal property in the 1960s, and to accept a campesino political identity that would enable them to successfully petition the government for a land reform *ejido* (communal land). De la Peña shows how the failure of that pragmatic strategy to end ethnic discrimination and restrain illegal logging enabled the old Council of Elders to reemerge and challenge the new ejido authorities politically, with the support of external actors. These actors ranged, over the course of time, from left-wing activists and liberation theology clerics to university teams developing environmental conservation projects and social projects aimed at the "rescue" of cultural traditions. The entry of university teams was facilitated by favorable correlations between local dynamics and broader national and global trends. De la Peña argues that while contemporary "indigenous culture" as knowledge and practice has been shaped by these interventions, it has not been created ex nihilo: today's identities reflect a resignification of local history in terms of active and creative forms of resistance rather than simply the work of outsiders. Nevertheless, these processes do not produce a uniform "subaltern subjectivity" but a multiplicity of different subject positions including those who still defend the National Peasant Confederation model, Zapatista sympathizers, and those who engage in "New Age" expressions of indigeneity.

Interesting points of convergence emerge between shifting visions of Mexico's indigenous communities and the vicissitudes of the quilombo in Brazil, the subject of the next chapter by Ilka Boaventura Leite, who has been actively involved in the land-titling struggles of the community of Casca in Rio Grande do Sul, in the south of Brazil. Portuguese colonial legislation branded the quilombo, defined as any assembly of more than five blacks, as subversive, and the use of the term "quilombo" to denote communities formed by runaway slaves made it into an icon for the struggles of Afro-Brazilians. Leite shows that as a "transhistorical" concept quilombo has come to denote resistance in a wide variety of senses. After the Constituent Assembly of 1988, however, it acquired a formal-juridical meaning as part of a pact between state and society to remedy the historical injustice of slavery by granting communal land titles to black communities. Leite shows how tensions arise from the judicial assumption that reparations have been made to those who have resisted by surviving on the margins of society and are now being incorporated into the nation. Leite recognizes the danger that old forms of domination may be reproduced in the institutionalized quilombo. But she also shows how the polysemic metaphor of the quilombo fortifies new movements and demands, especially in urban contexts, while frustration with the slow legal progress and the opposition of big landowners and agribusiness has prompted the quilombola movement to take direct action and consequently face police repression.

In this "post-utopian" context, it seems that rights cannot be obtained without reasserting the activism of the transhistorical quilombo in new ways. This is one of the issues that Maria Gabriela Hita explores in analyzing the politics of Bairro da Paz, a poor urban neighborhood of Salvador created by a land invasion in the 1980s that has built its identity around its original resistance to eviction and continuing militancy, despite the development of more cordial relations with public power. Some of the young black people that have emerged as new political actors in this community explicitly embrace the idea of declaring their *bairro* an "urban quilombo." Yet as Hita demonstrates, despite their clear ethnic consciousness, links to the militant black movement, and tendency to critique the capitalist system, these new political actors hold positions with many ambiguities in regard to the state, public-private partnerships, and the values of a global consumer society. Nevertheless, as Hita shows by comparing the youth groups with the community Residents' Council and some of the religious associations that play an important part in community politics, despite the existence of the same kind of "polyphony" of subaltern voices that Zárate and de la Peña identify, Bairro da Paz has maintained a degree of collective coherence in its negotiations with public authorities. More marginal actors, such as women associated with Bairro da Paz's nonelite *terreiros*, have not been excluded. While sharing the concerns of other contributors about the negative impacts of political clientelism and the deradicalizing potential of some NGO interventions and neoliberal approaches to managing "participation" and the politics of difference, Hita points out that community activists' consciousness of these problems might be one way of diagnosing what is new about today's resistance in a community that has built its identity around that very concept.

The final two chapters in this section return to Mexican examples. Helga Baitenmann continues the discussion of the implications of factionalism within subaltern populations by examining how campesinos use the new agrarian courts created after the constitutional changes that ended land redistribution in 1992. She takes her cue from William Roseberry's observation that the existence of land conflicts between peasant communities and haciendas, or between peasant communities and the state, should not blind us to the fact that today and in the past some of the most violent conflicts have occurred within and between indigenous and peasant communities themselves. In using the post-1992 agrarian institutions to pursue ongoing conflicts over land, peasant groups or individuals ask the courts to issue an *amparo*, a legal recourse originally introduced as a protection against procedural abuses by the state. Although the amparo was of great importance to landlords in the early years of land reform, it can now be an instrument by which one part of the state determines that another part of the state did not treat peasant claimants correctly. Baitenmann shows how neoliberal changes to agrarian reform have ironically led to an extended, rather than diminished, state involvement in matters of rural land tenure, since the courts have had to expand legal procedures beyond what was envisaged by the 1992 reforms. Furthermore, by privileging the resolution of violent conflicts over procedural formalities, the courts have in practice created a form of grant making. In this sense, a new agrarian reform program has been produced in which peasant resistance has played a central role, albeit not via the kinds of scenarios originally envisaged by critics of the neoliberal approach to agrarian matters.

Matthew Gutmann rounds off this section with a trenchant critique of the notion of subaltern agency that has dominated both resistance and social movement theory. Even if there are virtues in not painting subalterns as hapless and passive, and strong evidence that protests and defiance of existing power relations have changed history, he argues that an exagger-ated celebration of popular agency has left us bereft of theoretical tools to analyze not only failed resistance but also the frequency of compliance, collaboration, apathy, and passivity. Using ethnographic examples from a neighborhood in Mexico City with a long history of activism, and Oaxaca, the scene of a major mobilization against an unpopular state government that brought together a plurality of dissident social and political forces vio-lently repressed by federal government police action, Gutmann critiques the political as well as theoretical positions that have dominated the aca-demic field of resistance theory. He proposes a more dialectical approach that reflects the inspiration of Gramsci, as well as anthropological ana-lyses of rituals of protest that maintain, rather than undermine, existing power relations. Arguing that if resistance theories become no more than a means of opposing utopian dreams of worlds free from poverty, racism, and militarization, they are part of the problem rather than its solution, Gutmann proposes that his own concept of "compliant defiance" can pro-vide an ethnographically grounded framework for reintegrating the analy-sis of covert and sporadic acts of everyday resistance and overt organized protests, while tackling the need to understand the dialectics of mobiliza-tion, apathy, resignation, and self-blame.

CHAPTER TEN

Tracing Resistance

Community and Ethnicity in a Peasant Organization

MARGARITA ZÁRATE

The term "resistance" has become common currency in the discourses of diverse movements. It is used by peasants, students, trade unions, and religious minorities within the politics and infrapolitics of the subordinate. This chapter discusses the shapes that resistance took in a rural indigenous organization that has been depicted as combative and independent from the state. Community and ethnicity were at the center of this organization's actions; past and present were remembered and recreated in their struggle. Yet, as in every social movement, the protagonists, their motivations, and their actions were as diverse as they were controversial.

Community and Ethnicity: Weapons of Resistance

In my own work, *En busca de la comunidad: Identidades recreadas y organización campesina en Michoacán* (1998), I had argued that peasants—the subalterns—are not socially homogeneous but that their adoption of gender and ethnic identities was fluid and constituted a negotiated domain of "facts" and "meanings." Sherry Ortner (1995) argues that those who resist do more than simply oppose domination, more than merely produce a virtually mechanical reaction. They have their own politics, not only between bosses and *comuneros* or between landowners and peasants, but within every local category of tension and friction: women and men, parents and children, adults and adolescents.[1] Therefore, those occupying different subject positions will have different, even opposing, but still legitimate, perspectives on the situation. The Unión de Comuneros Emiliano Zapata (UCEZ, Emiliano Zapata Union of Communal Landholders) deserves its reputation as an important example of an independent rural movement, particularly at the end of the seventies, a decade in which peasant movements acquired a central role in Mexico.

Founded in Tingambato, Michoacán, in 1979, the UCEZ was a "reactive" response to significant repression and demands for land that had been ignored. Within four years, the UCEZ had become the second most important peasant organization in Michoacán, representing the demands of almost 150 communities and *ejidos*. With a strong agrarian orientation and predominately "indigenous" membership, the UCEZ was also the peasant organization with the greatest capacity for resolving agrarian disputes. The three "communities" discussed here have divergent histories and situations. Zirahuén has a history of combative behavior toward the state and other outside agencies, while emphasizing both the past and present to form its "ethnic" identity. Essential to Zirahuén is its lake, which has been threatened by pollution from outside. Concerns about the water's purity intertwine with issues of land cultivation and the struggle for land, which combined would ensure long-term reproduction of "community." The second community, Ixtaro, is a mestizo pueblo within an old hacienda that does not now have and never has had the legal status of *comunidad indígena* (as an agrarian or Indian village). The third is an urban community with the social characteristics of the urban *colonias populares*: the Colonia Comunal Emiliano Zapata, born of a land invasion in March 1990. Each of these communities is located in the southeastern municipality of Salvador Escalante in Michoacán (Zárate 2007, 154).[2]

In my earlier work (Zárate 1998) I argued, however, that analysis of the UCEZ's independence and radicalism must be nuanced and, with this intention, I discussed the organization's impact on three particular communities in the state of Michoacán (Zirahuén, the Colonia Comunal Emiliano Zapata, and Ixtaro), in which the struggle for land and building a sense of community were its principal tasks. I discussed the UCEZ's ambiguous and contradictory relations with official and state representatives, their appeal to and reinterpretation of national legislation, their subsequent exaggeration and readaptation of classic agricultural demands, and their relationship with actors of diverse political views. This analysis of local processes sheds light on the complex nature of the UCEZ's work, and on its concrete results, while demonstrating how these processes also formed the organization.

Gender and the Communal Project

Women's activism in the UCEZ showed similarities to women's activism in other social movements (including urban movements), because the UCEZ provided women with leadership roles and faced the difficulties and benefits of their participating. Each member's experience as a woman, a friend, and a wife was recreated and redefined in and through the "struggle." Being a woman was constructed through maternity, thus privileging the sphere of the private, and reinforced by the gender stereotypes of some of the male members of the organization, who considered motherhood an "impediment" not only to work in the fields but to political participation, a prejudice reinforced by the belief of some leaders that women were less capable of making decisions than men.

The constant UCEZ demands to participate in trips, meetings, and demonstrations put a great burden on young women with small children. These women admitted that they faced significant difficulties in adapting to the demands of their new situation. Their domestic role certainly constrained and defined their activities, but the fact of having children was not a problem in itself and, from another perspective, could be considered a motivation. For these women, having children and needing a home provided the principal impetus to participate in a struggle for land. For example, Salud, from Zirahuén, emphasized how the land would be her daughters' inheritance. Throughout these testimonies, there was a recurring insistence that "women defend the family." Activism in the UCEZ was part of defending the family.

Religion and gender roles also intertwined; the chapel in the Colonia Comunal Emiliano Zapata provided an organizational center for women, around which they arranged other activities such as parties or keeping watch for suspicious strangers and police who might be coming to evict the residents. As Patience Schell argues (chapter nine), women's "natural" roles could provide them with a legitimate discourse to engage in politics, challenge the state, and defend their religious faith. Besides, having a chapel inside the colonia constituted a blow against the secularist aims of the UCEZ, while demonstrating the deep roots of conflictual identities in Michoacán and how they transcend the ideological programs of organized movements. The secularism of the leaders, however, caused tensions. Efrén Capiz's (the main UCEZ leader) discomfort was revealed the day that the colonia celebrated its third anniversary on the festival of St. Rosario de Tlapa, whose image had been given by a "rich man" (the owner of a sawmill) to the chapel. The donation of this image was significant since it foregrounded important tensions and contradictions, centered on religion and power issues that permeated not only this colonia, but also Ixtaro and Zirahuén. An ambiguous relationship existed between comuneros and the *patrones* (old and new employers), reflected in the way the economically powerful came to occupy a central role in the community's relationship with the sacred. The contradiction between the secular tendencies of the UCEZ and a deeply rooted popular faith emerged again when Capiz showed his frustration that the chapel had been built at all, at the expense of a communal education and meeting place. The construction of this community space was again postponed, to construct primary school classrooms and a kindergarten. In Michoacán, this type of conflict had historical precedents, as Marjorie Becker argues: "For example, in 1934 the cardenistas [supporters of President Lázaro Cárdenas] organized the Congreso Femenil Socialista in Pátzcuaro. Tarascan women dressed in traditional blue shawls heard speeches extolling 'schools, rather than churches; workshops, rather than seminaries; cooperatives, rather than saints and alms boxes'" (1987, 458). But when the women presented their demands, these demands for rural investment reflected their own priorities: "The women asked for churches, for their cooperatives; for workshops, for schools for their children; and for arms to defend the government" (459).

During the twenties and thirties, Ixtaro experienced the conflicts associated with *agrarismo*, the agrarian reform movement, and the Cristero Rebellion (see chapter eight). Jesús's testimony very clearly describes his experience of these turbulent times for Ixtaro's inhabitants, the role of popular religious faith, and the anti-agrarista activities of the church and its priests, aided by the sharecroppers associated with the hacienda: "I remember when the Cristeros came, they organized an assembly in the square. At the same time, another assembly gathered to divide the lands of the hacienda. There were many sharecroppers, some of them had cultivated with four or five ploughs and they told people: 'don't take part in the land redistribution because the priest won't allow us to confess.' They did not want the land redistribution." Thus, the economic and social power associated with the old landowning class had been preserved not only by economic means, but also by a strong association with Catholic symbols, within a hierarchical social system.

Roger Keesing (1992) proposes that any analysis of resistance must focus on the actors' consciousness, thus searching for a political motivation; without political motivation resistance becomes displaced resistance. Following this line of thought, Schell (chapter nine) discusses how religion and gender trigger and offer strategies to defy conditions seen as unfair, while supporting Patricia Pessar's argument (chapter six) that the Enlightenment's secularism permeates the academy. In this same vein, Ortner identifies a certain hostility toward religion, stemming from Marxism, in the work of diverse authors. In the best of cases this leads us to marginalize religious factors, providing only "thin" cultural analysis (Ortner 1995, 181). Pessar's analysis of millenarian movements in Brazil shows that if religion is marginalized, we lose sight of the fact that religious norms and symbols in rural Brazil provided ethical and conceptual guides with which the rural inhabitants forged their material and social lives. In the three communities discussed here, Catholicism served both to justify and reinforce economic inequalities and yet offered a space from which resistance to such inequalities could be organized.

Gender combined not only with religious belief but also with ethnic identity through practices and discourses of honor, the purity of blood, and norms and sanctions related to being female or male. Women's participation, and their motives and practices, transgressed, conveyed, and mocked the hegemonic norm. As Susan Gal (2002) argues, silence is an important means of resistance. The testimonies of women members of the UCEZ indicate their respect for women who speak up, and not only to challenge those who wanted to take their lands, but also to challenge UCEZ leaders or their husbands. One of these women questioned the role of the leader in her particular community: "He only wanted deaf and dumb people." For other women, speaking up was difficult. Another one said, "I didn't say anything during the assemblies. We were asked our opinions, our thoughts. And I thought, what if I say this and it's wrong?"

According to Gal, there is a close relationship between gender, the use of speech or silence, and the exercise of power, but at the same time the relationship is not a direct one. On the contrary, she argues that silence, like any other linguistic form, gains different meanings and has different material effects within specific cultural and institutional contexts. Silence and inarticulateness are not necessarily evidence of powerlessness in and of themselves; silence can also be understood as a strategic action. Similarly, relationships of gender and domination are perpetuated and sometimes subverted in social institutions such as schools, courts, and political assemblies. Speaking is frequently used to judge, define, and legitimate those who speak. Thus, verbal interaction, whatever its end may be, is frequently the site of struggle over definitions of power. It is through linguistic practices that those who speak within institutions impose their understanding of people and their actions upon others. This capacity to force others to accept one's representation of the world and act accordingly is another aspect of symbolic domination. But this does not happen without resistance: devaluated strategies and linguistic genres can be celebrated despite extended denigration. Language is a politicized field through which oppositional thought is enacted and through which cultural territory is preserved. Language, in this sense, becomes disputed territory.

Past and Present of the Community—Practices and Discourses of Resistance

In my previous work (1998), I have discussed the importance of the concept of community in people's experience through their diverse discourses, and evaluated the UCEZ's project as an attempt to rebuild an idea of community while the UCEZ faced devastating social change: the depopulation and abandonment of the Mexican countryside. Here James Scott's central contention is pertinent: "The bond between domination and appropriation means that it is impossible to separate the ideas and symbolism of subordination from a process of material exploitation. In exactly the same fashion, it is impossible to separate veiled symbolic resistance to the ideas of domination from the practical struggles to thwart or mitigate exploitation. Resistance, like domination, fights a war on two fronts" (1990, 188). Thus, a central element of both discursive and organized social practices of resistance revolve around the search for community. The UCEZ movement found itself rooted in what Alan Knight (1992) called the continuity of protest.

The symbolic importance of Emiliano Zapata, the revolutionary general who fought for land restitution and whose name the organization took, was evident in people's testimonies. For these people, Zapata was "the person who fought for the land and defended the rights of the people and because of that, [our organization] was given his name." Or, as another resident expressed it, "Emiliano Zapata was someone who struggled for land and liberty, which before was just for the landowners." Others referred to the decision of the UCEZ leader, Efrén Capiz, to explain the choice: "Our colonia is called Emiliano Zapata because Capiz said that this was the name that we had to give it," or another would say, "Capiz said that Emiliano Zapata was a good name because he always struggled for land." Others explicitly presented Capiz as the heir of Zapata: "Before that man [Capiz], Zapata always fought for the lands, for the wellbeing of the poor, for the revolution." The UCEZ attempted to recreate what they understood as the collective forms of work and decision-making within indigenous communities and underlined the importance of the communal assembly as an organ of decision-making. This approach did not simply derive from the participation of the indigenous communities, but also reflected how the UCEZ leadership based its activism upon their interpretation of community governance. This project conceived the recuperation and the updating of indigenous practices as a means of resistance and cultural reproduction when confronting the transformative power of capitalism.

The UCEZ's official discourse underlined the importance of a "communal culture" as a form of resistance when confronted with economic exploitation and the plundering of land. Yet this discourse about communalism had a wide spectrum of meanings. Its principal meaning came from the emphasis on the legal defense of communal lands as opposed to private property. However, the UCEZ's practices went beyond constitutional legislation. Helga Baitenmann (chapter fourteen) offers an illustrative discussion of how, through law and its practical application, the legal, the illegal, and the extralegal coexist. Likewise, the UCEZ, by questioning the judicial system, reinterpreted the law to validate the diversity of political cultures in rural Mexico. One of the UCEZ's distinctive features came from Capiz's idea of community, which fused notions of utopia, *indigenismo*, and socialism in a synthesis that attracted the widest possible range of actors for the movement, but sacrificed stability. The notion of community also builds on a shared past and traditions. Anthony Cohen (1985) argues that it would be a mistake to characterize such approaches as being simply traditionalist, thus implying that a community was stuck in its own past and unable to face the present.

In the case of these three communities, the past has been used as a resource in diverse ways, through selective construction that resonates with contemporary concerns. For most community residents, the past is selectively remembered for current purposes and without historical rigor. This is shown in loose categories such as: "the old days," "when I was young," "our ancestors' times," and "in time immemorial." The last phrase is most often used as part of an argument to "recover" ancestral lands: "They have been our lands from time immemorial." To paraphrase Cohen, history is wonderfully malleable, for academic historians or for anyone else. Even when there is not a conscious intention to distort history, it is always built on interpretation. The imprecision of these references to the past in UCEZ testimonies, timeless and disguised as history, is what makes them a particularly apt apparatus for expressing the continuity of the past and present symbolically, and for reaffirming the cultural integrity of the community faced with its apparent subversion by the forces of change.

This point is also illustrated by Guillermo de la Peña's analysis of ethnogenesis in southern Jalisco (chapter eleven), in which he found that sustainable development promoted the renewal of ancestral knowledge. Likewise, past and present become equally relevant for Ilka Boaventura Leite's discussion of the quilombo (chapter twelve); she found that those excluded from citizenship, victims of racism, referred both to their slave past and to occupied land to demand legal recognition. Luis Nicolau Parés (chapter seven) found a similar process in his analysis of Candomblé, in which the continuity between past and present is central; as a black activist commented, "Black women in Candomblé have been resisting for centuries and we are still here to resist whether they like it or not" (147).

These processes echo Cohen's notion of the atemporality and use of history already mentioned; they also point to the centrality of the cultural concept of tradition, which Raymond Williams (1981, 187) also defined as "reproduction in action," since tradition, "our cultural heritage . . . is self-evidently a process of deliberate continuity, yet any tradition can be shown, by analysis, to be a selection and reselection of those significant received and recovered elements of the past which represent not a necessary but a *desired* continuity." Desire is not abstract, he explains, but rather, it resides in the context of existing social relations. Selectivity is also central in the way certain meanings and practices are chosen and others are excluded from the past and present. Even more crucially, some of these meanings and practices are reinterpreted, diluted, or understood in ways that support, or at least do not contradict, other elements within the dominant culture.

The Ejército Zapatista de Liberación Nacional (EZLN, Zapatista Army of National Liberation) uprising of 1994 in Chiapas gave a breath of fresh air to land demands in these communities, and the UCEZ took part in some of the meetings to support this new Zapatista movement. Capiz attended the Primera Reunión Nacional de Indígenas y Campesinos (First National Meeting of Indigenous Peoples and Peasants, March 13–14, 1994) in Chiapas, at which he gave a speech that emphasized the struggle for land through the mythology of national heroes: Miguel Hidalgo, José María Morelos, Pancho Villa, and Emiliano Zapata. Also mentioned were the martyrs of the guerrilla struggles in the state of Guerrero in the sixties and seventies: Genaro Vázquez and Lucio Cabañas. The meeting reiterated indigenous peoples' right to have their own government, make their own laws, and defend their cultures and traditions. Both the EZLN and the UCEZ shared a strong rejection of the reforms made to constitutional Article 27 that had enshrined land redistribution. Regarding the end of land reform the UCEZ and the EZLN had similar views, according to Neil Harvey: "The end of agricultural reform in Chiapas and other states also canceled out the hope of a piece of land for thousands of *campesinos* (peasants). In this respect, we should distinguish between effects which are directly measurable in terms of land purchases, etc. and those which operate more at the level of expectations, hopes and fears. It seems clear that the end of the land reform constituted a symbolic break with the past, but one which offered no guarantees of improvement for the future" (1994, 25). The UCEZ was founded within a wider context of structural conditions that determined its development. The peasant movement was a product of a long historical process of plundering land and exploitation; this process was exacerbated over the last quarter of the previous century by the way the new form of capitalist accumulation in the countryside intensified the pressure on land and natural resources, as well as increasing the rate of migration to the United States. From the early 1980s, neoliberal changes included a decline in state investment in rural development, a precipitous fall in agricultural credit, the end of subsidies for seeds and fertilizers, the end of guaranteed pricing, and the deregulation of markets, as well as the implementation in 1994 of the North American Free Trade Agreement and the reform to Article 27 (see chapter fourteen, this volume) (Espinosa and Meza 2000, 87).

Natural resources were also under increasing pressure. John Gledhill argues that despite legislation and mechanisms for policing and conservation, there is continuing devastation of the forestry resources of Michoacán, illustrating how a combination of social inequality and political impunity lead to disastrous environmental consequences. "External demand for timber is insatiable, the profits of overexploitation are high for entrepreneurs and poorly paid state functionaries make poor policemen. Those who run the illegal logging operations are notorious for their excellent connections with leading members of the ruling party in the capital and are frequently to be found playing the role of the principal bosses (*caciques*) of the ruling Partido Revolucionario Institucional (PRI) within the regions in which they operate, if not openly, then as leading power brokers behind the scenes" (Gledhill 1995, 11).

The extraction of oil and minerals, cattle raising, the intensive exploitation of forests for timber, the appropriation of irrigated lands, accelerated urban development, and the intensification of the process of migration have been based on despoilment and subordination. Although the UCEZ emphasized its own legality, its actions followed a consistent pattern in its ambiguous and contradictory relationship to power; this is exemplified by its relationship with Cardenismo (both in the thirties and in its reincarnation in the eighties and nineties), with the law, and with political parties and other political organizations. William Roseberry (1994, 363) explains this hegemonic process as follows:

> We can also see how forms and languages of protest or resistance *must* adopt the forms and languages of domination in order to be registered or heard. "Y venimos a contradecir" is a powerful statement of community solidarity and opposition, but to be effective it is addressed to the proper colonial authorities, it follows (ritualistically) the proper forms of address and order of presentation, and it is registered in the proper colonial offices. It recognizes and addresses power even as it protests it, or it decries the abuse or misuse of power, implicitly recognizing a legitimate use of the same power. To the extent that a dominant order establishes such legitimate forms of procedure, to the extent that it establishes not consent but prescribed forms for expressing both acceptance and discontent, it has established a common discursive framework.

However, such frameworks have a problematic and fragile nature; they can be broken, for instance, by the languages of solidarity used by subordinate groups.

Through collected oral histories, I tracked the historical roots of agricultural conflict in these communities; some testimonies focused on the role of the Catholic Church and its alliance with the rich. Other testimonies focused on the experiences of living on haciendas; many alluded to the use of violence; some, the eldest, remembered how the foreman did not allow them to glean in the cornfields and how they were beaten with a snake-skin belt when they tried. Another woman remembered how the patrones sent horses to chase them when they harvested the corn on hacienda land. As Roseberry argues, with reference to Scott: "The dominated *know* they are dominated, they know by whom and how; far from consenting to that domination, they initiate all sorts of subtle ways of living with, talking about, resisting, undermining and confronting the unequal and power-laden worlds in which they live" (1994, 357).

It was precisely the UCEZ's emphasis on the recovery of land that fostered a sense of security and legitimacy for its participants. The insistence on land "recovery," as opposed to invasion, is an example of the power of language and the importance of discursive resources in convincing people to join the UCEZ. The term invasion is rejected for its connotation of illegality, showing the UCEZ's determination to make use of existing loopholes in national legislation.

In the case of the UCEZ, factionalism, controversies over leadership styles, struggles for resources, *caciquismo* (boss politics), and new external pressures definitely became the central features of the situation in the mid-1990s, when I finalized my fieldwork. The cases analyzed—Zirahuén, the Colonia Comunal Emiliano Zapata, and Ixtaro—showed how UCEZ organizing followed different trajectories, depending on the nature and context of each local situation. The case of Zirahuén, for example, showed that indigenous historical roots and the defense of "the community" underscored the whole process, even as a deep factionalism that was historically rooted in the community was also updated. Similarly, old problems regarding leadership and caciquismo reappeared in modern forms. Factional discourses were centered on demands and counterdemands to conform to the "true community." Legality was an important theme, particularly in relation to legitimacy. The emphasis placed on holding historic land deeds illustrated two essential elements of legitimacy of landholding: the official acknowledgement of communal property (be its origins colonial or recent); and the concern for the stigmatizing and "authentication" of the actors who had been subjects of discrimination and social marginalization due to their ethnic identity and poverty. In Zirahuén, the dedication with which people defended their lands, forests, and particularly the lake was notable. The conservative and resistant position of the comuneros faced with "modernization" and "development" was also a reflection of their desire to recover the imagined, remembered, historical community. Thus, although the conflict that took place in Zirahuén on one level represented traditional struggles for recovering land, this conflict also constituted a creative response to social conditions of capitalist modernization.

In Ixtaro, economic differences and the breakdown of relationships of patronage and clientelism with landowners are of fundamental importance. Sharecroppers were the main instigators of the land takeover. As owners of ploughs and oxen, they were actually better off than others in the settlement. Landowners in that area were related by kinship, so that the new patrones were in a sense seen as a continuation of the old *hacendados*. Furthermore, the remains of the hacienda are still in the center of the community, and the hacendados' heirs live there. Some people did remark on the outside origin of those people, on their skin, hair color, and blue eyes. At least one name of a nearby hamlet, Españita (which used to be property of the hacendado's family), is a constant reminder of this origin. Nevertheless, in some accounts, land, a lot, the house, and the church are seen as presents given by the hacendados, who are therefore, in this case, also seen as constitutive of the community. Furthermore, some people considered themselves *rancheros* and Ixtaro is known widely as a *rancho*.[3]

The Colonia Comunal, in contrast, represents a model of partial proletarianization, pointing to the importance of growing corn as complementary to wage labor, even in urban contexts. Nonetheless, families tended to abandon this practice, despite its apparent advantages, because it could not fulfill their subsistence needs. Thus, being part of the UCEZ provided residents with a sense of belonging and identity that accomplished an important function within their social resistance against exploitation, domination, and the inequality that they suffered.

In practice, however, in all three cases, communal land tenancy was lived as "private property" or a "little piece of land." Within each community, people openly defended their right to have a small plot to grow corn, as well as the additional option to work anywhere as wage workers, rather than committing themselves unconditionally to the demands and the organization of collective action for land. Only a few had completely abandoned rural life, but they were trapped in a dilemma, between their intention to rebuild the community and the real difficulties that they faced as individuals.

In 2005, shortly after Capiz's death, the sixth meeting of the Congreso Nacional Indígena en la Región Centro Pacífico (National Indigenous Congress of the Central Pacific Region) took place in Zirahuén. In the congress's documentation, Zirahuén is called the Caracol Zapatista Erupción de Rebeldía (Zapatista Conch Shell Eruption of Rebelliousness). The Declaration of Zirahuén eulogized Capiz for his role in the land struggle and for his dignity, while recognizing "the struggle of Zirahuén's community for the defense of their lands, mountains and water, with a spirit which is the legacy of General Emiliano Zapata and . . . their decision to confirm their vocation of autonomy by constituting the Zapatista Conch Shell Eruption of Rebelliousness in the Blue Lake of Zirahuén, to fully exercise their rights, and to resist the aggressions of the Mexican state and big money that desires their lands, through the development of tourist and urban projects and the destruction of their territory, including the lake's existing biodiversity."[4] The Colonia Comunal Emiliano Zapata's struggle, similar in many ways, arose from changes at a regional level: the growth of urban centers and the lack of services and employment opportunities. But this case shows, with particular clarity, that it is difficult to recover old social practices in a changing world. Thus, transformations at the level of "traditional" family sustenance, for instance, were most in evidence in the Colonia Comunal, and in Ixtaro, where the contradictory character of relationships among subalterns and elites was illustrated. Jesús, for instance, maintained a nostalgic vision of the hacienda and the patrones:

> I worked very hard in the hacienda of the Barreras, with don Genaro. He gave me the plot where I live. At that time, everything was cheaper, I earned fifty cents per week and it was enough. We were given a *cuartillo*,[5] five measures of corn, one liter of beans. Monday was the day that we were given everything. With five cents, I could buy lots of bread. Those times were good because everything was cheap. Afterwards, I did not have ejidal land. Only a little land was distributed. Most of the people remained day laborers. Don Genaro died leaving some lands opposite Picuarembo and the rest of them were sold to other landowners.

His wife María added, "I would like those patrons to be here now. A cow cost twenty-five pesos, an ox thirty. Go and see if you can buy one now!"

Scott's analysis of peasant attitudes toward the past and present illustrate a similar process:

> As in any history, assessing the present forcibly involves a re-evaluation of what has gone before. Thus, the ideological struggle to define the present is a struggle to define the past as well. Nowhere is this more apparent than in the accounts given by poor villagers, who have had the least to be thankful for over the past decade and whose current prospects are bleak. They have collectively created *a remembered village and a remembered economy* that serve as an effective ideological backdrop against which to deplore the present. They remember when rents were paid after the crop was in and reflected the actual harvest. They remember the time before mechanization, when large landowners sought them out as tenants and when rents were modest. They remember when harvest work was plentiful and larger farmers curried favor with them by giving advance wages, loans, and *zaka* gifts and throwing larger feasts to which they were invited. (1985, 179)

Ethnicity and Recreation of Identity

In my previous work (1998), I examined the link between UCEZ membership and ethnic identity. In discussing ethnicity, it is vital to "investigat[e] the importance of ethnicity *in people's lives*" (Eriksen 1993, 134). Ethnicity is the systematic and enduring communication of cultural differences between groups that see themselves as distinct. Ethnicity appears when cultural differences are perceived as relevant to social interaction. Accordingly, ethnicity is both relational and situational: the ethnic character of a social encounter is contingent upon the situation. In other words, it is not absolute. Thus, my starting point was to consider ethnicity as a relationship between and among groups: ethnicity exists *between* and not inside such groups.

Ethnic identities, groups, and beliefs about culture or shared history are creations, either due to historical circumstances, key events, or unexpected consequences of political projects. As a result, we must consider J. D. Y. Peel's critical observations (1989) regarding the presentist orientation in social anthropology and the necessity of taking historical accounts more seriously, both as sources which document facts more or less accurately and as serious attempts by the "natives" to understand their past.

In this respect, some of the comuneros, mainly in Ixtaro, had even more utilitarian goals from their identity. They were fighting for land and so, as Jonathan Okamura (1981) indicates, they "selected" their ethnic identity accordingly. It is difficult, however, to draw an inflexible border between those objectives that are instrumentally motivated and other motivations. For instance, Modesta, a combative activist of the indigenous community of Ixtaro, was a convinced "community maker." Nevertheless, she also had personal hopes to obtain land for herself and that the UCEZ could win more government investment through political pressure. Modesta was also very aware of her place in a highly differentiated society; moreover, she related class stratification to skin color and ethnic group. Pointing to such processes, Scott argues that "it is precisely the fusion of self-interest and resistance that is the vital force animating the resistance of peasants and proletarians" (1985, 295).

One of the categories UCEZ members contested was *gente de razón* (people of reason), part of the package of hegemonic ideas imposed by the colonial order, which has been used more generally to distinguish Indians (as people "without reason") from mestizos. Being "people of reason" demarcates a racist and discriminatory category excluding only Indians. Reason means, in this context, the capacity to think, judge, and be "civilized." In two testimonies, there was an explicit reference to reason. In Salud's statement, in spite of wearing the "vestido de razón" (or in other words the *vestido de mestizo*), she is an Indian. Relia, a comunera from Zirahuén, was more specific when she said that people who have "another reason" have another way of dressing. Yet it is noteworthy that Relia talked about people who have another reason in a more relativistic and comprehensive sense. It would seem, then, that she rejects the discriminatory connotation of the phrase, but in a way that implicitly accepts an idea of innate spiritual differences between social categories that may serve as a means of revalorizing stigmatized identities, but has also played an important role in the defense of both ethnic and gender inequalities against the claims of liberal and egalitarian ideologies in postcolonial Latin American societies.

Generally, members of the UCEZ from these three communities defined their own identities in terms of *raza* (race), blood, and their Indian past.

The majority identified themselves as "Indians," leaving aside the racist and pejorative implications of this category from the point of view of the non-Indians (Bonfil Batalla 1981). Alcida Ramos, examining the transformations to the term "Indian" as a result of the pan-Indian movement in Brazil, notes a similar trajectory:

> They have transformed *Indian* from a derogatory term to a key concept in their politics of contact . . . The appropriation of Indian by the Indians has exorcised the heaviest spells of discrimination associated with the term. Of course, this does not mean that discrimination no longer occurs. What it means is that discrimination is now expressed in other ways . . . But Indian is no longer a dirty word. In fact it has gained legitimacy by the use to which it is put and the context in which it is used. The Indian is now a well-known political figure on the national scene. (Ramos 1998, 119–20)

Likewise, the UCEZ used Indian identity to promote and effectively affirm a political identity, when faced with an official discourse whose popular meaning is of the inferiority of Indians and of *mestizaje* as a route toward progress and which has sought, in practice, to divide and to fragment "popular movements." Some of the testimonies of the members explicitly discussed how belonging to the UCEZ provided them with an Indian identity. Ethnic identity issues and belonging to the community also provided strong foundations upon which they reclaimed social dignity and defended themselves against discrimination in their daily lives.

But at the same time, embracing an Indian identity did not necessarily mean eschewing a mestizo one. Capiz himself emphasized a mestizo identity, while at the same time stating that he shared the same blood with the Indians, in a speech made during a demonstration in Morelia, capital of Michoacán state.[6] From this position he could reconcile two apparently contradictory perspectives, relativizing essentialist positions in order to give priority to the Indian comuneros' land demands. "Many say that not all people belonging to the UCEZ are Indian, many people are mestiza. So what. Do we, mestiza people, not share the same origin and the same blood of our ancestors? We are really Indians, in the same way as there are real [Indian] communities. For this reason, this meeting and this parade have been named 'Indian Dignity.'" Similarly, in a reflection about the concept of mestizaje and the ethnic-racial auto-ascriptions in Cuzco, Perú, Marisol de la Cadena (2000) asserts that the Cuzco comuneros defined themselves as mestizos, and thus as non-Indians. However, mestizo identity was so broad that it included indigenous people with urban education and even allowed for the continuation of regional customs, which the Cuzco population called *auténticas* or *neto* (authentic) and which anthropologists termed "indigenous."

To summarize, the UCEZ's practices and discourse combined and sought to mediate, although not without problems, two contemporary political cultures. On the one hand, they had appropriated symbols that are associated with national elite culture, "attempting to shift the balance of power by subverting particular symbols from within" (Hale 1994a, 28). The most obvious example of this appropriation is the reference to Emiliano Zapata and other national heroes. On the other hand, the UCEZ questioned, not without ambiguity, popular visions that implicitly or explicitly replicated the "premise of a natural hierarchy between Indian and mestizo culture" (Hale 1994b, 27) and the premise of the inevitable assimilation of the former by the latter.

The UCEZ also used an "Indian identity" to establish the "justice" of their own demands, in contrast to the injustices of colonialism. The UCEZ materials produced in 1992 for the Movilización quinientos años de resistencia, lucha y dignidad del Indio (Five Hundred Years of Indian Resistance, Struggle and Dignity Movement) used this discourse to argue for tearing down the statue of a Spanish conqueror in the city of Morelia. An allusion to 500 years of resistance was present in the struggle against discrimination of the black Candomblé activists discussed by Parés (chapter seven). In a similar way, Felipe Castro Gutiérrez (chapter two) points to the importance of native responses to conquest in contemporary political discourse, for instance in the formation of the Consejo Mexicano 500 años de Resistencia Indígena, Negra y Popular (Mexican Council of 500 Years of Indigenous, Black and Popular Resistance). Furthermore, the UCEZ frequently alluded to the need to join anti-imperialist struggles globally. By identifying all the rural poor as Indian and by suppressing or incorporating the category of mestizo, the UCEZ used its historical narrative to strengthen the basis of its legitimacy. Nevertheless, the use of racial categories inside the narratives of the comuneros indicates some degree of internalization, within individual actors' consciousness, of national stereotypes of *blanqueamiento* (whitening) and *racismo lego* (uninformed racism), for example, in their insistence on the amount of Spanish blood (related to "purity of blood") that they had. Claudio Lomnitz-Adler (1992) argues that the notion of purity of blood served to engrave other notions upon popular consciousness, such as the "negative" characteristics, like lack of beauty and stubbornness, attributed to the Indians. In some of the declarations made by the people from Ixtaro and Zirahuén, for instance, categories such as "stubborn" or "de razón" were employed but with an "inverse" meaning, as proposed by Keesing (1992). Udelia and Guadalupe, a couple from Ixtaro, remarked, "We feel that we are Indians, what else? We are stubborn Indians who adopt nothing which is not befitting us." This last statement suggests that a categorization given by others is being assumed as one's own, through an inversion of its evaluative connotations. It was clear, however, that some people inside Ixtaro actually accepted the dominant and strictly negative stereotype about alleged Indian stubbornness, indicating a "lack of reason." Moreover, as a community that had learned to see themselves as non-Indian, Ixtaro was deeply influenced by the discourse that mestizo culture represents a form of progress. Finally, the UCEZ's complex discourse about ethnic identity simultaneously served both political purposes and to satisfy the necessity of belonging and compromise, that is to say, of "making community." Their language may have been one of ethnicity, but the nature of the social boundary itself suggests a model of fundamental divisions of class and power from the perspective of the poorest sectors of society. The ethnic language was a means to talk of class.

*   *   *

Regardless of whether it is taken as a metaphor or as a euphemism, the notion of resistance remains central to reflection and analysis, from our perspective as actors within an academic environment and from the perspective created and recreated in the center of social movements, characterized by its diversity of actors and of culturally informed agencies. The discussion on ethnicity, resistance, and community led us to consider the permanence of hegemonic practices and discourses of legality, gender, religion, and the way they are transformed from counterhegemonic practices and discourses, in contradictory and ambiguous ways, while other practices doubtless reinforce the hegemonic order through complicit relationships of clientelism and patronage. Yet the action of the indigenous movements and the re-creation of "national" projects through a new discourse of inclusion of differences and identity politics allowed the reconfiguration of a hegemonic order.

The continuity between past and present was fundamental in power discourses; the past became the central ingredient, making new forms of identity politics, re-creating, reinventing, and selecting identities and traditions. The cases in Mexico and Brazil examined in this book offer consistent evidence of this process. The "profundity" of tradition was evident in the case of Emiliano Zapata. Esteban Krotz (1988, 140) mentions that his statements and juridical orders contained, among other ideas, a utopian vision of a life without exploitation, with communal control over resources, in which "the land belongs to the person who works it." Community and ethnic identity became tools of resistance in this peasant-indigenous organization. Both became the ideal vehicle for different motivations and interests and offered a common language of struggle. In practice and in discourse, ethnicity allowed the display of the subaltern status of these comuneros: before colonial domination there were no Indians, no customs, just as Keesing (1992) argues that the inhabitants of Malaita did not have, nor could have, *kastom*; they had their ancestors and norms. No less important is John Monteiro's assertion (chapter one) that it is not enough to talk about the relations between subaltern peoples and structures of domination; processes of ethnogenesis must also consider conflicts between subalterns. But the conceptualization of resistance is made complex precisely because of the different types of agency and agendas of the actors, in other words, their internal politics. The examination of resistance draws our attention to the subject's active self-creation. The subjects' discourses and practices allow us to recognize their creativity, their complicity, and their ambiguity.

Notes

Translation by Mónica Morales Moreno

1 "Comunero" refers to members of a communal landholding community (by analogy with members of indigenous communities).
2 Settlements built without title to land, which may be formalized and regularized subsequently.
3 "Rancheros" are small farmers or cattle raisers who are not indigenous and live in dispersed settlements (see Barragán, Hoffman, and Linck 1994).
4 Online in Spanish at http://www.derechoshumanos.org.mx, accessed September 1, 2009, author's translation.
5 A Spanish measure of weight, particularly for maize.
6 Recorded in *Por Esto!* 291 (November 1987): 49.

CHAPTER ELEVEN

Resistance, Factionalism, and Ethnogenesis in Southern Jalisco

GUILLERMO DE LA PEÑA

When we talk about "ethnic resistance" in Mexico, two images come to mind: the hooded figures of the Zapatista Army of National Liberation (EZLN) in Chiapas, broadcast on television since January 1994, and the "Aztec warriors" who dance for tourists in Mexico City's main square as representatives of a movement to restore the ancestral culture of "deep Mexico." These dancers have little to do with what is actually happening in indigenous communities (Galinier and Moliner 2006), and although the Zapatistas of Chiapas have certainly drawn attention to the importance of the "ethnic question," neither are they representative of Mexico's indigenous groups, who are mostly poor peasants and migrants swelling the population of informal workers in big cities and day laborers in commercial agriculture.

The most significant demonstrations of ethnic resistance occur among these precarious and heterogeneous groups, found throughout the length and breadth of the country. While the postrevolutionary state favored the reproduction of ethnic identities and different collective memories, *indigenismo*, the official ideology and policy concerning indigenous peoples that prevailed until the 1970s, made contradictory claims about the need to merge races and identities in the "crucible" of a modern, nationalist, and *mestiza* society (de la Peña 2002). Consequently, *lo indio* became equivalent to "otherness," poor and backward, while *lo mestizo* became *lo nacional* (Bonfil Batalla 1996). Although from the 1930s onward some popular movements that defined themselves as "Indian" questioned this dichotomous vision, the emerging organizations of educated indigenous people generally accepted nationalist homogenization (Iwanska 1977).

Since 1970, and the exhaustion of the postrevolutionary regime, numerous communities and organizations have raised the banner of ethnic demands to justify the defense of communal lands, reject the hostility of the dominant society, search for better models of coexistence, and assert the right to determine solutions to local problems through truly representative authorities (Mejía and Sarmiento 1987; Warman and Argueta 1993; Dietz 2004; de la Peña 2006a). In 1992, five centuries after Christopher Columbus's voyage, many organizations joined an inter-American network that labeled itself the Frente 500 Años de Resistencia (500 Years of Resistance Front). For its part, since it opened the economy to the global market, the Mexican government has limited its social policies to the most "vulnerable" groups—including indigenous populations. Additionally, it has reformed the constitution to recognize, if in a limited way, the social, political, and cultural rights of indigenous peoples.

Within this context, we can understand the growing phenomenon of reinvented communities (de la Peña 2003), which entail processes of ethnogenesis. Following Christopher Hill (1996) and Miguel Bartolomé (2006), I adopt a complex approach to analyzing these processes. The "reinvented communities" are not purely fictitious; they require a credible narrative—at least partly based on traditions, living memory, and documents—that justifies the recovery of a collective identity. Ethnogenesis, or re-ethnicization (Gros 2000), implies that a group gradually becomes aware of itself, and presents itself to others as a distinct social subject whose members accept that they share a culture.[1] However, such self-awareness would not occur if it did not offer a collective advantage: for example, the possibility of claiming rights from the national state or international society (Tully 1995; Karlsson 2003).

In Latin America, the expression of popular demands as claims for cultural rights reflects the abandonment of certain social policies—especially agrarian reform—as well as the advance of discourse, laws, and official actions that recognize and promote multiculturalism (Yashar 2005). However, consciousness of the inherent rights of cultural diversity can largely be explained through external information: from the state, from political parties or churches, or from social movements and civil associations. Thus, ethnogenesis becomes a vast field of vertical and horizontal relationships, which may include manipulations, alliances, and patronage.

Additionally, ethnogenesis usually requires new leadership, which can generate factional conflict. It also requires new "organic intellectuals" who articulate discourses that others consider subversive.

Is ethnogenesis a form of resistance? The answer to this question is controversial. According to indigenismo, ethnic cultures' persistence depended on the perpetuation of precapitalist production relations in areas of the country ("regions of refuge") controlled by regional oligarchs (Aguirre Beltrán 1967). This control excluded part of the population from access to the economic, political, and cultural resources of the modern nation, thereby delaying their "acculturation." Other authors, however, insist on indigenous villages' collective agency in the defense of their culture and identity, understood as resources and "vehicles of survival" (Adams 1995). For example, Edward H. Spicer's classic study of indigenous people in northwestern Mexico and the southwestern United States uses the term resistance when analyzing the partial failure of the religious, linguistic, political, economic, and cultural assimilation that successive "cycles of conquest" aimed to impose (Spicer 1962). Spicer (1971) proposed the concept of a "system of persistent identity" to refer to the type of organization that made the resistance of minority groups against colonial or national powers viable. Subsequent work has applied this concept not only to remote hamlets and corporate communities but also to well-connected villages, to urban groups, and even to international migrants (Castile and Kushner 1981; Pérez Ruiz 2002; Fox and Rivera-Salgado 2004; Martínez Casas 2007). Processes of ethnogenesis in contemporary Mexico thus help us to understand the more general phenomenon of ethnic resistance.

This chapter analyzes community and ethnic reconstruction in the Sierra de Manantlán, a region in southern Jalisco that, since 1940, has experienced repeated confrontations between *campesinos* (peasants) from the community of Ayotitlán and invading outsiders, including ranchers, loggers, and mining companies. Throughout these conflicts, the people of Ayotitlán have been called "indios" by their opponents, in contrast to "mestizos," the term which vaguely denotes all who are "not indios." In practice, the dichotomy is not so clear, and the terms are applied situationally. Additionally, the Ayotitlans are internally divided through family and factional rivalries and because of alliances forged with external actors, including businessmen, government officials, progovernment and radical agrarian organizations, priests, progressive schoolteachers, and university groups from Guadalajara and Autlán. University groups introduced ecological protection programs—culminating in the creation of the Reserva de la Biosfera de Manantlán (the Manantlán Biosphere Reserve)—and programs for social development, community building, and the recovery of indigenous culture. Moreover, after the Chiapas uprising in 1994, Manantlán's inhabitants were also, for the first time, included in government indigenista programs. Thus, indigenous identity, ethnicity, and culture are notions pervasive today in internal and external negotiations, although their meanings vary. I will examine the use of ethnic resistance here not only in agrarian conflict but also in the mediations, negotiations, alliances, and disagreements between actors differentiated by both interests and lifeworlds (Long 2001).

The Setting

The Sierra de Manantlán forms part of the border between the states of Jalisco and Colima. There, on the southwestern slopes of the mountains, is the community of Ayotitlán, around sixty rancherías (small agricultural or ranching hamlets) spread over more than fifty thousand mostly forested hectares. Currently, only ten of these settlements have more than a hundred inhabitants. Almost six hundred people live in the *cabecera* (communal capital), also called Ayotitlán, with its old Franciscan chapel, along with a small clinic, a school, and some government offices. Until the 1970s, the cabecera was only accessible along paths, but since then rudimentary roads have opened.

The extreme dispersal of the population is related to the precariousness of the *coamiles*, sloping land where people practice "slash and burn" agriculture. Cultivated fields must be rotated every few years. Hamlets are formed by members of an extended family, usually related through patrilineal ties. When the family outgrows the land's productive capacity, the youngest leave and establish a new farm. In addition to agriculture, traditional economic activities include the manufacture and sale of artisanal products, although seasonal migration to the coastal plantations is also frequent, and often necessary for survival.

The Fight for Lands and Woods: 1921–1980

In June 1921, the indigenous community of Ayotitlán formally requested confirmation of permanent title to their ancestral lands, which had been partially invaded by large estates during the second half of the nineteenth century. Their petition failed: the National Agrarian Commission (CNA) demanded presentation of the colonial land grant and "proof of dispossession."[2] The file was not closed, however, and the CNA did order the withdrawal of several logging companies that had invaded the local mountains. Yet after 1940, logging companies returned and multiplied. This unleashed a conflict, at times violent, in defense of the woods against the invading *talamontes* (illegal loggers), led by the Consejo de Mayores (Council of Elders), the traditional indigenous authority, though lacking official status (Durán Legazpi 1987; Rojas 1996). Ayotitlán, along with Cuzalapa and Chacala (also indigenous villages), was dependent on the mestizo authorities of Autlán municipality, and, after a new municipality was formed in 1946, on those of Cuautitlán. Many people in the municipal capital did not hide their distrust of, or even contempt for, the *inditos* (little Indians). From the start of the twentieth century, when the Cuautitlán parish priest established Ayotitlán's first school, the indigenous language, customs, and political organization had been persecuted. When the postrevolutionary government introduced rural schools, their mission was to impose the Spanish language.

During the 1950s, the community again requested land deeds. The talamontes—protected by a powerful family of politicians and military men from Cuautitlán—responded by propagating the idea that the indios were dangerous and violent. Because communal boundaries were not officially defined, there were several clashes between the inhabitants of Ayotitlán, Cuzalapa, and other neighboring villages.[3] In 1956, uniformed soldiers invaded the Tenamaxtla hamlet, where the Consejo de Mayores was meeting, burning down houses and massacring those who did not flee. The survivors stopped appearing in public. To replace the Consejo, a communal assembly created the Comité Provisional de Bienes Comunales (Provisional Committee for Communal Goods), which registered with the federal agrarian authorities in order to continue the struggle, although the mayores retained backstage influence on collective decisions.

Scared and discouraged, the Ayotitlans consciously minimized the signs of their stigmatized ethnic identity. By the beginning of the 1960s, both the Náhuatl language and traditional clothing had fallen from use. During the same period, the National Peasant Confederation (CNC), the rural arm of the ruling Institutional Revolutionary Party (PRI), proposed to the Comité Provisional de Bienes Comunales that they stop petitioning for confirmation of their old communal landholdings and instead request land for an *ejido*, a state land grant for communal use. This all occurred within the context of a national campaign to widen agrarian reform's benefits to potentially rebellious groups (de la Peña 2007). Granting an ejido did not imply recognition of the indigenous community's previous rights: the federal authorities decided the area of the assigned land and number of beneficiaries. The CNC officials argued that the ejido eliminated the insuperable problem of documenting the community's historical rights, and that becoming members of an ejido would end racial discrimination (since they did not have rights recognized for being "indios") and give them the PRI's protection.

Although the Consejo de Mayores opposed it, a majority voted for the ejido in the communal assembly. Thus, in January 1963, the Ejido of Ayotitlán was founded, with a grant of 55,332 hectares, of which only 6 percent was defined as "cultivable land." In July of that year, the Comisariado Ejidal (Ejido Executive Committee) was formally established and 776 *ejidatarios* (members) received temporary possession of 50,332 hectares, 5,000 less than the amount originally approved. A month later, a presidental resolution confirmed that first amount.[4] Yet maneuvering by the loggers delayed definitive possession of the ejido until 1977, and even then the final grant—for reasons never explained—was only 34,700 hectares (Durán Legazpi 1987, 283–84).[5] Meanwhile, the talamontes continued to log, under the pretext of previous permissions. One of these organizations maintained control of a huge forested area, and judicial authorities even arrested some Ayotitlans who attempted to protect the woods.[6] In 1968, with CNC support, a 10,330-hectare extension of the ejido was obtained, which benefited 842 families. Officially, however, these lands were not handed over until 1981. Factional conflicts—between those who supported the Consejo de Mayores and *cenecistas* (members of the CNC)—delayed the production of a definitive list of ejidatarios and boundaries, while the ejido authorities could not stop the invaders destroying the forest, since they could not prove the definitive demarcation of their land.[7] In addition, the Peña Colorado Mining Consortium invaded Ayotitlán's lands from the southeast in order to exploit the rich iron deposits found there (Durán Legazpi 1987, 284–86).

New Political Actors and the Creation
of the Manantlán Biosphere Reserve

Traditionally, parcels of communal land were distributed annually within each hamlet, through agreements among families. The person in charge of organizing this cyclical distribution was named the *cabezal* (head), periodically selected by the Consejo de Mayores. But new agrarian rules and political pressure from the invaders prompted the disappearance of traditional authorities. However, in the 1980s, the defenders of the communal land regime reinvigorated their activism, with the support of new actors. These included priests inspired by liberation theology and rural teachers linked to the leftist Revolutionary Peasant Alliance (Alianza Campesina Revolucionaria, ACR) (Torres and Cuevas n.d.).

Since the mid-1970s, researchers and students from the University of Guadalajara had also explored the mountains, attracted by the diversity and rarity of flora and fauna, and by news of the presence of wild *teosinte* (*Zea perennis*), a distant ancestor of maize. Researchers not only found teosinte, but also an older and previously unstudied species: *Zea diplo-perennis* (Guzmán 1978). Consequently, the university created an extensive research and ecological protection program, installing its Laboratorio Natural Las Joyas in the heart of the mountains, which became the center of several international scientific projects (Jardel 1992; Gerritzer 2002). The researchers also carried out socioeconomic studies, seeking solutions to the Sierra population's marginalization (León and Gutiérrez 1988; Rojas 1996).

Meanwhile, seeking to legitimize itself, the Ejido Executive Committee took the mining company, loggers, and even the federal and state authorities to court. Nevertheless, the forest's devastation only stopped in 1987, when a presidential decree created the Reserva de la Biosfera Sierra de Manantlán (Manantlán Mountain Biosphere Reserve), championed by university researchers, members of the Ayotitlán community, and the ACR, with the support of the state government and international scientific institutions.[8] The reserve, 139,577 hectares, includes almost the entire Ayotitlán ejido. In its 42,000-hectare central zone, all activities that could damage the resources (flora, fauna, and mineral deposits) or change land use are prohibited. The felling of trees was suspended for fifty years in the rest of the reserve. The resident population, however, was allowed to continue its traditional activities, under the supervision of reserve authorities. Forest police enforced the withdrawal of the logging companies.

Many initiatives now arose to promote "sustainable development" using the inhabitants' culture as a starting point. These initiatives involved the revival of ancient knowledge and customs (Robertson Sierra 2002; Moreno Badajoz 2004), with the participation of the Consejo de Mayores, along with the ACR and university researchers. Particularly important was the presence of local, educated young people who had worked at the Laboratorio Natural Las Joyas or in socioeconomic investigations in the area. In July 1993, the Unión de Pueblos Indígenas de Manantlán (UPIM, Manantlán Union of Indigenous Villages) was established to channel resources from public, private, and university institutions into the region. The UPIM has also promoted human rights and environmental and cultural sustainability. After the Chiapas rebellion in 1994, the Instituto Nacional Indigenista (INI) and the newly founded Procuraduría de Asuntos Indígenas de Jalisco (Jalisco Agency for Indigenous Affairs) started programs in the Manantlán mountains. That same year, the University of Guadalajara's Unidad de Apoyo a Comunidades Indígenas (UACI, Indigenous Community Support Unit) was founded to offer legal advice on agrarian rights, to stop neocolonial aggression toward community culture, and to support cultural reconstruction (see UACI 2000).

The UACI encouraged the people of Ayotitlán to found community committees, which set up consciousness-raising workshops following the paradigm of Brazilian educator Paulo Freire. These centered on the recovery of collective memory and finding solutions to community problems (UACI 2000). A workshop about governance and citizens' rights drew up a communal statute to foster consensus among the people of Ayotitlán, which opened up a new space for the Consejo de Mayores. Other workshops discussed the community's agrarian and economic problems, as well as strategies for developing forestry, medicinal plants, commerce, and domestic industry (improving techniques of embroidery, weaving, and wood carving). Every aspect of traditional culture has merited a workshop examining ancestral memory and cataloguing lost beliefs and practices. The UACI also promoted exchanges between Ayotitlans and people from other indigenous villages, particularly Huicholes from northern Jalisco and Náhuatl communities from the south of the state. In 1995, it negotiated funding with the INI for a group from Ayotitlán to attend the EZLN-sponsored Congreso Nacional Indígena, in Mexico City. Six years later, funded by the University of Guadalajara, the Ayotitlans attended another indigenous congress in Nurío, Michoacán.

Cataloguing and Remaking Tradition

The identity and culture workshops have reconstructed a worldview that combines traditions with Náhuatl culture from central Mexico (UACI 2000). Its cornerstone is a firm belief in the active and ubiquitous presence of ancestors, "the *señores*" or "little old men." These ancestors, for example, make the large trees opposite the old chapel in the cabecera bloom year round, so that people remember where their roots are and that communal unity is founded on fidelity to origins. The people who leave the community return, thanks to those trees; it is said that "he who cuts them down, will die" (Higareda 2000, 180; Robertson Sierra 2002, 13). The ancestors live inside the hills and control nature, continually manifesting themselves in it. Some elderly people bear witness to having entered the world of los señores. They were amazed by the lush landscape and heard wise words, spoken in the language of the ancient Mexicans, reminding them that human life depends on the gifts of the earth, the nourishing mother who must be thanked with offerings and rituals (Robertson Sierra 2002, 156–58).

The UACI promoted the revitalization of traditional arts and crafts as valuable patrimony and also as a means to produce essentials and earn money (Robertson Sierra 2002, 75, 158–64). Ayotitlán *equipales* (armchairs with a leather seat), for example, are well known and other workshops have reinvigorated the production of wax candles, vessels made of varnished pumpkins, clay ceramics, embroidered cloths, tiles, and adobe bricks. It has again become important to learn the Náhuatl terms for primary materials and artisan objects, and the indigenous communities have asked for Náhuatl to be taught in schools to recuperate the use of their ancestral language.

Traditional medical practices also remain common (Higareda 2000). Three fields are distinguishable: *parteras* (midwives), herbalist-massagers, and *medicos de rama* (traditional healers). Despite attacks from biomedical professionals in the region's public clinics, the practice of the healers not only remains vigorous but has been strengthened by the UACI's promotion of communication between local therapists and those further afield.

Reanimation of religious festivals has been another remarkable achievement of the cultural workshops. Celebrations in honor of Christ, the saints, or the Virgin Mary happen every month in different settlements (Camacho 2000; Robertson Sierra 2002, 176–79). Each sacred icon has its *mayordomo* (steward), who ceremonially changes each year. Aided by his wife and family, the mayordomo provides music, fireworks, flowers, candles, food and drink, and arranges a Mass. These celebrations bring together families from the many settlements of Ayotitlán, and from other communities.

The Meaning of Recovered Ethnicity: Five Testimonies

According to the UACI model, community rituals constitute a symbolic space wherein solidarity is recreated and collective memory catalyzed. Through the performance of "customs," history itself is incorporated into everyday life. Rituals maintain belief in the world of the ancestors, enable the benevolent wisdom of the healers, and give artisan work significance. The postcolonial syncretic culture of the saints and the Virgin distributes and reproduces practical responsibilities that express belonging to a community. The discourse of the reinvention and recuperation of community, culture, and identity—the ethnogenetic discourse that constitutes "us"— promises a life in harmony with man and nature. But it also provides a formula for political action based on reclaiming history and a worldview. The way this discourse is presented, however, depends on its position in a complex social situation, as I will now illustrate with five individual testimonies. The ethnographic present is 2001.

"Only" seventy-eight years old, Don Juventino presents himself as the youngest member of the Consejo de Mayores. Although he only had one year of schooling, he is literate and enjoys showing off Ayotitlán's ancient origins: "Tenochtitlán, the capital of the Aztec Empire, was going to be founded here. The God Huitzilopochtli had announced to the priests that they would find an island in the middle of a lake and there they would see an eagle sitting on top of a cactus, eating a snake. But the mountains blocked the view of the lake, and the priests passed by without seeing it; but others who were cleverer did see it and stayed. So we say that we are the original Mexicans." This wisdom comes from the spirits who live in the old Franciscan chapel and deep in the mountains, and who talked to the elders: "We need to recover the Consejo de Mayores' influence." He remembers sorrowfully the times his father and other elders had to hide from the murderous loggers who colluded with corrupt authorities. Fortunately, Juventino says,

> Don Zeferino [one of the mayores] is still alive, he has looked after our documents [land titles], where you can see that our community is very large, our lands stretch to the Pacific . . .[9] The Consejo de Mayores was dead, but then the young people of the UACI called don Zeferino and other old people who knew how things were before. An anthropology professor came from Mexico [City] to help us with our traditions . . . Today we are once again learning to enjoy all our festivals.
>
> The real authority is that of the elders, they have the responsibility of naming the municipal delegate, only for a year; they have to punish those who do not behave properly, and defend the community . . . This community has always been attacked, my father said that during the Revolution as well, the armies came and killed people, and then the loggers did the same.

For don Juventino, what the UACI does is very good, although he does not seem to know much about the biosphere reserve. He enjoys the interest of the urban students who work with the local youth to revive old customs: "We'll see if our young people stop leaving. Each time we sow less, because we have fewer hands." And he is very happy to have attended the national indigenous congresses and have met the Zapatistas.

In contrast to don Juventino, who sees local history as the resistance of "true Mexicans" against aggressive invaders, Ildefonso believes that internal disputes have caused the main conflicts in Ayotitlán. He belongs to a cenecista family; he began primary school in Ayotitlán and finished it in Cuautitlán. Aged fifty-something, he has been president of the Ejido Executive Committee and a CNC delegate several times.

Since he was young, Ildefonso has denounced the ineptitude and corruption of the federal government's agrarian functionaries, who for decades delayed the demarcation of the ejido boundaries. But he believes that if Ayotitlans had continued to petition for the restitution of communal lands, they "would still be waiting . . . Who can deny that we have a road, albeit a bad one, thanks to the ejido? Before, we had to walk the hills, on foot or by mule." All the same, he offers his own ethnicist discourse:

The indigenous communities have suffered terrible poverty, despite being those who have taken care of Mexican lands. Here, the mestizos took away a great deal of our land, but that was because we indios were always fighting amongst ourselves and forgot to pay our taxes, so that while we fought, they bought the title deeds from the tax collector . . . In 1921, when the Mayores made a demand for the return of the lands, they were very naïve and did not receive legal advice, so they didn't come away with anything. And now that we have an ejido, we have still not received all the land that is legally ours, because the ignorant people just keep on fighting.

Ildefonso disapproves of the UACI and the biosphere reserve: "Those from the university are all lefties . . . in reality, we, the people, are not very important to them. Thanks to the ejido, the timber companies paid us money for the trees they cut down. Now they have made the reserve and we no longer have this money; they don't even let us touch the woods." Ildefonso does not lament losing the Náhuatl language or traditional dress, but recognizes that racial aggression caused this loss: "The government in Colima didn't like . . . our countrymen who went to work or sold avocados and apples from here in the mountains, they had to buy or rent trousers because if they didn't, they would be put in jail." As for ethnic demands, he believes that indigenous communities should become independent municipalities. "Ayotitlán should separate from Cuautitlán and have its own municipal president, but not a Consejo de Mayores, which is just a joke." He also argues that indigenous people should have "serious" representatives in congress. As for the INI's programs, and other government assistance programs, they are paternalistic, unfair, and badly run.

Manuel is around forty-five. His parents migrated to Autlán when he was an adolescent, where he went to secondary school, but he didn't continue his studies, because his family moved back to the mountains. He has been a member of the ACR and the UPIM, taken part in many workshops and training courses promoted by the Las Joyas laboratory and the UACI, and today is one of the leaders of a production cooperative. From Manuel's point of view, it was the ACR that initiated change in the Sierra: "We had our first contact in 1979. At that time there was a complete and shameful complicity among the timber companies, the municipal authorities, and the Ejido Executive Committee. Also, the mining consortium was increasingly encroaching on our land from Colima [with government complicity]

... So, the ARC organized protest demonstrations, in Guadalajara and even in Mexico [City]. When the university researchers started to come, the ARC helped them to become aware of the problems in the countryside." Manuel proudly narrates how the ACR and the UPIM led the people to support the university researchers and technicians from the ecology ministry in the creation of the biosphere reserve. He deplores what the ejido authorities have done:

> We went to see the governor of Jalisco. Then we were able to kick out the loggers and now we are in peace. The reserve put an end to the irrational exploitation of the woods, which had dried up the water sources and destroyed the wild fauna . . . It is a shame that those who control the ejido are inefficient and corrupt. It is true that they contracted a lawyer who managed to get the timber companies to pay compensation, but this money was shared out amongst the leaders and CNC sympathizers. They aren't even capable of completing the ejidal census, and they also wanted to cheat with that, so they did not register us in the National Agrarian Register.

Manuel maintains that the Consejo de Mayores has unified people and fought against poverty and alcoholism: "The solution to our problems is in our human capacities, not in being exploited and devouring our resources until we have none left. The mayores know our history, our way of life, our culture and they can bring us optimism. To be ourselves, we depend on them." But Manuel's greatest hope is for his cooperative's sustainable development project, which has obtained technical help from the biosphere reserve, the University of Colima, and the agricultural ministry, and public and private funding: "Today we have 125 members. . . . Our main project is apiculture, and it is working very well, but we also have small coffee, hibiscus and blackberry plantations, and we have just started to produce coffee liquor and soap. We have a shop in Telcruz and we also export to Guadalajara and Mexico City. We're going slowly, but if we are united, we will go far."

Roberta is about forty and one of the best-educated people in the Sierra. Supported by a teacher at the school in Ayotitlán who lived in Cuautitlán, she finished primary and secondary school in the municipal capital. Women "were not allowed to study, but [she] rebelled . . . [she] had the support of [her] grandfather, who knew how to read and write: he wrote the community's letters." In 1981, she began work as a literacy teacher at the National Institute for Adult Education. With this salary she could afford high school studies in Guadalajara. But she stayed in contact with the Sierra and, influenced by the researchers at Las Joyas, decided to study agronomy at the University of Guadalajara, returning in 1992 as an assistant researcher there.

Roberta was one of the founders of the UPIM, one of whose main objectives was, she states, to overcome the enmity between CNC and ACR supporters:

> In the 1980s, the sawmills were at their height and a good part of the ejidatarios agreed that they wanted to continue selling [wood], because the CNC's lawyer—who also had business with the timber merchants—had obtained payments for the ejido. But the payment was not fairly shared out, and many people were unhappy . . . It was very difficult to coordinate everyone, there were over 1,600 ejidatarios, and many didn't get anything . . . The felling was excessive and the trees were running out . . . We started UPIM as a community group, linked to the church and in 1993 we registered it as a civil association. . . . We wanted the union to achieve a reasonable use of the woods and we also wanted to defend migrant workers working on agricultural land, because they had no protection. We also wanted, and still want, to work with ejidatarios to get the federal government to hand over or compensate for the 15,000 hectares that are missing from the definitive grant.

The UPIM has 500 registered members, but in practice almost 2,000 people participate in different activities. There are even a good number of people from the CNC. "What happens is that those from the CNC don't want us to be considered indigenous, or as an indigenous community, because they think that the land would be taken away from us." But she recognizes that there is also a political question: the ejidos have an intrinsic link with the CNC, which in turn forms part of the campesino sector of the PRI. The agrarian community regime, however, allows more independence. For Roberta, the UPIM could and should achieve a change of agrarian regime and gain municipal autonomy:

> Cuautitlán's municipality has 15,000 inhabitants; there are 9,000 of us from Ayotitlán, whilst there are only 6,000 mestizos, and they have treated us really badly . . . This is why it is important to regain

our identity, to defend ourselves as what we are, find our own dignity within ourselves, and this is only possible if we identify and value what we are, where we are, and what we have. Thus from the beginning we have supported the UACI in its recovery of our culture . . . Although only a few people still speak Náhuatl, we want children to learn it in schools.

Roberta is optimistic because the reserve has consolidated the protection of the woods, and because the Consejo de Mayores is helping people from Ayotitlán unite, with the support of the UACI workshops. She is also optimistic because the municipal authorities, at first suspicious of the UPIM and the Consejo de Mayores, respect them and agreed to collaborate in seeking federal government support to expand public services. The UACI has worked with government ministries to secure support for a host of projects: organic agriculture, bakeries, nixtamal mills, electrification by solar panels, small-scale irrigation, and water purification, as well as training for all these activities. However, Roberta admits that there is still much to do.

At twenty-nine, Mercedes is known in the region as a healer, but also for her links to the EZLN national congresses. She finished primary school in the community center. She declares herself to be conscious of being an indigenous woman from experiences both inside and outside her community. From childhood, she saw women abused by alcoholic men: "There was no justice for abused women; they did not recognize their value . . . What started to give us alternatives were the workshops on natural medicine. Now, women no longer let themselves be treated like that, and they denounce the beatings." Roberta promoted the natural medicine workshops, supported by the UACI in 1994 and 1995. She organized women of all ages and backgrounds, and introduced them to Mari-Chuy, a young healer from Tuxpan—another Nahua community in southern Jalisco—who had founded a community health center in her village, and did not hide her sympathies for the EZLN (de la Peña 2006b, 485–88). Focusing on regaining local curative traditions, they also talked about nutrition, possible uses of local resources, and the value of women's work. Mercedes continues:

The husbands and fathers did not oppose the workshops much. Here people knew about plants, but we also learnt to prepare syrups, ointments, and tinctures. I spent a week in Tuxpan learning to give massages; it was the first time I had left the community . . . later my friends persuaded me that we should set up a health center here in the community, although I was unsure. With time, I agreed; I helped two disabled girls to recover, as well as another who had hit her spine and a boy who had a dislocated hip. I cleanse people charged with negative energy.

In January 1996, she traveled to Chiapas to participate in the First Indigenous Forum, organized by the EZLN. Other meetings that year and in later years took her to Sierra Huichola, Oaxaca, Mexico City, Veracruz, and finally to Europe:

At the San Cristóbal [Chiapas] forum, there were about 5,000 people [in workshops]. I went to the women's workshop, and the debate was huge, they talked about ethnic rights, but also about the rights of indigenous women. . . . [We said that] we could have our own land, as women, independently of our husbands. . . . I started to wake up, because before I had been asleep. We are human beings and we think [as well as men]. . . . Those four days meant a lot . . . I didn't even know what had happened in Chiapas, and so I started to read the newspapers.

With the *huicholes* [those from the Sierra Huichola], we had intercultural meetings. The men there didn't want the women to go, but yes [they did], thanks to Mari-Chuy, who told them off. I also told them off, I said: "How will we progress? If we don't participate we will never do anything. The women want to come, and women always move forward. And you only want polygamy and why not polyandry?" In the end, the women did come. If a woman is silent, she dies . . .

. . . But what was amazing was my trip to Europe. I trust Mari-Chuy a lot, but I said to her, what are we going to do with our children, with our sisters? I fell ill [because of the anxiety I felt] and I couldn't even walk. Mari-Chuy cured me with dressings. . . . The Rural Workers' Union invited me to Seville, and I gave talks about the reality in Mexico, about the women, about the lack of respect for indigenous people. People even cried, and they asked me a lot of questions. It took away my embarrassment at speaking; I think it's harder here than there . . . Later, I went to other cities giving talks. I realized that you have to talk from the heart.

In Tuxpan and in the Sierra de Manantlán, Mari-Chuy and Mercedes have carried out an INI-funded program about the recovery of traditional medicine and women's development.

*   *   *

I began this chapter referring to Edward Spicer's use of the term "resistance" and the Frente 500 Años de Resistencia. In both cases, resistance signified a long-term process, involving opposition to cultural assimilation and political exclusion. Such a vision of cultural resistance does not necessarily correlate with revolutionary projects of seizing state power. In many senses, it is related to James Scott's "weapons of the weak" (1985), with its emphasis on everyday and nonviolent forms of rebelliousness motivated by what Edward Thompson (1971) called "moral economy."

Authors such as John Womack (1969), Eric Wolf (1969), Jean Meyer (2005), Arturo Warman (1976), Alan Knight (1986), and John Tutino (1990) have shed light on why militant popular movements emerged in early twentieth-century Mexico. Tutino suggests three main conditions: the collective feeling of injustice in the dominated sectors; attribution of this injustice to the actions of the government, a specific dominant sector, or both; and the perception of weakness in the guardians of public order. Scott's approach shows that, when the perception of weakness does not exist, resignation is not the only alternative.

The inhabitants of Ayotitlán felt injustice because of the invasion of their lands and the persecution of their language, beliefs, and customs. Yet their feelings of defenselessness and pessimism reflected the effects of what Gonzalo Aguirre Beltrán (1967) called a *proceso dominical*, a process of postcolonial domination in which an indigenous sector in an obvious situation of disadvantage is subordinated to mestizo or white social actors who control strategic economic, social prestige, and political-administrative resources. Yet the Ayotitlán case does not support Aguirre Beltrán's assumption that abandoning ethnic identity could transform this situation.

In the 1970s, a group of Ayotitlans accepted the CNC proposal to petition for an ejido that would legally constitute them as campesino clients of the revolutionary regime, rather than as indigenous people. Yet becoming ejidatarios did not end outsiders' predations or ethnic discrimination. This situation reinforced the influence of radical priests and teachers, who connected local people with the ACR. The revitalized Consejo de Mayores accused the new agrarian authorities and cenecistas of being corrupt intermediaries for the timber companies and the municipality. Alliances with external actors transformed the conflict, culminating in the creation of the reserve, the loggers' expulsion, and the foundation of the UPIM. The appearance of the UACI allowed greater access to public resources. But the connections of people from Ayotitlán to the EZLN congresses also fostered a new discourse in which the demands of *lo indígena* became synonymous with the fight against exclusion. This became strategically relevant when constitutional changes in 1992 and 2001 proclaimed the Mexican nation "multicultural," recognizing certain indigenous rights. Indigenous identity also became advantageous because of social programs targeted at "vulnerable groups."

In Ayotitlán, ethnogenesis was forged through changes in existing political relations. Resistance became visible as a resignification of history and local culture, but to understand this process, the complex field of vertical and horizontal relationships through which conceptions are elaborated about the ethnic "us" must be taken into account.

The narratives presented in the previous section show the differentiated composition of subaltern subjectivities. They also show the different perspectives from which local actors articulate themes of culture, identity, and interethnic relations in relation to personal and collective situations. Don Juventino expresses the optimism of someone who, after painful vicissitudes, has regained a position of prestige in his community, partly thanks to the UACI. Ildefonso, in contrast, feels his mediating power and prestige diminished because the Las Joyas laboratory, the UACI, the INI, and the biosphere reserve have abolished much of the Comisariado Ejidal's authority. Manuel and Roberta define themselves as active participants in a process of change and consider the interventions of the UACI, the ACR, and the church highly positive. Mercedes emphasizes the persistence of gender discrimination but also the doors that have been opened for women through the tradition of healing and more external contact. The narratives show how the distinction between the "internal" and the "external" is affected by Ayotitlans' participation in organizations outside their community, for example Ildefonso in the CNC and Mercedes in networks of alternative medicine.

Discursive differences reflect this variety of perspectives. Don Juventino is emotional and open, Ildefonso officialist and cautious; Manuel and Roberta use politically charged language, and Mercedes uses "New Age" terms. All five identify themselves as members of a collective that has suffered numerous historical injuries. But Ildefonso, without explicitly defending the loggers, argues that their presence was beneficial, when they could be charged for logging. For Ildefonso, the community's problems are down to "the ignorant, the lefties, and quarrelsome people." Manuel, in contrast, blames the local authorities colluding with invaders, and Roberta blames a lack of dialogue. Both highlight the negative role of the CNC leaders. For Mercedes, defense of community and the dignity of indigenous people makes no sense without women's equal participation. Like Roberta and Manuel, she believes that historical claims cannot be dissociated from the defense of human rights.

Don Juventino associates indigeneity with the Aztec foundational myth, concluding that the Mayores should recover their authority because they know where the people of Ayotitlán come from. Lo indígena is thus defined by ancestry and justifies hierarchy. Ildefonso, however, says that the Consejo de Mayores is a "joke." For him, identifying as indigenous represents not only a past of racial discrimination, but also the possibility of establishing an independent municipality (in which he could be PRI candidate for municipal president). Mainly preoccupied with social and economic development plans, Manuel recognizes ethnicity's value as a unifying banner and a symbol of solidarity. Roberta sees the recuperation of identity as a step toward autonomy and justice, while Mercedes views the indigenous world as internally unequal, but once its ancestral wisdom has been retrieved, it will transcend the local and open up to the world.

I want to end by discussing ways in which my analysis relates to other contributions in this volume. Parallels with the case discussed by Margarita Zárate (chapter ten), for instance, are clear, but they extend to processes in other times and places. Patricia Pessar (chapter six) teaches us the strategic value of "traditional" culture (and especially religion) in the search for a different modernity. Ilka Boaventura Leite (chapter twelve), analyzing the different interpretative visions of the *quilombo*, provides us with a suggestive model to understand ethnic movements in Mexico as well as different interpretative visions of the indigenous community. Luis Nicolau Parés (chapter seven) demonstrates the historicity of Candomblé, examining essentialist interpretations of identity revitalization movements that ignore phenomena of cooptation and the multiple affiliations of the participants, while also highlighting the importance of subversive cultural and religious differences in the production of a historical consciousness that allows antihegemonic narratives. In his turn, John Gledhill poses a key question: Does it make sense to talk about community, and utopian, resistance in a context dominated by the neoliberal economy? Our response in this collective work is to reiterate the significance of subaltern thought and projects in the march of history. It may be true that global problems cannot be solved locally, but global solutions would be worthless without local recovery of social agency and participation.

Notes

Translation by Lucy Lawton.

This work is based on research conducted during the period 1999–2002, within the collective project "Social policies towards indigenous people in Mexico: Actors, mediations and spaces of identity," under my coordination and with support from CIESAS, CONACYT, and the Ford Foundation. I would particularly like to thank my assistants Alejandra Navarro, Rocío Moreno, Carlota Rivera, and Cristina Alfaro, and my generous friends at the UACI of the University of Guadalajara, especially Margarita Robertson, Jaime Hernández, César Delgado, and Samuel Salvador. I also wish to express my gratitude to my informants in Ayotitlán, whose anonymity I must respect, and to all those people who received me in the Manantlán Sierra.

1 What is important is not that the cultural components are unique and "original," but that within the group they are considered different and emblematic (Barth 1969).

2 Registro Agrario Nacional (RAN), Archivo General Agrario (AGA), Dotación de Tierras, Memorándum, Ejido Ayotitlán, Municipio de Cuautitlán, Exp. 23/834-3643-236, May 18, 1975, sheets 74–75. The constitution of 1917 recognized two forms of social property: the agrarian community (for the recuperation or confirmation of a collective ownership that had existed since the colonial period) and the ejido (a gift from the new regime to a group of petitioners).

3 RAN, AGA, ibid., Exp. 23/834-832, October 17, 1953, and August 10, 1954.

4 RAN, AGA, Acta: Resolución Presidencial, Ejido Ayotitlán, Municipio de Cuautitlán, Exp. 23/834-152, August 28, 1963, sheets 3–16, and September 23, 1963, pages 37–50.

5 RAN, AGA Dotación de Tierras, Acta, Ejido Ayotitlán, Municipio de Cuautitlán, Exp. 23/834-152, May 6, 1977, sheets 17–22, 24–29, 76–78.

6 RAN, AGA, ibidem, Exp. 23/834-832, March 24, 1969, sheet 263; July 31, 1972, sheet 298; Exp. 23/834-262, March 22, 1976, sheet 30.

7 RAN, AGA, Dotación Ejidal, Ejido de Ayotitlán, Municipio de Cuautitlán, Exp. 23/834-832, June 10, 1975, sheet 359.

8 "Decreto por el que se declara la Reserva de la Biosfera de la Sierra de Manantlán," Diario Oficial de la Federación, March 24, 1987, 10–22.

9 Over ninety years old, Don Zeferino is considered the wisest of the mayores.

CHAPTER TWELVE

The Transhistorical, Juridical-Formal, and Post-Utopian Quilombo

ILKA BOAVENTURA LEITE

The drums have burst into rhythm and song, resounding not only on Marques de Sapucaí Avenue but throughout the country, as part of the Carnival tribute in 2007 to the "Brazilian Africas." A crowd of millions of people have gathered together in rows of seats or watching the parade on television, following the Samba School Beija-Flor drumbeat from Nilópolis while they sing the refrain:

> Sou quilombola, Beija Flor
> Sangue de Rei, comunidade
> Obatalá anunciou
> Já raiou o sol da liberdade
>
> [I'm the quilombola humming bird
> Royal blood, community
> Obatalá has spoken
> The sun of freedom has begun to shine.]

According to the Yorubas, Obatalá is the greatest of all the orishas, the creator of the universe and Lord of all creatures living and dead, whose power extends beyond words. As the king of the community, he is depicted in the samba as announcing to quilombolas everywhere that the sun of freedom is now shining. In contemporary Brazil, "quilombo" is a term that signifies transformation. It is heard everywhere, from popular demonstrations to political affairs of state.

As much as the quilombo signifies transformation, the term quilombo

itself does not refer only to historical facts and past events; each day it acquires new meanings. It represents what Marshall Sahlins (1997) refers to
as a "metaphorical process," in which old words acquire new meanings
to explain new events. The increasing prevalence of the word *quilombo* in
Brazilian society marks subtle changes in Brazilians' perceptions of their
identities and results from changing representations of its significance in
racial and ethnic terms.[1]

More than a century after the abolition of slavery in Brazil, the term
quilombo continues to evolve new meanings, not all of them associated
with its previous historical sense as a community established by runaway
slaves. In 1994 the Palmares Cultural Foundation defined the quilombos
as "any black rural community composed of descendants from slaves,
who survive through subsistence agriculture, with cultural manifestations strongly linked to the past." Later on, the concept was widened to
include urban areas, as well as to include various other reinterpretations
and re-creations of an African cultural legacy that are taking place now
(see Hita, chapter thirteen). From being a form of opposition to the regime
of slavery, the quilombo thus came to signify the enjoyment of full citizenship through its inclusion in land tenure regularization, housing, health,
and educational and cultural policies. It thus became a political project, a
project to change the present situation of Afro-Brazilians.

The current literature on the quilombo is intimately tied to the concept
of resistance, as a reaction against slavery and its consequences. It was in
this sense that the concept of quilombo became an icon for the struggles
of Africans and their descendants in the diaspora. The quilombo encapsulates a long historical experience and its main line of development has
produced to-and-fro movements that have often put pressure on dominant
structures and institutions, including the juridical order and the legal system, to modify their own structures and principles of organization. Slave
flights, rebellions, and even assassinations of masters spanned centuries
of resistance to the slave regime. The existence of a parallel society of the
kind represented by the quilombo of Palmares, which lasted more than a
century, is emblematic of what happened throughout the colonial period
and from independence in 1822 until legal abolition in 1888. In 1596, colonial expeditions began to the region of the Serra da Barriga, where escaped slaves already existed and the quilombo was being established.
From 1655 to 1694, more than forty military expeditions were dispatched
to put an end to Palmares. Even after its destruction in 1694 and the death

of Zumbi, its leader, in 1695, around twenty-nine expeditions were still responding to attacks from dispersed groups that had been part of the quilombo (F. Gomes 2006). The enslaved Africans and their free descendants cultivated their own forms of organization despite prohibitions, including the cults of Candomblé (see Parés, chapter seven). In Brazil it is difficult to find another word with such strength, vigor, and power to mobilize and unite people.

The quilombo's present role is closely associated with denouncing new forms of social injustice that derive from the continuity of these relations of domination. The demise of institutional slavery did not result in substantial loss of the term's previous meaning, because many of those practices and relations of domination changed very little, or, when they did change, continued to be seen as they were before. Therefore, we can conclude that the end of slavery did not eliminate the association of the quilombo with resistance and opposition. However, more recent changes in the formal juridical status of quilombos, from a form of protest to a right, from a posture of opposition to a form of state policy, invite us to think about whether it is possible to assume that the concept still connotes the same sense of resistance. Modifications to the juridical and epistemological status of quilombos, and in political practices associated with them, suggest more substantial changes in the term's uses and meanings, necessitating the introduction of new questions, such as those of invisibility, the condition of denial of citizenship that leads to the absence or expropriation of territorial rights, on the one hand, and compensatory and affirmative social actions, on the other.

The recent creation of hundreds of quilombola associations in the country has focused on the quilombo as a form of resistance, derived from the period of slavery, a symbol of protest, revenge, and rebellion. The concept of resistance has also been used in academic analyses of social movements and struggles. Some authors favor a more restricted understanding of resistance that applies only to collective phenomena, while others use it in interpersonal relations and aspects of personal identity.[2] But in his introduction to this book John Gledhill emphasizes the central role that resistance has played in the analysis of a wide variety of social movements in Latin America, linking the debates around resistance to broader issues of conceptualizing power relations and hegemony.

In response to this book's aim of subjecting resistance to a process of rethinking in the light of past critiques, I will address some of the main discourses that emphasize the quilombo as resistance, focusing on the term's uses, contexts, and meanings, and attempting to demonstrate its paradoxes and discrepancies. I face the challenge of trying to understand the quilombo as a discourse of power that, as was described by Foucault (1996), has a productive as well as a repressive role in the history and social dynamics of subjectivity, and in the methods and instruments of social transformation. I want to discuss the significance of this term in diverse social contexts in contemporary Brazil, and through this, its recent impact from the point of view of theoretical discussions in the social sciences.

Throughout this chapter, I will demonstrate, using empirical examples, some based on my own field research in quilombola communities (I. Leite 2004), how changes in the uses and meanings of the term illustrate the metaphorical process mentioned above. I will present the concepts of the transhistorical and the juridical-formal quilombo and attempt to distinguish the meanings of resistance associated with each of them. Lastly, I will make some final observations about what I mean by the term the "post-utopian quilombo."

The Transhistorical Quilombo

The term quilombo has come to include the most diverse forms of reaction to domination instituted since the era of slavery, irrespective of their degree, type, and intensity. As a result, it does not denote a single set of facts, a specific relation, or rigid chronological frameworks, but a set of diverse situations whose range makes it difficult to establish rigid criteria for defining what a quilombo is and to confirm that we are talking about a phenomenon that concerns the establishment of an identity.

Slave insurrections and various other demonstrations against the slave system during the colonial period transformed the quilombo, especially the quilombo of Palmares, which, as I noted earlier, was the longest-lasting example of an independent domain organized by runaway slaves, into an icon of the struggle against colonial domination. By the late nineteenth century, many abolitionists used the specter of the quilombo in their discourses to talk about the conditions of inequality imposed by slavery, about racism and the revolts that resulted from it, and above all, to press for social changes relating to labor, landed property, and educational rights.

In the 1930s, the Brazilian "Black Front" recuperated the idea of the quilombo to denounce both the ideology of *embranquecimento* ("whitening") and the exclusion of black people from the republican project associated with the modernization of the country. The work of Celia Marinho de Azevedo (1987) analyzes the thought of the reformist elites in the final years of slavery, describing the disciplinary measures adopted to substitute European immigrants for former slaves, and the image of the "black wave" that provoked such strong reactions among the Brazilian elites. The Brazilian Black Front was created by Abdias do Nascimento in the 1930s to denounce the marginalization of black Brazilians and propose their inclusion in social policies. With the advent of the New State and the suppression of democracy by Getúlio Vargas in 1937, the Black Front was closed down. But in 1944 Abdias created the Experimental Theater of the Negro, and the newspaper *O Quilombo* concentrated the debate on the condition of the black population and their projects and demands. In 1950, the first Congress of the Black Brazilian took place, the fruit of mobilizations throughout the country that were subsequently stifled by the military coup of 1964. In 1968, Abdias went into exile in the United States, only returning to Brazil in 1983, when he was elected a congressman. His work, focused on the idea of a "quilombista movement," was fundamental, along with his presence in the National Constituent Assembly that drafted a new constitution in 1988.

From 1930 onward, the quilombo appeared once again, and thanks to the claims of militants of the black movement and members of parliament, was eventually taken to the National Constituent Assembly, to be transformed into a juridical device able to promote the effective entrance of Afro-descendants into the new institutional order. The text of the constitution grants blacks specific cultural and territorial rights: Article 68 envisages the regularization of the land rights of the "remainders of the quilombo communities," associating this with the full set of fundamental human rights (CFB/1988, título I, on fundamental rights and guarantees, título II, cap. II, on social rights), and beyond these, also recognizes the right to specific cultural practices and protection of cultural patrimony (CFB/1988, Articles 215 and 216 on Brazilian cultural patrimony).

The majority of black associations, many created after 1988 and representing groups seeking land rights regularization, only became aware of the quilombo as a constitutional right some years after the proclamation of the federal constitution in 1998. Since then they have developed a series of propositions based on their own experiences, presented in meetings throughout the country. These propositions are based on constitutional rights, but also grounded in shared narratives about the nature of the territorial conflicts that had persisted in the country for over a century. During these meetings, leaders over eighty years old recounted the stories of their ancestors seeking innumerable times to legalize their lands. The oral histories, presenting an alternative version of history to the formal, legal one, ultimately discredited the dossiers, maps, and land titles of their adversaries, exposing the frauds utilized by the bureaucracy to cheat these communities out of their customary rights to land. This is what happened in Casca, a community in Rio Grande do Sul, in which the original owner of the *sesmaria* (colonial land grant), upon his death in 1824, willed his land to the "black" community (I. Leite 2004). The black groups never concerned themselves with making maps of their property or inscribing their names in cadastral registers. When they inherited these lands, they observed territorial limits that corresponded with their memories of past land use, environmental landmarks, and management of the ecosystem, reflecting their continuous usufruct of these lands from the time of their ancestors. The maps made almost a half-century later were based on a fundamentally different relationship to land and relied upon official bureaucratic instruments used to formalize, register, and legitimize land ownership and, in this case, to steal the land from its existing occupants. In this as in many other cases, the use of written documentation effectively denied locally embedded ideas of rights to land, rights that only became visible through the oral histories of the groups, because they are not recorded in any document.

In the past twenty years, there have been hundreds of encounters throughout Brazil of black groups that are today organized into local, state, and national associations. Collective practices of land usufruct are becoming a target of intense debate within these community associations, most of which are members of the National Association of Quilombos (CONAQ), which is attempting to unite all of these local associations and to make alliances with other social movements in order to achieve greater legitimacy and leverage in dealings with government. CONAQ is the vehicle through which the claims of these black groups are presented to the national state. For example, in the north of Brazil, the quilombo movements are networking with the indigenous movements, rubber tappers, fishermen, and riverine populations, discussing land rights and common property systems. Meetings of the leaders of black communities with the aim of strengthening practices of collective land appropriation are also uniting communities in different countries, including residents of the Brazilian Amazon, French Guyana, Guatemala, Colombia, and Venezuela. These movements are looking for successful transnational strategies to apply to local problems. National and international campaigns of solidarity with the "quilombola cause" took these organizations to the United Nations Durban Review Conference in Geneva in 2009, created to evaluate progress toward the goals established by the World Congress against Racism and Racial Discrimination in 2001. Dialogue between CONAQ and nongovernmental organizations resulted in a campaign in defense of quilombola rights in Europe and other parts of the world. The Manifesto for the Defense of Quilombola Rights of June 2009 describes the actions of the movement in the federal supreme court and the national congress.

Thus, although quilombo is a word that has been in use since the colonial period, its capacity to signify a variety of forms of escape from, protest against, and aspirations to transform existing relations of domination has given it an enduring capacity to undergo resignification through time, up to the present era of human rights and antiracist and multicultural politics. Through the trajectory described above, it becomes clear that the quilombo is a transhistorical concept that embraces different periods, contexts, and situations, the common denominator being its symbolization of the refusal to accept different kinds of domination.

The Juridical-Formal Quilombo

Since 1988 the quilombo has been gradually transformed into a right through constitutional Articles 68 (regulated by Decree 4887/2006), 215, and 216 of the federal constitution of 1988. Thus, in the two decades since the constituent assembly, the quilombo has shifted from simply forming part of the discourse of social movements into becoming an instrument of state policies. We therefore need to consider the implications of this new juridical-formal quilombo.

As Alfredo Wagner Almeida (2005) has observed, the quilombola question has become the subject of extensive and multifaceted national action on the part of the executive power.[3] However, governmental actions and rhetoric reveal extensive disagreements over the judicial consolidation of territories and the implementation of social policies. At present, the social programs targeted at quilombola communities are slowly being put into effect, while the process of land titling has been relatively insignificant. From 2007 to 2008, no new quilombola land was titled. Also visible is a tendency toward the intensification of the judicial controversies based on questioning the principles and criteria used to define what a quilombo should be. On one side are those who reaffirm it as a transhistoric concept, focusing on its semantic dislocations; on the other side are those who try to delete its references to the past, and to tradition, and denounce the political instrumentality of the use of the term quilombo by those seeking rights to land. As a result of this struggle over definitions, statistics are being constantly reformulated, either to increase or reduce the number of quilombos. Some figures aim to justify the distribution of resources from the public budget. Current official estimates point to the existence of more than three thousand quilombo communities in Brazil. Yet, the UNEGRO, one of the organizations of the black movement, asserts that there are more than four thousand quilombos.[4]

In the quilombos, the federal government saw an opportunity for greater visibility and political capital, depicting itself as a government of the people. For the subaltern groups, seeking the official titling of a quilombo often involves confronting serious structural conflicts, of a kind that sometimes date back to the slave and immediate postslavery period. Almost two centuries have passed and Casca is still fighting for titles to lands that became subject to dispute with other parties (I. Leite 2004). For black communities, the post-1988 judicial context demands, among other things, the rethinking of internal and external alliances and strategies and the basis on which political support can be obtained in order to engage the legal system. The present legislation envisages a preliminary stage in which all conflicts must be resolved by the community before titling can take place, which creates a vicious circle from which it is difficult to break out.

The first Land Law was enacted in 1850 as the slave system was called increasingly into question. The law intended to distribute public lands to "Brazilians" and "Foreigners" (European immigrants). The various legal strategies employed were claimed to have universal application but in fact applied only to a minority. Africans and their slave descendants were excluded from the distribution of land through a subtle mechanism of territorial expropriation: the law denied Africans and their descendants full Brazilian citizenship by placing them in the special liminal category of *libertos* (Africans and their descendants), a category that gave them no rights under the law. The 1850 law, which transferred public lands to private ownership, favored large landowners and the accumulation of large properties (L. O. Silva 1996). In this clearly racist moment, which favored big landowners and European immigrants alike, the libertos, the poor, and all those labeled indigenous were displaced, principally because they could not present documentary proof of their rights of occupation or because they could not pay the taxes charged to have their properties registered. These supposedly universal provisions thus created numerous legal ways of expropriating the land: expulsions, removals, enclosure and the registering of "vacant" land, the forced and arbitrary division of community lands understood by the owners to be inalienable, and the seizure of lands for failure to pay taxes (for Mexican parallels, see de la Peña, chapter eleven).

The invisibility of rural black communities in Brazil for more than a century demonstrates the hegemonic legal order and at the same time exposes a form of symbolic violence to which these groups were forced to submit. This hegemonic order operated by criminalizing those who fought to remain on their lands or in their *terreiros de Candomblé*, as described by Luis Nicolau Parés in chapter seven.

The form of violence practiced in the expropriation of land arises from the way some technologies of control are inaccessible to a world without literacy, exercised through the state apparatus of legislation, the deployment of the police as an instrument of public order, and the private appropriation of public resources. Currently, extensive legislation, particularly Federal Decree 4887, defines the process by which quilombos should be officially recognized and legalized. What is significant about this contemporary framework is that the law appears to incorporate sectors of the Brazilian population who had previously been de facto disenfranchised as far as territorial rights were concerned. But in fact the judicial process exposes longstanding land conflicts, as the hostile reaction of the Party of the Liberal Front (now renamed the Democratic Party) indicates. This party, which represents agribusiness and other national and international business interests, is seeking a constitutional amendment to nullify the law. From a human rights perspective, however, this law is consistent with the international rights conventions to which Brazil is a signatory, particularly International Labor Organization Convention 169 and the UN Convention on Human Rights. This legislation introduces criteria by which Afro-descendants can identify collectively as a quilombo community. In addition, it reestablishes the principle of communal land rights for qui-lombos, a crucial and historic innovation.

Besides being incorporated into the ambit of government social poli-cies, the quilombo has also been incorporated by the Federal Public Min-istry and by several groups within Brazilian civil society, such as political parties, NGOs, trade unions, Afro groups, theater companies, churches, academic research institutes and groups, and other agencies including international ones.[5] Since legal recognition was introduced, the quilombo has become a right, thus becoming the subject of a growing number of judicial disputes. For instance, the Agrarian Reform Ministry (INCRA) re-ported in January 2007 that there were 463 lawsuits in the state of Pará as a result of quilombolas' requesting the government acknowledge the lands they occupy. In some states, interests opposed to the acknowledgement of the quilombola communities enjoy the support of local governments. This reaction started in 2004, after the Party of the Liberal Front, a party of the center-right renamed the Democrats in 2007, mounted its challenge to the constitutionality of the decree that regulates Article 68.

In 1998, during my first visit to the community of Casca, today officially recognized as a quilombola community, I was asked by the local leader about the meaning of the term quilombo. He explained that in that region, the term conveyed a strong sense of insubordination, and that it was also a word used to describe inappropriate and socially unacceptable behavior. For him, "quilombo" represented situations that inverted the social order, associated with other terms such as reveling, disorder, confusion, fight-ing, street riots, and shacks or shanties (reflecting the residence of large numbers of blacks in shantytowns in Brazilian cities). This man, already in his late seventies, returned again and again to the subject because he could not understand how the word quilombo, from something negative, had been transformed to refer to something apparently positive for the black communities. "I have seen on television that it is going to be good for the blacks, a right! Is the quilombo a right to make a mess?" he asked himself, trying to change his question into a joke, or perhaps doubting the effectiveness of the application of the law. Indeed, what had changed was not only the meaning of the word quilombo, but its effect, its link to new events that were starting to modify the entire local reality.

What he was really trying to understand was not only the change in the meaning of the term quilombo, but the fact that it meant something that he could not understand. Now, ten years after this episode took place, I have more perspective and can understand the reasons for his perplexity over the term, and his concerns. The quilombo, in the sense of struggle, opposition, and protest, has now become part of the juridical order; it has become a right within the legal order. The initial sense of confrontation and antagonism, of something marginal to national institutions and official power, has been effectively transformed. The redefinition of quilombo connotes new events and relations, including those resulting from questioning the old relations shaped by slavery.

This old man, having been for more than twenty years the administrator of the land left to the slaves, feared that now he would gradually lose his legitimacy as a traditional leader. This was because he had used his black phenotype as a justification, legitimated by the racial domination instituted since the colonial period, for committing a number of acts that broke the rules of succession and inheritance of the patrimony of the group. He now feared that all this could undermine his authority and control. His suspicions and fears derived from the questioning of his legitimacy by the heirs, which had begun many years earlier but was now becoming anchored in the law. When the quilombo entered the juridical-formal order, what he feared most in fact happened: although black like others in the community, his status as a relative and member of the group has been questioned, and this could be the initial step for his removal as leader. Now I realize why it was so important to him at that particular moment to understand not only the apparently simple change in the meaning of the term, but its direction and its implications.

The old criteria on which local social organization, traditions of succession, and the administrative-political system rested have been revised and redefined. Traveling back and forth to Casca for field research during the past ten years, I have been able to follow the successive changes that have also occurred in the perception of the map of the territory, which resulted from the application of the procedures of Article 68 and Decree 4887. Yet it remains important to remember that, like so many others, the Casca community has not achieved its ultimate goal, since its land rights have still not been confirmed through official titling.

The transhistorical concept of quilombo has connected the African diaspora to the conquest of territory. Discussion about land rights brings to the surface various other kinds of rights, including the right of return to ancestral lands, the right to have a home, and the right to receive schooling and have access to health care.[6] In the metaphorical process associated with the quilombo, the quilombolas are viewed as slaves' descendants, that is, as people who have been deprived of citizenship. The rights the quilombo confers are thus rights that concern all those rendered invisible by racism. These rights apply to a large portion of the Brazilian population, both rural and urban. The quilombo today covers a very full list of demands, its significations disseminated through all aspects of social life. In all of them, the quilombo signifies the reaffirmation of rights that have still not been fully won.

The sound of the Carnival drums and the refrain sung by thousands of samba dancers at Marques de Sapucaí are part of these new events. Presenting an *enredo* (a samba plot) centered on the Orixá Obatalá to pay homage to quilombos, Beija-Flor Samba School from Nilópolis won the title of 2007 Carnival Champions of Rio de Janeiro. This would be an event of little importance to our analysis were it not for the visit to the samba school of a Brazilian government minister and staff responsible for the government's agrarian and Afro-Brazilian heritage policies (including the "Brazilian Quilombola Program"). The visit was widely announced in the press and aimed to support and reinforce the theme of the carnival performance, considered to coincide with the policies of the current government.[7] In the show, it was possible to see, among the *Baianas* (women wearing the full white dresses associated with mothers of saints in the world of Candomblé in Bahia), clowns, and *pierrôs* (pierrots), four quilombola communities to which homage was paid. One of them was the Casca community, already mentioned in this chapter.[8]

Thus, a popular festivity also became a political act. But for whom? The government, through its official representatives, established their new obligations with the people. The quilombo, for both government and people, embodied the idea of change, which was stated several times in the refrain of the samba plot: "I'm quilombola community and freedom."

The quilombo, which was initially a set of land policies, has come to incorporate and synthesize the ethnic pluralism expressed in the new constitution: Brazil is represented as a multiethnic country and the state as the manager of this diversity. The idea of *mestiçagem* (racial mixture) as a founding myth and part of the imaginary of the nation assumed a secondary place in this Carnival context of multiple identity references (Da Matta 1987). In its place and through this ritual, the quilombo becomes an important part of national identity.

In contrast to previous representations of the nation, such as the *mes-*

tiço, or a Brazil of graceful *mulatas*, the new points of reference in the definition of Afro-Brazilian identity extend beyond the boundaries of the nation itself to the Brazilian Africas. The politics of territorial recognition associated with this new conception are presented as originating from harmony between society and the state. The quilombos' struggle for recognition and reparations, now inserted in contexts that suggest a successful social pact, floats behind the carnival masks; yet these masks hide territories in war and Africas that have never become effectively Brazilian.

Those responsible for implementing the law, mainly working from within the federal justice ministry, whose basic role is to respect and implement the constitution, also demonstrate in their discourses that sometimes they consider and recognize that the meaning given to the term "quilombo" by protest movements, and by anthropological studies, is in accordance with the text of the law (Rocha 2005). Some judges, when they adopt the principle of multicultural law, judge according to this logic. The justice ministry accepts the citizenship demands of subaltern groups and interposes itself as a mediator between divergent interests in its actions of control, monitoring, and application of the laws that compose the federal constitution.

In a public civil action in 2005 by the INCRA and the Palmares Cultural Foundation in favor of the Silva Family Quilombola Association (the first officially recognized urban quilombo in Brazil), the judge gave his opinion based in the following arguments: "To assure protection to those who have resisted for a long time and fought for their survival in the margins of the established order."[9] In this case, the official discourse used the idea of resistance in the same sense as the black social movements used it, to justify the necessity of recognizing their claims, a recognition that at the same time has not been carried through in practice up to the present day, since the lands have not been titled.

In his judgment, the judge made use of the transhistorical concept of the quilombo when presupposing that the end of slavery did not represent an end to relations of domination. The idea of resistance becomes the foundation of the right to a quilombo, legitimates it, and transforms it into an act of reparation (see also Hita, chapter thirteen). Yet the effective possibility of reparations is now established by the state through laws that make recognition of quilombos dependent on the state. From that point on, the quilombo stops representing resistance by movements that operate "on the margins of the established order" and starts being managed by the state, thus integrating this resistance into the body of the nation.[10] Now that it has become part of a utopian national project, in this new context the state must promote the quilombo's complete incorporation and integration through formal recognition of land rights, affirmative action policies, and support for social and economic development.

Resistance in its earlier sense is thus a condition for recognition, but ceases to be relevant once official recognition has been granted. When it becomes a right, the quilombo does not lose its explicit relation with the idea of African resistance to slavery, but this resistance now represents part of the grounds for state recognition, which brings the quilombo in from the outside, from the context of the African slave diaspora, to the inside, to the context of the nation. Once it is "nationalized," the concept of resistance that is integral to the transhistorical quilombo undergoes an inversion of its previous meaning: rebellion is transformed into a social pact.

This process disrupts and transforms the metaphorical meaning of the transhistorical quilombo, in particular its continuing association with a variety of forms of resistance to domination. From the point of view of state policies, the incorporation of the quilombo into Brazilian society inverts the idea of resistance as conflict into the idea of resistance as order. The struggle of the quilombolas is spreading and is everyone's struggle. The idea of resistance itself becomes one that actually begins to mask the antagonisms and slow rhythm of substantive changes.[11]

The implications of this transformation manifest themselves in the new kinds of political compromises and alliances that the leaders of quilombola communities are now obliged to make, both to secure official recognition and to gain access to state social development programs. The quilombo as a form of oppositional politics is in danger of turning into the opposite, a political instrument that government can manipulate in a way that leads to the maintenance, acceptance, and institutionalization of forms of domination that do not represent a real break with past patterns.

It is important to remember, however, that the juridical-formal quilombo is a lawful right, and as such does not in itself promote attitudes of deference, alienation, and subalternity. The gap between promise and reality in the implementation of both the law itself and the new social policies associated with state support for quilombos is producing a new field of tensions and conflicts that I term manifestations of the emergence of a "post-utopian" quilombo.

The Post-Utopian Quilombo

Given the delay in legal resolution and the slowness of the process of regularization of land titles, some quilombola associations have sought to publicize their demands through occupations of the land that had been expropriated from them. At same time, conservative Brazilian media that reflect the views of the political right and oppose movements seeking to achieve social justice for "racially" defined groups have reinforced the challenges mounted in congress to the legitimacy of the constitutional right introduced in Article 68 and implemented in Decree 4887.[12] This unfavorable climate provided a pretext for the strengthening of actions by rural interest groups who defended the private property of large landowners and agribusiness tied to international capital. Opponents of Decree 4887 argue that, because of these new rights, a racializing of social conflicts is occurring that is actually detrimental to the achievement of social justice in a society in which most people are the product of mixing between European, African, and Amerindian populations. They argue that initiatives focused on political organizing are more important than initiatives focused on race. These arguments that depict the quilombo as divisive are gaining increased attention and supporters.

During the twenty years of the quilombo's constitutional existence, Brazil has gained a prominent place in international politics and in the global economy and has been recognized as an emerging world power. Nevertheless, the rhetoric of equality is still permeated by the backstage role in Brazilian politics of clientelistic relations that sabotage the principles of the constitution. Powerful economic groups with a strong influence on government, principally in export agriculture and the economic sectors that produce paper and cellulose, have lobbied strongly against the application of the law on the grounds that lands transferred to quilombos will not be used to promote "the objectives of development." It is important to see here that different concepts of development are in play when it is a question of making land available for "social interest" uses that will reduce poverty directly, or putting it at the disposal of large-scale transnational capital. As part of the same tactics of domination used in the past, these practices sustain Brazil as a country of inequality, violence, and injustice. The protests by the quilombola movement have invariably been met with repressive police action, which demonstrates that the power of resistance attributed to the juridical-formal quilombos is not sufficient for them to achieve their rights without the activism of the transhistorical quilombo. Yet the existence of a legal framework for pursuing rights claims now serves to delegitimize more militant action.

Brazil today is living in what has come to be considered a "postmodern" condition, that is, with all the types of insurgent action that are called postmodern. On the one hand, the quilombo seems to call into question existing power structures, their legitimacy, and the methods used to maintain them. Yet on the other hand, it seeks to become part of those structures, to the extent that the right to a quilombo becomes grounded in the law. It therefore becomes pertinent to ask questions about other possible meanings of the quilombo and the different senses of resistance that it encapsulates. The answers will emerge from future developments that remain difficult to foresee. But perhaps it is a question of a dynamic play of forces that makes deepening democracy a planetary utopian project.

The quilombo as a constitutional right resonates with this planetary project, and for this reason has been seen as a phenomenon that disturbs national identity, since it challenges and confronts the clientelism that runs through the structures of the state. In consequence, the quilombo in the two senses of resistance that it has embodied is a type of power that crosscuts state and society in their most diverse forms: first, when it disrupts fixed identities based on kinship, region, and nation; and second, when it implants doubts about the state's capacity to determine citizenship rights and order territorial space. From this perspective, it seems possible to conclude that both the transhistorical and juridical-formal quilombo integrate state and society.

This new context is what I call the post-utopian quilombo. The notions of the postmodern and the postcolonial, as they have emerged in contemporary social theory, do not mark a fixed chronological moment, but represent a change in the concepts of culture and power. Some conceptions of hegemony have cast doubt both on the capacity of subaltern groups to analyze and act on situations of oppression, and also on that of dominant groups to negotiate and concede. Yet as Matthew Gutmann shows in chapter fifteen with Mexican examples, we can and should still understand how subaltern groups gain historical agency and produce effective and transformative political movements, without romanticization or setting aside the contradictory aspects of such processes.

The current context therefore compels us to continue thinking about the concept of resistance, linking it to new configurations of power, especially those initiated in the process of African decolonization. These new realities stimulate us to think about resistance as a right, and the right of resistance, which are important corollaries of liberal doctrines. They can only exist when some space exists for dissent, for the incorporation of different lifestyles, and for environmentally sound practices. It is in this sense, as was understood by Gramsci, that civil society and the state are not separate; they overlap and are engaged in a radical dialectical practice that leads in unpredictable directions but nevertheless maintains an impetus towards historical change.

Notes

1 According to official statistics, the numbers of those identifying themselves as *negros* (blacks) in Brazil is growing. About 90 percent of the inhabitants of the areas designated as "remainders of quilombos" are self-proclaimed black people ("negros," "pretos," or "morenos"). From this index we deduce what is known as "African ancestry," but it is important to recognize that this represents a transformation of earlier Brazilian ideas about racial differences based on skin color, with the current emphasis on African ancestry reflecting a reidentification based on a political and organizational criterion.

2 For example, in her analysis of trade union struggles in Couço, Portugal, Paula Godinho has argued: "An attitude of resistance . . . is contrary to one of giving up, of succumbing, that is considered passive. It integrates the vocabulary and constitutes a vital need that human beings always feel whenever the thresholds of survival are at stake. It is used in the collective sense, a fight for life, but also to designate a set of values that are common to a group and, without which, life isn't worth living. It also constitutes a way to demonstrate adhesion to the values a group has in common, even if said group has a minority position. Resistance constitutes therefore a culture, since it determines that a group shares common ideals and habits, which help them to continue to exist" (2001, 32, translated by the author).

3 Official institutions involved in implementing quilombo-oriented programs include four agencies of the presidency of the republic, the holders of which have ministerial status: the Special Office for Racial Equality Policies, Secretariat of Human Rights, and, both supporting the President's Office, the Casa Civil, and the Institutional Security Cabinet. They also include six ministries (agrarian development, culture, education, health, justice, and social development), plus the Palmares Cultural Foundation, National Health Foundation, and National Institute of Colonization and Agrarian Reform (A. W. B. Almeida 2005, 27).

4 In all the regions and states of the federation, the "remaining quilombo areas"

are identified. In 2002, the Palmares Cultural Foundation acknowledged having already "catalogued" 843 quilombos, of which 510 were in the northeastern region, 212 in the northern region, 88 in the southeast, 18 in the central Western region, and 15 in the south of Brazil. Since then, the numbers have continued to rise. The INCRA of Minas Gerais recently announced, in a preliminary survey, the existence of 387 quilombola communities in that state alone. The Special Office for Racial Equality Policies (SEPPIR) revealed, in January 2007, the existence of 3,250 quilombola communities, comprising 2.5 million people. At the same time, figures for certifications are almost irrelevant: in 2004 there were 2; in 2005, 4; in 2006, 14, involving 1,947 families and 28,725 hectares.

5 The Brazilian Association of Anthropology, in partnership with the federal government, opened a competition in 2004 to finance anthropological studies, monographs, and essays on the quilombola territories. The Channel Foundation has bestowed master's scholarships on quilombola women.

6 Brazil signed Convention 169 of the International Labor Organization in June 1989, although the federal senate did not ratify it until July 2002. This convention establishes the rights granted to ethnic minorities. The fundamental criterion is considered to be the ethnic self-identification elements that broaden the bond between social and ethnic rights. Article 14 stipulates, "The ownership and property rights over the lands on which the interested people live will have to be acknowledged." Article 16 introduced the right to return, under the following terms: "Whenever possible, these people will be entitled to return to their traditional lands as soon as the causes that motivated their departure and resettlement have ceased to exist."

7 In an interview with the press, Rui Leandro dos Santos, general coordinator of the regularization of the quilombola territories program in the Institute of Colonization and Agrarian Reform (INCRA), declared, "The victory of the Beija-Flor is also an achievement of these communities. This type of victory is important to the quilombola cause, because it draws the attention of the general population to the problems surrounding the acknowledgement of the legacy that Afro-descendants left to Brazilian culture. It also highlights the issue of land regularization of thousands of Brazilian quilombola communities, a right the INCRA and the federal government seek to guarantee by all means—through the SEPPIR [Special Office for Racial Equality Policies] and the Brazil quilombola program." Santos also said he went with the other representatives of INCRA to the headquarters of Beija-Flor before Carnival to find out about the details of the plot or script of the samba and the costumes involving the quilombola communities: "We went to the school, we talked to the constituents and we clarified any doubts they might have had regarding what we're doing for the communities. We presented details of the politics of the federal government regarding the quilombolas and told them that our actions are making it possible for Afro-descendants, who have been neglected for centuries in Brazil, to recover

their rights" (INCRA website news section, February 6 and 21, 2007, http://www
.incra.gov.br/).

8 The lyrics of the samba from Beija-Flor also mention the quilombola community of Pedra do Sal, which is currently undergoing a process of land regularization at the INCRA in Rio de Janeiro, and pay tribute to the quilombola communities of Ilha de Marambaia, also in Rio, and Kalunga, in Goiás.

9 "Ação de Manutenção de Posse" number 2005.71.00020/04–4, *Justiça Federal*,
July 12, 2005.

10 Decree 4887, which regulates Article 68 of the constitution, mandates that the
titles of the lands that have a collective use must be granted to the association,
with a clause of inalienability.

11 A. W. B. Almeida (2005, 39–44) correlates official recognition, demarcation, and
certification, three separate steps in the process of land regularization.

12 Recent articles in the *Jornal Nacional* of the TV Globo Network, in the weekly
magazines *Veja*, and *Exame* (www.exame.com.br), and in the newspaper *O Estado de São Paulo* have questioned the legitimacy of the quilombo.

CHAPTER THIRTEEN

From Resistance Avenue to the Plaza of Decisions

New Urban Actors in Salvador, Bahia

MARIA GABRIELA HITA

In this chapter, I examine the impact of a history of resistance on the vigorous associational life of Bairro da Paz (Neighborhood of Peace), a low-income settlement in the city of Salvador, Bahia. This is a history impressed on the consciousnesses of neighborhood residents, recorded in the names of streets and public spaces. Originating in the popular urban housing movement of the 1980s, this community's forms of struggle have been updated by a mix of social, political, religious, and cultural actors with an increasingly democratic profile. These actors are central to my ethnographic description of the case, and are my point of departure for broader reflections on the contemporary meanings and practices of resistance.

Neighborhood residents developed their self-image as people who "resist" through struggles to affirm less stigmatized identities. I argue that the gains from these struggles were as much the result of transformations undergone by Brazilian society at large (including changes brought about by neoliberal state projects), as fruits of the robust popular movement that developed in this community. I begin by sketching the principal changes in politics and urban policy that shaped this community's role within the popular urban movement during the 1980s and 1990s. I then consider its specific history in ethnographic detail. Resistance was initially associated with struggles for land and clear opposition to the state, but as relations with public authorities and civil society changed, so did the types of social actions in which residents were involved, without eliminating an "emphasis on demands."

I then discuss how various organizations came together to create the Fórum Permanente de Entidades do Bairro da Paz (Permanent Forum of Organizations of Bairro de Paz, or "the forum"). Through an analysis of this new social actor, some of the groups that form it, and an engagement with theoretical literature on resistance, I explore how the myth of resistance in Bairro da Paz has been reinvented, and old meanings updated in new modes of practicing resistance, so that some are conserved while new modes are introduced. Inverting the significance of some of James Scott's (1990) ideas, I conclude by proposing official transcripts of subaltern ethnic consciousness as a new form of resistance that uses the "weapons of the strong."

Housing Policies of the 1990s

Brazil's urbanization was characterized by sharp social inequalities. Large, destitute areas with minimal infrastructure coexisted with affluent neighboring districts with greater provision of amenities. The lack of affordable public housing caused rural migrants living in precarious conditions to invade empty spaces in defiance of urban regulations. In Salvador, with a population of just over 3 million in 2000 (P. H. Almeida 2006), 60 percent of a total of approximately 700,000 housing units were in areas of irregular occupation, and the housing deficit was nearly 100,000 homes (Gordilho 2000). Disadvantages in access to housing were greatest for poor black citizens; 80 percent of Salvador's population is of African descent.

The struggle for urban reform in Brazil has gone through various phases: it was driven in the 1940s by the action of the Comitês Democráticos Populares contra os Despejos (Popular Democratic Committees against Evictions), in the 1950s by the Sociedades dos Amigos dos Bairros (Societies of Friends of the Neighborhoods), and in the 1980s by the Movimento Urbano de Favelados (Urban Movement of the Residents of Favelas), which supported land invasions throughout the country (Kowarick 1994; Teixeira 2001). The constitution of 1988 marked a decisive change, reflecting the transition from a military "developmentalist" state to liberal democratic governance (Caldeira and Holston 2004). Enshrining new individual and social rights, the constitution reflected the contribution of social movements, including those for housing and the rights of women and black citizens, to the struggle to restore democracy.

At the level of local politics in Bahia, change occurred in official attitudes to housing problems because the center-left candidate Waldir Pires won control of the state government in 1987, defeating the dominant *carlista* group, led by three-time governor and senator for Bahia Antônio Carlos Magalhães, popularly known as ACM, a conservative ally of the military dictatorship, business leaders, and the northeastern landed class. At this time the national project Minha Casa (My House) sought to forge partnerships between the state and slum communities. From 1989 to 1996—a period that covered the left-wing mayorships of Lídice da Mata and Fernando José—the realization of these programs was, however, limited to municipal funding. Therefore it was only possible to fund emergency projects for people who lost their homes, for the relocation of land invaders, and for the legalization of land ownership.

In 1997 and 1998, after the United Nations Habitat II conference, there was a significant rise in urban investment across Brazil, thanks to the extensive financial support offered by international and federal bodies. One visible change in this new policy model was the prioritization of improvements to the infrastructure of poor areas by maintaining their original populations in place, as opposed to the policy of relocating invaders to housing complexes in peripheral areas that had been the norm in previous decades. The number of houses constructed in this period was almost double that during the two previous administrations (Gordilho 2000).

While these changes broadened the rights to the city of disadvantaged groups, public-private partnerships and other neoliberal policies often also insidiously reproduced previous structural and social inequalities. Public investments in housing and sanitation programs in the poorest areas in Salvador during the 1990s remained timid compared with the scale of investment in support of leisure projects, public transportation, and facilities that supported the city's economic reorientation to global tourism and service industries (P. H. Almeida 2006).

This reorientation is exemplified by the development since the 1980s of the Avenida Paralela (Parallel Avenue), on which Bairro da Paz is located. The main area of high-income development in the city today, it provides access to the "Green Line" of coastal resorts to the north, and includes the state government administrative center, built by ACM, as well as upscale

developments constructed after Bairro da Paz was established: the Alphaville condominium, the Faculdade de Tecnologia e Ciências (FTC, University of Science and Technology), Imbuí, a middle-class residential area,
and the Parque Aquático de Diversões (Aquatic Amusement Park). In 2008,
work began on a new science and technology park. Bairro da Paz thus appears as a stain of poverty in a zone of high purchasing power.

The most recent national developments to impact Bairro da Paz are
the two presidential terms of Luis Inácio "Lula" da Silva of the Partido dos
Trabalhadores (Workers Party, or PT). Between 2002 and 2010, the Lula
governments developed a series of effectively articulated public policies
grouped under the master program Fome Zero (Zero Hunger). These included stipends for families and school attendance similar to the Oportunidades program of neoliberal Mexican governments (González de la
Rocha 2006; see also de la Peña, chapter eleven) and other initiatives designed to enhance social inclusion.

Citizens' Movements in the 1980s and 1990s

Despite the contemporary world's tendencies toward individualism—
tendencies that are the products of consumer society and the emphasis
on survival on the part of the most excluded—countervailing attitudes oriented to collective action continue to reappear. Since the 1990s, there has
been a prodigious proliferation of NGOs and "new social movements" that
have strengthened civil society and actively participated in struggles for democratization. Many themes previously absent from the public sphere—
such as issues of gender, youth, the elderly, and ethnicity—began to command new global political agendas. This has resulted in what some call
a "new political culture" of "citizen participation" characterized by new
modes of expression associated with a heterodox and emancipatory vision
of politics (Teixeira 2001; Castells 2002; Jelin 2004; Touraine 2005). Yet, as
Charles Hale (2002) points out, some changes are also a product of a top-
down project of neoliberal multiculturalism that selects and promotes the
types of cultural rights that are in the interests of the ruling system.

This new political paradigm is, paradoxically and simultaneously, the
result of both the crisis and precariousness of welfare states, the discred-
iting of party political systems, and the deepening of class conflicts, and
also of a growing political awareness on the part of various sectors seeking
to advance their social participation. Despite the reduced preoccupation

with capturing state power and the greater fragmentation that characterizes new movements, the logic emerging through their practice is also one
of greater respect for plurality and the search for normative consensus
vis-à-vis basic questions, presaging a "new institutionalism" based on the
practice of more democratic relations. Furthermore, these new types of
social action tend to operate through networks, articulating diverse associational movements and attempting to combat fragmenting tendencies.[1]

In Bairro da Paz (and Salvador more generally) the organizational support offered to popular groups since the 1970s by the Centro de Estudos e Ação Social (CEAS, Center for Studies and Social Action) has been
essential. Reflecting the developments just outlined, the CEAS, founded
by Jesuits and lay groups committed to liberation theology, has recently
shifted its focus of action, previously centered upon support for unions,
homeless people, and residents' councils, toward investment in the cultural activities of black youths and "re-Africanization" movements of the
kind described by Luis Nicolau Parés in chapter seven. Such new forms
of popular mobilization have enjoyed considerable success in Salvador,
for many movements have institutionalized themselves and formed inter-
nationally recognized NGOs with an ethnic character, as in the case of
Olodum, which, since 1983, has been concerned with social action in the
Maciel-Pelourinho community, or that of Timbalada in Candeal, led by the
singer Carlinhos Brown (Gordilho 2000).

From the Resistance of the Malvinas to the Peace of the Decisions

Bairro da Paz, located directly on the Avenida Paralela, was known before
1987 as the "Malvinas Invasion," because the community emerged during
the war fought between Great Britain and Argentina over possession of the
Malvinas, or the Falkland Islands.[2] The name echoes the violent confrontation between the "invaders" and the municipal powers that tried to evict
them. In 1982 and 1983, the city authorities made no fewer than eighteen
attacks on their shacks, although the dwellings the authorities destroyed
were patiently rebuilt at night through collective efforts, a clear act of resistance to state repression.

In 1983, following negotiations with the *favela* movement of which they
were a part, two thousand families relocated to Fazenda Coutos, in the distant Subúrbio Ferroviário. Yet despite the prefecture's efforts to repress the
Malvinas invasion and the number of different parties with interests in the

occupied land, including real estate developers, politicians, and environ-mentalists, the movement was never deactivated.[3] Subsequent waves of invaders were soon to be added to the first groups that arrived at the be-ginning of the 1980s. This invasion of land of high real estate value split public opinion in Bahia between those who believed the settlers should be evicted and those who supported their fight for permanent residence rights in the area. When the election of Waldir Pires as governor in 1987 did secure the invaders the right to remain on the occupied lands, the settlement was renamed "Bairro da Paz," a name that symbolized the new status the invaders had won, the victory of the popular organization, and a desire to adopt a less stigmatized self-image. In this conjuncture, the legal occupation of the land was negotiated for residents who lived in a polygonal area with greater urbanization, around the main square. These residents now started to collaborate with city authorities in exercising con-trol over excessive growth of the neighborhood's population. Residents of the other five areas of the bairro adjacent to the polygon, where housing conditions were more precarious, benefited less from the settlement. De-spite the fact that public squares, churches, crèches, and schools were also beginning to arrive in these areas, there were constant complaints about their lower levels of urbanization and lack of paved streets and sanitation.

The Malvinas was the most combative standard-bearer of Salvador's Movimento dos Favelados (a precursor of the contemporary Sem Teto homeless movement). The consciousness of being the product of strong resistance to state repression is recurrent in the collective memory of residents and community leaders, strategically imprinted by the record-ing of this facet of community history in the names chosen for streets, squares, and public places. The name of the main avenue at the entrance to the neighborhood is Avenida da Resistência (Avenue of Resistance), which connects Avenida Paralela to the six subregions of the settlement. On this avenue one finds the greatest concentration of shops, churches, and facilities of NGOs that are active in the bairro, and continuing along it one arrives at the main square of Bairro da Paz, called Praça das Decisões (Plaza of Decisions).[4] This square benefits from the best facilities and has the highest property value. The bus routes that serve the community also converge on this square. The main Catholic church (which has six depen-dents serving the other areas) can also be found there, along with one of the three primary schools, the only and still-temporary secondary school, and the largest supermarket. Further along Rua da Paz, other important community and Catholic church buildings can be found, including those occupied by a group of nuns from India, a building occupied by an Italian priest, the substantial buildings of the Fundação Dom Avelar Brandão Vilela (Dom Avelar Brandão Vilela Foundation) and Cidade Mãe (Mother City) project, as well as the headquarters of the residents' council.

The first phase of urbanization occurred between 1990 and 2000, although action was tightly linked to election periods and the interest of politicians in the bairro's votes. Some of the first facilities secured were preschool crèches. The community crèches were run by women who had played a prominent role in the formation of the first associations and militant struggles, and these initiatives received support from feminist groups. The case of Bairro da Paz illustrates the prominent presence in popular, religious, urban, and rural struggles of female actors of differing ideological orientations, ranging from socially conservative charitable positions to militant Marxist and feminist ones, a fact complementing the cases discussed by Patience Schell in chapter nine and Margarita Zárate in chapter ten.

The Santa Casa de Misericórdia (Sacred House of Charity, a traditional Catholic institution) targeted Bairro da Paz for philanthropic work, as did other religious groups and NGOs that have become part of the internal network of actors operating in the community. The development of Bairro da Paz can also be understood as a process of "ethnogenesis," in the sense defined by Guillermo de la Peña in chapter eleven, given that it concerns the construction of both a community identity and a local, ethnic identity. This is because some of its internal factions, discussed later in this chapter, define Bairro da Paz as "black" and an "urban *quilombo*," a place of settlement for a black population that claims possession of the land as recompense for the past injustices committed against its ancestors. Ilka Leite provides an extended discussion of the quilombo, including this version, which she terms "post-utopian," in chapter twelve.

Since 2000, philanthropic crèches have appeared. Today there are a total of six Catholic crèches (together offering approximately 700 places), and one Spiritist crèche (150 places), besides the four smaller community crèches already mentioned, one of which is linked to a Candomblé *terreiro* (temple). One community crèche, that of Dona Celina, who joined the *carlista* political network of Antônio Carlos Magalhães, was closed down after she was accused of corruption. Today all the crèches rely on municipal or state support in some way, but those founded by charitable organizations enjoy more stable funding; thanks to better facilities, institutional sponsorship, and professional staffing, they are better able to meet the requirements of the New Guidelines and Bases for Infant Education implemented by the ministry of education in 1996. It is through such institutions that the state has managed to distribute food (through programs like Prato Amigo) and other types of benefits targeted at needy families.

Additionally, Bairro da Paz has a health center, installed in 2002, a police station, and, most recently, a digital inclusion telecenter. The telecenter is connected to the Internet thanks to financial partnerships between the current residents' council, Petrobras (the national oil company), and the Instituto de Formação Tecnológica (Institute of Technology Studies), an information network for the third sector. Young people are the main users of the center, and other NGOs, crèches, and the Centro de Convivência (community center) have been equipping rooms with computing facilities in order to provide similar services. The Centro de Convivência do Bairro da Paz, a sports and cultural center, was inaugurated in 2005, located outside the neighborhood and financed by the owners of the rich neighboring Alphaville condominium and the private FTC university. Despite the provision of these facilities, their quality and quantity remain inadequate to meet the needs of a population the size of Bairro da Paz.

There is a strong sense within the community's leaderships that what gains have been made have resulted more from struggle and popular organization than state concessions. Yet the relation between the state and the community did change over the years. The state, once an agent that repressed the residents during Brazil's military dictatorship, became a promoter of infrastructure development though private-public partnerships in the era of democratic opening. The emergence of new types of leadership and social action is a direct consequence of the broader political developments already described, as well as the internal evolution of the community itself. The first associations formed by residents played an important role in the initial phases of resistance but were corrupted by the clientelistic politics of elites. With the resumption of CEAS's activities in the area and greater support from the Catholic Church, the years after 1988 saw a new type of community leadership consolidated in the formation of a new residents' council.

New Types of Community Leadership

From within the web of actors in Bairro da Paz that confront and enter into conjunctural coalitions with each other, I will describe three positions: those of the residents' council, religious groups, and cultural groups. All exemplify a more democratic style of leadership in their different ways, as heirs to the citizenship movements of the 1980s and 1990s. In order to demarcate their distinguishing features, I highlight the types of projects that they represent, their principal enemies, and the positions they have adopted in the Fórum Permanente do Bairro da Paz.

As in any popular neighborhood, there is visible disputation and competition for access to resources between internal factions in Bairro da Paz. Conflicts and alliances reveal the party-political, religious, and social differences that divide these groups, the diversity of experiences of poverty, and the differing positions local groups occupy vis-à-vis wider networks. There are frequent criticisms of the mediating role of community institutions in the distribution of resources and benefits, and many complaints of favoritism toward friends and relatives. This shows how the circulation of goods tends to create clientelistic subgroups within community networks, as well as how the absolute scarcity of resources prevents equal distribution to all. The legitimacy of each group varies according to the clientele that is judging it, and according to the quality, amount, and durability of the resources that it manages to acquire and circulate, the type of project in which it is involved, and the networks to which it is connected. Because of this, of all the groups currently operating in Bairro da Paz, the current residents' council, while one of the strongest, also has many critics.

The Residents' Council

The Conselho de Moradores was created in 1993 by dissident members of the residents' association led by Dona Celina. Today's council is more democratic, transparent, professional, and critical than its predecessor, sympathizing with the political stance of the PT. Although its formation resulted from the advice of the CEAS, which was oriented to liberation theology, it also enjoys the support of the Italian lay organizer Clementina, representing a more conservative faction of the Catholic Church, one closer to the Vatican line, that funds the Dom Avelar Brandão Vilela Foundation.[5] The council is the state's right hand in the community and its central body in cultivating third-sector and private partnerships. It is this confluence of external support that makes it so powerful.

Among its main rivals are older associations linked to the clientelist networks of *carlismo*, such as the association Unidos para Vencer (United to Overcome). This is a vehicle for the leadership of a single individual, a man known as Mr. Marcelo, an authentic community leader who found a space through which to channel his projects in the Permanent Forum of Organizations of Bairro de Paz. Another of the older associations is the Associação Luis Eduardo Magalhães (named in honor of the son, since deceased, that ACM groomed as his political heir). The community crèches, including the Candomblé crèche, still form part of the network of these older associations. They are occasionally joined in some disputes by dissident youth and cultural groups, which fought without success for greater representation on the residents' council, and found in the forum a more level playing field for contention and empowerment relative to other groups in the community. These youth groups take varied stances among themselves and are therefore fragmented, at one moment opposing proposals of the council, at another moment converging with them. Though they have never aligned themselves with the opposition networks just described, some Evangelical groups are also frequent opponents of the council.

Among the council's main allies are Catholic institutions with which it has established important partnerships. Much of the community's leadership has become entangled with the Catholic networks by belonging to multiple institutions simultaneously and accumulating offices. The council also relies at times on the support of public authorities and richer neighbors, such as the FTC and Alphaville, with which it brokered the concession of the community center. The center's location outside the community and the limited number of people who benefit from it nevertheless draw criticism from the council's opponents.

Religious Networks

In Bairro da Paz there are four broad religious groupings: the powerful Catholic network, an Evangelical network, a Spiritist network, and Candomblé groups (or *povo do santo*, "people of the saint"). Each mobilizes significant symbolic social capital as well as material resources. All aid in the distribution of donations of food, blankets, and clothes, as well as in the provision of education and health services. It is these religious groups that people ask for help, and not simply those that practice the religions they espouse. In Bairro da Paz, due to their greater poverty, the povo do santo and Evangelicals are concentrated more on the receiving side of donations, which often come from Catholic and Spiritist organizations. Religious associations are important spaces of sociability, creating solidarity and a sense of belonging that "dignifies" their members. Studies have shown that they have a greater impact on improving the quality of life than other types of networks (Lavalle and Castello 2004). The Spiritist network is the community's weakest, since the Spiritists have not gone beyond charitable work and the establishment of a well-equipped crèche to develop a community of religious practice inside the bairro.

The Catholics have a particularly prominent position because they have the support of secular leaders in the community and operate within well-defined pastoral constituencies (with a predominance of women), youth groups, and Bible circles, and because they are able to count on the institutional legitimacy, inside and outside the community, of their church. They are prominent, too, thanks to their striking physical presence in Bairro da Paz's infrastructure, occupying around thirty buildings strategically positioned throughout the six areas of the community. The presence of Catholic groups in the forum strengthened since its formation, indicating the types of projects Catholics prioritize. Yet although a majority of the population of Bahia declares itself Catholic, it is common for Bahians to participate in other cults, sometimes simultaneously. In 2006 we discovered some forty Evangelical churches and eighteen Candomblé terreiros in Bairro da Paz, all an intrinsic part of the daily life of the community, vying with the Catholics for position and recognition.

Despite decades of marginalization, at present Candomblé is showing signs of empowerment, operating as an important marker of ethnic identity for black youth groups, as evidenced by the respect those youths express for the terreiros of their communities. Candomblé temples are often associated with networks of mutual aid, and some of their *pais e mães de santos* (fathers and mothers of saints, the spiritual leaders of the Candomblé religion) have played significant roles in the community. For example, the terreiro Ladê Padê Mim, the oldest in the Bairro da Paz, was led by the distinguished Mãe Zenaide, who also managed the crèche associated with Candomblé. Zenaide's is not an "elite terreiro" in the sense discussed by Parés in chapter seven, but the relative invisibility of Ladê Padê Mim within the hierarchy of temples in Salvador as a whole changes when it is compared with other temples within the community.[6] It enjoys internal prestige and also receives municipal support to ensure the survival of its crèche, food donations via the Prato Amigo program, and further resources from the Instituto Ação Comunidade (Community Action Institute) and from the Secretaria Municipal de Educação e Cultura. Other terreiros in the community are now organizing themselves to offer community services in order to be able to enjoy such state aid.

Ladê Padê Mim was extremely active during the initial phases of the forum. After the illness and death of its leader, its representation in the forum passed to Claudionor, a young musician trained by Carlinhos Brown's Timbalada, who founded the local group Etnia. The clientele of Ladê Padê Mim is basically formed by Claudionor's family and neighbors, networks that usually crosscut each other. There are visible conflicts between terreiros, although confrontations become more dramatic when they involve Evangelicals. Members of Ladê Padê Mim reported aggressive episodes of religious intolerance on the part of the Igreja Universal do Reino de Deus (Universal Church of the Kingdom of God), which constructed its huge building directly in front of their terreiro.

The relationship between Ladê Padê Mim and Catholic groups is one of mutual respect, even though the terreiro complains that its crèche is losing clients after the opening of new Catholic crèches. The impressive presence of the silent Zenaide, dressed as a mãe de santo, at Catholic-sponsored events was a symbol of the rapprochement between the two churches, a mark of willingness to negotiate and recognize her authority in the community. But during the mayorship of João Henrique Carneiro, an Evangelical, the terreiro complained about discontinuation of the support received under former administrations, although this was restored after the forum made representations to the prefecture.

Among the Evangelical groups of Bairro da Paz, I wish to highlight that of a Baptist pastor called Valmir, who occupied a post in Jõao Henrique's administration. Valmir is another critic of the residents' council, whose Catholic leaders, supporters of the Workers Party, accuse him of using his church for political proselytization. As far as Valmir is concerned, there is no contradiction between church-building and the use of his political contacts to augment his congregation and further his dreams of social ascension. With municipal support, he developed distributions of basic food and mattresses to the needy and organized large-scale events, such as a health week in partnership with the Faculdade São Camilo, which in 2006 offered gynecological and pediatric services through two mobile units. However, owing to a lack of water and a level of demand beyond expectations, these services proved chaotic and deficient. Nevertheless, the event brought Valmir increased visibility, was followed by others, and increased the clientele of his church. Currently he has congregations in three different neighborhoods. His participation in the forum was brief, and he left definitively in the face of hostility from members of the residents' council, though his construction of a new house in another community was another factor. The continual opening of new churches, especially Evangelical churches, is a clear sign of the penetrative power of these belief systems among the poorest, suggesting that there is still unsatisfied demand for spiritual services in these neighborhoods.

Cultural and Youth Groups

These consist mainly of young people who identify themselves as black. In Salvador, black youths are one of the main targets of new social policies, and members of cultural groups have proved important partners in the promotion of ethnic awareness and the government, third sector, and private business provision of symbolically valuable community services. These groups are politicizing debates and changing public agendas. Bairro da Paz has a variety of dance, music, and theater groups, including ones dedicated to *capoeira* (a dance and martial art), *maculelê* (a dance of African origin), *pagode* (a subgenre of the samba of Rio de Janeiro), *forró* (country music and dance), reggae, hip-hop, and rock. Today, many of these groups belong to the Juventude em Ação (Youth in Action) network that works with the CEAS. Several are connected to re-Africanization movements, which leave their mark on their consciousness and critical ethnic discourses. They struggle to strengthen citizenship independently of party politics, paving the way for processes of self-management in community practices. As mentioned earlier, there is some support among these groups for Bairro da Paz to be declared an urban quilombo.

In the early days of the forum, youth groups provided an important equilibrating force through the clarity, plurality, and transparency of their positions. Nonetheless, their presence and ongoing representation within the forum has been complicated by several factors, including their special interests and need to promote cultural events, their unstable position in labor markets as freelancers, internal divisions provoked by competition for resources, and a lower tolerance of traditional political models. They frequently appear and disappear, returning in moments when new cultural events must be prepared. They justify their position by expressing resentment against the leaders of the residents' council who have regular employment in community institutions and do not need to struggle for a livelihood.

Bairro da Paz's cultural groups have developed new ways of participating in society and creatively articulating themselves with national and international networks influenced by international black youth cultures and by the global brands they consume. But despite these new influences, they also show signs of reorienting themselves to older local traditions and values. Their identities are forged locally, but transcend the frontiers of the purely local. The participation of these young persons in debates about global dynamics is self-conscious and critical, and has been facilitated by access to information via the Internet. Their capacity to communicate with the other groups allows them to master different codes and work with polysemic and heterodox cultural identities, simultaneously participating in more than one social world, turning them into what Lorenzo Macagno (2003) calls "nomads of post-colonial modernity."

Myths of Resistance and the Associational Fabric of Bairro da Paz

A richly woven fabric of associations, bolstered by strong internal leaderships and the support of external groups, gives Bairro da Paz a distinct identity. Community actors have been articulating their history of struggle in newer expressions of social agency, within each group and collectively in the forum, in a way that reworks but reproduces a foundational myth of resistance, once again paralleling the process of ethnogenesis described by de la Peña in chapter eleven.

In April 2007, the forum was established as a broad and inclusive network of community organizations in partnership with the Federal University of Bahia (which offers technical assistance to the forum), NGOs, religious, political, and cultural groups operating in the bairro, and two state institutions, CRAS and SEBRAE.[7] With its mantra of inclusion, the forum, regardless of the religious and political differences among its members, sought to combat the fragmentation, duplication, and overlapping of initiatives produced by the proliferation of NGOs in Bairro da Paz by strengthening collective actions. The emergence of organizations of this kind suggests that popular social networks can remain robust in the face of the tendencies toward individualization and fragmentation associated with neoliberal capitalism (Auyero 2000).

But the bairro's lively associationalism was as much the product of external support as of community leaderships that continued to rework its founding myth to promote a sense of common interests. The basis on which the forum developed, following the format of the World Social Forum, was the creation of a framework for dialogue with local authorities through the presentation of the community's own diagnoses of its principal deficits in the provision of education, health, infrastructure, public security, and culture and leisure facilities. In the context of the Lula government, the forum has continued to advance as a space for community decision-making in which decisions are preceded by extensive debate on the issues and based on collective consensus between the distinct groups that make up the forum. The legitimacy of this model for action is the result of a self-conscious reflection on problems of factional divisions, individualism, and the uneven distribution of benefits on the one hand, and, on the other hand, a collective effort, albeit one that did not come to pass without its own share of conflicts, to act jointly with authorities to find the best way of addressing the principal needs of the community and the city.

Implications for Rethinking Resistance and Resistances

Whereas for Foucault (1978) power is less institutionalized and for James Scott (1990) less pervasive when seen from the perspective of hidden subaltern resistance, for Lila Abu-Lughod (1990) resistance is the best way of diagnosing power, which is always relational. To these points Sherry Ortner adds that resistance studies cannot afford to dispense with ethnography, which shows how resisting groups, instead of merely expressing opposition to the dominant, express their own political vision, which can be "creative and transformative." But Ortner suggests that before anything else, we should recognize the polyphony of subalternity, an idea similar to the insistence by Donna Haraway (1991) on the need to be aware of the position from which each and every one speaks. Following this reasoning, an exploration of the internal politics and divisions of dominated groups also reveals their ambivalence and the ambiguity of the modes of resistance they adopt, as Zárate also notes in chapter ten.

Bairro da Paz was born in a context of struggles against the effects of a capitalist power structure that developed on the basis of expropriating subaltern groups, reproducing their exclusion and position as losers. The history of this neighborhood exemplifies the emergence of innovative types of action that have transformative potential despite their ambiguities and the constraints imposed by the neoliberal capitalist context that circumscribes them. Since the time of their struggle to secure the right to reside on invaded land, residents have struggled to deepen their rights to the city and achieve a less symbolically stigmatized visibility. From an initial situation of direct confrontation with the state, they began to forge alliances and more constructive modes of interaction with both the state and civil society, even including real estate developers, while still strengthening their ability to act as protagonists of popular demands. The recurrent "emphasis on demands" in the discourses of community leaders and the format adopted for negotiations with the state through the forum underscore the importance of the continuing reinvention of the community's founding myth of resistance at different moments, following the flow of new and, at times, contrasting, global tendencies.

The transition from the "Malvinas War" to the peace achieved after the community's consolidation did not occur in an unequivocal manner. During this transition, there were several important changes in a direction contrary to that which Alan Knight discusses in the conclusion of this book when he refers to transitions from hidden resistance to revolt. The first concerns the change of identity expressed in the change of the community's name: an identity associated with war, violence, and marginality changed to one that stressed peace, dignity, and citizenship. The broader relationship between the state and civil society also changed in this period, and the subsequent proliferation of community partnerships with private and public organizations indicates how that change reoriented the dynamics of everyday life in the following decades. Another significant transition was a move away from the emphasis on unitary, collective action inspired by a utopian "search for the promised land," an emphasis steadily toned down after the consolidation of the settlement in order to better accommodate the emerging multiplicity of individual interests and those of the different factions that constitute the community today. Even so, a sense of solidarity was not lost, and the forum has reestablished the centrality of collective action through coalition- and consensus-building. It points to a new type of agency and self-expression articulating new styles of resistance and modes of dialogue in negotiation with authorities. Yet in comparison with the original expression of resistance to the state by the Malvinas invaders, acts of resistance now seem more diffuse, often seem to pull in different directions, and are not always readily visible.

That community leaders in Bairro da Paz are aware of the reproduction of internal inequalities is evident in the critical postures that they adopt in debates in the forum, hence the search for more democratic solutions and attempts to empower the most fragile groups. Yet criticisms of the advantages enjoyed by the leaders of the strongest networks, the Catholic networks and residents' council, continue. At the same time, the voices of the community's weaker coalitions have been gaining influence, illustrated by the rising prestige enjoyed by Evangelical and Afro-Brazilian groups, the role of black youths who can choose manifestations of art and culture in order to reject marginalization and drug trafficking as their only options, and the centrality of the role of women as important religious leaders and as leaders in the development of health and education activities in popular organizations. These are examples of a social tendency to recognize the value of a plurality of once stigmatized social actors.

Nevertheless, there is now a multiplicity of "hidden transcripts" (J. C. Scott 1990) that concern the internal politics of the bairro itself. They are detectable in the gossip-mongering and everyday criticisms that groups make of each other, the manner in which different religious cults confront each other as they strive for recognition, the diversity of alliances formed, and the recent empowerment of black youth groups. It is through these daily forms of hidden resistance that those who suffer from situations of inequality through poverty and sexual, racial, or age discrimination search for opportunities to make material gains. Once resistance in Bairro da Paz became entangled in the constant disputes over access to resources and diverse benefits that followed the end of violent conflict with the state, the field of disputes between the dominant and the dominated became more open, negotiated, and explicit in one sense, but less visible in others, since there was diffuse resistance within the community's own power relations.

Alliances between community actors and the state or NGOs, and a greater tendency toward bureaucratization and professionalization of leaderships (Foweraker 2001; Teixeira 2001), do not necessarily make movements less resistant or less radical, despite the danger of being co-opted by dominant groups (see Gledhill's introduction). On the contrary, as is lucidly pointed out by Knight in his conclusions, this simply indicates the complexity that power relations always manifest: "In the process [of resisting], 'resisters' have to acquire some of the 'weapons of the strong,' literally and metaphorically" (342). In this regard, the projects of black youths in Bairro da Paz demonstrate the ambiguity of their type of agency. Despite their sharpened ethnic consciousness, links with radical black movements, and general critiques of the capitalist system, and without being totally manipulated within the private-public partnerships on which they depend, they often end up submitting to the values of global consumerism, oscillating between discourses that are simultaneously ones of critique and cooptation, authenticity and globalization, and thus occupy a paradoxical position in local-global relations. Nonetheless, the negotiation of personal advantages does not *exclude* resistance, for this has taken on another guise. It is reconstructed as the product of the unjust diaspora forced upon their ancestors, and the heritage of past systemic inequalities.

It is in their knowledge of the law, their defense of ethnic rights, and their development of partnerships with the public and private sectors that these groups are learning to use the "weapons of the strong." In utilizing the languages and discourses of the strong to criticize their own subaltern world and those who dominate it, they are thus producing hidden transcripts that are "different." Charles Tilly describes hidden transcripts as having something in common with "internal monologues and muttering under one's breath, with the crucial difference that people in a given structural position create them collectively and share them" (Tilly 1991, 596). The move toward making transcripts more open and collective produces what I call "official transcripts of subaltern ethnic consciousness," an inversion of the sense of Scott's original concepts. The incorporation of ethnic discourses by black youths in Bairro da Paz represents such an inverted "subaltern official transcript" because these discourses are characterized more by open confrontation than conformity, and the youths express a resistance that they want others to emulate. Their ethnic and class inequality and exclusion remains evident, but the demand for recognition of their alterity gives them greater public visibility.

Thus, it is more accurate to understand these processes as a "relocation" of the meanings of resistance that, in this specific case, has nothing to do with a lack of awareness. In demanding a guarantee of rights through the discourses of citizenship, these meanings have ceased to present themselves as a reaction, becoming instead a demand for affirmative action. These groups are seeking guarantees of a new position in a society that valorizes alterity through the right to be different, a right the official transcripts of universal citizenship and racial democracy framed by the dominant tend to deny.

To what extent does my ethnographic account of disputes and "polyphony of the subalterns" in Bairro da Paz permit us to think about not just new types of agency, but also resistances? If we accept Foucault's conception of power as diffuse and omnipresent, the same could be said of resistance, which needs to be identified and analyzed in each specific situation and relation. From this perspective, we could consider the conflicts and critiques that emerge among the internal factions of impoverished communities a good way of identifying new types of resistance, so often directed at the tricks and traps of power itself.

Notes

Translation by Richard Reed

1 Elenaldo Teixeira (2001) distinguishes "citizen participation" from "community participation" because the objective of the former is not just to provide services for the community or to organize it; and she distinguishes it from "popular" participation because it does not restrict itself to restorative actions and simple opposition to the state.

2 The invaded land belonged to the Visco family, but in 1987 became public property after they defaulted on taxes owed to the municipality.

This section draws on the research project "Pobreza, Redes Sociais e Mecanismos de Inclusão/Exclusão Social" (Poverty, Social Networks, and Mechanisms of Social Inclusion and Exclusion), directed by the author and financed by FAPESB, the Bahian State Foundation for Research Support, and the Center for Metropolitan Studies of CEBRAP, the Brazilian Centre for Analysis and Planning. For more details of the history of the neighborhood, see Hita and Duccini (2007).

3 Among the groups competing for control of this land were large construction firms (especially OAS Construction Company Ltd., connected with ACM) with interests in the upscale development projects that now surround the bairro. Simultaneously, environmentalists argued for the conservation of the zone as a reserve of Atlantic forest.

4 At the beginning of the 1980s, the area around this square was still thick Atlantic forest. A core group met there in order to plan strategies to resist eviction and

negotiate with the authorities: the name "Plaza of Decisions" reflects this past role.

5 Named after a Bahian archbishop whose political orientation was center-right, the foundation, created in 1987, has developed a large number of social assistance programs in Bairro da Paz and is responsible for building much of its infrastructure.

6 The "elite" terreiro Ilê Axipá (founded by Mestre Didi), visited by eminent figures in Bahia, is found at the borders of Bairro da Paz, but not felt to be part of the community in any way by its residents.

7 The Centro de Referencia e Assistência Social (Centre for Referral to Social Assistance) and the Serviço Brasiliero de Apoio as Micro e Pequenas Empresas (Brazilian Support Service for Micro and Small Businesses), respectively.

CHAPTER FOURTEEN

Contestation in the Courts

The Amparo *as a Form of Resistance to
the Cancellation of Agrarian Reform in Mexico*

HELGA BAITENMANN

Mexico has a long history of peasant resistance to state projects. One reason for continued rural resistance over the past two decades has been the official cancellation in 1992 of Mexico's longstanding land reform program, in which successive governments expropriated and redistributed over half of Mexico's total surface area to 3.5 million land recipients organized into thirty thousand *ejidos* and agrarian communities in the decades following the revolution of 1910–20.[1] In some regions, land reform beneficiaries have refused to participate in the land-titling program intended gradually to privatize the sector (Reyes Ramos 2008; Rivera Herrejón 2000). And throughout the country, hundreds of thousands of *campesinos* (peasants) have flooded the new agrarian courts created by the reforms in 1992 in order to contest unfavorable court sentences in the form of an amparo. In the process, they have in practice extended Mexico's agrarian reform program.[2]

The postrevolutionary agrarian reform was officially concluded in 1992 when the administration of President Carlos Salinas de Gortari (1988–94) amended Article 27 of the 1917 constitution, canceling the state's obligation to grant land to the landless. One significant question confronting the architects of the reform, however, was what to do with the approximately 10,600 land petitions still pending before the Ministry of Agrarian Reform—the infamous *rezago agrario* (agrarian backlog).[3] To eliminate this backlog, the Salinas government created a new agrarian court system within the national judiciary, replacing the executive-controlled agrarian administration that had served as a proxy agrarian court for the better part of the twentieth century (Chávez Padrón 2003). Between 1992 and 2009, the Agrarian Supreme Court in Mexico City and the 49 agrarian district courts delivered verdicts on over 500,000 legal cases. In that same period, rural dwellers challenged unfavorable court decisions by filing over 90,000 amparo suits. In almost 26,000 of these suits, the federal courts granted amparo protection.[4]

In order to explore the evolving meanings of resistance in contemporary rural Mexico, this chapter examines fifty amparo suits published in the federal register, the *Diario Oficial de la Federación*, between 1992 and 2010, suits that were filed with the post-1992 agrarian court system. What is striking about these cases is that they challenge the dichotomies implicit in much of the resistance literature. The first section of this chapter explains why.

The case files highlight how campesinos resorted to state protection against court resolutions, creating disputes between governmental authorities. Court officials allied with the subaltern to cancel another court's judgment. Moreover, one court forced the other to hand down another decision in conformity with the amparo judgment. This interplay between campesinos and the various governmental authorities involved in an amparo suit greatly complicates notions of resistance premised on a state-society dichotomy.

Agrarian court records also highlight the limits of a conceptualization of resistance premised on a simple subaltern-elite opposition. Whereas the core idea underpinning Mexico's postrevolutionary agrarian reform was that the state would side with landless campesinos against large landowners, the court cases summarized in the second part of this chapter reveal a multifaceted landscape in which this class-based dichotomy is difficult to sustain.

Most remarkably, the court cases show that resistance often involves factional disputes within and between rural population centers. Several authors in this volume (Gledhill, Pessar, Zárate) cite William Roseberry's 1994 work on hegemony. In his later work, however, Roseberry moved away from the concept of hegemony to focus on the meaning of local conflict. "In analyzing agrarian politics," he wrote, "we often focus on one type of conflictual relation—between communities and haciendas, say, or between communities and the state—and draw conclusions based on how communities respond to particular elite initiatives" (1999, 16). Yet Rose-berry found that "some of the sharpest conflicts" occurred within and be-tween indigenous communities in the form of factional disputes, and he stressed "that this internal difference and conflict mattered and that it also shaped the politics of twentieth century Mexico" (1998, 29). Indeed, cam-pesinos most often resort to amparo protection as part of factional dis-putes. The difficulties involved in resolving these disputes have been the single most important reason why the courts have been unable to erase the agrarian backlog.

While factional violence has complicated and indefinitely postponed the conclusion of the agrarian reform program, it has also had a dynamic effect. The second section of this chapter takes up Lila Abu-Lughod's proposition that "where there is resistance, there is power" (1990) in order to show that resistance is a key element in what Gilbert Joseph and Daniel Nugent (1994) called "everyday forms of state formation." In fact, resis-tance to the conclusion of the agrarian reform program has created post-1992 agrarian legislation, because court decisions that have binding legal effect in essence constitute new agrarian laws. Moreover, at a time when the agrarian reform program has been canceled, campesino pressure has created two new types of land reform, one based on alternative grants (monetary grants substituting for land) and the other based on selective land purchases. In view of the fact that the cancellation of the postrevolu-tionary agrarian reform program has actually created new forms of state involvement in rural Mexico, the conclusion asks whether the almost two-decade-long effort to end the agrarian reform might not (paradoxically) be more fruitfully understood as a new type of land reform (as opposed to a counterreform).

Breaking Down Oppositional Categories

Amparo case files clearly show how campesinos negotiate their rights with a state that is multifaceted and does not always govern in unison; they de-mand land in ways that do not always conform to class-based archetypes and that often involve factional struggles.

Multiple States

All amparo cases involve intragovernmental disputes. The case of San Sebastián, a town in the central western state of Jalisco, serves as an example of how this works. Here in 1939 a group of landless campesinos petitioned for a land grant. A year later, engineers and surveyors from the Jalisco Agrarian Commission conducted a census. Because land grants in Mexico were inalienable concessions of land collectively granted to twenty or more landless campesinos, settlements had to have at least that many potential agrarian-rights beneficiaries. Agrarian engineer Miguel Güitrón identified 380 rights-bearing individuals among the town's total population of 824. As with other amparo cases, government delays were prevalent. It is not clear from the court documents why it was not until 1979 that agrarian engineers actually surveyed the land within a seven-kilometer radius of the settlement (an agrarian legal requirement with antecedents dating from the colonial period), and why it was not until 1982 that the governor of Jalisco provisionally granted to the petitioners 4,360 hectares of mountainous rain-fed land. And yet, the grant was not formalized with the required "presidential resolution."

As part of the post-1992 effort to resolve the agrarian backlog, engineers conducted a new survey in San Sebastián and found only 460 hectares of land that had not, in the intervening forty-two years, been granted to other ejidos and that therefore could be legally expropriated. In 1997 the Agrarian Supreme Court formally granted San Sebastián beneficiaries the available 460 hectares. The issuance of this court sentence allowed campesino representatives to file an amparo suit at the collegiate court against the Agrarian Supreme Court and the Thirteenth Agrarian District Court. In 2002, the collegiate court granted them "the protection of federal justice" on the grounds that the Agrarian Supreme Court had modified the governor of Jalisco's resolution of 1982 without having properly surveyed the properties within the specified seven-kilometer radius from the population center.

With the help of the collegiate court, the campesinos (partially) upheld the governor of Jalisco's resolution and annulled the judgment of the Agrarian Supreme Court and the Thirteenth Agrarian District Court and reopened the entire case. Martha Beatriz Suarez and Teodoro González led the court's "executive brigade" responsible for conducting a new survey and census. These agrarian engineers identified within their survey area fifty-six properties of various extensions, some in the form of ejidos and agrarian communities and others that were privately owned—and many of them so poorly surveyed that their boundaries actually overlapped. Among these fifty-six properties, the surveying brigade found a dozen private properties that exceeded the pre-1992 size restrictions on rural private ownership (a hundred hectares of irrigated land). As a result, in 2004 (over a decade after the cancellation of the agrarian reform) the remaining forty land solicitors received a 1,260-hectare land grant.[5]

Manifold Classes

Inequality in contemporary Mexico is undeniably profound, and in some states landowners still brutally dominate regional politics. Nevertheless, most of the present-day land struggles that find their way into the courts do not conform to the subaltern-elite dichotomy implicit in some resistance studies.

In the historical literature, the amparo has been most often discussed as the legal procedure that landowners employed to seek judicial protection in order to block land reform initiatives threatening their properties.[6] Indeed, amparo suits have allowed landowners to block many land petitions, as in the case of Zoyatepec, in the central state of Puebla, where landowners filed an amparo to block a land petition in 1974 that then remained unresolved until 2003.[7] An examination of post-1992 amparo cases, however, shows that this old class-based dichotomy has hidden from analysis the many small property owners who seek state protection to prevent the expropriation of their lands. The town of San Lucas Huarirapeo, in the central western state of Michoacán, is one of many such examples.

In 1983, San Lucas Huarirapeo received a presidential resolution confirming, titling, and transferring 290 hectares of communal lands to 138 beneficiaries. Two groups of small property owners subsequently solicited amparo protection against this presidential resolution. In 1993, the Ministry of Agrarian Reform invalidated the presidential resolution of 1983 and forwarded the matter to the newly created agrarian courts. Three years later, the court negotiated an agreement between the members of the community's governing board and the small landowners, in which the former promised to respect the latter's property. Although the amparo has often been a political tool for large landowners, in this and in other post-1992 cases it has also protected individuals such as María de los ángeles

Baca Martín de Reyes, who in 1975 had purchased two half-hectare properties known as "El Capulín" and "Joya de San Lucas." With the agreement of 1996 in place, the agrarian court could in 1999 recognize and title 105 hectares of land to benefit the settlement of San Lucas Huarirapeo, while explicitly excluding the small properties of twelve women, like Baca Martín, and thirteen men.[8]

Fractured Proceedings

Perhaps the most striking characteristic of the post-1992 amparo cases is that they often involve violent factional struggles. Many authors in this book follow James C. Scott's injunction about Mexico: "One must always speak of popular culture and resistance to [hegemonic] projects in the *plural*" (1994, xi). In fact, Margarita Zárate (chapter ten) notes that subalterns are socially heterogeneous and have fluid gender and ethnic identities; Juan Pedro Viqueira (chapter three) alerts us to the heterogeneous behavior of the subaltern; and Guillermo de la Peña (chapter eleven) reminds us that internal divisions are traversed by multiple alliances with external actors. This section adds another variant to Foucault's (1978, 95–96) contention that "resistance is never in a position of exteriority to power" by proposing that where there is resistance, there is factionalism. In fact, almost all of the fifty post-1992 amparo cases examined here involve conflict within or between, or within and between, subaltern groups, particularly groups of settlers (or "squatters") fighting against each other, or boundary conflicts between long-established villages (oftentimes former indigenous pueblos).

One common strategy for obtaining land in Mexico has been to settle on vacant federal or private lands. More often than not, however, vacant or underused lands have been invaded not by one but by a number of groups, who often end up in violent fights with each other. Many of these land disputes have become deeply enmeshed in the agrarian reform program, which the courts then have had to sort out.

The history of La Mutua, a settlement in the central state of San Luis Potosí, is one of many instances in which contending settler groups have engaged in violent fights over land. Here, in 1980 the area called Rancho El Estribo (comprising 4,500 hectares) was expropriated, divided into four sections, and converted into federal property to benefit a state-run agricultural research center. Three of those four sections were used as ecological and research reserves. The fourth area, El Plan del Guajolote (measuring 938 hectares), had been occupied by a number of settler groups, including groups named Charcos del Oriente, "Km 42," El Sarnito, and La Mutua. In 1981, one group of settlers submitted a petition for a land grant from the federal property, El Plan del Guajolote. A few months later, the San Luis Potosí agrarian commission conducted a census and surveyed the properties within a seven-kilometer radius of the population center. They identified 204 potential agrarian subjects, but they claimed there was no land available for the grant. On these grounds, the agrarian commission denied the land petition. Nevertheless, land petitioners continued to press their case. In response, the state delegate of the Ministry of Agrarian Reform ordered two additional surveys, one in 1983 and one in 1984. Neither survey produced different results.

La Mutua settlers refused an offer to form a new ejido population center elsewhere, and in 1997 they filed an amparo suit against the agrarian administration instead. They received amparo protection in 1999, which annulled the unfavorable decision in 1984 and obliged agrarian staff to conduct yet another survey. In 2001 the Agrarian Supreme Court awarded La Mutua settlers the 300 hectares they had, by then, possessed and cultivated for a full two decades. However, no sooner had the court made the grant than another group of La Mutua representatives filed an amparo suit against it, claiming that the decision had favored the wrong La Mutua representatives. In this instance, as in many other cases, there were factional struggles not only between groups, but also within them. One splinter group was led by Roberto Ahumada, who represented the original land petitioners from 1981, and another splinter group was led by Blas Gutiérrez, who represented another sixty-five La Mutua campesinos. The infighting dragged on until at least 2004, when the Agrarian Supreme Court issued another decision in the case.[9] Knowing what happened after that, however, would require further in-depth fieldwork in the community, for as Hugo Santos Gómez explains in his analysis of court procedures in the state of Oaxaca, "Solutions that are exclusively legal do not guarantee results that are accepted as legitimate by the parties" (1999, 158, author's translation).

The other type of factional dispute that stands out in post-1992 amparo cases involves very old boundary disputes between long-established villages, as in the case of Santiago Tochimizolco, in the central state of Puebla. Santiago Tochimizolco is one of many communities whose request to be included in the federal executive's "communal land recognition and titling program" went hand-in-hand with efforts to resolve border conflicts with another community. Indeed, in 1939, representatives of Santiago Tochimizolco requested land restitution that would also resolve a long-festering conflict over boundaries with neighboring San Francisco Huilango. It was not until 1954 that they received a presidential resolution recognizing their communal rights over 710 hectares of land. The community representatives, however, refused to accept the resolution on the grounds that it did not settle a boundary conflict involving another ninety-one hectares of land disputed by neighboring villages. Six months later, they filed an amparo suit before the supreme court.

It took the supreme court sixteen years to rule on the amparo suit. In 1971, the court revoked the presidential resolution of 1954, allowing residents of Santiago Tochimizolco to reopen their case file. Yet, it is not clear from the court documents why this then became one of the thousands of unresolved agrarian cases. It was not until 1995 that the Agrarian Supreme Court determined the authenticity of Santiago Tochimizolco's land titles dating from 1579 and 1610, and in 2002 it ruled in favor of Santiago Tochimizolco and against neighboring San Francisco Huilango.[10]

This example is typical of many cases in the states of Guerrero, Oaxaca, and Chiapas, where boundary disputes between communities span several centuries and where the amparo plays a key role in the (perhaps temporary) resolution of intervillage struggles over land.[11] These boundary disputes have become so prevalent in the post-1992 efforts to resolve the agrarian backlog that the courts have had to issue what is in effect post-1992 agrarian legislation.

The Post-1992 Land Reform

In filing amparo suits, campesinos have not only reopened agrarian case files, prolonging the completion of the agrarian reform, they have also created a new, post-1992 land reform. First, they have expanded the courts' role in agrarian matters and fostered the creation of new agrarian laws in the form of judicial precedents. And, second, they have pressured the government to create two new forms of land reform, one based on alternative grants to land (monetary compensation in the form of infrastructure or development projects) and the other based on land purchases made by the Ministry of Agrarian Reform in order to settle "social conflicts" (a euphemism used by government officials to signal that violent conflicts are occurring in a particular locality) that are otherwise irresolvable within existing legislation.

The New Agrarian Laws

In the fifty amparo cases reviewed for this chapter, judicial precedents play a role in expanding the agrarian courts' jurisdiction over important national matters such as village boundary disputes. In Mexico, five consecutive court decisions that make the same finding set judicial precedent, thereby binding judges who subsequently decide comparable cases. In fact, Stephen Zamora et al. characterize judicial precedent as one of several "sources of law" in Mexico (2004, 83).

It is not surprising that one of the judicial precedents expanding the agrarian courts' jurisdiction involved five case files from the state of Oaxaca, where almost 90 percent of all land is collectively owned in the form of ejidos and agrarian communities. One of these rulings concerned the boundary dispute between San Isidro Huayapam and Santa María Asunción Cacalotepec, in the predominantly indigenous Mixe District of the Sierra Norte of Oaxaca. Here, until the end of the 1950s, Huayapam had been part of the municipality of Cacalotepec. Huayapam, with higher-quality lands and a growing population, however, challenged the authority of the municipality, and in 1959 it legally seceded from Cacalotepec and joined Santa María Alotepec (see Santos Gómez 1999).

In 1967, San Isidro Huayapam received a 4,200-hectare grant as part of the federal government's communal land recognition and titling program. Cacalotepec responded by filing an amparo suit claiming the land was within their jurisdiction, and in 1971 the supreme court reversed the grant and ordered federal agrarian officials to reopen the case. In the 1980s the Agrarian Department initiated so-called boundary-conflict proceedings, and in 1987 a presidential resolution granted Cacalotepec 11,000 hectares of land, including the 4,200 claimed by Huayapam. In the same year, Huayapam filed a dissenting legal action specific to the "boundary-conflict proceedings." Under the terms of the then-prevailing Federal Agrarian Reform Law of 1971, if one of the parties disagreed with the presidential resolution regarding land boundaries, the complainant could file a dissenting legal action before the supreme court.

The case file was not resolved by the time the laws were reformed in

1992 and Huayapam subsequently became one of five supreme court rulings involving Oaxaca that delegated to the agrarian courts all unresolved case files involving pre-1992 *juicio de inconformidad agraria por límites* (boundary-conflict proceedings decisions). By confirming the authority of the agrarian courts to include what used to be supreme court matters, this judicial precedent in effect expanded the agrarian courts' jurisdiction beyond that granted to them in the laws of 1992.[12]

Alternative Grants

Whereas before 1992 land conflict resolutions could only be solved as part of a zero-sum game in which one village's land gain meant another's loss, campesinos have forced the executive branch of government to create, and the agrarian courts to accept, a new mode of land conflict resolution. The land conflict between San Lorenzo Texmelucan and Santo Domingo Teojomulco, both of which are located in Oaxaca's de Sola de Vega district, is a case in point.

Here, in 1941 the municipal authorities and residents of the mainly *mestizo* (that is, nonindigenous) community Santo Domingo Teojomulco solicited the recognition and titling of their communal lands. In 1966 a presidential resolution recognized and titled some 19,000 hectares. Six years later, however, the neighboring Zapotec indigenous community of San Lorenzo Texmelucan filed an amparo suit against the presidential resolution on the grounds that the Teojomulco grant included 6,000 hectares of *their* communal lands. In fact, both communities had titles to the same lands issued by the Spanish Crown on the same day in October 1521.[13] In 1973 the supreme court gave amparo protection to Texmelucan against the presidential resolution of 1966, but the conflict was not settled.

In 1996, the agrarian courts assumed responsibility for resolving the long-running and very violent boundary dispute between Texmelucan and Teojomulco. Ten years and at least 200 deaths later, the Unitary Agrarian Tribunal authorized an agreement whereby Teojomulco would allow Texmelucan to keep the disputed 6,000 hectares in exchange for government funding for various infrastructure and development projects, including a water treatment plant allegedly costing 40 million pesos (or about 3.2 million dollars).[14]

Selective Land Purchases

Other pending legal cases involving social conflict that could not be resolved within the 1992 legal framework have been settled at the margins of existing legislation. Whereas the essence of the postrevolutionary agrarian reform program was to expropriate land from private properties exceeding specific limits or to turn national land into social (or ejido) property, many post-1992 grants have involved outright purchases of land by the Ministry of Agrarian Reform.

This was the case of San José Itho, a town in the central state of Querétaro. Here, residents applied for land restitution in 1967. In the 1970s, the agrarian administration restituted 360 hectares from the properties of María Luisa Perrusquía Sarabia to 200 agrarian-rights-bearing individuals. However, when San José Itho residents submitted their land titles for authentication, paleographer María Guadalupe Leyva concluded that the nineteenth-century documents she received were not land titles; rather, they were documents from a lawsuit filed in 1849 against San José Itho by the neighboring village of San Pedro Tenengo. She stated that what was required in this instance was not paleographic authenticity but legal interpretation. In the end, the restitution failed on the grounds that San José Itho residents had no land titles and could not prove that the hacienda had appropriated their lands. Not even the backing of the Independent Peasant Confederation (the Central Campesina Independiente, an important national peasant organization) allowed them to push the restitution forward.

After the reforms of 1992, the San José Itho residents filed an amparo suit against the Ministry of Agrarian Reform and the Agrarian Supreme Court. A federal court granted them an amparo on the grounds that San José Itho residents had solicited the land restitution when the Agrarian Code of 1942 was in force, and Article 219 of the code stated that when individuals solicited restitution, they were automatically petitioning for a land grant as well—a form of protection for land petitioners in case the restitution request failed, as was often the case. On these grounds, the court had to reopen the case. But because surveyors could not identify private properties exceeding pre-1992 size limits to landholdings, the state government of Querétaro purchased 100 hectares from the Perrusquía Sarabia lands and 73 additional hectares from another landowner, and in 2004 the Agrarian Supreme Court formally granted 173 hectares from these lands to the San José Itho land petitioners.[15] Although this type of land grant is not contemplated within existing legislation, many case files involving private purchases cite a judicial precedent from 1994 allowing the Agrarian Supreme Court to make grants of federal, state, and municipal land even when pre-1992 procedural requirements had not been fulfilled.[16]

One such example involves campesinos from Tres Bocas (Veracruz). In 1931 Tres Bocas residents solicited a land grant. Five years later, sixty-two agriculturalists received 540 hectares from the Santa Elena hacienda. Although the federal executive had issued a positive presidential resolution, the land beneficiaries were only awarded 106 hectares, mainly because the hacienda owners managed to protect most of their property by dividing its ownership into smaller parcels that were within the size limits stipulated for private rural property.

Nevertheless, Tres Bocas residents kept up their pressure on the government, and in the 1970s they acquired an additional 400 hectares. A formal investigation subsequently showed that this supplementary land grant was of inferior quality to the original land endowment in 1936. Members of the ejido board representing the original sixty-two land reform beneficiaries continued to demand the fulfillment of their "agrarian and economic needs," and so another group from Tres Bocas petitioned for a further land extension. Federal agrarian officials denied the extension in 1988, on the grounds that there was no more land available for expropriation within a seven-kilometer radius of the population center. There were so many land conflicts in this region that, in the early 1990s, Ministry of Agrarian Reform officials, citing the 1994 judicial precedent allowing the Agrarian Supreme Court to make grants of federal, state, and municipal land even when pre-1992 procedural requirements had not been fulfilled, negotiated the purchase of 130 hectares of land from the Santa Elena hacienda.[17]

Campesinos have so heavily pressured the Ministry of Agrarian Reform to conduct these "selective land purchases" that, in 2003, the government included this new land grant modality in its social program called "National Accord for the Countryside." The purpose of the selective land purchases is to deal with the accumulation of cases that have received negative court resolutions but where the petitioning groups are already in possession of the lands. For this, the Ministry of Agrarian Reform organizes an "eligibility committee" composed of government and campesino representatives. After the land is formally appraised, the committee negotiates the land purchase with the owners. The Ministry of Agrarian Reform, check in hand, purchases the private property, notarizes the purchase, and gives birth to a new post-1992 generation of ejidos.[18] The only way to conclude Mexico's historic agrarian reform program has been to expand the jurisdiction of the new agrarian courts and to establish new procedures for making land grants, and the post-1992 agrarian procedures have in effect created a new (albeit different) type of land reform.

Peasant Resistance and the Post-1992 Land Reform

Campesinos have in practice resisted any swift completion of Mexico's postrevolutionary agrarian reform program by, among other things, filing amparo suits to contest unfavorable court decisions. They have done so in ways that complicate notions of resistance premised on state-subaltern dichotomies. As the case studies in this chapter illustrate, resisters engage a multilayered state by seeking court protection to resist state actions. The case studies also question the concept of resistance, when premised on the elite-popular oppositional category. Rather than contesting elite injustices, campesinos prolong the conclusion of the agrarian reform by engaging in ongoing and often violent struggles with other equally underprivileged groups. As many of the case studies illustrate, the government's incapacity and negligence, from the 1920s to 1992, often fomented such factionalism. Either way, factional struggles within and between rural population centers and peasant groups were the very motor of resistance to the planned completion of the agrarian reform program in 1992.

Moreover, as in the case of other neoliberal policies that were intended to reduce the role of the state in society or the economy, the role of the state in rural Mexico has in fact expanded (Snyder 2001). Resistance to the closure of the agrarian reform program has also had the unintended effect of extending court involvement in rural matters regarding rights to land. Courts have had to expand legal procedures beyond what was anticipated by the reforms of 1992. As this chapter has illustrated, the courts have even created a new form of grant-making that privileges monetary resolutions of violent conflicts over procedural formalities.

This situation takes us back to Joseph's and Nugent's (1994) proposition regarding the importance of understanding the role of resistance in processes of state formation, and to Roseberry's preoccupation with the productive role of factionalism in twentieth-century, and now twenty-first-century, Mexico. If we consider the experience of the last two decades as a new type of land reform program—one in which the new ejido form of private property and the new form of agrarian community semiprivate property continue to be the most important land-tenure arrangements in Mexico (Pérez Castañeda 2002; Robles Berlanga 2008)—then it is certainly a land reform program in which campesinos have played a central role.[19]

There is perhaps no better illustration of resisters' involvement in a state project than the case of the campesinos from the Castaños community in the northern state of Coahuila, who in 1991 petitioned federal authorities for a land grant to create a "new ejido population center." After complicated legal negotiations, in 2003 the Agrarian Supreme Court granted them ninety-seven hectares of rain-fed land that had previously been expropriated from an alleged drug dealer. They named the new ejido population center "Lic. Carlos Salinas de Gortari."[20]

Notes

Many thanks to John Gledhill and Patience Schell for inviting me to participate in this collective project and to the Manchester seminar colleagues for their inspiration. I also thank Kevin J. Middlebrook for his comments and Juan Carlos Pérez Castañeda for his generous counsel on agrarian law (all remaining errors are mine). I dedicate this paper to the memory of Bill Roseberry.

1 The colonial term "ejido" (public or communal pastures and woodlands) was adopted for the land grants made by postrevolutionary governments. Ejido land could not be sold, mortgaged, or transferred in any other way than by inheritance to a family member. Agrarian laws differentiated between two types of land endowments: the *dotación*, or granting of land by state fiat to rural dwellers with no ancestral claims to land, and the *restitución* of lands to those communities that could prove that their communal lands had been illegally seized during the implementation of nineteenth-century liberal laws. The Agrarian Code of 1943 created the *comunidad agraria* (agrarian community) as a form of organization for restituted land that was slightly different from that of the ejido.

2 Here the term "campesino" (used in its inclusive, masculine form although the discussion identifies women who appear in court materials) includes all rural dwellers engaged in agriculture, livestock production, or both.

3 Chiapas, for example, had 3,000 unresolved cases, some of them outstanding for eighty years (García de León 2002, 61–62).

4 The figures include amparos filed at the Tribunales Colegiados de Distrito, also called "indirect amparos" (see Tercer Informe de Gobierno del Presidente Felipe Calderón Hinojosa, http://tercer.informe.gob.mx/). An amparo is a "uniquely Mexican legal institution" (Zamora et al. 2004, 259) that encompasses a set of federal judicial procedures by which individuals and collectivities (associations,

cooperatives, land reform beneficiaries, and so forth) may contest a law or the action of a government agency. There is no English term that is a precise equivalent. The discussion employs the terms "amparo petition" and "amparo suit" interchangeably, following Zamora et al. (2004, 257–86).

5 *Diario Oficial de la Federación* (hereafter DOF), April 28, 2004, *Sentencia pronunciada en el juicio agrario 363/96*, San Sebastián, Municipality of San Sebastián, Jalisco.

6 In Mexico's postrevolutionary agrarian history, landowners were the first rural class to gain the right to file an amparo suit. Venustiano Carranza's Agrarian Law of 1915 granted landowners the right to resort to the amparo when agrarian procedures violated their individual guarantees and property rights. In 1934, in a government shift toward accelerating land distribution, an amendment to Article 27 of the Constitution abolished landowners' amparo rights. In 1947, however, the administration of Miguel Alemán (1946–52) reversed course and again modified Article 27, restoring landowners' right to file an amparo suit.

7 DOF, October 6, 2003, *Sentencia, expediente 115/01*, Zoyatepec, Tecali de Herrera, Puebla. Other backlog cases dealing with landowners' amparos include, for example, DOF, July 26, 1999, *Sentencia, juicio agrario 326/93*, Matancillas, Ojuelos, Jalisco; DOF, August 6, 1999, *Sentencia, juicio agrario 548/97*, Villela, Santa María del Río, San Luis Potosí; DOF, May 30, 2003, *Sentencia, juicio agrario 45/2001*, Artículos, Durango, Durango; and DOF, March 22, 2007, *Sentencia, juicio agrario 1019/93*, Salvador Urbina, Ángel Albino Corzo, Chiapas.

8 DOF, March 23, 2006, *Sentencia, juicio agrario 24/97*, Indios y El Tule, Tonalá, Chiapas. See also, DOF, August 28, 2002, *Sentencia, juicio agrario 557/2001*, San Guillermo, Miahuatlán de Porfirio Díaz, Oaxaca; DOF, October 15, 2002, *Sentencia, expediente 480/98*, Tenzompa, Huejuquilla el Alto, Jalisco; and DOF, November 4, 2004, *Sentencia, expediente 005/2004*, Teucizapan y Anexos, Ixcateopan, Guerrero.

9 DOF, December 16, 2005, *Sentencia, juicio agrario 53/2000*, La Mutua, El Naranjo, San Luis Potosí. See, also, DOF, April 20, 2000, *Sentencia, juicio agrario 11/93*, Santa María Ajoloapan, Hueypoxtla, Estado de México; DOF, September 30, 2000, *Sentencia, juicio agrario 948/9*, Mesa del Toro, San Matín Chalchicuautla, San Luis Potosí; DOF, April 14, 2005, *Sentencia, juicio agrario 185/93*, La Sauceda, San Diego de la Unión, Guanajuato; DOF, June 23, 2005, *Sentencia, juicio agrario 1112/93*, San Juan de Avilés y Puentes Aramberri, Nuevo León; DOF, March 14, 2007, *Sentencia, juicio agrario 980/94*, La Peñita, Acuitzio, Michoacán; and DOF, December 22, 2008, *Sentencia, juicio agrario 111/93*, General Francisco Villa, Tijuana, Baja California.

10 DOF, May 22, 2007, *Sentencia, expediente 306/2000*, Santiago Tochimizolco and San Francisco Huilango, Tochimilco, Puebla.

11 See, for example, DOF, July 27, 2000, *Sentencia, expediente TUA.XII-205 y 247/93*, Paraje Montero and Malinaltepec, Malinaltepec, Guerrero; DOF, December 17,

2003, *Sentencia, expediente 287/96*, San Andrés Yaá and San Melchor Betaza, Villa Alta District, Oaxaca; and DOF, July 15, 2002, *Sentencia, juicio agrario 1221/93*, El Carrizal, Motozintla, Chiapas.

12 *Gaceta del Semanario Judicial de la Federación* 60 (1992, 17), Jurisprudencia J/2a, 12/92: "Juicios de inconformidad agraria por conflicto de límites. La segunda sala de la Suprema Corte de Justicia de la Nación, carece de competencia legal para conocer de los." See also DOF, July 28, 2004, *Sentencia, expediente 99/95*, San Miguel Ixitlán, Puebla, versus San Pablo Tequixtepec, Oaxaca; DOF, January 17, 2006, *Sentencia, expediente 41/92*, Villa Tejupan de la Unión, versus San Cristóbal Suchixtlahuaca (both Oaxaca); and DOF, November 12, 2008, *Sentencia, expediente 228/96*, Santiago Tilantongo versus Santa María Tataltepec (both Oaxaca).

13 Red Oaxaqueña de Derechos Humanos, 2001, "Segundo Informe," 37.

14 "Compensan a Teojomulco con 40 mpd por invasión de Texmelucan," http://www.e-consulta.com (September 22, 2008).

15 DOF, July 20, 2004, *Sentencia, juicio agrario 06/2003*, Emiliano Zapata (previously San José Itho), Amealco, Guanajuato.

16 *Boletín Judicial Agrario* 26 (1994, 43), Jurisprudencia del pleno del TSA: "Ampliación de ejido por incorporación de tierras al régimen ejidal. Procede decretarla de plano aun sin haberse tramitado procedimiento ampliatorio, cuando la afectación recae en tierras propiedad de la federación, de los estados o de los municipios o fueron puestas a su disposición para satisfacer sus necesidades agrarias." See also DOF, August 10, 2000, *Sentencia, juicio agrario 422/92*, Petac/Halacho, Halacho, Yucatán.

17 DOF, September 19, 2000, *Sentencia, juicio agrario 442/94*, Tres Bocas, Martínez de la Torre, Veracruz. Other such cases involving purchases to resolve "social conflicts" include, for example, DOF, August 6, 1999, *Sentencia, juicio agrario 038/93*, Chaliguey, Valparaíso, Zacatecas; DOF, March 14, 2007, *Sentencia, juicio agrario 980/94*, La Peñita, Acuitzio, Michoacán; DOF, June 16, 2008, *Sentencia, juicio agrario 6/2008*, Zapotal de Zaragoza, Tuxpan, Veracruz; DOF, February 9, 2000, *Sentencia, juicio agrario 20/98*, La Trinidad, Guasave, Sinaloa; and DOF, February 9, 2000, *Sentencia, juicios agrario 404/96*, Los Alpes, Mapastepec, Chiapas.

18 Juan Carlos Pérez Castañeda, personal communication with the author. See also Mondragón (2004) and "Acuerdo Nacional para el Campo: Por el desarrollo de la sociedad rural y la soberanía y seguridad alimentarias" (April 28, 2003), http://www.senado.gob.mx.

19 This is not to say that this "new" land reform is necessarily positive in terms of social justice, poverty alleviation, or agricultural productivity. For a sobering evaluation of the effects of the Procede titling program, see Robles (2008).

20 DOF, April 22, 2004, *Sentencia, juicio agrario 8/2003*, Lic. Carlos Salinas de Gortari, Castaños, Coahuila.

CHAPTER FIFTEEN

Beyond Resistance

Raising Utopias from the Dead in Mexico City and Oaxaca

MATTHEW GUTMANN

Is radical transformation no longer imaginable, or is it the fantasy
of human control over human destiny that has vanished?
—Wendy Brown, *Edgework*

In my earlier writing about democratic citizenship in a working-class
neighborhood of Mexico City, I employed the phrase "compliant defiance"
to help decipher the roller-coaster politics there and more generally in
the Mexican capital (Gutmann 2002). In 2002, residents of Colonia Santo
Domingo, the neighborhood in question, were clearly unhappy with many
aspects of political life and for decades had showed their defiance in all
manner of open and silent protests against governmental abuse and ne-
glect. At the same time, most people, most of the time, tolerated political
life with a resigned, compliant shrug and a knowing wink: What could you
do about political life stacked against *la gente humilde*?

The term "compliant defiance" is meant to capture a widespread sen-
timent among my friends and neighbors in Santo Domingo that directly
associated political knowledge and actions with something far less positive: the responsibility and, moreover, the culpability ordinary citizens in
Colonia Santo Domingo shared in their own social problems. My intent
was to explore issues of power and knowledge and to acknowledge what
my friends and neighbors in Santo Domingo emphasized to me when they
held themselves and others accountable for their political thoughts and
actions, regardless of who they were or how little power they evidently had.

One aspect of this exploration of compliant defiance was to critique the

term "agency," as it was used in the previous two decades in scholarly writing, for instance, with regard to social movements. Agency often stands in
contrast to culpability and as such has been a useful concept in challenging determinist thinking, giving the dispossessed a fuller voice in deciding their own fates, victories, and tragedies. Generally, however, agency
has referred to the politically progressive efforts of *los de abajo* only when
they are able to break free of what are often held to be preexisting structural and systemic constraints. How one understands failures or situations
when the poor dare not even attempt to break out are subjects analysts
have been more reluctant to address. At the least, agency has been absent
as a concept when the issue of compliance arises, if it is entertained at all.
For whatever reason, then, agency is used to capture aspects of defiance
but has been less useful in helping us conceptualize compliance.

As John Monteiro demonstrates so carefully in chapter one, the meanings and implications of indigenous "collaboration" with colonial powers
and projects in Brazil have ramifications for scholars of social movements,
protests, and resistance. Yet the lopsided and often wooden analysis of
those who would resist remains common, as Juan Pedro Viqueira notes
in chapter three, in simplistic analyses of elites and the dominated, as if
the two neatly lined up against each other in actual social confrontations.
Thus the propensity to romanticize the politically successful among the
dispossessed has unfortunately resulted in feeble analysis with respect to
the politically unsuccessful—those who are not successful, those who try
but fail, those not interested, or those who are just not aware. Even to mention the possibility of poor people who may not be "aware," of course, con-
jures up images of false consciousness and other concepts that are themselves abjured today. Yet political passivity, whether considered an aspect
of agency or not, remains paradoxically uncharted territory.

What, we might ask with tongue only slightly in cheek, is wrong with
"blaming the victim"? If agency is wonderful to behold and defend, then
the implications of agency for situations in which the powerless are less
successful must be explored. If agency describes successful incursions of
los olvidados into the power arenas, we need to know more about agency's
opposites. If agency comes about, in part, when Manuel Azuela's (1938)
legendary social underdogs understand their plight and thus seek to lessen
their misery, we must also understand the implications of *mis*understandings and *mis*steps.

One reason for agency's popularity relates to the historical context in which the term became popular among academics, a time that saw the advent of resistance theory as well. Agency and resistance both arose in the 1980s, when thinking about large-scale social change, at least in Europe and the United States, seemed to nearly all observers foolhardy, outdated, possibly suspect, and indubitably dangerous. As John Gledhill (2004b, 341) has written, "In a world in which the triumph of the market economy is taken for granted, it seems increasingly difficult to specify 'realistic' strategies for those at the bottom of global society that do not entail enhancing their capacity to function in market society." It is thus not surprising that the ideas of political thinkers like James Scott (1985; 1990) seemed appealing precisely because they were proudly grounded in goals that appeared more feasible, small-scale, and pragmatic.

Weapons of the Politically Demoralized

As is well known, James Scott (1985; 1990) counsels that we should learn to better appreciate covert and unorganized forms of resistance. This part of his argument is the one usually and positively utilized by scholars of Mexico, Brazil, and beyond. The other half of his thinking, however, needs to be addressed as well: that these forms of resistance have become the only viable ones for the exploited and oppressed today, and are therefore the most reasonable focus of scholarly attention. Moreover, Scott frequently and explicitly opposes the two forms. Despite disclaimers, he pits gradual, incremental, and all but hidden change against self-consciously directed and radical change: "Petty acts of resistance . . . [have] thus changed or narrowed the policy options of the state. It is in this fashion, *and not through revolts*, let alone legal political pressure, that the peasantry has classically made its political presence felt" (1985, 35–36, emphasis added). Scott says that "persistent practice of everyday forms of resistance underwritten by a subculture of complicity can achieve many, if not all, of the results aimed at by social movements" (1987, 422).

It is perhaps no accident that Scott's star rose precisely in a period of retrenched conservatism in the United States, the 1980s. In this decade, the permanence of capitalist social orders seemed more realistic than it did in the 1960s, a period Scott has dismissed as inspiring inappropriate romanticism for national liberation movements and the like from Eric Wolf and others. Preferring to argue for the "pragmatic adaptation to the realities" of their lives (1985, 246), Scott cautioned that peasants, for example, must recognize that these realities set "limits that only the fool-hardy would transgress" (247). Overt resistance (much less rebellion) was therefore reckless and unwarranted.

At the same time in the United States, when many left-leaning intellectuals were licking their wounds after the antiwar and civil rights movements, and later, after the soul-searching triggered by the collapse of the Soviet empire, theories of resistance emerged that seemed to offer a panacea for those unable to believe in capacious theories, much less the titanic social change once known as socialism. Gone were the days, such as those described by Luis Nicolau Parés (chapter seven), in which intellectuals played an open and influential role in the political debates and events of the day. Like some of the new social movement analysis, resistance represented another theoretical current, often based more on identity than on class categories. As the new century approached, resistance theory also began to attract attention in Latin America (see the discussion in Coronado Malagón 2000).

Undoubtedly, resistance theory attracted disenchanted postsocialist converts in part because of the desire of many intellectuals to support social underdogs and their hope that greater social equality could be realized. Yet as with approaches to agency, much of the allure of resistance is romantic in nature (see Abu-Lughod 1990; Kearney 1996). In his analysis of the quixotic qualities of resistance theory, Harry Sanabria suggests instead that "we center more of our efforts on *ineffective* and *unsuccessful* resistance in order to understand better the contexts in which successful resistance can be achieved" (2000, 57). In other words, as with agency, so too with resistance; we must account for both the successes and the failures, for both activism and passivity, if these concepts are to be truly helpful in understanding social change.

For a variety of reasons, including economic crises and frustrations with electoral politics, progressive change has appeared to be less realizable to many in Mexico in the first decade of the twenty-first century than in the 1980s. Many scholars in Mexico, as elsewhere, began to reconceptualize the working classes and their ability to alter their political worlds. Analytically, resistance theories complemented newly translated French poststructuralist theory, attributing power (and culpability) to everyone everywhere. Nonetheless, as John Gledhill suggests in his introduction, Foucault did contribute in important ways to offering a means to recognize resistance within a more nuanced understanding of power relations.

Thus, scholars utilizing resistance theories could continue to focus on the poor and oppressed while redirecting their energies to microencounters of conflict and subterfuge, within the context of greatly diminished expectations for the people unburdened by material and intellectual riches.

In academic circles in Mexico, late modern realism has included a shift away from "class analysis," as illustrated in the influential works of Néstor García Canclini (see, for example, 1982; 1989; 1995a). The parallels are striking between the wholesale replacement of working-class theories with others focused on "popular classes" and the rise in status of resistance theories. Universalist theories of classes and class struggle were replaced with more standard sociological categories of "urban citizenry" and "popular consumers." The ambiguities of delineating lines of demarcation for those suffering from grinding inequalities and those who perpetrate such cruelty became, for a growing number of scholars, opaque.

In an insightful paper on political culture, Guillermo de la Peña (1990, 105) insists that we treat the concept of class as profoundly historical. We must cease to view class as a magic wand to categorize groups of people in order to predict social behavior. Instead, de la Peña argues, for class to retain its salience, it must be a concept alive with the possibility of real people constructing real (and really) complex interpretations of their daily lives. It is more than coincidence that a reevaluation of the constitution and consequence of classes occurred as doubt and ironic uncertainty were on the rise, and as modernist (meta)truth and teleology were met with unchecked uncertainty or even scorn. Although there is much to be altered and amended in class analysis, the key problem for those who would shuffle the concept off to ironic oblivion may be that, like their overdetermining ancestors, they have too little insight into and no plan to help resolve poverty, disease, and raging inequalities.

With these thoughts as a backdrop, and keeping in mind the dialectical versus dichotomous concept of compliant defiance, I now turn to several ethnographic encounters in order to highlight, first, how people in Colonia Santo Domingo, Mexico City, implicate themselves in discussions of political activity and immobility, and, next, critical approaches to political consciousness and consensus in Santo Domingo and in the southern Mexican city of Oaxaca, where in 2006 an enormous social movement erupted aimed at toppling the state government.

To begin, a discussion about blame.

Resistance and Burros

"A lot of people talk these days about democracy as the goal of all kinds of social struggle," I commented one day in 1997 to Gabriel, a mechanic friend.

"But ask those wise guys if they go to the marches, if they go to the meetings. 'Do you go out and raise hell?' Everyone talks about democracy," Gabi complained.

"The Zapatistas, too?" I asked.

"The Zapatistas practice democracy more because the groups who are prepared are the ones who are marginalized. Why? Because they are the groups who actually can see to it that democracy functions. But that's when people get together and analyze things so democracy doesn't become, as I was saying, ten burros and a genius."

Which of course raised the obvious question: "And who's to say who are the burros and who are the geniuses?"

"The burros are the ones who talk about democracy and don't practice it," Gabriel responded, barely managing to keep a straight face.

"Are you a genius or a burro?" I needled him.

"A burro," he replied, laughing. Recovering his composure, he added in a half-serious, half-playful tone, "But I'm not a mountain burro, because even burros have hierarchies. There are burros who are more burros than I am and there are burros less burros than I am. What I do think is that there's a lack of *educación* and that the level of educación in our country is very low." By "educación" Gabriel was talking about formal schooling, but also an awareness of social relations, a social consciousness and conscience, thus highlighting points by de la Peña and Viqueira that show in different ways the heterodox views, goals, and practices of those like Gabriel who have little reserve cultural or economic capital.

"But even in countries where the level of formal education is very high there are assholes all over," I commented.

To which Gabi retorted, "And in the end, who's to blame?"

"I don't know," I lied, because I knew where this line of argument was leading. "Tell me," I requested.

"The people," Gabriel told me. "The people" bore some responsibility for their own misery, because only the people, if they became "educated" in the sense of being conscious of their situation, could do something to rectify their lives.

Who is responsible for what conditions is a persistent theme for Gabriel and one that has colored many of our discussions over a period of almost two decades. Whether at the level of social misery and conflict or in more intimate ways when confronting personal foibles and proclivities, Gabriel has always been among my most intellectually restless of friends. His commentary is regularly spiced with an assignment of blame leaving no one unscathed, yet in his estimation, not everyone is equally at fault.

Years earlier, in 1993, Gabriel and I sat in the June sun on a wall atop the extinct volcano Xitle in the mountains ringing southern Mexico City, talking politics and his problem with *las copas*.

"You must have begun drinking when you were six," I teased Gabriel.

"No, even before that," he corrected me. "You know why I began before? Because maybe I've inherited something from my father. Maybe I began when I was conceived. That's when I began to drink. It might be. It might be something inherited."

"Genes?"

"Might be. Maybe an escape; it's the most likely. Sometimes, because of the way I think, I feel like I don't fit, in my family or in society. Maybe I don't have the channels for me to realize my potential. Sometimes I end up saying that only drunk and asleep can I forget how screwed up things are, because sometimes I don't have anyone to talk to about all my experiences, my worries, my traumas, my complexes. Because in my family, I feel. . . . In my marriage, I am not understood."

"And your friends? Can't you talk to them?" I asked.

"Sometimes we clash. I like to talk about everything, and I can't do it with them. Like religion. And when I make them see some mistake in their way of looking at it. I figure if they weren't my friends, I wouldn't tell them about their mistakes. I could give a shit. But that's why we fight sometimes."

Gabriel's thirst for knowledge and for debate on questions philosophical and political is largely a matter of beliefs and conversations. He has participated in marches to support the Chiapas Zapatistas, and he continues to argue against voting as a means to fundamental change in Mexico. But mainly, in the almost twenty years I have known him, Gabriel talks. He talks openly, sarcastically, and sometimes vehemently about current events, music, indigenous protests, agnosticism, student politics, snake tacos, the naming of children. He talks with friends, family, acquaintances, and basically anyone he can stop on Huehuetzin Street—in

Colonia Santo Domingo—who wanders by during the twelve- to fourteen-hour shifts Gabriel works six days a week. There, from eight in the morning and often until nearly midnight (using flashlights, a lamp, and even cigarette lighters), Gabriel repairs all manner of vehicles in the street and sidewalk in front of his cubbyhole workshop.

Colonia Santo Domingo, on the south side of Mexico City, was settled by "parachutist" squatters beginning in September 1971. Almost forty years later, well over 150,000 people live in the colonia, only a fraction of whom can find gainful employment there. Since 1971, settlers have built the streets, brought in electricity, water lines, and more recently helped lay the pipes for sewage. In many respects, Santo Domingo is typical of other colonias in the city, in that it is populated overwhelmingly by poor men and women living close together, sharing and fighting over whatever they have. In other ways, however, Santo Domingo is a unique neighborhood, because of its particular history, especially that experienced by women in their capacities as organizers and leaders in the physical and moral construction of the area.

In chapter ten, Margarita Zárate similarly underscores the relationship of broad social divisions—such as ethnicity and gender—to very local political turmoil and change, while at the same time referencing world events that have seemingly nothing to do with the immediate struggles at hand, such as the naming of a neighborhood Colonia Kuwait, during the First Gulf War (1990–91). So, too, in Colonia Santo Domingo, the participation of women in neighborhood, citywide, and national political events was a source of constant debate in homes and families, as well as an indication of profound transformations with respect to broader gender relations. These changes can be seen in the participation of women in remunerated employment, the fact that girls began keeping pace with boys in years of formal education received, and women's participation in diverse political mobilizations. In a related fashion, Patience Schell (in chapter nine) shows how in the 1920s the activities of elite conservative Catholic women fit as well under the rubric of resistance. With regard to both gender and religion, Schell argues, these women faced bona fide opprobrium and exclusion that can only be understood in a larger fabric of social inequalities.

One of the fascinating aspects of studying Colonia Santo Domingo has been precisely the fact that women and men often have personal experience participating in various forms of social protest and resistance. Yet if one were inclined to seek representative samples and describe a "typical" resident of the colonia, doubtless most people, most of the time, want absolutely nothing to do with protest or even to participate in any form of public politics. In the fluctuations between political activity and passivity, and the contradictory analyses that my friends and neighbors offer of their and others' involvement, I find solace in the conclusion that few people in Santo Domingo, if any, are ever truly indifferent to social change, large or small. How they express their concerns regarding issues as diverse as the cost of sewer pipes, the visit of Rigoberta Menchú to a nearby liberation theology church, or municipal and federal elections is, of course, a lesson in diversity and contradiction. No matter, their political horizons extend far beyond simply putting up a defensive fight against mounting humiliation and subjugation.

In part this reflects a Gramscian (1971, 333) notion of "contradictory consciousness," whereby the popular understandings, identities, and practices of the members of subordinate classes simultaneously embody that which has been inherited from past generations and that which unites them in contemporary struggle against dominant social classes. Such conditions are indeed more than merely ideational and, to paraphrase Kate Crehan (2002, 192), stem from the very contradictions between classes themselves. From this understanding we may in turn grasp distinctions between social resistance as a form of protest against insurmountable odds and rebellion that challenges preexisting class relations.

Talking about Cosmic Significance

One recurring discussion with Gabriel over the years has concerned the question of significance: the significance of parents and how children inherit certain traits from them; the significance of political events and movements in effecting real change in society, especially as that change might relate to the inequality between rich and poor, Indian and mestizo; the significance of what people say in relation to what they think and do; and, perhaps on the grandest of all possible scales, the ephemeral significance of humans in a cosmic universe. This last topic led us to a conversation in 1993 about the television series *Cosmos*.

"I watch Carl Sagan in the documentaries. He seems very good. This is one intelligent guy. Now, I haven't studied what I have learned. [Working] people don't have access to the kind of learning he does . . . there's no information . . . it's a small nucleus [of people who can do this kind of study-ing]. For people who work and sometimes don't have time or are tired, it's easier to have a documentary to watch. It's more practical and you can learn. I think it would be good to propose to the university [Universidad Nacional Autónoma de México, UNAM] something like this for people.

"I know a book exists, but I haven't had the opportunity to read it. It's translated into Spanish, and, truth is, I think it's got some really interest-ing things. It's helped me to understand more. When you understand what we are, well, you learn everything.

"Unfortunately people aren't attracted to the program, at least the youth aren't. How come? Actually, there's a lot of interest. I've read some astronomy books that have fallen into my hands, and everything Sagan says I have read in other books. These are the books they sell over there [by the university], and as they're less expensive, I buy them. Sometimes I find them tossed away. I've found really good books in the garbage, and the truth is that a book is a treasure."

Gabriel talked of acquaintances employed at UNAM who had argued with him about Sagan, telling him that in the university they had already learned everything Sagan discussed in his program, that he had nothing new to offer. Gabriel continued,

"So I know more about Sagan than I do about the university. The univer-sity gives classes at one in the afternoon, at two, and no worker can attend. So, I told these people I was arguing with, 'Do you know what the value of Carl Sagan is? For me, the value is that he's giving information, that you can learn from him. That's his value, and that's why I defend him. What's a university worth if it's out of reach? And the truth is that you need a lot, a lot of time to learn, because there's so much to learn. And there's not enough time in the schedules of the workers.

"I have the videos" of *Cosmos*, Gabriel told me. "I had them taped. You don't see the picture well, but you can more or less make it out. It's really interesting because at any given moment it makes you feel like a flea, and at the same time it makes you feel important. Because I'm realiz-ing what it is all about. I'm realizing that I'm learning things that I never even thought I was going to learn, learning about the nature of life. And I think, 'Even though it's no more than a passing fancy, I've learned a lot.' We want to have this *capacidad* [ability, knowledge]; I would like to have this capacidad."

In Santo Domingo, as elsewhere, popular theories of genetic inheritance have become a type of secular cosmology, imbuing those in the know with the capacity to explain the most perplexing of enigmas about human existence and cosmic infinity. To take the most obvious example, genetics is held by some to offer the key to understanding all sorts of human behavior. For instance, Gabriel discusses his penchant for alcohol in terms of inherited traits, linking his proclivities to biological roots and in the process deriving some absolution for his sins. Although his remarks are often offered offhandedly, Gabi is not alone in attributing drinking proclivities to genes (see Gutmann 1999). In this way, problems like alcoholism may be characterized as beyond the reach of rational remedies; if they are caused by "inside forces" that are amenable only to evolutionary mutations, then what is a poor problem drinker to do but accept this biologically derived fate?

At the same time, Gabriel discusses his pursuit of knowledge and his anger at those who demean such learning as unsophisticated, insinuating that Gabriel is less truly well informed. What constitutes correct understanding, when has someone achieved a real, conscious grasp on an issue, and how are these things measured? Far from being confined to cloistered, scholarly towers, these questions permeate daily street discussions—at least if Gabriel directs the conversation.

It is easy enough to support Gabriel's claims to the right to knowledge. And we may, and should, admire Gabi's refusal to bow to the snobbishness of those who argue that Sagan dumbed down his program for the masses. If such determination and thirst for learning is not simply a good in itself, then when men like Gabriel become more learned, even more self-aware, there are implications for political life. And surely they may learn without seeking the permission of condescending saviors. But if this self-awareness is to result in more than the romantic valorization of poor people and their ability to break through unflattering portraits of themselves, such knowledge must be measured against ignorance and complicity. John Monteiro's discussion (chapter one) is relevant with respect to understanding the meaning and applicability of collaboration between subject peoples and those in socially dominant circumstances. No matter how loath theorists of change may be to attribute to the dispossessed any responsibility for their misery, cooptation, and duplicity, the recognition of this self-awareness requires it.

Historical Motivations and Social Expectations

Let us now turn to Oaxaca, where a major social conflict in 2006 holds lessons for the contemporary study of social expectations, agency and apathy, and resistance. As they have each year for more than two decades, in May 2006, 70,000 teachers in Oaxaca, Mexico, occupied the Zócalo (central square). They declared that their sit-in would persist until the state government met demands for better pay and working conditions. The *plantón* had become a regular part of negotiations each year between the teachers' union, Sección 22, and the governor. That year, however, it was different. In the middle of the night of June 14, the governor ordered state police to dismantle the sit-in and clear the teachers out of the downtown area.

In the next five months, a massive social conflict unprecedented in the history of Oaxaca ensued. Eventually hundreds of thousands of citizens, including thousands of university students and a smaller number of professors, became involved in public ways to demand that Governor Ulises Ruiz Ortiz resign from office. As part of a broad coalition known as the Asamblea Popular de los Pueblos de Oaxaca (Popular Assembly of the Peoples of Oaxaca, the APPO), protesters occupied and broadcast from twelve radio stations, while others erected barricades throughout the city. In late October, President Vicente Fox sent over 4,000 members of the Federal Preventative Police to quell the upheaval.

The governor never resigned. Instead, twenty-three persons were assassinated by government supporters and none of the killers were brought to trial. Hundreds of protesters were illegally arrested, with over 140 of them sent to prison in the state of Nayarit, over twenty hours' drive from Oaxaca. Human rights commissions received over 1,200 complaints—including from students, professors, and others from Oaxaca universities and other institutions of higher learning—alleging torture and harassment at the hands of the authorities.[1] In June 2007, I led a fact-finding delegation of the Latin American Studies Association to Oaxaca to study the impact of the conflict in 2006 on academic freedom of expression.

For much of 2006, universities and institutions of higher learning in Oaxaca were significant sites for conflict and social movement organizing, while students and, to a lesser extent, professors from these academic centers participated in the APPO and other forms of protest. This was especially true of the Universidad Autónoma "Benito Juárez" de Oaxaca (UABJO), where pitched street fighting took place just outside the campus from June through November. Moreover, on June 14, 2006, university students and faculty seeking to "democratize the media" took over the radio station of the UABJO, Radio Universidad. During the conflict, they used the station to broadcast messages and information.

Throughout the conflict, the UABJO rector, Francisco Martínez Neri, made concerted attempts to preserve the autonomy of the university, declaring, "We would defend the participation of any professor and any student" in the social protests. After university students took over Radio Universidad, there were personal attacks on Martínez Neri, such as announcements on a government-allied radio station that persons were headed to his house to burn it down.

The events of November 2, 2006, were especially complex. As Martínez Neri later recounted, after hearing on the radio that the police were trying to enter the university, he called the Mexican president, the secretary of the interior, and the federal police that had entered Oaxaca only days before, demanding that "they withdraw from the university." When he arrived at the university himself, he "observed that a group of state police was trying to force a door [in order] to enter" the university, and helicopters from the federal police were dropping tear gas within the university, which had become, in his words, "a war zone." Nonetheless, despite government pressure, the rector defended the university's autonomy and the police were unable to occupy the campus.

In the last twenty years, when Mexico has experienced a "democratization" of political processes, the party that had long controlled virtually every political office at federal and local levels, the Institutional Revolutionary Party (PRI), has lost one election after another, including the last two presidential elections. In contrast, in the last decade, the PRI has redoubled its political authoritarianism in Oaxaca. The conflict in 2006 stems in good measure from the PRI's corruption, cronyism, and corporatism; the state's political climate is characterized by intolerance, intimidation, and violent suppression of independent social movements. The social polarization that occurred in the course of events in 2006 resulted from a generalized conflict in Oaxaca's society reflecting obvious and extreme social inequalities and was the product of a social movement whose scale and impact was extraordinary.

"The repression against the popular movement in Oaxaca," notes Salomón Nahmad, "provides evidence of state terrorism" (2007, 24). He continues, "A deep chasm in Mexican society is leading to great polarization." Certainly "polarization" was a term heard repeatedly in Oaxaca in 2007. There were systematic attempts by Oaxaca's government and police, and later by federal authorities and police, to intimidate, threaten, punish, and even murder those who expressed opposition to the governor and to the violent state repression. A climate of fear, polarization, and impunity that was fomented and sponsored by the government's out-of-control "dirty war" of 2006. In a sense, such polarization is nothing new in Oaxaca, with the indigenous peoples of the state excluded now and historically from seats of power, as they have been in Jalisco (discussed by Guillermo de la Peña in chapter eleven).

Although the percentage of university professors who openly supported these social movements was small, the state government's persecution of these individuals served to intimidate intellectuals more generally. In the years preceding the conflict Dr. Víctor Raúl Martínez, a professor-researcher at the UABJO, was well known locally for his activities with a variety of academic, civic, and religious organizations. He was also a columnist for the newspaper *Noticias* and a regular commentator on Radio HIT.[2] In the course of its investigations, the delegation interviewed Dr. Martínez and his family about their experiences. Because he was active in the APPO and the Pueblos Indígenas Foro de los/de Oaxaca (Indigenous Peoples' Forum of Oaxaca) in November 2006, he received threats on his life and against his family in the form of telephone calls to him, his wife, and two of his brothers. His photograph was among twenty-five published on an anonymous website that announced: "These are the delinquents who have kidnapped your city. Grab them wherever you see them or go find them in their homes!" By July 2007, five of the twenty-five persons had reportedly been killed. Dr. Martínez himself was threatened repeatedly on Radio Ciudadana.

One of the most remarkable developments in the 2006 conflict pertained to the role of women. One reason for women's participation as leaders and activists was the fact that despite having passed a legislative agenda in 2003 and 2004 pledging gender equality—through issues as diverse as the inclusion of women candidates in elections, free childbirth, and justice for indigenous women prisoners—the state government had done nothing to fulfill these promises. From the beginning of the social upheaval, women were at the forefront of marches, forums, and decision-making of all kinds in the movement, though unlike the women discussed by Patience Schell (chapter nine), these women activists were overwhelmingly poor and indigenous. On August 1, over 2,000 women took over the state-run television channel Canal 9, saying, "We are tired of hearing lies." On August 21, in the middle of the night, the transmission tower was destroyed. In response, the women and others from APPO took over twelve radio stations. Also on that day, the Coordinadora de Mujeres de Oaxaca Primero de Agosto (August First Oaxacan Women's Coordinating Committee) was formed to promote and protect women's presence in the social protests.

In the context of state terrorism and the ensuing social upheaval, we may well ask ourselves what it means to "be reasonable" about the chances for large-scale social change. Or, to paraphrase the query of political philosopher Wendy Brown (2005, 99), what does it mean for scholars to be working in a time when we have lost the belief in the possibility and the viability of a radical overthrow of existing social relations? In particular, Brown calls for scholars to "recuperate a utopian imaginary," and it is this vision that I wish to contrast to the dreary realism of so much resistance writing.

Roger Bartra noted that in the 1980s and 1990s in Mexico, although many believed that the new social movements would provide the impulse for "the great transformation" that would incorporate the nationalist and populist social programs they demanded, social disparities of nearly every kind continued to widen, notwithstanding the fact that these movements successfully mobilized tens of thousands of citizens (1999, 70–71).

The conflict and social movement in Oaxaca in 2006 took place amid brutal government repression against social protest. Yet also noteworthy is the fact that this repression was met with what the director of the UABJO's Radio Universidad described as "an effervescence of popular initiative." And for everyone in Oaxaca, regardless of political viewpoint, the changes that occurred were seen as producing "a before and an after," a sense that "Oaxaca will never be the same." A reflection of this transformation is perhaps found in the flourishing artistic workshops of youth in the universities and in the surrounding villages, and in the *rebeldía oaxaqueña*, as evidenced in the new "music from the barricades."

In June 2007, among those who called themselves "the opposition," there was still an effervescence of utopian feelings about the previous year. In interviews with over two dozen intellectuals, artists, human rights workers, liberation theology clergy, and students, I witnessed a remarkable optimism and celebratory mood. People talked about the APPO as a "movement of movements," an acephalous coalition that embodied what some considered the ancient virtues of indigenous community assemblies, *usos y costumbres*, instead of corrupt electoral politics. Others pointed to the social mobilization against the governor and government, unprecedented in the history of the state.

During the 2006 conflict, universities and institutions of higher learning and individual researchers, teachers, cultural workers, and intellectuals associated with universities, schools, and nongovernmental organizations performed a vital role in establishing a civic space for information, debate, and independent social protest. The key struggle took place in the streets, during massive *megamarchas* and at barricades erected by youths each night for weeks on end. The universities and their employees nonetheless played a crucial role not only by participating alongside other citizens, but also by helping to articulate the demands of various social actors involved in the conflict, including indigenous peoples and women.

The UABJO and Rector Martínez Neri, in particular, were at the center of the conflict almost daily. The UABJO played a critical role in maintaining the dignity and autonomy of scholarly debate, an engagement with social problems and participation in social affairs, in disseminating views and news otherwise unavailable in society, and being a refuge from police and *parapolicía* attacks that became almost routine. The administration, faculty, and students of the university protected academic independence and efforts to resolve the conflict peacefully.

Nonetheless, June's optimism was conspicuously weaker by the end of 2007, as the PRI won virtually every state election that year, the protesting teachers seemed far less visible, and the APPO was no longer able to maintain its constant presence in the city and countryside of Oaxaca. Avenues of significant social change once again seemed blocked, nonnavigable, or razed. So how are we to take stock of the final outcome of the struggle and resistance in Oaxaca during 2006?

In her analysis of what she terms "post-utopian" quilombos in Brazil (chapter twelve), Ilka Boaventura Leite shows how double meanings have operated as an element of resistance. The meanings in question are utilized by quilombo organizations as rebellion has itself "become a social pact" and social antagonisms have become masked. In this way, perhaps, the quilombo experience stands both in contrast to the utopian goals of the APPO and many of the Oaxaca activists of the summer of 2006, yet notably parallel in the end, as the idea of resistance replaced "the slow

rhythm of actual changes." Young and older activists alike were tremen-
dously encouraged by the outpouring of support for their struggle. Not surprisingly their enthusiasm often got ahead of their ability to bring about
lasting change in Oaxacan society. The attempts to move beyond resistance to utopian social transformations seemed ultimately beyond reach
in Oaxaca, as it had seemed among the quilombos of Brazil. So, finally,
there appeared for the moment to be no political space beyond resistance.

Activism and Apathy

Yet I hasten to add that none of the events in Oaxaca should be taken to
mean that scholars should focus exclusively on activists, on rebellions, or
on intentional forms of opposition to various forms of status quo. Among
other things, in the very "apolitical" and "apathetic" interstices beloved by
historians and anthropologists one may find that the uninvolved and uninformed are never quite so, and that visions of better worlds can also be
the stuff of daily life for those who seem to shun public politics.

Jumping back in time, and returning to the Mexican capital, following the financial crisis of 1994–95, a particularly heated topic of debate in
Colonia Santo Domingo concerned the *marchas* and *plantones* (demonstrations and occupations) that were being carried out by various groups
protesting austerity measures. Invariably, the opinion a person in the colonia may have held about the protests that blocked traffic was determined
more by general political sympathies than by how much and how often he
or she had been personally inconvenienced by the events. Whether or not
the protests were viewed with contemptuous scorn or accepted as a necessary nuisance, such political activities were undoubtedly seen as one
of the only means that poor people had at their disposal to change social
policies. Or more precisely, marchas and plantones were among the few
options available for open street protests. As such, these street politics are
exemplary of a defiant politics, in which defiance "presumes intent," in the
words of Susan Eckstein (1989, 11).

Obviously, marches, sit-ins, and other occupations did not begin in
1994. In fact, in Santo Domingo, such protests constitute an important
part of local history, dating from its earliest days. Since the first days of
the invasion of Santo Domingo in September 1971, when men and women
gathered around rock piles and discussed how to contend with municipal
authorities and periodic police incursions into their makeshift squatter

camps, it has been similarly difficult to distinguish between activity that constitutes hidden forms of resistance and that which represents overt confrontational politics.

In January 1997, Juan and Héctor offered to give me a ride to the north side of the city. We tried heading in their car straight through downtown but quickly found ourselves in a traffic jam. We never figured out what had caused all the traffic, but as we sat there going nowhere, both Juan and Héctor launched into a spirited condemnation of marches, protests, and occupations in general. It did not matter, Héctor insisted, leaning over to look at me in the back seat, who might be demonstrating—students, campesinos, workers, or some other troublemakers—the demonstrations were futile, disruptive, and most annoying. Juan, who was driving, added that all I had to do to learn about the ineffectiveness of protests like these was watch the news. Weren't the TV announcers correct that so many stopped cars greatly exacerbated the already-high wintertime pollution? They explained it all quite clearly on television, Juan said, and he was convinced that this analysis of protesters being out of sync with the population overall was accurate and fair.

Among Santo Domingo's residents, such contrarian opinions and their varied practical relationship to such activities, are integral to local political processes and struggles. As Marc Abélès has argued, political meetings and street demonstrations are major rituals in many societies. That street demonstrators "brandish symbols of antagonism," such as slogans and banners, amid shouts and heckles, serves to illustrate "an undercurrent of violence." And such rites "punctuate circumstances in which political life takes a more agitated turn" (1997, 324). For those like Juan and Héctor, who usually disapprove of demonstrating, these rituals of protest have become a lightning rod spurring them to further resentment. For the protesters themselves, their understanding of the significance of their actions is undoubtedly more varied. For some, participation in these activities is seen as the only option left them. Others, however, may suspect that even the more agitated rituals sometimes represent little more than another means to legitimize those whose policies they target.

Moreover, odd as it may seem, protest does not always entail actual opposition to the target of dissent. Protests can also be ritualized and used to legitimize the status quo. Paraphrasing Max Gluckman's (1960) famous discussion of rites of rebellion, David Kertzer has shown that "in spite of their apparent delegitimating intent, such rites can serve to reinforce existing power inequalities. . . . [as] people are able to ventilate their natural resentments of occupying inferior places in society and, in so doing, allow the system to continue" (1988, 54–55). Acting as safety valves and sops, protests can validate the powers that be, as Stanley Brandes (1988) has shown in his analysis of fiestas in rural Mexico. But insofar as protests actually defy existing social relations, they can upset them. Either way, however, rarely is resistance in the form of public protest so one-sided that it represents some kind of pure political action untainted by competing interests among the "resisters."

Political resistance, like other forms of political struggle, is a contradictory phenomenon, often described in the well-known formula, one step forward, two steps backward. In Mexico City and Oaxaca, in *colonias populares* like Santo Domingo and citadels of higher learning like the UABJO, in the 1990s "socialism" ceased to be discussed or even contemplated as a way of radically reorganizing society. Instead, it seemed, "democracy" became the watchword of social change, *the* ethical endpoint and *the* aim of social struggle. Like its socialist forebear, democracy offers utopian visions of a world in which poverty, racism, militarization, and inequality are progressively eradicated by participating citizens in free elections and civic organizations. And though overused and underdefined today, democracy, like the concept of agency, can be very useful in describing aspects of citizens' defiant assertions of their political rights.

The other side of the coin, political compliance and resignation to the status quo, is less easily conceptualized with standard understandings of democracy, agency, or in the case at hand, resistance. As with the concept of democracy, if theories of resistance can help us to address novel ways of resolving the plagues of poverty, racism, and militarization, they are to be encouraged and embraced. If, on the contrary, theories about the rituals of resistance offer no more than blanket critiques of utopian attempts to raise from the dead the dream of human control over human destiny, then they are part of the problem.

Notes

My thanks to John Gledhill for his comments at every stage of my thinking regarding resistance and related concepts (see especially Gutmann 1993 and 2002), to my colleagues in the Rethinking Histories of Resistance in Brazil and Mexico Seminar for their painstaking engagement with the place of resistance in the history of social change, and to Catherine Lutz for her magic blue pen.

1 The views expressed in this chapter are my own and do not necessarily reflect those of the delegation or LASA.

2 Dr. Martínez (2007) has also provided one of the first scholarly studies of the conflict and protests. See also Comisión Civil Internacional de Observación por los Derechos Humanos 2007; Esteva 2007a; 2007b; Osorno 2007; and Gutmann 2008.

Rethinking Histories of Resistance in Brazil and Mexico

ALAN KNIGHT

In this chapter, I offer a general discussion of resistance, drawing on the rich set of examples provided in the rest of this book. As a historian of Mexico, I know much less about Brazil than about Mexico, and much less about anthropology than history. While these two disciplines share a measure of kinship within the great extended family of the social sciences, they are second cousins rather than siblings, hence, while history generates plenty of debates (usually of a specific, low-to-middle-range kind), it is usually methodologically, theoretically, and conceptually poorer; although I would see this as a genteel kind of poverty, the product of modest wants rather than intellectual bankruptcy. I mention this in light of my later discussion of concepts, which may seem both ignorant and dismissive. Finally, in conclusion, I touch on the contrasting approaches of historians, who often deal with dead and distant peoples, and anthropologists, who may be bound to "their" contemporary communities by ties of experience, affection, and solidarity.

Definitions

The central concept of this project is resistance, a protean concept that, it seems, can accommodate a vast range of phenomena "from revolutions to hairstyles" (Hollander and Einwohner 2004, 534). We can try different strategies to pin down protean concepts of this kind. One strategy involves etymology: chasing down the origins of words. In this case, however, the chase takes us into the unpromising realm of physics and hardly helps. An alternative "genealogical" approach would be to focus on the paternity of the concept: when and why it was born. Here, there seems to be some consensus. Resistance theory—or, more loosely, the notion of resistance—is a relatively recent construct, which helped fill a gap left by the decline of cognate theories and notions, while responding to (perceived) events in the "real world," as discussed in John Gledhill's introduction to this book. These theories included class and class consciousness, class-based move- · ments, including "social revolutions," the grand metanarrative of dialectical materialism, and "really existing socialism." Their decline, linked to the end of the Cold War, the atrophy of Marxism, and the supposed triumph of neoliberalism, left a theoretical vacuum, into which flowed several new conceptual currents. Scholars focused on the "new social movements," "identity" (as opposed to "class") politics, and bottom-up, incremental, decentralized political mobilization (as opposed to top-down, revolutionary vanguardism). At a time when radical and progressive "dreams [had] lost their luster," resistance theory offered a different perspective, allied to a dose of optimism (M. Brown 1996, 729).

In Brazil and Mexico in particular, the so-called new social movements of the 1980s and 1990s challenged the political status quo, as represented by declining authoritarian or semiauthoritarian regimes, while highlighting key issues (such as land in Brazil and debt and public services in Mexico) and displaying the capacity of "civil society" to act independently of a sclerotic state (for example, after the Mexico City earthquake of 1985). Of course, there was a good deal of slippage between the political and academic worlds. With the restoration—or establishment de novo—of electoral democracy, political parties and elections acquired greater clout, especially when leftist parties proved capable of winning national or, as in Mexico City, major regional elections. By the beginning of the twenty-first century, the new social movement boom was waning, certainly in the academic world, probably in the real world too. But, given the accumulated inertia of research programs, doctoral degrees, academic appointments, and funding priorities, academic trends take time to adjust. Even if the current crisis portends a prolonged period of depression and socioeconomic protest, the academy may cling to "identity politics" for years to come.

Whatever the causes, it seems clear that the grand leftist metanarratives of the 1960s and 1970s gave way, during the 1980s and 1990s, to more modest, "de-centered" mininarratives. In my own field (Mexican revolutionary studies), the great unitary revolution became "many revolutions," or just "a great rebellion," and other great revolutions—the English, the

French—were similarly cut down to size (Knight 1992). Our theoretical bearings also shifted: studies of "great" or "social" revolutions (Brinton 1938; B. Moore 1966; Wolf 1969), which posited grand global patterns of causality, "stages," and outcomes, gave way to more particularist approaches, which asked not only "Why Men Rebel" (a title Ted Gurr would probably not get away with today) but also "why men and women do *not* rebel" and, thus, why they comply, albeit grudgingly, or seek small respites and advantages without challenging the entire edifice of power (Gurr 1970). James Scott's (1976; 1985) shift from the political economics of peasant revolution to the "weapons of the weak" exemplified this shift: not because Scott had radically changed his mind, but rather because he had switched his focus (from the macropolitics of revolutionary Vietnam in the 1940s and 1950s to the micropolitics of conservative Malaysia in the 1960s and 1970s) and this shift happened to suit the mood of the times. Hence the weapons of the weak became—like "imagined communities" and "invented traditions"—a reiterated mantra, even among those, I suspect, who had never read Scott's book.

As tends to happen when grand metanarratives collapse, the extinction of supposed conceptual dinosaurs (social revolution, socialism, and dependency) favored the rapid evolution of a swarm of small, busy, burrowing mammalian competitors. One of those—resistance—has now grown to substantial proportions; it is, perhaps, the elephant of the post-Jurassic era. But, as this book shows, resistance consorts and competes with a host of other post-Jurassic concepts, some of quite ancient pedigree, some relatively new mutations whose fitness for survival remains as yet unknown. Reviewing the contributions to this book, I encountered

1. *big, old concepts* that survived the mass extinction (prolonging the evolutionary metaphor, one might call them sharks): elite, power, hegemony and counter-hegemony, legitimacy, democracy, culture and subculture, domination, subordination, mentality, modernity, ethnicity, utopianism, populism, clientelism, citizenship, false consciousness;
2. *big new concepts* that have sprung up and multiplied, mammalian-fashion, alongside resistance: agency, subalternity, alterity, imaginary, identity, negotiation, metanarrative, transnationality and postmodernity. And, finally,
3. *small new concepts* struggling to survive and procreate:[1] governmentality, materiality, horizontality, translocality, transutopianism, trans-

behavioralism, varieties of power ("vertical" and "oblique"), varieties of resistance ("endo" and "exo"), polynucleated power fields, and so on. We might call them the conceptual voles of the post-Jurassic.

The point about this quick semantic census is not to rehash old arguments about the utility—or disutility—of jargon and neologisms. There are plenty of occasions when jargon and neologisms can be useful (Knight 2002, 148–49). Rather, the point is to flag the risks of such semantic fecundity. The purpose of concepts is to help us understand the world, past and present. For a concept to help, it should be reasonably clear and consensual: clear, so that its meaning cannot be endlessly contested; and consensual, in that there is some broad agreement among scholars as to what that meaning is, so that they can constructively deploy it in debate. Of the list presented above, the first category (the sharks) consists of concepts that, being old and familiar, come with a lot of theoretical baggage; but for that reason we can unpack the baggage and achieve some measure of clarity. Thus my conception of the state is Marxist or Weberian or Thomist. Or, when I refer to democracy, I mean representative liberal democracy on the lines of Dahl's polyarchy (Dahl 1971). Even if, since one *politólogo*'s polyarchy may be another's "bourgeois democracy," we do not achieve complete consensus, we at least know roughly where we are coming from, hence debate need not proceed along multiple parallel paths that never meet.

The second and third categories (elephants and voles) have not acquired the same baggage; they are travelling light and can be rather skittishly evasive. Category two concepts we encounter quite frequently, but we do not know if, between encounters, the concept has remained constant. They may be familiar, but they remain, as yet, ill-defined and "insufficiently theorized."[2] Hence their proliferation, especially their careless and unexplained proliferation, tends to generate confusion. A fortiori, category three concepts, being new, unfamiliar, and (often) unexplained, do not promote comprehension and enlightenment. Perhaps they will eventually make the grade and achieve promotion to category two concepts—that is, they will catch on and become familiar, if still somewhat inscrutable, conceptual friends. Eventually, given time and effort, they make it all the way to category one status, as established, proven, "successful" concepts.[3]

I draw three conclusions from this swift overview: first, following

William of Ockham, we should not multiply concepts, unless we think they are really necessary; so, we should resist overpopulating category three. Second, as and when category three concepts acquire currency—become successful "memes," as Dawkins et al. would say (Blackmore 1999)—we should make sure to debate and define what they mean. Thus, finally, we should try to promote category two concepts to category one, which means supplying them with clear, useful, consensual definitions and, no less important, the attendant bibliography that enables those definitions to be achieved—definitions being, to my mind, not a priori Platonic notions, but working formulations based on the creative interplay of theory and practice. Perhaps one practical outcome of this book might be to promote—or, at least, make a case for promotion of—the concept of resistance from category two status (familiar but vague and contested) to category one (familiar but bolstered by useful theoretical and practical knowledge). Thus, we turn an elephant into a shark.

Typologies

So, I now turn to the central concept of resistance. Since, as this book shows, resistance is a protean phenomenon, capable of assuming many guises, it seems to me unavoidable that we break it down into categories or subtypes. This should not be an exercise in simple pigeonholing; the distinctions that follow usually form part of continua, not discrete categories.

The Emic-Etic Binary

I start with a basic distinction between resistance as it is defined by contemporary actors and as it is defined ex post facto by scholars (we could play around with "subjective or objective" and "emic or etic" labels). For historians, this distinction is often crucial; for contemporary analysts—anthropologists and sociologists, for example—it may be less salient. On the other hand, social scientists working in the present can probe motivation more thoroughly, since historians often have to infer motivations from behavior. Thus, when we ask whether actors *conceive* of their actions as "resistant" or not, historians may be hard put to provide answers. An additional, crucial, and arguably neglected point is if the *targets* of resistance—again, in emic or subjective terms—discern resistance? Do employers, landlords, or state officials (let's, for the moment, call them elites) identify certain actions—usually, "subaltern" actions—as resistant?[4] It is, I think, historically common for elites to exaggerate (subaltern) resistance, to make it sound more extreme and bloodcurdling than it really was.[5] They may do this for tactical reasons, in order to smear their opponents and, perhaps, to justify top-down repression. In Latin America, as in the United States, varieties of the "Red Scare" have been apparent since 1917 (Deutsch 1999). But, quite often, exaggerated fears seem to have been quite genuine: hence the Grande Peur of the French Revolution (Lefebvre 1973), or the fears of *chilangos* that they would all be murdered in their beds when the Zapatistas entered Mexico City in 1914, which, of course, did not happen (Womack 1969, 219). Indeed, it may be that tactical elite scaremongering serves to stoke the fires of genuine elite fear. Just as elites, perhaps, come to believe their own high-minded and self-justifying "public transcripts" (about good government, paternalism, and noblesse oblige; Abercrombie, Hill, and Turner 1984, 3), so too, perhaps, they come to believe their own alarmist scare stories. A key consequence is that popular radicalism—by which I mean the radicalism both of goals and methods—is often exaggerated, as it was in the case of the Zapatistas. To the extent that (historical) sources tend to be produced by elites, they may display a systemic bias in favor of subaltern radicalism. I am not sure if any such bias exists in the anthropological literature, which tends to focus on the agents of resistance, the subalterns, rather than the targets, the elites. This preliminary distinction leads immediately to a second, which is perhaps more immediately relevant.

Intentionality

Does resistance have to be *intentional* to qualify as resistance? Some scholars are firmly of this view (Hollander and Einwohner 2004, 542–43; Castro, chapter two). If the putative "resisters" do not think that they are resisting—that they are mounting a concerted or considered challenge to their superiors, a challenge that is, perhaps, "counter-hegemonic" (Seymour 2006, 305)—then some say it is meaningless to talk of resistance: resistance must be deliberate and purposive, not simply an unconscious by-product of behavior that lacks any such underlying motive.

Motives are certainly important, but they are hard to get at (especially for historians). Who is to say whether petty stealing and foot-dragging are really intentional resistance, even "counter-hegemonic resistance"?

(J. C. Scott 1990, 188). Intentions are hard to get at not just for want of raw data (historians may find it hard to "open windows into men's souls," as Queen Elizabeth I put it, but anthropologists in the field can at least try); it is also a question of "indexicality"—that is to say, a question of what people might themselves understand by "resistance," however that term is translated.[6]

However, outcomes are even more important. They tend to be more accessible, and they may hinge upon unintentional as well as intentional resistance. Or, as sometimes happens in history, unintentional consequences exceed conscious intentions (modest ambitions may spawn grand outcomes; though, even more often, grand ambitions spawn modest outcomes).[7] The consequences of unintentional resistance can be seen in several contrasting contexts. For example, scholars stress the importance of solidarity: beliefs and practices that foster solidarity can—potentially or actually—fortify resistance. Thus, Candomblé may facilitate resistance even if its practitioners do not conceive of it as inherently contestational (see Parés, chapter seven). (Again, elites may still feel threatened and thus perceive resistance where none is intended.) Similarly, in times of war, popular resistance to conscription, culminating in mass desertion, can undermine not only armies, but entire empires, such as the Russian empire (J. C. Scott 1986, 6). A contrasting example—admittedly far removed from our comparison—concerns trade union activity.[8] At the height of trade union militancy in the UK in the 1970s, it was plausibly argued that wage claims, backed up by effective strike action, were eroding profits and pushing companies to the wall, even threatening a systemic crisis of capitalism in the United Kingdom (Glyn and Sutcliffe 1972). While some employers—and some government ministers—alleged that militant unionists were consciously bent on such an outcome, this was almost certainly not the case: the "objective" radicalism of potential outcomes (declining profits and, eventually, a capitalist crisis) far outran the "subjective" radicalism of most union members, who were seeking better pay and job protection, not the destruction of capitalism. Of course, the experiment was not allowed to run its course, since, following the "winter of discontent" in 1979, the Thatcher government came to power, intent on breaking the power of the unions, which it did.

It is hard to say, in cases like these, whether objective (system-threatening) consequences arose from circumstances in which purposive (subaltern) resistance was absent or present, but less subjectively radical than the objective outcomes. In other words, Brazilian slaves or British workers may have subjectively entertained notions of resistance, loosely defined, without intending to mount the kind of objective threat to the system that they did (or, recalling my previous point, that elites *believed* they did). To go back to the Zapatistas: the original Plan of Ayala of 1911 was a moderate document that conceded the sugar plantation a place in Morelos society; the Zapatistas initially sought to adjust the balance between village and hacienda that had been drastically upset by thirty years of the Pax Porfiriana. As John Womack begins his classic study: "This is a book about country people who did not want to move and therefore got into a revolution. They did not figure on so odd a fate" (Womack 1969, ix). However, the moderate Zapatista challenge was bitterly resisted and the result was Zapatista radicalization leading to Zapatista revolution. Again, the objective outcome—the eventual destruction of the Morelos sugar estates— went beyond initial subjective goals (a common enough consequence in revolutions; Skocpol 1979, 17–18). This brings me to my third distinction.

Radicalism and Thresholds

If intentionality counts, it seems reasonable to ask how *radical* intentions are. Or, to put it differently, is the resistance in question trivial, limited, moderate, militant, radical, root-and-branch, or even revolutionary? Many recent resistance studies concern actions that are fairly low key, discreet, evasive, and quotidian (i.e., the famous "weapons of the weak"; J. C. Scott 1985). Quite rightly, I think, social scientists have shifted their attention from the great rebellions and revolutions—the relatively rare thunderstorms of resistance—in order to focus on smaller, more extensive and, perhaps, cumulative events: the "normal" rainfall patterns over years and decades. This shift raises some interesting questions and problems. First, as several scholars point out, there is a risk of diluting the concept of resistance (M. Brown 1996, 730; Gutmann 2002, 42, 114). All societies embody a measure of conflict. Should we dignify every example as a case of resistance, thus "lumping" phenomena which should be "split," while at the same time exaggerating social conflict at the expense of social cooperation and cohesion? (M. Brown 1996, 729, 734). Joe Foweraker asks, regarding the new social movements, what threshold must be crossed for a minor conflict to qualify as resistance (1995, 24–25).

I have already suggested that subaltern intention, elite perception, and objective consequences are all relevant but not necessarily commensurate. If, for example, a single sharecropper, fallen on hard times, breaks habit and conceals a fraction of his crop from the landlord, not out of any conscious intention of challenging the landlord's authority; and if, in addition, the landlord remains unaware and such concealment, being a rare occurrence that sharecroppers in general do not emulate, remains an isolated case and poses no objective threat to the profitability of the enterprise, then it seems rather a stretch to call this resistance and to include it in the same category as strikes, land reform petitions, *tomas de tierras*, and rebellions, all of which are acts of deliberate confrontation that are overt, collective, organized, and, in many cases, sustained (Tarrow 1994, 4–6). We could, by way of contrast, call the sharecropper's action "pilfering" (it is individual, self-interested, and clandestine, lacking normative significance).[9] Or, more positively, we could term it a "survival strategy" (Ortner 1995, 174–75). Of course, if the sharecropper makes a habit of it (and gets away with it); if the idea catches on and other sharecroppers follow suit (thus, individual actions acquire a collective character, involving horizontal solidarity); if the profitability of the hacienda suffers and the landlord tries to stop the concealment, then we enter a situation of clear-cut resistance and conflict, rather as the cotton plantations of Mexico's Laguna region did during the late Porfiriato and revolution (O'Hea 1966).

My cautious conclusion is that, while it is valid to stress intentionality, we should not make intentionality a *necessary* criterion of resistance, given that probing motives is often difficult, especially for historians. Elite perceptions also matter, and if resistance, just as beauty, is in the eye of the beholder, then elite beholders should also be taken into account. Finally, cumulative pilfering might, at some murky point in the process, eventually become a form of discreet collective action that combines solidarity, intent, organization, and, most importantly, practical consequences.

The preceding discussion concerns the *lower* threshold, at which, for example, pilfering becomes resistance. Should we also demarcate an upper threshold, where resistance—with its connotations of low-level, evasive, "moderate" action, characteristic of the weapons of the weak—gives way to more extreme, overt, violent, and radical protest, the kind of protest that, a generation ago, attracted major scholarly attention? (B. Moore 1966; Wolf 1969; Tilly, Tilly, and Tilly 1975). Again, the answer to this question is partly heuristic and semantic: We can adopt very wide definitions of resistance stretching from, say, petty pilfering to outright social revolution. Or we can try to achieve greater precision by slicing up the continuum, either by introducing other terms (protest, revolt, revolution: there is an ample, if somewhat dated, bibliography) or by qualifying the portmanteau term "resistance." In chapter eight of this book, Jean Meyer has usefully done this with his distinction between *Resistenz* and *Widerstand*, the latter denoting more open, radical, and violent confrontation. In the same spirit, Felipe Castro (chapter two), following Jan de Vos, offers a triple typology: open, concealed, and negotiated resistance. Such distinctions are useful: first, because they broaden our field of comparison and, second, because, in actual historical processes, defining the upper threshold at which resistance becomes revolt and the metaphorical weapons of the weak are traded in for real machetes, Winchesters, and AK-47s may not be such a clear-cut liminal point.

It is not clear-cut because the shift from moderate to radical resistance or protest, or from *Resistenz* to *Widerstand*, may conceal several different and overlapping transitions. It can denote

1. a shift in *means* (in what Tilly calls the actors' "repertoire of contention"; Tilly 1986, 390), from peaceful to violent, covert to overt, local to national, individual to collective, or sporadic to sustained (Tarrow 1994, 4–5, 31–2);
2. a shift in *ends*, from petty, self-interested "pilfering" (pilfering as an individual survival strategy) at one extreme all the way up to ambitious, even Utopian, projects of social transformation at the other; and
3. a shift in *social relations*, as low-level skirmishing gives way to broader and deeper social conflict, as—irrespective of the aforementioned means and ends criteria—the stakes of the conflict become greater, the social polarization sharper, the sheer exuberance of contention more palpable.[10]

These three shifts may coincide, as they have in some major revolutions and rebellions, when conflict intensifies, goals become more radical, and social polarization—some of a distinctly expressive kind—snowballs. This rather rare triple conjunction is neatly summed up in the notion of "the World Turned Upside Down" (C. Hill 1975).

But usually there is no such triple conjunction. Consider some of the possible permutations.[11] A protest may be violent, but relatively modest and moderate in terms of its goals (as were, for example, most village riots in colonial Mexico; Taylor 1979; Castro, chapter two). Thus, the authorities can make some pragmatic concessions, the social polarization—and consequent repression—may remain limited, and the system trundles on much as before. (Compare this classic Mesoamerican pattern with the extensive, radical, polarizing revolts of late-colonial Andean America, which, of course, elicited savage repression—Flores Galindo 1994; Walker 1999.) On the other hand, some nonviolent movements,examples of *Resistenz* rather than *Widerstand*, have entertained radical, system-changing goals: British Chartism in the early nineteenth century, for example (Tilly 1995); Mahatma Gandhi's Quit India movement; or, perhaps, the mass strikes that occurred in São Paulo's ABC region in the late 1970s and early 1980s (J. D. French 1992). Regarding Meyer's case study, I would argue that Catholic opposition to the Mexican revolutionary state was more durably successful in the 1930s, when *Resistenz* prevailed, than it had been in the 1920s, when, in the form of the Cristiada, *Widerstand* was the preferred strategy. For that, Schell's redoubtable Damas Católicas can claim some of the credit.

Perhaps a rough rule of thumb can be advanced: in many cases, where the authorities enjoy superior coercive power, as they usually do, a commitment to violent protest plays into the authorities' hands, since they can resort to force on grounds of tit-for-tat, claiming, after Weber, that they should enjoy a "monopoly of the legitimate use of force" and that dissidents who infringe that monopoly deserve harsh treatment.[12] Thus, as Sidney Tarrow observes, violence "gives authorities a mandate for repression" and may make repression politically acceptable, even in some subalterns' eyes (1994, 104). Perhaps for this reason, the old anarchist tactic of "propaganda by the deed" has not been noticeably successful (Ford 1982, 4–5; Hobsbawm 1982, 15). Nor, I would add, have political assassinations or recent terrorist plots been successful, in respect to the supposed goals of the plotters. More importantly, it is for this reason that "death by government" ("democide") has been much more extreme and extensive in Latin America than "death by revolution" or "death by subversion" (Rummel 1994).[13]

Of course, context is crucial. In the face of Nazi anti-Semitism, Germany's Jewish community adopted a pacific, legalist stance that tragically failed. In occupied Denmark, however, passive resistance helped save almost the entire (admittedly small) Jewish population (Kurlansky 2007, 134). Most regimes, and not just liberal-democratic regimes, entertain some notion of proportionate response (analogous, we might say, to the notion of "just war," which also transcends particular regime types;

Walzer 1992). Proportionate response means—if only for reasons of regime self-interest—trying to counter nonviolent protest with nonviolent means, legal, political, "ideological," and even religious means. Thus, the Tehuantepec rebellion of 1660 was allegedly calmed by the bishop, who paraded through the town "in full pontifical robes" as the rebels prostrated themselves before him (Hamnett 1971, 13; compare Rudé 1980, 48–49, for a late medieval German precedent). Proportionate response also means not gratuitously massacring civilians, especially women and children. Catholic activists in revolutionary Mexico, being well aware of this, sometimes placed women on the front line (literally) of civic protests (Schell 2003, 182–83). The significance of the Tlatelolco massacre of October 1968 was not just that Mexican citizens were killed by the forces of the state, but that those citizens were peaceful demonstrators, mostly young, urban, middle-class students, and that they were killed in the middle of Mexico City. The Mexican state had been killing peasant activists out in the sticks for decades (Gutiérrez 1998; Castellanos 2007), but those victims were more easily depicted as violent subversives than the students of 1968. Peasant activists were more expendable; they got what they deserved. Once resistance turns violent, or is seen to turn violent, the gloves come off and the state can resort to its usually superior coercive power with less fear of criticism or reprisal. Hence the Díaz regime had little difficulty in quashing the small, radical, clandestine, and insurrectionary Partido Liberal Mexicano in 1906 and 1908; but was at a loss for how to deal with the mass-based, peaceful protest of Madero's Anti-Reelectionists of 1909–10 (Knight 1986, vol. one, chapter two). I am not arguing that peaceful resistance is in all cases a preferable strategy; the character of the regime—Habsburg, Bourbon, British colonial, Nazi, PRIísta—clearly makes a big difference. But I would suggest that many regimes, when faced with challenges from below, would almost prefer a gloves-off, violent challenge to one that is peaceful, civilian, and "moderate." And it is a common strategy of regimes to try to provoke their opponents into counterproductive violence.

Who Resists?

So far, I have discussed definitions of resistance, the question of intentionality, and degrees of radicalism (upper and lower thresholds). An additional concern must be the sociopolitical makeup of resistance and, logically, of the targets of resistance, too. There is clearly an assumption throughout most of this book that we are talking about popular or subaltern resistance, what might reasonably be called the resistance of "common folk" (Eckstein 1989, 1). Generically and semantically, of course, "resistance" need not be so limited. Powerful vested interests resisted Cárdenas's reforms in Mexico, as they did Goulart's populist policies in Brazil on the 1960s. Cárdenas bent with the wind; or, as some historians now say, he made some tactical retreats when confronted by the "weapons of the strong." That is, he did not face armed right-wing insurrections (which, like Cedillo's, were few and futile), but more subtle stratagems of capital flight, propaganda, political lobbying, and activism. It was this conjuncture of anti-Cárdenas resistance that spawned the Partido Acción Nacional (PAN; Knight 1994; Fallaw 2001). Examples of elite, well-to-do, or "bourgeois" resistance are common: the Brazilian plantocracy's resistance to abolitionism; the elite and middle-class xenophobia of Buenos Aires in 1919; the antipopulist military coups of the 1960s and 1970s in South America; and the *cacerolazos* of Allende's Chile. Thus, just as we could debate whether the concept of resistance should be confined to intentional action, we could also ask whether we are concerned only with resistance that is somehow popular, subaltern, or bottom-up. And, if so, why? Should not "uncivil movements" of "superordinate" resistance figure as well? (Payne, 2000).

An open-minded and eclectic response might be to admit any form of resistance, whatever the social or political makeup of the resisters and their targets. If the Ku Klux Klan can be counted as a "social movement," could it not be considered a form of racist resistance, too? (Foweraker 1995, 15). However, the great majority of resistance studies focus on popular or subaltern resistance, or both. In this book, only Patience Schell's chapter could be said to address resistance that emanates from relatively better-off social groups. Of course, the justification for including the Damas is that they confronted an oppressive state that sought to curtail or eliminate certain religious freedoms they held dear. This case reminds us that resistance can be deployed against both states and socioeconomic elites. And, as the Brazilian cases demonstrate, resistance can be deployed against official or established churches too, and certainly against ethnic or racial elites. Thus, even if the Damas were far from being *socioeconomic* subalterns, they saw themselves as—and, arguably, in some objective sense, they were—*politically* subject to an oppressive anticlerical state. In other words, hierarchies of subordination and superordination can be rigged according to different principles: socioeconomic, political, religious, ethnic, racial, gendered, and generational. Often, such hierarchies cohere, displaying a kind of functional interdependence, as in the case of the Spanish empire, at least until the Bourbon reforms began to prize the mutually supporting hierarchies apart (Taylor 1996). Conversely, "great" revolutions may involve the simultaneous subversion of several intertwined hierarchies—political, socioeconomic, religious, and generational. More commonly, run-of-the-mill resistance focuses on particular hierarchies—slave owners, factory bosses, state officials, the Catholic clergy—and does not involve frontal assaults on the entire edifice of power and privilege. Indeed, resistance in one sector of contestation (for example, in the church) may tend to promote quiescence in another (hence, for example, the apparent political conservatism of Latin American Protestantism; Eckstein 1989, 31–32). On the other hand, resistance may spill over, especially where hierarchies are closely intertwined and interdependent: "No bishop, no king, no nobility," as King James I pithily put it (C. Hill 1975, 32). We could refer to this as the contagion effect, which can operate both in reality and in perception—especially in fearful, elite perception.

Mexico in the 1920s was an odd case, precisely because of the 1910 revolution, which had brought substantially greater political than socioeconomic change (in the 1930s, the socioeconomic deficit would be somewhat made up). A regime of revolutionary newcomers now held power, distributing land, supporting labor unions, and combating the clergy. The "relative autonomy of the (Mexican revolutionary) state" made it entirely possible for groups which remained *socioeconomically* privileged—but were now *politically* derogated—to turn against the state, deploying—as Fallaw describes for Yucatán—the "weapons of the strong" (Fallaw 2001). Meyer also gives examples of successful Catholic colonization or cooptation of the state; or, to put it the other way round, the state's calculating collusion with vested interests, including the Catholic hierarchy.

If there are good reasons for keeping the Damas Católicas on board (at least with the qualification just mentioned), there are also good reasons for focusing chiefly on subordinate resistance (thus, on groups, well represented in this book, who are clearly socioeconomically, and sometimes also legally and ethnically, subordinate, like Brazilian slaves or Indians). In other words, we are not concerned with superordinate or elite resistance—with military coups and middle-class protests, carapintadas and *cacerolazos* (Payne 2000). There are two reasons for this. One is normative: if we aspire to a more just and less unequal society, we may wish to focus on the victims of injustice and inequality, the better to understand their predicament and further their cause. As I note in conclusion, this seems to be a common assumption, but it is open to serious question.

The second reason for focusing on subaltern resistance is empirical, rather than normative, and, in my view, much more compelling. Elites are by definition powerful: they enjoy a measure of economic, social, political, and cultural power. Otherwise they wouldn't be elites. Subalterns don't enjoy such power; that's why they are subalterns. True, there may be intermediate groups whose location, interests, and identities are open to dispute. Yet the fact that class (or ethnic) divisions have not achieved binary simplicity does not prevent us from distinguishing elites and subalterns, while recognizing, where necessary, the role of those caught in the middle. Indeed, most, if not all, social or cultural categories tend to be frayed at the edges. Just as it may be difficult to say where the elite (or the bourgeoisie) stops and where the subalterns (or the workers, peasants, and common folk) start, so too it is hard to draw a definite line between, say, literates and illiterates, Indians and mestizos, or between citizens, subjects, and parochials (Almond and Verba 1989). So, fuzzy borders are not an unusual or insuperable problem.

The previous point addresses the problem of complexity: we can accept that things are complex—fuzzy at the edges—without concluding that complexity and fuzziness make analysis impossible, or that, having identified complexity and fuzziness, we have done our jobs and can all go home in a glow of scholarly satisfaction. Similarly, we must recognize that history marches on and that we are dealing with processes and not timeless truths. Hierarchies change and sometimes hierarchies tumble, as in Mexico after 1910. Even then, the usual result is a rejigging—not a complete abolition—of hierarchies. After 1910, the church and landed class lost power, while the state, the revolutionary military, and their popular allies gained power. Hence the Damas can be seen, at least in some measure, as political subalterns. Compared with Mexico, Russia and Cuba experienced more thoroughgoing revolutions, but hierarchies (of a very different kind) remained.

In the vast majority of societies, at least since the Neolithic revolution and the rise of the state, hierarchies have been entrenched (but not unchanging). This palpable fact governs any study of resistance. We could call elite control and repression of subordinates resistance. But there are several objections to this eclectic approach: again, it excessively expands and thus dilutes the concept of resistance; and, more importantly, it suggests that all resistance, from above or below, on the part of elites or subalterns is much of a muchness, that the same ideas, goals and methods can be discerned. But this is not the case. Subaltern or popular resistance differs from elite control and repression, in ways that I will shortly examine.

We should clear up another related point (which may also seem obvious). Subalterns are not homogeneous and they are often found in conflict with one another. The squabbling pueblos of Oaxaca are notorious (Kearney 1972; Dennis 1976). The Mexican Left, which supposedly stands for the subaltern, is nearly as bad. The Zapatistas, whom Womack depicted as united and mutually loyal, in fact fell prey to feuds and factions (Brunk 1995). Yet more remarkably, subalterns can usually be found on both sides of the barricades when major revolts and revolutions are on the agenda. When, in 1712, the Tzeltal Indians of Chiapas mounted a serious armed challenge to Spanish colonial rule (which, by most objective standards, was discriminatory and oppressive), many Indians—as Juan Pedro Viqueira shows in chapter three—opposed the rebellion. In Brazil, a century later, some slaves, usually Brazilian born, sided with their masters against the protests and insurrections of fellow slaves, usually African born (Reis 1993, 50, 142–43). Thus, definable subalterns are to be found fighting—or resisting?—fellow subalterns. We have to recognize "everyday forms of peasant collaboration" as well as peasant resistance (Ortner 1995, 175, citing Christine Pelzer White). While we should note and seek to explain this common phenomenon (was it the product of elite policies of divide-and-rule, of rational subaltern self-interest, or of lamentable "false consciousness"?), I doubt we should refer to it as resistance, thus lumping it in with actions that display a clear subaltern "them-and-us" logic. Subalterns who—for whatever motive—ally with elites in a situation of social polarization (as they did in the Tzeltal rebellion) are not practicing resistance. They may be self-regarding rational actors or victims of "false consciousness," or both, but they are clearly shoring up, rather than resisting, the prevailing social, economic, political, and religious order.

How Do They Resist?

"Resistance," therefore, should be reserved for conflicts in which a demonstrable inequality pertains, and in which that inequality is in some senses at stake. These are what James Scott calls "power-laden situations" (J. C. Scott 1990, x). Foucault might respond that all situations are "power-laden," and "where there is power, there is also resistance," and Lila Abu-Lughod would cap that with "where there is resistance there is also power" (1990, 42). So, perhaps resistance, like power, is everywhere, vested in every human action and relationship. Fine, but in that case our *explanandum*—the thing we are trying to explain—becomes so pervasive and ethereal that it defies explanation; we have concept-dilution of homeopathic proportions, hence my attempt to draw some loose boundaries around the concept itself.

Resistance, then, derives its character in part from the social—and political, ethnic, and cultural—makeup of the conflict (broadly speaking, subalterns against elites). Resistance is also characterized by the modality of the conflict. Since elites enjoy power, they can fight—they can resist resistance—by typically elite methods, whereas subalterns, qua subalterns, have to use different methods. Resistance is no less characterized by its goals, the basic issues at stake, and potential outcomes. Successful subaltern resistance entails a measure of popular empowerment, material redistribution, or both. These dimensions of conflict hang together, giving the notion of resistance a measure of analytical coherence. For example, subalterns are by definition disadvantaged, economically, politically, or ethnically. They have fewer resources (in per capita terms) and, if they step out of line, they risk incurring the rigor of the law (often an arbitrary or personal kind of "law" that is stacked against them). Hence, as Scott rightly stressed, subaltern resistance often has to be covert and pragmatic. Subalterns do, however, possess some limited advantages that elites do not. They are, almost by definition, more numerous. They know the lie of the land (literally, in many cases). They possess "local knowledge," and they have a strong incentive to fathom the minds of their masters.[14] The masters, on the other hand, can afford to be more cavalier, hence the common phenomenon of landlords, bosses, *políticos*, and colonial officials who grossly misjudge the temperament and intentions of their subordinates—attributing to them, at times, a spurious docile passivity and, at other times, a wild-eyed radicalism that, as I have said, may be greatly exaggerated.

On the basis of these limited and largely cognitive assets, subalterns rely on rumor, gossip, evasion, and duplicity to extract small advantages from the system. Cumulatively, this process might have systemic effects: for example, undermining the slave "futures" market in Brazil (see Slenes, chapter five) or the productivity and profits of commercial enterprises. The familiar litany of complaints about "lazy natives" or, as Manuel Flon saw them, subversive Indian layabouts, is an effect of this process (see Castro, chapter two). However, in most cases, enterprises and systems can live with this low-level resistance. It may even function as a useful safety valve, keeping the engine of exploitation going. For resistance to become more pervasive, collective, overt, and radical (in terms of methods or goals), and thus socially threatening, subalterns have to take a great many more risks (not least the risk of resorting to violence and thus inviting repression); and they have to achieve a measure of solidarity, to make their numbers count and to overcome the problem of "free-riders," those who, in a situation of conflict, wait and see, hopeful of deriving benefits without incurring risks (Olson 1965).

A shift up the scale of resistance therefore has both organizational and ideological implications, as the "repertoires" of resistance change (Eckstein 1989, 10; Tarrow 1994, 33–45, 105–7). Overt resistance requires overt organization: nocturnal machine-breakers turn to trade unionism; disgruntled campesinos litigate and petition for land; small guerrilla bands (some of them "social bandits") cohere into larger forces that, in rare instances, achieve the critical mass of Pancho Villa's División del Norte. In the process, "resisters" have to acquire some of the "weapons of the strong," literally and metaphorically. Depending on circumstances, they need weaponry, finance, and means of communication, even an incipient bureaucracy. The trend may be broadly civilian (the formation of trade unions) or military (the División del Norte, again). They may also feel obliged to seek out allies, as Zapata did, though not necessarily of pure subaltern status (Womack 1969, chapter ten). They may feel impelled to make necessary compromises and deals and, in order to overcome the free-rider problem, to resort to heavy-handed methods, ranging from forced military recruitment to the kind of "pressing" that Gilbert Joseph and Allen Wells describe in their account of Yucatec Maya mobilization (1996, 232, 244). A similar process has been discerned in the more recent evolution of the new social movements of the 1980s and 1990s, which, as they grew, also had to come to terms with a state apparatus they had previously tended to spurn (Foweraker 1995, 62–63, 70–71). We could see this as a kind of necessary loss of innocence, as an infant resistance (or new social) movement grows, consolidates, and acquires the necessary weapons of the strong that will enable it to operate overtly and collectively in the world of mass macropolitics. While romantics may lament the loss of innocence, there is a certain inevitability about this process. Unless the state "withers away"—a Utopian promise which, as far as I can see, has rarely if ever been fulfilled—resistance and social movements have to achieve some sort of modus vivendi with the state, assuming they cannot take it over entirely.[15] That was the conclusion the Catholic hierarchy correctly reached in Mexico in the late 1920s.

Ideology

The process I have just described may also have an ideological dimension. I mentioned how, as the Mexican Revolution progressed and social polarization increased, the Zapatistas acquired more radical agrarian goals, which they sought to apply nationwide, not just in Morelos. Of course, the trend may go in a different direction, as power and success restrain an early popular radicalism, perhaps to the point where that old villain, "Thermidorian reaction," heaves into sight. Apart from the French Revolution, examples might include the Bolivian Movimiento Nacionalista Revolucionario, especially after 1956, and any number of lesser movements—syndical insurgencies, for example, that began as subversive, democratic protests, but veered toward clientelism and careerism (e.g., the Poza Rica section of the Mexican oil-workers union; Olvera 1992). Some theorists of "great" revolutions believe that each historical case experiences a common trajectory, characterized by discernible stages: a moderate stage, a radical stage, and finally a "reaction" stage (Brinton 1938). This seems to be both a priori fanciful and a posteriori wrong. A more plausible rule of thumb, perhaps a sort of Hempelian "covering law," would be Robert Michels's "iron law of oligarchy," which posits a tendency toward the concentration of power in the hands of a directing minority, such as Mexico's *comisariados ejidales*, discussed by Helga Baitenmann in chapter fourteen.

While, in organizational terms, this may make sense, it does not follow that concentration of power always means a loss of ideological radicalism. In ideological terms, the "stage" theory of revolutions is not very convincing. The Cuban Revolution, though controlled by a narrow and enduring *camarilla*, has not hit the Thermidorian buffers. Peru's Sendero Luminoso was intensely centralized and radical at the same time. The civic movement that sprang up in the Mexican state of Guerrero in the early 1960s evolved from a broad, popular, democratic base to become more narrow, radical, militant, and violent (Castellanos 2007, 101 and following).[16] In other words, ideological trends obey no very clear pattern, whether at the level of major revolutions or lesser social resistance movements. It all depends on the circumstances.

That does not mean, of course, that ideology is unimportant. The days when serious historians talked of "prepolitical" peasants, locked in their tiny parochial microcosms, unable to rise above mundane—usually material—concerns or to formulate broad encompassing visions, are long gone (Hobsbawm 1959). Recent research on Mexico has, indeed, stressed the *prise de conscience* that affected large swathes of rural and provincial Mexico as early as the late Bourbon and independence periods (Guardino 1996; 2005). Quite quickly, it seems, "parochial" Mexicans—Indians, mestizos, and mulattos—began to talk of citizenship and citizens' rights and, even more importantly, began to participate in elections and incipient political associations, like Oaxaca's "oil" and "vinegar" factions (Guardino 2005). This phase of politicization was loosely liberal-democratic; but, as several chapters in this book demonstrate, religion—be it Catholic, Candomblé, Kongo, or millenarian—could also afford a powerful mobilizing and sustaining ideology.

While the nature of the ideology espoused by resistance movements is obviously important—Catholics and Communists tend to think and operate differently—I would suggest that the presence of *an* effective ideology may be just as important as the nature of the ideology per se. After all, ideologies are shifting and fungible. Liberalism or nationalism, for example, can be vehicles both for popular dissent and progressive causes (anticolonialism, reform of the suffrage) and for elite, antipopular, even reactionary projects (fascism, neoliberalism). Religion is similarly fungible: as Edward Thompson's brilliant dissection of Methodism shows, the same sect could legitimize factory owners of the Gradgrind variety in Manchester and—in the shape of "primitive Methodism"—early working-class solidarity and organization (E. P. Thompson 1968, chapter eleven). Latin American Catholicism can similarly be found on both sides of the political barricades: it is "not just an opiate," but—from *Rerum Novarum* (1891) to *Vatican II* (1963)—has served as a spur to progressive action (Eckstein 1989, 39; Levine and Mainwaring 1989). Meanwhile, crosscutting these explicit ideological affiliations are ex post categories devised by scholars: the Tillys' dichotomy of "reactive" versus "proactive" protest (Tilly, Tilly, and Tilly 1975, 50–55) and George Rudé's comparable division of popular ideologies into "inherent" and "derived" (1980, 30–33).

Useful though they may be, these typologies tend to be overly idealis-
tic, stressing the power of ideas (political or religious, "reactive" or "proactive") at the expense of historical context and collective interests. Zapatismo was a successful revolutionary movement, even though its ideology
was retrospective, restorationist, and "reactive" (Knight 1986, 1:309–15).
Thus, ideologies of resistance may be important less for their formal ideational content than for their practical role in facilitating protest. Such ideologies serve two related functions: they make sense of the world, linking
specific, local struggles to grander causes; and they help foster solidarity,
by giving participants common ideas, rituals, and a sense of dignity. As
several analyses rightly stress, "resistance" may have a strongly material
emphasis, but notions of dignity and autonomy also seem to figure promi-
nently: people object to being unjustly treated not just because it deprives
them of "life, liberty, and the pursuit of happiness," but also because it
is basically unjust (J. C. Scott 1990, 22–23). Hence, when the tables are
turned, we get the counterhumiliation of elites, such as the *ladino* women
of Chiapas in 1712, an example, perhaps, of "expressive" resistance against
"instrumental" resistance (see Viqueira, chapter three). It is for this reason, too, that rational-actor models of protest are inherently limited (see
Zárate, chapter ten; Eckstein 1989, 4–5): they miss the sense of injustice
and moral outrage that often characterizes protest (B. Moore 1978, 29).[17]
Thus, whether the grand ideology happens to be Candomblé, Christianity,
or communism, it helps locate a specific struggle and its participants
within a grander story, a story replete with heroes, martyrs, and didactic
narratives. It may also, in organizational terms, help local participants link
up with powerful supralocal allies. In some (religious) cases, allegiance
may also promise supernatural solace and assistance. Within the group,
too, the associated rituals afford a basis for initiation and solidarity, a particularly crucial factor in societies where subaltern organization is risky
and hard to sustain (see Slenes, chapter five, and Parés, chapter seven).

"False consciousness?"

Does it matter if the ideology is a pack of lies? Let me finally turn to the
question of "false consciousness." I would distinguish between a "thick"
and a "thin" version of this contentious thesis. The thin version recognizes
that, for example, Catholicism and Communism are not easily compatible;
they cannot both be right. Resistance movements have been premised on

both (perhaps most obviously in the case of *the* Resistance in France after 1940). To the extent that either ideology can confer the kind of benefits I have just mentioned, they can serve their turn: in the French case, they both bolstered resistance to the German occupation. Similarly, a range of "churches," broadly defined, have bolstered slave and black resistance in both Brazil and the Caribbean: Catholic, Candomblé, Santería, Anglican, Baptist. The choice of one or an other church derives from local or national circumstances; to put it differently (and pretentiously), it is a question of "historicity." The important thing is not *which* ideology or "metanarrative" is chosen, but that there should be one and that it should be effective; its truth-value is secondary to its mobilizing and sustaining function. Confronted with movements of this kind—movements of subaltern resistance premised on ideas that we might find bizarre and even delusionary—we might nevertheless soft-pedal our intellectual misgivings on the grounds of practical efficacy. One does not have to be an Islamic "fundamentalist" to appreciate why Hamas has a strong following in Gaza.

The thin version of false consciousness therefore gives priority to efficacy over truth-value. Of course, efficacy begs several questions, not least the criteria against which efficacy should be judged. Scott's analysis suggests that there are discernible subaltern "interests": in order to evaluate the notion of "hegemony," he argues, we must "assess the ways in which subordinate groups may be socialized into accepting a view of their interests as propagated from above" (J. C. Scott 1990, 19–20). Often, we can clearly identify when the interests of an individual or group are either advanced or prejudiced. Being sold into slavery, having your village lands expropriated, losing your job in a recession, and being imprisoned without due process are all prejudicial to your interests. If we include considerations of personal dignity and autonomy among interests, the list grows even longer. In many cases, derogations of material or political interests also involve slights against individual dignity (for example, for workers in Porfirian Mexico; R. Anderson 1976). We may not be able to calibrate the relative weight of, say, material, political, and psychological factors (is the worst thing about unemployment the loss of income or the loss of dignity?), but when they tend in the same direction, there is no crucial dilemma. We can therefore reasonably speak of subaltern *interests*, and thus of actions or decisions that promote or prejudice those interests, and of the implications of a given ideology on those actions or decisions. The interests of black Africans were prejudiced by slavery; the interests of

Brazilian Indians are prejudiced by indiscriminate logging. Ideologies of resistance—to slavery or logging—may not all be "true" (they could, for example, take contrasting liberal, Catholic, Communist, or millenarian forms); but they could still be effective, by exerting a strong appeal, fostering solidarity, and addressing the needs (interests) of the oppressed.

The thick version of false consciousness comes into play when ideology militates against interests, when, in other words, subalterns are seen to act counter to their interests, apparently as a result of their misconstruing those interests, of their being under the influence of a persuasive but "deceptive" ideology. A good example would be lower-class Republican voters who, swayed by nationalism and religion, supported George W. Bush in 2000 and 2004. These voters exercised a free vote, yet their material interests were not served by Republican policies and their reasons for supporting Bush included American nationalism and Evangelical Christianity. We could add, by way of further explanation, that the ideological hegemony of religion and nationalism is actively maintained by a barrage of media—film, TV, talk radio, country music, and the Evangelical pulpit. Thus, to put it rather simply, we have a "general public always easy prey to manipulation by television" and "the crude politics of getting the people to vote against their own interests by frightening them with the Red Menace," or whatever "horrendous foreign enemy" can be conjured up (Vidal 2004, 6, 84, 109).

Of course, Scott (1990) argues that false consciousness and ideological hegemony are often illusory: subalterns maintain a facade of compliance, or even eager endorsement, behind which they grouse, grumble, and resist. In many cases, he is probably correct. He is particularly correct when dealing with highly authoritarian and hierarchical societies, in which there is no such thing as a "free vote," and in which, therefore, apparent compliance may be no more than apparent and the state and socioeconomic elites, lacking the will or the power to manufacture ideological hegemony, rely, instead, on extreme and exemplary coercion.[18] Several of the chapters in this book deal with societies of this kind (e.g., slavocratic Brazil). I would guess that Scott's analysis fits those societies pretty well. In other contexts, however, the "poor Bushite Republican" example raises more tricky problems, since Scott cannot entirely dismiss Gramscian arguments of hegemony (or, in more extreme form, imputations of false consciousness). He can, I think correctly, distinguish between thick and thin hegemony: the first entailing eager endorsement, the second grudging compliance—

more or less what Gutmann calls "compliant defiance" (Gutmann 2002; J. C. Scott 1990, chapter four). Regarding contemporary Mexico, quite a lot of what passes for political quiescence, "consensus," or "hegemony" is, I think, grudging and cynical, based on a realistic expectation that the authorities are self-interested and that things are unlikely to change dramatically for the better. (We should note that this expectation extends to much of the political Left as well). Sidney Almond and Gabriel Verba (1989) drew similar conclusions some forty years ago; since then—since 1982, in particular, I would guess—grudging compliance has been common, irrespective of whether the PRI or the PAN has occupied Los Pinos. The hegemony of the Mexican state has tended to be of the thin variety (Knight 2007a).

The same could not be said of poor Bushite Republicanism, which, at least in its heyday, seemed to be vigorous, vocal, and antithetical to the interests of many poor Republicans. This anomaly, if indeed it is an anomaly, could have several explanations: poor Bushite Republicans, being stupid and uneducated, failed to perceive their own interests; were briefly conned, and have since woken up to that fact; or (emically) rated their own interests differently and, according to their own "bounded rationality," saw Bushite Republicanism as the best available vehicle for their aspirations.

Analogous problems are apparent in our own—Mexican and Brazilian—cases. When the rebels of Tehuantepec bowed to the bishop in 1660, they were perhaps engaged in a typically Scottian act of public deception; but perhaps they genuinely revered the bishop and respected his authority. Some fifty years later, during the Tzeltal rebellion, plenty of Indians supported the Crown against the rebels. Two centuries later, tens of thousands of Mexican Catholics resisted the revolutionary state; many were of lower social class than the Damas Católicas and, in resisting the state, they were, in some measure, resisting land reform and supporting the landed class. While their motives were mixed (again, grudging compliance with local landlord power was a factor), most recent studies stress the autonomous role of religion (Meyer 1976; Butler 2004). Thus, like poor Bushite Republicans, poor Cristeros made their political choices partly on the basis of religious beliefs, beliefs influenced, in the Cristero case, by an unusually powerful regional Catholic Church. Republican voters were also influenced by nationalism; and we do not have to accept the facile description of nationalism as a "secular religion" to recognize that nationalism,

like religion, offers a set of normative criteria that transcend those associated with collective or individual interests. Interests may seem to mandate one course of action (demanding land, voting Democrat), but religion
or nationalism can trump interests by invoking the superior claims of God
or the patria. These are noncommensurate criteria (unless we mistakenly
believe that religion and nationalism can always be reduced to some prior
interest for which religion and nationalism are just contrived facades).[19]
And where such noncommensurate criteria are involved, it is very difficult
to make the "etic" argument that, say, the rank-and-file Cristeros, being
victims of false consciousness, betrayed their own class interests by resisting the revolutionary state and supporting a phalanx of landlords and
priests. They could reply that they were fighting for their immortal souls:
What greater interest could there be than that? The real false consciousness, they might add, was that of the *agraristas* who, for a pittance of poor
land, became the hired Cossacks of the atheistic state.

So, too, with nationalism. In Britain, before conscription was introduced in 1916, men volunteered and fought in part because of powerful patriotic beliefs that permeated society. If we believe that those beliefs, and the action they mandated, were not conducive to the interests
of the volunteers (who, of course, died in droves), then we are in false-
consciousness country. And we only get out of it by postulating noncommensurate norms: voluntarily dying for your country (like being martyred
for your religion) can be justified if patriotic or religious values are allowed
to trump interests. I should add that while this argument applies particularly forcefully to subaltern classes, it *can* apply to elites as well (many
British elite families suffered heavily from First World War mortality). And
the argument does not necessarily apply to *all* wars, since some—for example, a good many wars of national liberation and the Second World
War, at least from the British or U.S. viewpoint—could be said to involve a
genuine collective interest, including the defeat of an oppressive colonialism. The argument similarly applies to most religions, but not all: apart
from its transcendental claims, Brazilian millenarianism also brought
very practical worldly benefits, by way of community order and stability in
times of upheaval (Della Cava 1968).

Finally, if false consciousness or something like it exists, should scholars, when they encounter it, stoically accept it or, rather, set out to subvert
it, thus helping the subalterns see the truth of their plight? Should scholars

therefore study resistance theories so that those theories can "help us to address novel ways of resolving the plagues of poverty, racism, and militarization"? (Gutmann, chapter fifteen). For anthropologists the problem is, I believe, quite familiar, the classic formulation being: should anthropologists try to restrain "traditional" local practices that are palpably abusive — infanticide, honor killings, drunken violence — at the risk of being seen as "pushy and judgmental aliens" (Gutmann 2002, 14). Historians, working at greater chronological distance, and usually dealing with dead people on the basis of written records rather than fieldwork, face no such practical dilemma. The historical die was cast long ago and no belated ex post intervention can make things better. However, historical research might have some beneficial future impact (for another time and place), and, certainly, several influential Latin American historians seem to see themselves as political activists, in the sense of writing history with one eye (if not two) on the practical political impact of their work (Joseph 2001; Stern 2001). And even when the motive is not so explicit, a creeping tendency to romanticize and legitimize subaltern resistance is sometimes apparent. Perhaps most commonly this takes the form of drawing a veil over subaltern sins, while stressing the nobility of the subaltern cause (see, for example, Ortner's critique of Clendennin's portrayal of Mexico's Maya; Ortner 1995, 177–78). Whitewashing the subaltern, Brown suggests, is a logical consequence of the decline of the old Left and the rise of postmodernism (mentioned above). As the old normative struts are kicked away, social scientists of progressive bent have "few options other than to make their case through rhetoric that projects moral fervor" (M. Brown 1996, 729).

Speaking as a historian, for whom these dilemmas are less acute, I think such instrumental or romantic engagements are best avoided (Knight 2007b, 351–60). Of course, we all have our political preferences, and they may seep into our work, but so do typos and split infinitives. That is no reason to encourage them. Deliberately writing history to suit present and future political causes (in this case, by whitewashing subalterns) seems to me ill-conceived for at least four principal reasons:

1. It is likely to be counter-productive (that is, it preaches to the converted and offends the rest);
2. It is paternalistic (in effect, it censors the people being studied);
3. It rather arrogantly assumes that history matters in the "real world"; and

4. Most importantly, it mixes up "is" and "ought," empirical data and value judgments, which should be kept apart. We may want our subalterns to be enlightened and egalitarian; and we may want the world to be enlightened and egalitarian, too; but these are normative aspirations (not necessarily shared by all, hence point one above) and they cannot affect what, in J. H. Hexter's phrase, actually "happened to happen" in history.

I readily concede that the anthropologist's dilemma is different and more acute (since objection three above counts for less, they may actually be able to achieve practical positive results; see, for example, de la Peña, chapter eleven). If research serves to compromise subaltern resistance, or to give aid and comfort to elites (as Stoll's critique of Rigoberta Menchú presumably did), should that research not be done? (Arias 2001). Or, when done, not published?[20] And does it matter if, in pursuit of subaltern resistance, Menchú got a few—quite important—facts wrong? Perhaps the end justifies the means.

My personal feeling is that, at a time when respect for the unvarnished truth seems to be wilting, there should be a powerful bias in favor of following the old *Easy Rider* slogan to "tell it like it is," even if, at times, the telling of it may prove unpalatable—when, for example, we find credulous or cruel subalterns behaving opportunistically and self-seekingly.[21] After all, they probably learned all that sort of thing from their supposed betters.

Notes

1 By using "small," I do not refer to the scope or significance of the concept, but rather its relative novelty, and hence its lack of scholarly citation, discussion, and salience.

2 It may be that, within some "epistemic communities"—for example, subgroups of academics who speak the same, sometimes arcane language—these concepts *are* seen as "sufficiently theorized." I am speaking on behalf of that convenient imaginary creature, the "intelligent lay reader."

3 The process is analogous to that described by E. H. Carr (1964, 12–13) whereby, with time, research, and debate, a "mere fact" becomes a "historical fact."

4 I am using "elites" simply as shorthand for "those who are not subalterns and who have power over subalterns" (an ugly alternative would be "superordinates"). I do not think an excursion into "elite theory" (Pareto, Mosca, etc.) is necessary.

5 After 1789, even moderate movements of social and political reform were, in Britain, regarded as dangerously radical: "The result," Malcolm Thomis and

Peter Holt argue, "was often the creation of revolutionaries where none had previously been" (Tarrow 1994, 76).

6 "Indexicality," as I understand it, refers to the basic problem of interpretation that arises as concepts are traded across cultural boundaries (which may or may not be linguistic); thus, apart from "translation" in the literal sense, it is questionable how far terms like "resistance" can be taken to mean the same thing in contrasting contexts (Welch 1993, 6–7).

7 The lack of fit between goals and outcomes is particularly apparent in the history of revolutions that, as Theda Skocpol (1979, 14–18) argues, are less purposive and voluntaristic than is often supposed: "Revolutions are not made; they come."

8 There are no case studies of trade union resistance in this book, even though unionization must surely qualify as a principal form of resistance in urban industrial societies (including contemporary Mexico and Brazil). Some scholars, it is true, regard unionization a little askance: being "centralized, hierarchical and often clientelistic" organizations, unions have sometimes been differentiated from "social movements," which are supposedly "decentralised, non-hierarchical . . . open, spontaneous, fluid and participatory" (Foweraker 1995, 43). For similar reasons, unions have also been termed "interest groups" rather than social movements (Tarrow 1994, 15). I am not persuaded that these distinctions, to the extent that they are empirically valid, should debar trade unions from consideration in this context; resistance can be—and sometimes has to be—hierarchical, and maybe centralized and even clientelistic.

9 Eckstein (1989, xi) includes "pilfering" along with "footdragging . . . and passive non-compliance" (see also Scott 1990, 118).

10 While a good deal of resistance—especially low-level, quotidian, discreet resistance—can be analyzed in terms of instrumental calculation by "rational actors," there is much more to it than that. Some protest involves "expressive" or "affective" actions: cutting loose, having a good time, flaunting a new-found freedom, humiliating old oppressors. This aspect of resistance is captured in the phrase current during the Mexican Revolution (and other rebellious or riotous events in Mexico): "Ir a la bola" (to join the party). Clearly, this differs from classic Scottian resistance.

11 Hollander and Einwohner (2004, 544) offer a more elaborate typology of resistance involving seven categories multiplied by three perspectives to produce twenty-one variants.

12 Of course, the authorities strive to "delegitimize" protest in other ways too: for example, by regularly portraying political rebels as criminal "bandits" (Womack 1969, 72, 106–7, 121, 138, 166).

13 An extreme but exemplary case would be the massacre in El Salvador in 1932, when rebels may have been responsible for up to thirty-five deaths and the government killed 10,000 in response (T. Anderson 1971, 134–37).

14 This seems to me a crucial point that would repay further investigation. James Scott (1990) stresses subaltern canniness and percipience; Gutmann (2002, 118–19, 123, 135) expresses doubts and points to the limitations of subaltern knowledge and horizons. I think both are right; that is, in some situations, subalterns possess a thorough and shrewd grasp of circumstances (as Scott argues); in others, they are constrained by a lack of information (and education) or by flagrant misconceptions about the world (for example, notions of "naive monarchism," to the extent that they are genuinely held and are not mere discursive facades). I should add that elites are similarly fallible. I return to this point, very briefly and superficially, when, in conclusion, I touch on "false consciousness." The interesting task, in my view, would be to distinguish between circumstances in which subaltern canniness is apparent and those in which it is not. I suspect that the contrasting patterns obey a kind of situational logic and are not merely random.

15 I am referring, of course, to the benign and progressive "withering away" of the exploitative state proposed by Marx, not the kind of "state failure"—or outright state collapse—that is associated with civil war, balkanization, and warlordism.

16 The PRIísta state was probably happy with this trend and even encouraged it.

17 Unless, of course, we read "injustice" as "disutility." However, recasting complex human feelings in terms of a basic binary, utility-disutility, not only grossly simplifies, by reducing noncommensurate values to a phony common currency; it also leads to a reductio ad absurdum, whereby any course of action—including St. Simeon Stylites' sitting atop his pillar with his withered arm held aloft—could be said to maximize utility (in this case, Christian-ascetic utility).

18 Not surprisingly, many of the examples deployed by Scott (1990) derive from systems of serfdom and slavery, such as Tsarist Russia and the antebellum South, and focus on "slaves, serfs, untouchables, the colonized and subjugated races" (J. C. Scott 1990, xi). Literate, liberal, urban, industrial societies figure very little.

19 Of course, religion can sometimes afford a facade behind which political and personal opportunism lurks. A relevant example is given by Butler (1999).

20 In this case, motives might be relevant: Was Stoll seeking celebrity, money, or the plain unvarnished truth? But motives are hard to get at, and may well be mixed.

21 I refer not just to diplomats—who are "sent abroad to lie for their country"—or politicians, who readily do so both at home and abroad, but also to journalists working for supposedly reputable broadsheets, such as the *New York Times*, and even to historians (see Hoffer 2004).

Bibliography

Abbeville, Claude d'. 1614. *Histoire de la mission des pères capuchins en l'Isle de Maragnan et terres circonvoisines*. Paris: De l'Imprimerie de François Huby.

Abélès, Marc. 1997. "Political Anthropology: New Challenges, New Aims." *International Social Science Journal* 49, no. 3: 319–32.

Abercrombie, Nicholas, Stephen Hill, and Bryan S. Turner. 1984. *The Dominant Ideology Thesis*. London: George Allen and Unwin.

Abu-Lughod, Lila. 1990. "The Romance of Resistance: Tracing Transformations of Power Through Bedouin Women." *American Ethnologist* 17, no.1: 41–55.

Acuña, René, ed. 1987. *Relaciones geográficas del siglo XVI: Michoacán*. Mexico City: Universidad Nacional Autónoma de México.

Adams, Richard N. 1995. *Etnias en evolución social*. Mexico City: Universidad Autónoma Metropolitana-Iztapalapa.

Agier, Michel. 1992. "Etnopolítica: A dinâmica do espaço afro-baiano." *Revista de Estudos Afro-Asiáticos* 22: 99–115.

Aguirre Beltrán, Gonzalo. 1967. *Regiones de refugio: El desarrollo de la comunidad y el proceso dominical en Mestizoamérica*. Mexico City: Instituto Indigenist Interamericano.

Albert, Bruce, and Alcida Rita Ramos, eds. 2002. *Pacificando o branco: Cosmologias do contato no Norte-Amazônico*. São Paulo: Ed. Unesp.

Alencastro, Luiz Felipe de. 2000. *O trato dos viventes: Formação do Brasil no Atlântico Sul*. São Paulo: Companhia das Letras.

Almeida, Alfredo Wagner Berno. 2005. "Os quilombos e o mercado de terras." *Porantin* 272: 6–7.

Almeida, Maria Regina Celestino de. 2003. *Metamorfoses indígenas: Identidade e cultura nas aldeias coloniais do Rio de Janeiro*. Rio de Janeiro: Arquivo Nacional.

Almeida, Paulo Henrique. 2006. "A economia de Salvador e a formação de sua região metropolitana." In *Como Anda Salvador e sua Região Metropolitana*, edited by Inaiá Maria Moreira de Carvalho and Gilberto Corso Pereira, 11–53. Salvador: Editora da UFBA.

Almond, Sidney, and Gabriel Verba. 1989. *The Civic Culture: Political Attitudes and Democracy in Five Nations*. London: Sage.

Amoroso, Marta Rosa. 1992. "Corsários no caminho fluvial: Os Mura do Rio Madeira." In *História dos Índios no Brasil*, edited by Manuela Carneiro da Cunha, 297–310. São Paulo: Companhia das Letras.

Anderson, Gary Clayton. 1999. *The Indian Southwest, 1580–1830: Ethnogenesis and Reinvention*. Norman: University of Oklahoma Press.

Anderson, Rodney. 1976. *Outcasts in Their Own Land: Mexican Industrial Workers*. De Kalb: Northern Illinois University Press.

Anderson, Thomas P. 1971. *Matanza: El Salvador's Communist Revolt of 1932*. Lincoln: University of Nebraska Press.

Andrade, Manuel Correia de. 1965. *A guerra dos Cabanos*. Rio de Janeiro: Conquista.

Andrade, Marcus Ferreira. 1998–99. "Rebelião escrava na comarca do Rio das Mortes, Minas Gerais: O caso Carrancas." *Revista Afro-Ásia* nos. 21–22: 45–82.

Andrews, George Reid. 1991. *Blacks and Whites in São Paulo, Brazil, 1888–1988*. Madison: University of Wisconsin Press.

———. 1992. "Racial Inequality in Brazil and the United States: A Statistical Comparison." *Journal of Social History* 26, no. 2: 229–63.

Apter, Andrew. 1992. *Black Critics & Kings: The Hermeneutics of Power in Yoruba Society*. Chicago: University of Chicago Press.

———. 2004. "Herskovit's Heritage: Rethinking Syncretism in the African Diaspora." In *Syncretism in Religion: A Reader*, edited by Anita Maria Leopold and Jeppe Sinding Jensen, 160–84. New York: Routledge.

Arias, Arturo, ed. 2001. *The Rigoberta Menchú Controversy*. Minneapolis: University of Minnesota Press.

Arruda, João. 1993. *Canudos: Messianismo e conflito social*. Forteleza: Edições UFC/SECULT.

Arruti, José Maurício. 2004. "Recuperação da memória do lugar auxilia laudo antropológico." *Com Ciência* 52. http://www.comciencia.br/, accessed November 1, 2008.

———. 2006. *Mocambo: Antropologia e história do processo de formação quilombola*. Bauru: Edusc/Anpocs.

Auyero, Javier. 2000. "The Hyper-Shantytown: Neo-Liberal Violence(s) in the Argentine Slum." *Ethnography* 1, no. 1: 93–116.

———. 2007. *Routine Politics and Violence in Argentina: The Gray Zone of State Power*. Cambridge: Cambridge University Press.

Azevedo, Celia Maria Marinho de. 1987. *Onda negra, medo branco: O negro no imaginário das elites, Brasil, século XIX*. Rio de Janeiro: Paz e Terra.

Azuela, Manuel. 1938. *Los de abajo: Novela de la revolución mexicana*. Mexico City: Pedro Robredo.

Azzi, Riolando. 1977. *O episcopado do Brasil frente ao catolicismo popular*. Petrópolis: Editora Vozes.

Bajtín, Mijail M. 1989. *Estética de la creación verbal*. Mexico City: Siglo XXI.

Barabas, Alicia. 1986. "Rebeliones e insurrecciones indígenas en Oaxaca: La trayectoria histórica de la resistencia étnica." In *Etnicidad y pluralismo cultural:*

La dinámica étnica en Oaxaca, edited by Alicia Barabas and Miguel Bartolomé, 213–56. Mexico City: Instituto Nacional de Antropología e Historia.

Barickman, Bert J. 1999. "As cores do escravismo: Escravistas 'pretos,' 'pardos,' e 'cabras,' no Recôncavo Bahiano, 1835." *População e Família* 2, no. 2 (July–December): 7–62.

Barragán López, Esteban, Odile Hoffman, and Thierry Linck, eds. 1994. *Rancheros y sociedades rancheras*. Zamora: El Colegio de Michoacán, ORSTOM and CEMCA.

Barreto, Murilo de Sá. 1998. *Testemunho, servico e fidelidade*. Juazeiro do Norte: Paróquia de Nossa Senhora das Dores.

Barth, Fredrik. 1969. *Ethnic Groups and Boundaries: The Social Organization of Culture Difference*. Boston: Little, Brown.

Bartolomé, Miguel Alberto. 2006. *Procesos interculturales: Antropología política del pluralismo cultural en América Latina*. Mexico City: Siglo Veintiuno Editores.

Bartra, Roger. 1999. *La sangre y la tinta: Ensayos sobre la condición postmexicana*. Mexico City: Oceano.

Bastide, Roger. 1986. *Sociología de la religión*. 2 vols. Ediciones Jucar: Madrid.

———. 1996. "Continuité et discontinuité des sociétés et des cultures afro-américaines." *Bastidiana* 13–14 (January–July): 77–88.

Becker, Marjorie. 1987. "Black and White and Color: Cardenismo and the Search for a Campesino Ideology." *Comparative Studies in Society and History* 29, no. 3: 453–65.

Bernasconi Giannetto, Adriana. 1999. "Catálogo de Archivo de Unión Femenina Católica Mexicana, 1921–1929." B.A. thesis, Universidad Iberoamericana.

Bethell, Leslie. 1970. *The Abolition of the Brazilian Slave Trade: Britain, Brazil and the Slave Trade Question, 1807–1869*. Cambridge: Cambridge University Press.

Beverley, John. 1999. *Subalternity and Representation: Arguments in Cultural Theory*. Durham: Duke University Press.

Birman, Patrícia, and Márcia Pereira Leite. 2000. "Whatever Happened to What Used to Be the Largest Catholic Church in the World?" *Daedulus* 129, no. 2: 271–90.

Blackmore, Susan. 1999. *The Meme Machine*. Oxford: Oxford University Press.

Bloch, Marc. 1997. *Apologie pour l'histoire ou Métier d'historien*. Edited by E. Bloch. Paris: Armand Collin.

Boaventura, Edivaldo. 1997. *O parque estadual de Canudos*. Salvador: Secretária de Cultura e Turismo.

Boccara, Guillaume. 1999. "Etnogénesis mapuche: Resistencia y restructuración entre los indígenas del Centro-Sur de Chile (Siglos XVI–XVIII)." *Hispanic American Historical Review* 79, no. 3: 415–61.

Bonfil Batalla, Guillermo. 1981. *Utopía y Revolución: El pensamiento político contemporáneo de los indios en América Latina*. Mexico City: Editorial Nueva Imagen.

———. 1996. *México Profundo: Reclaiming a Civilization*. Austin: University of Texas Press. First published in Spanish, *México profundo: Una civilización negada*. Mexico City: Secretaría de Educación Publica and CIESAS, 1988.

Borges, Dain. 1992. *The Family in Bahia, Brazil: 1870–1945*. Stanford: Stanford University Press.

Boulanger, André. 1974. *Yambe à l'aube des symboles: Essay d'anthropologie religieuse zela (République du Zaire)*. Vol. 21, ser. 2. Bandundu, Zaire: CEEBA.

Bourdieu, Pierre. 1977. *Outline of a Theory of Practice*. Cambridge: Cambridge University Press.

———. 1984. *Distinction: A Social Critique of the Judgement of Taste*. Cambridge: Harvard University Press.

Boxer, Charles. 1952. *Salvador de Sá and the Struggle for Brazil and Angola, 1602–1686*. London: Athlone.

Boyer, Christopher R. 2003. *Becoming Campesinos: Politics, Identity, and Agrarian Struggle in Postrevolutionary Michoacán, 1920–1935*. Stanford: Stanford University Press.

Brandes, Stanley. 1988. *Power and Persuasion: Fiestas and Social Control in Rural Mexico*. Philadelphia: University of Pennsylvania Press.

Bricker, Victoria Reifler. 1989. *El cristo indígena, el rey nativo: El sustrato histórico de la mitología del ritual de los mayas*. Mexico City: Fondo de Cultura Económica.

Brinton, Crane. 1938. *The Anatomy of Revolution*. New York: W. W. Norton.

Brown, Michael F. 1996. "On Resisting Resistance." *American Anthropologist* 98, no. 4: 729–35.

Brown, Michael F., and Eduardo Fernández. 1991. *War of Shadows: The Struggle for Utopia in the Peruvian Amazon*. Berkeley: University of California Press.

Brown, Wendy. 2005. *Edgework: Critical Essays on Knowledge and Politics*. Princeton: Princeton University Press.

Bruneau, Thomas. 1974. *The Political Transformation of the Brazilian Church*. Cambridge: Cambridge University Press.

Brunk, Samuel. 1995. *Emiliano Zapata: Revolution and Betrayal in Mexico*. Albuquerque: University of New Mexico Press.

Butler, Matthew. 1999. "The 'Liberal' Cristero: Ladislao Molina and the Cristero Rebellion in Michoacán, 1927–29." *Journal of Latin American Studies* 31, no. 3: 645–71.

———. 2004. *Popular Piety and Political Identity in Mexico's Cristero Rebellion: Michoacán, 1927–1929*. Oxford: Oxford University Press.

Cabral de Mello, Evaldo. 2004. *A outra Independência, o federalismo pernambucano, 1817 a 1824*. São Paulo: Editora 34.

Caldeira, Teresa P. R., and James Holston. 2004. "State and Urban Space in Brazil: From Modernist Planning to Democratic Intervention." In *Global Assemblages: Technology, Politics and Ethics as an Anthropological Problem*, edited by Aihwa Ong and Stephen J. Collier, 393–416. Malden, Mass.: Blackwell.

Callado, João Pereira. 1981. *História de Lagoa dos Gatos*. Recife: FIAM, Centro de Estudos de História Municipal.

Camacho, Eduardo. 2000. "Sobrevivencias de la estrategia educativa misionera en las formas simbólicas de la pastorela de Ayotitlán." In *Rostros y palabras: El indi-*

genismo en Jalisco, edited by Rosa Rojas and Agustín Hernández, 126–43. Guadalajara: Instituto Nacional Indigenista.

Campos, Roberta Bivar C. 2004. "Quando final dos tempos chegar." In *Antes do fim do mundo: Milenarismos e messianismos no Brasil e na Argentina*, edited by Leonarda Musumeci, 144–65. Rio de Janeiro: Editora UFRJ.

Canabal Cristiani, Beatriz. 1984. *Hoy luchamos por la tierra*. Mexico City: Universidad Autónoma Metropolitana-Xochimilco.

Candido, Mariana Pinho. 2006. *Enslaving Frontiers: Slavery, Trade and Identity in Benguela, 1780–1850*. Ph.D. diss., York University, Toronto.

Cardim, Fernão S. J. 1997. *Tratados da terra e da gente do Brasil, 1583–90*. Edited by Ana Maria de Azevedo. Lisbon: Comissão Nacional para as Comemorações dos Descobrimentos Portugueses.

Carmagnani, Marcello. 1992. "Un movimiento político indio: La 'rebelión' de Tehuantepec, 1660–1661." In *Patterns of Contention in Mexican History*, edited by Jaime Rodríguez, 17–35. Wilmington: University of California Press and Scholarly Resources.

Carr, Edward Hallett. 1964. *What Is History?* Harmondsworth: Pelican Books.

Carrillo Cázarez, Alberto. 1993. *Michoacán en el otoño del siglo XVI*. Zamora: El Colegio de Michoacán.

Carvalho, Marcus J. M. 1996. "Os índios de Pernambuco no ciclo das insurreições liberais, 1817–1848: Ideologias e resistência." *Revista da Sociedade Brasileira de Pesquisa Histórica* 11: 51–69.

Casarrubias, Vicente. 1945. *Rebeliones indigenas en la Nueva España*. Mexico City: Secretaria de Educación Publica.

Castellanos, Laura. 2007. *México armado, 1943–1981*. Mexico City: Era.

Castells, Manuel. 2002. *O poder da identidade*. Vol. 2. São Paulo: Editora Paz e Terra.

Castile, George P., and Gilbert Kushner, eds. 1981. *Persistent Peoples: Cultural Enclaves in Perspective*. Tucson: University of Arizona Press.

Castillo, Lisa Earl. 2008. *Entre a oralidade e a escrita: A etnografia nos candomblés da Bahia*. Salvador: EDUFBA.

Castro Gutiérrez, Felipe. 1996. *Nueva ley y nuevo rey: Reformas borbónicas y rebelión popular en la Nueva España*. Zamora: El Colegio de Michoacán and Universidad Nacional Autónoma de México.

———. 2003. "'Lo tienen ya de uso y costumbre': Los motines de indios en Michoacán colonial." *Tzintzun* 38: 9–34.

Chacon, Vamireh. 1990. *Deus é brasileiro: O imaginário do messianismo político no Brasil*. Rio de Janeiro: Civilização Brasileira.

Chalhoub, Sidney. 1990. *Visões da liberdade: Uma história das ultimas décadas da escravidão na Corte*. São Paulo: Companhia das Letras.

———. 2010. "Illegal Enslavement and the Precariousness of Freedom in Nineteenth-Century Brazil." In *Assumed Identities: The Meanings of Race in the Atlantic World*, edited by John D. Garrigus and Christopher Morris, 88–115. College Station: Texas A&M University Press.

Chalhoub, Sidney, and Fernando Teixeira da Silva. 2009. "Sujeitos no imaginário acadêmico: Escravos e trabalhadores na historiografia brasileira desde os anos 1980." *Cadernos AEL*, 14, no. 26 (first semester): 11–49.

Chávez Padrón, Martha. 2003. *Derecho procesal social agrario*. Mexico City: Editorial Porrúa.

Chiozzini, Daniel. 2005. "Território negro." *Patrimônio Revista Eletrônica do IPHAN* 1. http://www.revista.iphan.gov.br/, accessed September 6, 2008.

Ciudad Real, Fray Antonio de. 1976. *Tratado curioso y docto de las grandezas de Nueva España*. Edited by Josefina García Quintana and Víctor M. Castillo Farreras. Mexico City: Universidad Nacional Autónoma de México.

Cohen, Anthony P. 1985. *The Symbolic Construction of Community*. London: Routledge.

Cohen, Thomas M. 1998. *The Fire of Tongues: António Vieira and the Missionary Church in Brazil and Portugal*. Stanford: Stanford University Press.

Comaroff, Jean, and John Comaroff. 1991. *Of Revelation and Revolution*, Vol. 1, *Christianity, Colonialism, and Consciousness in South Africa*. Chicago: University of Chicago Press.

———. 1992. *Ethnography and the Historical Imagination*. Boulder, Colo.: Westview.

Comisión Civil Internacional de Observación por los Derechos Humanos (CCIODH). 2007. *Informe de la V CCIODH*. http://cciodh.pangea.org/, accessed March 12, 2008.

Consorte, Josildeth Gomes. 1999. "Em torno de um Manifesto de Ialorixás Baianas contra o Sincretismo." In *Faces da tradição afro-brasileira: Religiosidade, sincretismo, anti-sincretismo, reafricanização, práticas terapêuticas, etnobotánica e comida*, edited by Jéferson Barcelar and Carlos Caroso, 71–91. Rio de Janeiro: Pallas/CEAO.

Coronado Malagón, Marcela. 2000. "Los apodos de la resistencia: Estereotipos gentilicios zapotecas en el Istmo de Tehuantepec, procesos de identidad, movimiento social y producción discursiva." *Alteridades* 10, no. 19: 79–88.

Coronil, Fernando. 1994. "Listening to the Subaltern: The Poetics of Neocolonial States." *Poetics Today* 15, no. 4: 643–58.

Corrigan, Philip, and Derek Sayer. 1985. *The Great Arch: English State Formation as Cultural Revolution*. Oxford: Basil Blackwell.

Corrigan, Philip, Harvie Ramsay, and Derek Sayer. 1980. "The State as a Relation of Production." In *Capitalism, State Formation, and Marxist Theory*, edited by Philip Corrigan, 1–26. London: Quartet Books.

Costa, Emilia Viotti da. 1985. *The Brazilian Empire: Myths and Histories*. Chicago: Dorsey.

Costa e Silva, Candido da. 1982. *Roteiro de vida e de morte: Um estudio do catolicismo no sertão da Bahia*. São Paulo: Atica.

Craemer, Willy de, Jan Vansina, and Renée C. Fox. 1976. "Religious Movements in Central Africa: A Theoretical Study." *Comparative Studies in Society and History* 18, no. 4 (October): 458–75.

Crehan, Kate. 2002. *Gramsci, Culture, and Anthropology.* Berkeley: University of California Press.

Cunha, Manuela Carneiro da, ed. 1992. *História dos Índios no Brasil.* São Paulo: Companhia das Letras.

Cuoto, Manoel José Gonçalves. 1873. *Missão abreviada para despertar os descuidados, converter os peccadores e sustentar o fructo das missões.* Porto, Portugal: Sebastião José Pereira.

Curtin, Philip D. 1969. *The Atlantic Slave Trade: A Census.* Madison: University of Wisconsin Press.

Da Cunha, Euclides. 1944. *Rebellion in the Backlands.* Chicago: University of Chicago Press.

Dahl, Robert. 1971. *Polyarchy: Participation and Opposition.* New Haven: Yale University Press.

DaMatta, Roberto. 1987. "Digressão: A fábula das três raças ou o problema do racismo à brasileira." In *Relativizando: Uma introdução à antropologia social.* Rio de Janeiro: Rocco.

Dantas, Beatriz Góis. 1987. "Pureza e poder no mundo dos candomblés." In *Candomblé: Desvendando identidades (Novos estudos sobre a religião dos Orixás),* edited by Carlos Eugênio Marcondes de Moura, 121–27. São Paulo: EMW Ed.

———. 1988 [1982]. *Vovó Nagô e Papai Branco: Usos e abusos da África no Brasil.* Rio de Janeiro: Edições Graal.

Davis, David B. 2006. *Inhuman Bondage: The Rise and Fall of Slavery in the New World.* Oxford: Oxford University Press.

Dean, Warren. 1976. *Rio Claro: A Brazilian Plantation System, 1820–1920.* Stanford: Stanford University Press.

De Groot, Kees. 1996. *Brazilian Catholicism and the Ultramontane Reform, 1850–1930.* Amsterdam: Centre for Latin American Research and Documentation.

De la Cadena, Marisol. 2000. *Indigenous Mestizos: The Politics of Race and Culture in Cuzco, Peru, 1919–1991.* Durham: Duke University Press.

De la Peña, Guillermo. 1990. "La cultura política entre los sectores populares en Guadalajara." *Nueva Antropología* 11: 83–107.

———. 2002. "El futuro del indigenismo en México: Del mito del mestizaje a la fragmentación neoliberal." In *Estados nacionales, etnicidad y democracia en América Latina,* edited by Mutsuo Yamada and Carlos Iván Degregori, 45–64. Osaka: Museo Nacional de Etnología.

———. 2003. "Identidades y participación ciudadana en el México de la transición democrática." *Revista de Occidente* 269 (October): 88–107.

———. 2006a. *Culturas indígenas de Jalisco.* Guadalajara: Secretaría de Cultura del Gobierno de Jalisco.

———. 2006b. "Os novos intermediários étnicos, o movimento indígena e a sociedade civil: Dois estudos de caso no oeste mexicano." In *A disputa pela construcao democrática na América Latina,* edited by Evelina Dagnino, Aldo Panfichi, and Alberto Olvera, 467–97. São Paulo: Paz e Terra and UNICAMP.

———. 2007. "Civil Society and Popular Resistance: Mexico at the End of the Twentieth Century." In *Cycles of Conflict, Centuries of Change: Crisis, Reform and Revolution in Mexico*, edited by Elisa Servín, Leticia Reina, and John Tutino, 305–45. Durham: Duke University Press.

Della Cava, Ralph. 1968. "Brazilian Messianism and National Institutions: A Reappraisal of Canudos and Joaseiro." *Hispanic American Historical Review* 48, no. 3: 402–20.

———. 1970. *Miracle at Joaseiro*. New York: Columbia University Press.

Dennis, Philip A. 1976. *Conflictos por tierras en el Valle de Oaxaca*. Mexico City: Instituto Nacional Indigenista.

Deutsch, Sandra McGee. 1999. *Las Derechas: The Extreme Right in Argentina, Brazil, and Chile, 1890–1939*. Stanford: Stanford University Press.

Diacon, Todd A. 1991. *Millenarian Vision, Capitalist Reality: Brazil's Contestado Rebellion, 1912–1916*. Durham: Duke University Press.

Dietz, Gunther. 2004. "From *Indigenismo* to *Zapatismo*: The struggle for a Multi-Ethnic Mexican Society." In *The Struggle for Indigenous Rights in Latin America*, edited by Nancy Grey Postero and Leon Zamosc, 32–80. Brighton: Sussex University Press.

Dirks, Nicholas. 1996. Foreword to *Colonialism and Its Forms of Knowledge: The British in India*, by Bernard Cohn, ix–xvii. Princeton: Princeton University Press.

Domingues, Ângela. 2000. *Quando os Índios eram vassalos: Colonização e relações de poder no Norte do Brasil na segunda metade do século XVIII*. Lisbon: Comissão Nacional para as Comemorações dos Descobrimentos Portugueses.

Durán Legazpi, Juan Manuel. 1987. "Los juicios en los asuntos de comunidades indígenas." In *El Municipio en México*, edited by Brigitte Boehm de Lameiras, 280–92. Zamora: El Colegio de Michoacán.

Eckstein, Susan. 1989. "Power and Popular Protest in Latin America." In *Power and Popular Protest: Latin American Social Movements*, edited by Susan Eckstein, 1–60. Berkeley: University of California Press.

Eisenberg, Peter L. 1974. *The Sugar Industry in Pernambuco: Modernization Without Change, 1840–1910*. Berkeley: University of California Press.

Eriksen, Thomas Hylland. 1993. *Ethnicity and Nationalism: Anthropological Perspectives*. London: Pluto Press.

Esparza, Manuela. 2004. *Eulogio Gillow y el Poder*. Oaxaca: INAH.

Espinosa Damián, Gisela, and Miguel Meza Castillo. 2000. "Guerrero en cifras: Las dimensiones de la pobreza." In *Crónicas del Sur: Utopías campesinas en Guerrero*, edited by Armando Bartra, 75–102. Mexico City: Ediciones Era.

Esteva, Gustavo. 2007a. "Oaxaca: The Path of Radical Democracy." *Socialism and Democracy* 21, no. 2: 74–96.

———. 2007b. "The Asamblea Popular de los Pueblos de Oaxaca: A Chronicle of Radical Democracy." *Latin American Perspectives* 34, no. 1: 129–44.

Eyerman, Ron, and Andrew Jamison. 1991. *Social Movements: A Cognitive Approach*. Cambridge: Polity.

Fabian, Johannes. 1979. "The Anthropology of Religious Movements: From Explanation to Interpretation." *Social Research* 46, no. 1: 4–35.

Fáco, Rui. 1963. *Cangaceiros e fanáticos.* Rio de Janeiro: Civilização Brasileira.

Fallaw, Ben. 2001. *Cárdenas Compromised: The Failure of Reform in Postrevolutionary Yucatán.* Durham: Duke University Press.

Farage, Nadia. 1991. *As muralhas dos sertões: Os povos indígenas no Rio Branco e a colonização.* Rio de Janeiro: Paz e Terra/Anpocs.

Faria, Sheila de Castro. 1998. *A colônia em movimento: Fortuna e família no cotidiano colonial.* Rio de Janeiro: Ed. Nova Fronteira.

———. 2007. "Damas mercadoras: As pretas minas no Rio de Janeiro (século XVIII–1850)." In *Rotas atlânticas da diáspora africana: Da Baía do Benim ao Rio de Janeiro,* edited by Mariza de Carvalho Soares, 103–34. Niterói: EdUFF.

Fausto, Carlos, and Michael Heckenberger. 2007. *Time and Memory in Indigenous Amazonia: Anthropological Perspectives.* Gainesville: University Press of Florida.

Fernandes, Florestan. 1966. *A integração do negro na sociedade de classes.* 2 vols. São Paulo: Dominus Editora/EDUSP.

———. 1975. *Investigação etnológica no Brasil e outros ensaios.* Petrópolis: Editora Vozes.

Fernandes, João Azevedo. 2003. *De cunhã a mameluca: A mulher tupinambá e o nascimento do Brasil.* João Pessoa: Ed. UFPB.

———. 2004. "Selvagens bebedeiras: Álcool, embriaguez e contatos culturais no Brasil colonial." Doctoral thesis, Universidade Federal Fluminense, Niterói.

Fernández Aceves, María Teresa. 2000. "The Political Mobilization of Women in Revolutionary Guadalajara, 1910–1940." Doctoral thesis, University of Illinois, Chicago.

Ferraz, Lizandra Meyer. 2010. "Entradas para a liberdade: Formas e freqüência da alforria em Campinas no século XIX." M.A. thesis, Universidade Estadual de Campinas.

Ferreira, A. Rodrigues. 1974. *Viagem filosófica pelas capitanias do Grão Pará, Rio Negro, Mato Grosso e Cuiabá: Memórias, antropologia.* 1783–92. Brasília: Conselho Federal da Cultura.

Ferretti, Sergio. 1995. *Repensando o sincretismo.* São Paulo: EDUSP.

Figueira de Mello, Jeronymo Martiniano. 1978. *Crônica da rebelião praieira: 1848–1849.* 1850. Brasília: Senado Federal.

Fix-Zamudio, Hector. 2003. *Ensayos sobre el derecho de amparo.* Mexico City: Editorial Porrúa and UNAM.

Fletcher, Robert. 2001. "What Are We Fighting for? Rethinking Resistance in a Pewenche Community in Chile." *Journal of Peasant Studies* 28, no. 3: 37–66.

Florentino, Manolo. 1997. *Em costas negras: Uma história do tráfico de escravos entre a África e o Rio de Janeiro.* 2nd ed. São Paulo: Companhia das Letras.

———. 2005. "Sobre minas, crioulos e a liberdade costumeira no Rio de Janeiro, 1789–1871." In *Tráfico, cativeiro e liberdade: Rio de Janeiro, séculos XVII–XIX,* edited by Manolo Florentino, 331–66. Rio de Janeiro: Civilização Brasileira.

———. 2007. "Da atualidade de Gilberto Freyre." In *Ligações perigosas: Políticas raciais no Brasil contemporâneo*, edited by Peter Fry, Yvonne Maggie, Simone Monteiro, and Ricardo Ventura Santos, 89–94. Rio de Janeiro: Civilização Brasileira.

Florentino, Manolo, and José Roberto Góes. 1997. *A paz das senzalas: Famílias escravas e tráfico atlântico, Rio de Janeiro, c.1790-c.1850*. Rio de Janeiro: Civilização Brasileira.

Flores Galindo, Alberto. 1994. *Buscando un Inca: Identidad y utopia en los Andes*. Lima: Editorial Horizonte.

Flory, Thomas. 1981. *Judge and Jury in Imperial Brazil, 1808–1871: Social Control and Political Stability in the New State*. Austin: University of Texas Press.

Fogel, Robert W., and Stanley L. Engerman. 1974. *Time on the Cross: The Economics of American Negro Slavery*. 2 vols. Boston: Little, Brown.

Ford, Franklin L. 1982. "Reflections on Political Murder: Europe in the Nineteenth and Twentieth Centuries." In *Social Protest, Violence and Terror in Twentieth-Century Europe*, edited by Wolfgang J. Mommsen and Gerhard Hirschfeld, 1–12. London: Macmillan.

Foster, George. 1962. *Cultura y conquista: La herencia española de América*. Xalapa: Universidad Veracruzana.

Foucault, Michel. 1996. *A ordem do discurso*. 2nd edition. São Paulo: Loyola.

———. 1978. *The History of Sexuality, Volume 1: An Introduction*. New York: Pantheon Books.

Foweraker, Joe. 1995. *Theorizing Social Movements*. London: Pluto.

———. 2001. "Grassroots Movements and Political Activism in Latin America: A Critical Comparison of Chile and Brazil." *Journal of Latin American Studies* 33, no. 4: 839–65.

Fox, Jonathan, and Gaspar Rivera-Salgado, eds. 2004. *Indigenous and Mexican Migrants in the United Status*. La Jolla, Calif.: Center for U.S.-Mexican Studies, UCSD, and Center for Comparative Immigration Studies, UCSD.

Frank, Zephyr. 2004. *Dutra's World: Wealth and Family in Nineteenth-Century Rio de Janeiro*. Albuquerque: University of New Mexico Press.

Frazier, E. Franklin. 1939. *The Negro Family in the United States*. Chicago: University of Chicago Press.

Fregoso Centeno, Anayanci. 2006. "Dolores Palomar Arias, 1898–1972: La familia y la religión en la construcción del sujeto." In *Siete historias de vida: Mujeres jaliscienses del siglo XIX*, edited by Anayanci Fregoso Centeno, 41–65. Guadalajara: Universidad de Guadalajara.

Freire, Jonis. 2009. "Escravidão e família escrava na Zona da Mata mineira oitocentista." Ph.D. diss., Universidade Estadual de Campinas.

Freitas, Décio. 1990. *Palmares: A guerra dos escravos*. Rio de Janeiro: Graal.

French, Jan Hoffman. 2009. *Legalizing Identities: Becoming Black or Indian in Brazil's Northeast*. Chapel Hill: University of North Carolina Press.

French, John D. 1992. *The Brazilian Workers' ABC: Class, Conflict, and Alliances in Modern São Paulo*. Chapel Hill: University of North Carolina Press.

Freyre, Gilberto. 1971. *Novo Mundo nos Trópicos*. 1945. São Paulo: Companhia Ed. Nacional.

———. 1980. *Casa Grande e Senzala*. 1933. 20th ed. Rio de Janeiro: José Olympio Editora.

Fry, Peter. 2005. *A persistência da raça: Ensaios antropológicos sobre o Brasil e a África austral*. Rio de Janeiro: Civilização Brasileira.

Funes Rivas, María Jesús. 1998. *La salida del silencio: Movilizaciones por la paz en Euskadi, 1986–1998*. Madrid: Akal Ediciones.

Gal, Susan. 2002. "Between Speech and Silence." In *The Anthropology of Politics: A Reader in Ethnography, Theory, and Critique*, edited by Joan Vincent, 213–21. Oxford: Blackwell.

Galinier, Jacques, and Antoinette Moliner. 2006. *Les néo-indiens: Une religion de IIIème millenaire*. Paris: Odile Jacob.

Gálvez, José de. 1990. *Informe sobre las rebeliones populares de 1767*. Edited and introduced by Felipe Castro Gutiérrez. Mexico City: Universidad Nacional Autónoma de México.

García Canclini, Néstor. 1982. *Las culturas populares en el capitalismo*. Mexico City: Nueva Imagen.

———. 1989. *Culturas híbridas: Estrategias para entrar y salir de la modernidad*. Mexico City: Grijalbo.

———. 1995a. *Consumidores y ciudadanos: Conflictos multiculturales de la globalización*. Mexico City: Grijalbo.

———. 1995b. *Hybrid Cultures: Strategies for Entering and Leaving Modernity*. Translated by Christopher L. Chiappari and Silvia L. López. Minneapolis: University of Minnesota Press.

García de León, Antonio. 2002. *Fronteras interiores: Chiapas, una modernidad particular*. Océano: Mexico City.

Genovese, Eugene. 1974. *Roll, Jordan, Roll: The World the Slaves Made*. New York: Pantheon.

Gerritzer, Peter R. W. 2002. *Diversity at Stake: A Farmer's Perspective on Biodiversity and Conservation in Western Mexico*. Wageningen: Wageningen University, Circle for Rural European Studies.

Gledhill, John. 1995. *Neoliberalism, Transnationalization and Rural Poverty: A Case Study of Michoacán, Mexico*. Boulder, Colo.: Westview.

———. 2004a. *Cultura y desafio en Ostula: Cuatro siglos de autonomía indígena en la costa-sierra nahua de Michoacán*. Zamora: El Colegio de Michoacán.

———. 2004b. "Neoliberalism." In *A Companion to the Anthropology of Politics*, edited by David Nugent and Joan Vincent, 332–48. Malden, Mass.: Blackwell.

Gluckman, Max. 1960. "Rituals of Rebellion in South East Africa." In *Order and Rebellion in Tribal Africa: Collected Essays with an Autobiographical Introduction*. Glencoe, Ill.: Free Press.

Glyn, Andrew, and Bob Sutcliffe. 1972. *British Capitalism, Workers and the Profit Squeeze*. Harmondsworth: Penguin.

Godinho, Paula. 2001. *Memórias da resistência rural no Sul: Couço (1958–1962)*. Oeiras: Celta Editora.

Góes, José Roberto Pinto de. 2003. "São muitas as moradas: Desigualdades e hierarquia entre os escravos." In *Ensaios sobre a escravidão I*, edited by Manolo Florentino and Cacilda Machado, 201–16. Belo Horizonte: Ed. UFMG.

————. 2007. "Histórias mal contadas." In *Ligações perigosas: Políticas raciais no Brasil contemporâneo*, edited by Peter Fry, Yvonne Maggie, Simone Monteiro, and Ricardo Ventura Santos, 57–61. Rio de Janeiro: Civilização Brasileira.

Gomes, Flávio dos Santos. 2006. *Histórias de quilombolas: Mocambos e comunidades de senzalas no Rio de Janeiro, século XIX*. 1995. Revised and expanded edition. São Paulo: Companhia das Letras.

Gomes, Flávio dos Santos, and Olívia Maria Gomes da Cunha, eds. 2007. *Quase-cidadão: Histórias e antropologias da pós-emancipação no Brasil*. Rio de Janeiro: Fundação Getulio Vargas.

Gomes, Tiago de Melo. 2004. *Um espelho no palco: Identidades sociais e massificação da cultura no teatro de revista dos anos 1920*. Campinas: Editora da Unicamp.

González de la Rocha, Mercedes. 2006. *Procesos domésticos y vulnerabilidad: Perspectivas antropológicas de los hogares con Oportunidades*. Mexico City: Ciesas/ Publicaciones de la Casa Chata.

González de la Vara, Martín. 1992. "La rebelión de los indios pueblos de Nuevo México, 1680–1693." In *Organización y liderazgo en los movimientos populares novohispanos*, edited by Felipe Castro, Virginia Guedea, and José Luis Mirafuentes, 11–36. Mexico City: National Autonomous University of Mexico.

González Obregón, Luis. 1952. *Rebeliones indigenas y precursores de la independencia Mexicana en los siglos XVI, XVII*. Mexico City: Fuente Cultural.

Gordilho, Ângela. 2000. *Limites do habitar: Segregação e exclusão na configuração urbana contemporânea de Salvador e perspectivas no final do século XX*. Salvador: Edufba.

Gosner, Kevin. 1992. *Soldiers of the Virgin: The Moral Economy of a Colonial Maya Rebellion*. Tucson: University of Arizona Press.

Graham, Richard. 1999. "Free African Brazilians and the State in Slavery Times." In *Racial Politics in Contemporary Brazil*, edited by Michael Hanchard, 30–58. Durham: Duke University Press.

Gramsci, Antonio. 1971. *Selections from the Prison Notebooks*. 1929–35. Edited by Quintin Hoare and Geoffrey N. Smith. New York: International.

Grinberg, Keila. 2002. *O fiador dos Brasileiros: Cidadania, escravidão e direito civil no tempo de Antonio Pereira Rebouças*. Rio de Janeiro: Civilização Brasileira.

Gros, Christian. 2000. *Políticas de la etnicidad: Identidad, estado y modernidad*. Bogotá: Instituto Colombiano de Antropología e Historia.

Gruzinski, Serge. 1985. "La memoria mutilada: Construcción y mecanismos de la memoria en un grupo otomí de la mitad del siglo XVII." In *II Simposio de histo-*

ria de las mentalidades: la memoria y el olvido. Mexico City: Instituto Nacional de Antropología e Historia.

Guardino, Peter F. 1996. *Peasants, Politics, and the Formation of Mexico's National State*. Stanford: Stanford Universty Press.

———. 2005. *The Time of Liberty: Popular Political Culture in Oaxaca, 1750–1850*. Durham: Duke University Press.

Guedes, Roberto. 2008. *Egressos do cativeiro: Trabalho, família, aliança e mobilidade social (Porto Feliz, São Paulo, c. 1798–c. 1850)*. Rio de Janeiro: Mauad X/FAPERJ.

Guha, Ranajit. 1983. *Elementary Aspects of Peasant Insurgency in Colonial India*. Delhi: Oxford University Press.

———. 1988. Preface to *Selected Subalternal Studies*, edited by R. Guha and Gayatri Spivak. New York: Oxford University Press.

Gurr, Ted Robert. 1970. *Why Men Rebel*. Princeton: Princeton University Press.

Gutiérrez, Maribel. 1998. *Violencia en Guerrero*. Mexico City: La Jornada.

Gutman, Herbert G. 1976. *The Black Family in Slavery and Freedom, 1750–1925*. New York: Random House.

Gutmann, Matthew. 1993. "Rituals of Resistance: A Critique of the Theory of Everyday Forms of Resistance." *Latin American Perspectives* 20, no. 2: 74–92.

———. 1999. "Ethnicity, Alcohol, and Acculturation." *Social Science and Medicine* 48, no. 2: 173–84.

———. 2002. *The Romance of Democracy: Compliant Defiance in Contemporary Mexico*. Berkeley: University of California Press.

———. 2008. "Academic Freedoms Under Assault in Oaxaca: The LASA Delegation Report." *LASA Forum* 39, no. 1: 6–8.

Guzmán, Rafael. 1978. *El teosinte en Jalisco: Su distribución y ecología*. M.A. thesis, Universidad de Guadalajara.

Hale, Charles R. 1994a. *Resistance and Contradiction: Miskito Indians and the Nicaraguan State, 1894–1987*. Stanford: Stanford University Press.

———. 1994b. "Between Che Guevara and the Pachamama: Mestizos, Indians and Identity Politics in the Anti-Quincentenary Campaign." *Critique of Anthropology* 14, no. 1: 9–39.

———. 2002. "Does Multiculturalism Menace? Governance, Cultural Rights and the Politics of Identity in Guatemala." *Journal of Latin American Studies* 34, no. 3: 485–524.

Hall, Stuart. 1981. "Notes on Deconstructing the 'Popular.'" In *History and Socialist Theory*, edited by Rafael Samuel, 227–40. London: Routledge and Kegan Paul.

Hamnett, Brian. 1971. *Politics and Trade in Southern Mexco, 1750–1821*. Cambridge: Cambridge University Press.

———. 1992. "Absolutismo ilustrado y crisis multidimensional en el periodo colonial tardío, 1760–1808." In *Interpretaciones del siglo XVIII mexicano: El impacto de las reformas borbónicas*, edited by Josefina Zoraida Vázquez, 67–108. Mexico City: Nueva Imagen.

Haraway, Donna. 1991. *Ciencia, cyborgs y mujeres: La reinvención de la naturaleza.* Madrid: Universidad de València and Instituto de la Mujer/ Ediciones Cátedra.

Harding, Rachel. 2000. *A Refuge in Thunder: Candomblé and Alternative Spaces of Blackness.* Bloomington: Indiana University Press.

Harrison, Simon. 1999. "Identity as a Scarce Resource." *Social Anthropology* 7, no. 3: 239–51.

Harvey, Neil. 1994. *Rebellion in Chiapas: Rural Reforms, Campesino Radicalism and the Limits to Salinismo.* La Jolla: Center for U.S.-Mexican Studies, University of California, San Diego.

Hemming, John. 1978. *Red Gold: The Destruction of the Brazilian Indians, 1500–1760.* Cambridge: Harvard University Press.

Hermann, Jacqueline. 2004. "Dom Sebastão e a cidade do paraíso terrestre." In *Antes do fim do mundo: Milenarismos e messianismos no Brasil e na Argentina,* edited by Leonarda Musumeci, 58–78. Rio de Janeiro: Editora UFRJ.

Higareda, Yésica. 2000. "El arte de curar: La medicina de los antepasados: El testimonio de los médicos tradicionales nahuas." In *Rostros y palabras: El indigenismo en Jalisco,* edited by Rosa Rojas and Agustín Hernández, 171–200. Guadalajara: Instituto Nacional Indigenista.

Hijar Ornelas, Tomás de. 1999. "Beato Cristóbal Magallanes Jara (1869–1927)." *Semanario* 14 (November): 9.

Hill, Jonathan. 1975. *The World Turned Upside Down: Radical Ideas during the English Revolution.* Harmondsworth: Penguin.

———. 1996. Introduction to *History, Power, and Identity: Ethnogenesis in the Americas, 1492–1992,* edited by Jonathan Hill, 1–19. Iowa City: University of Iowa Press.

———, ed. 1988. *Rethinking History and Myth: Indigenous South American Perspectives on the Past.* Urbana: University of Illinois Press.

Hilton, Anne. 1985. *The Kingdom of Kongo.* Oxford: Clarendon.

Hita, Maria Gabriela, and Luciana Duccini. 2007. "Da guerra à paz: O nascimento de um ator social no contexto do 'nova pobreza.'" *Caderno CRH* 20, no. 50: 281–97.

Hobsbawm, Eric J. 1959. *Primitive Rebels.* Manchester: University of Manchester Press.

———. 1981. *Bandits.* New York: Random House.

———. 1982. "Political Violence and Political Murder: Comments on Franklin Ford's Essay." In *Social Protest, Violence and Terror in Twentieth-century Europe,* edited by Wolfgang J. Mommsen and Gerhard Hirschfeld, 1–12. London: Macmillan.

Hoffer, Peter Charles. 2004. *Past Imperfect.* New York: Public Affairs.

Hollander, Jocelyn A. and Rachel L. Einwohner. 2004. "Conceptualizing Resistance." *Sociological Forum* 19, no. 4: 533–54.

Holston, James. 1999. "Alternative Modernities: Statecraft and Religious Imagination in the Valley of the Dawn." *American Ethnologist* 26, no. 3: 605–31.

Hoornaert, Eduardo. 1974. *Formação do catolicismo brasiliero, 1550–1800*. Petrópolis: Editora Vozes.

———. 1981. *Cronica das casas de caridade: Fundadas pelo Padre Ibiapina*. São
Paulo: Edições Loyola.

———. 1997. *Os anjos de Canudos: Uma revisão histórica*. Petrópolis: Editora Vozes.

Ibarra Mendivil, Jorge Luis. 1989. *Propiedad agraria y sistema político en México*.
Mexico City: Miguel Angel Porrúa.

Iturribarría, Jorge. 1955. *Oaxaca en la Historia, de la época precolombina a los tiempos actuales*. Mexico City: Stylo.

Iwanska, Alicja. 1977. *The Truths of Others: An Essay on Nativistic Intellectuals in
Mexico*. Cambridge, Mass.: Schenkman.

Janzen, John M. 1979. "Deep Thought: Structure and Intention in Kongo Prophet-
ism, 1910–1921." *Social Research* 46, no. 1: 106–39.

———. 1982. *Lemba, 1650–1930: A Drum of Affliction in Africa and the New World*.
New York: Garland.

———. 1992. *Ngoma: Discourses of Healing in Central and Southern Africa*. Berkeley:
University of California Press.

Janzen, John, and Wyatt MacGaffey, eds. 1974. *Anthology of Kongo Religion: Primary
Texts from Lower Zaïre*. Lawrence: University of Kansas Publications in Anthropology.

Jardel, Enrique P., ed. 1992. *Estrategia para la conservación de la Reserva de la Biosfera Sierra de Manantlán: Documento base para la integración del programa de
manejo integral*. Guadalajara: Editorial de la Universidad de Guadalajara.

Jarvie, Ian. 1964. *The Revolution in Anthropology*. New York: Humanities.

Jelin, Elizabeth. 2004. "Ciudadania, derechos e identidad." *Latin American Research
Review* 39, no. 1: 197–201.

Joaquim, Maria Salet. 2001. *O papel da liderança feminina na construção da identidade negra*. Rio de Janeiro: Pallas.

Johnson, Paul Christopher. 2002. *Secrets, Gossip, and Gods*. Oxford: Oxford University Press.

Joseph, Gilbert M. 2001. "Reclaiming 'the Political' at the Turn of the Millennium."
In *Reclaiming the Political in Latin American History*, edited by Gilbert M. Joseph,
3–16. Durham: Duke University Press.

Joseph, Gilbert, and Daniel Nugent, eds. 1994. *Everyday Forms of State Formation:
Revolution and Negotiation of Rule in Modern Mexico*. Durham: Duke University
Press.

Joseph, Gilbert M., and Allen Wells. 1996. *Summer of Discontent, Seasons of Upheaval: Elite Politics and Rural Insurgency in Yucatán, 1876–1915*. Stanford: Stanford University Press.

Kantor, I. 2004. *Esquecidos e renascidos: Historiografia acadêmica luso-americana,
1724–1759*. São Paulo: Hucitec/Centro de Estudos Baianos da UFBA.

Karasch, Mary. 1987. *Slave Life in Rio de Janeiro, 1808–1850*. Princeton: Princeton
University Press.

Karlsson, Bengt G. 2003. "Anthropology and the Indigenous Slot." *Critique of Anthropology* 23, no. 4: 403–23.

Katz, Friedrich. 1988. "Las rebeliones rurales en el México precortesiano y colonial." In *Revuelta, rebelión y revolución: La lucha rural en México del siglo XVI al siglo XX*, edited by Friedrich Katz, 65–93. Mexico City: Ed. Era.

Kearney, Michael. 1972. *Los vientos de Ixtepeji*. Mexico City: Instituto Nacional Indigenista.

———. 1996. *Reconceptualizing the Peasantry: Anthropology in World Perspective*. Boulder, Colo.: Westview.

Keesing, Roger M. 1992. *Custom and Confrontation: The Kwaio Struggle for Cultural Autonomy*. Chicago: University of Chicago Press.

Kellogg, Susan. 1995. *Law and the Transformation of Aztec Culture, 1500–1700*. Norman: University of Oklahoma Press.

Kertzer, David. 1988. *Ritual, Politics, and Power*. New Haven: Yale University Press.

Kittleson, Roger A. 2005. "Women and Notions of Womanhood in Brazilian Abolitionism." In *Gender and Slave Emancipation in the Atlantic World*, edited by Pamela Scully and Diana Paton, 99–140. Durham: Duke University Press.

Klein, Herbert S. 1970. "Rebeliones de las comunidades campesinas: La república tzeltal de 1712." In *Ensayos de antropología en la zona central de Chiapas*, edited by Norman McQuown and Julian Pitt-Rivers, 149–70. Mexico City: Instituto Nacional Indigenista.

Klein, Herbert S., and Clotilde A. de Paiva. 1996. "Freedmen in a Slave Economy: Minas Gerais in 1831." *Journal of Social History* 29, no. 4: 933–62.

Klieman, Kairn. 2003. *"The Pygmies Were Our Compass": Bantu and Batwa in the History of West Central Africa, Early Times to ca. 1900*. Portsmouth: C.E. Heinemann.

Knight, Alan. 1986. *The Mexican Revolution*. 2 vols. Cambridge: Cambridge University Press.

———. 1992. "Revisionism and Revolution: Mexico Compared to England and France." *Past and Present* 134, no. 1: 158–99.

———. 1994. "Cardenismo: Juggernaut or Jalopy?" *Journal of Latin American Studies* 26, no. 1: 73–107.

———. 2002. "Subalterns, Signifiers and Statistics: Perspectives on Mexican Historiography." *Latin American Research Review* 37, no. 2: 136–58.

———. 2007a. "Hegemony, Counterhegemony and the Mexican Revolution." In *Counterhegemony in the Colony and Postcolony*, edited by John Chalcraft and Yaseen Noorani, 23–48. London: Palgrave Macmillan.

———. 2007b. "Patterns and Prescriptions in Mexican Historiography." *Bulletin of Latin American Research* 25, no. 3: 340–66.

Koelle, Sigismund W. 1963. *Polygotta Africana; or, a Comparative Vocabulary of Nearly Three Hundred Words and Phrases, in More than One Hundred Distinct African Languages*. 1854. Edited by P. E. H. Hair and David Dalby. Freetown: Fourah Bay College, University College of Sierra Leone.

Kowarick, Lúcio, ed. 1994. *Lutas sociais e a cidade: São Paulo, passado e presente.* 2nd ed. São Paulo: CEDEC and Paz e Terra.

Krotz, Esteban. 1988. *Utopía.* Mexico City: Universidad Autónoma Metropolitana-Iztapalapa.

Kurlansky, Mark. 2007. *Non-Violence: The History of a Dangerous Idea.* London: Vintage.

Lameiras, José. 1987. "Angel Palerm: Un indigenista original." In *La heterodoxia recuperada (en torno a Ángel Palerm)*, edited by Susana Glantz, 265–84. Mexico City: Fondo de Cultura Económica.

Lapassade, Georges, and Marco Aurélio Luz. 1972. *O segredo da Macumba.* Rio de Janeiro: Paz e Terra.

Lara, Silvia Hunold. 1988. *Campos da violência: Escravos e senhores na capitania do Rio de Janeiro, 1750–1808.* Rio de Janeiro: Paz e Terra.

———. 1995. "'Blowin' in the Wind': E. P. Thompson e a Experiência Negra no Brasil." *Projeto História* 12 (October): 43–56.

Lavalle, Adrián Gurza, and Graziela Castello. 2004. "As benesses desse mundo: Associativismo religioso e inclusão socioeconômica." *Novos Estudos* 68: 73–93.

Lefebvre, Georges. 1973. *The Great Fear of 1789.* New York: Vintage. Orig. pubd. 1932.

Leite, Ilka Boaventura. 2004. *O legado do testamento: A comunidade da Casca em perícia.* Florianópolis: NUER/UFSC.

Leite, Serafim S. J. 1938–50. *História da Companhia de Jesus no Brasil.* Vol. 8. Lisbon and Rio de Janeiro: Portugália/Civilização Brasileira.

León, Pedro, and Raquel Gutiérrez. 1988. *La reforma agraria en la Sierra de Manantlán.* Guadalajara: Documento de Investigación, Laboratorio Natural Las Joyas, Universidad de Guadalajara.

Lepine, Claude. 2005. "Mudanças no candomblé de São Paulo." *Religião e Sociedade* 25, no. 2: 121–35.

Léry, Jean de. 1994. *Histoire d'un voyage en terre de Brésil.* Edited by F. Lestringant, based on the 2nd complete edition. Paris: Livre de Poche. Orig. pubd. 1580.

Levine, Daniel H., and Scott Mainwaring. 1989. "Religion and Popular Protest in Latin America: Contrasting Experiences." In *Power and Popular Protest: Latin American Social Movements*, edited by Susan Eckstein, 203–40. Berkeley: University of California Press.

Levine, Robert. 1992. *Vale of Tears: Revisiting the Canudos Massacre in Northeastern Brazil, 1893–1897.* Berkeley: University of California Press.

Lévi-Strauss, Claude. 1967. *Structural Anthropology.* New York: Doubleday.

Libby, Douglas C., and Afonso de Alencastro Graça Filho. 2003. "Reconstruindo a liberdade: Alforrias e forros na freguesia de São José do Rio das Mortes, 1750–1850." *Vária História* (Belo Horizonte) 30 (July): 112–51.

Libby, Douglas C., and Clotilde A. de Paiva. 2000. "Manumission Practices in a Late Eighteenth-Century Brazilian Slave Parish: São José d'El Rey in 1795." *Slavery and Abolition* 21, no. 1: 96–127.

Lijphart, Arend. 1971. "Comparative Politics and the Comparative Method." *American Political Science Review* 65, no. 3: 682–93.

Lindoso, Dirceu. 1983. *A utopia armada: Rebeliões de pobres nas matas do tombo real*. Rio de Janeiro: Paz e Terra.

Lira González, Andres. 1972. *El amparo colonial y el juicio de amparo mexicano*. Mexico City: Fondo de Cultura Económica.

Lockhart, James. 1999. *Los nahuas después de la conquista*. México: Fondo de Cultura Económica.

Lomnitz-Adler, Claudio. 1992. *Exits from the Labyrinth: Culture and Ideology in the Mexican National Space*. Berkeley: University of California Press.

Long, Norman. 2001. *Development Sociology: Actor Perspectives*. London: Routledge.

López de Cogolludo, Diego. 1957. *Historia de Yucatán*. 5th ed. Prologue and notes by J. Ignacio Rubio Mañé. Mexico City: Academia Literaria.

López Monjardin, Adriana. 1996. "Los guiones ocultos de Chiapas: La resistencia cívica entre los indígenas." *Viento del Sur* 7 (summer): 1–23.

Lovejoy, Paul. 1997. "The African Diaspora: Revisionist Interpretations of Ethnicity, Culture and Religion under Slavery." *Studies in the World History of Slavery, Abolition and Emancipation* 2, no. 1: 1–22. http://www.yorku.ca/nhp/publications/Lovejoy_Studies%20in%20the%20World%20History%20of%20Slavery.pdf.

Lowden, Pamela. 1996. *Moral Opposition to Authoritarian Rule in Chile, 1973–90*. New York: St. Martin's.

Luna, Francisco Vidal, and Herbert S. Klein. 2003. *Slavery and the Economy of São Paulo, 1750–1850*. Stanford: Stanford University Press.

Luna, Francisco Vidal, and Iraci Del Nero da Costa. 1980. "A presença do elemento forro no conjunto de proprietários de escravos." *Ciência e Cultura* 32, no. 7: 836–41.

———. 1982. *Minas Colonial: Economia e Sociedade*. São Paulo: FIPE/Livraria Pioneira Editora.

Macagno, Lorenzo. 2003. "Cidadania e cidades (aventuras e desventuras do multiculturalismo)." *Espaço & Debates* 23, nos. 43–44: 51–59.

Machado, Helena Maria P. T. 1994. *O plano e o pânico: Os movimentos sociais na década da abolição*. Rio de Janeiro: UFRJ/EDUSP.

Maggie, Yvonne. 1992. *Medo do feitiço: Relações entre magia e poder no Brasil*. Rio de Janeiro: Arquivo Nacional.

Mainwaring, Scott. 1986. *The Catholic Church and Politics in Brazil, 1916–1985*. Stanford: Stanford University Press.

Malheiro, Agostinho Marques Perdigão. 1976. *A escravidão no Brasil: Ensaio histórico, jurídico, social*. 1866–67. 3rd ed. 2 vols. Petrópolis: Editora Vozes.

Mallon, Florencia. 1994. "AHR *Forum*: The Promise and Dilemma of Subaltern Studies: Perspectives from Latin American History." *American Historical Review* 99, no. 5: 1491–515.

Mansbridge, Jane. 2001. "The Making of Oppositional Consciousness." In *Opposi-*

tional Consciousness: The Subjective Roots of Social Protest, edited by Jane Mansbridge and Aldon Morris, 1–19. Chicago: University of Chicago Press.

Martínez Casas, Regina. 2007. *Vivir invisibles: La resignificación cultural entre los otomíes urbanos de Guadalajara*. Mexico City: CIESAS (Publicaciones de la Casa Chata).

Martínez Peláez, Severo. n.d. *Motines de indios: La violencia colonial en Centroamérica y Chiapas*. Puebla: Universidad Autónoma de Puebla (Cuadernos de la Casa Presno, 3).

Mattos [de Castro], Hebe Maria. 1998. *Das cores do silêncio: Os significados da liberdade no sudeste escravista—Brasil, século XIX*. 1995. 2nd ed. Rio de Janeiro: Ed. Nova Fronteira.

———. 2000. *Escravidão e cidadania no Brasil monárquico*. Rio de Janeiro: Jorge Zahar.

———. 2008. "'Terras de Quilombo': Land Rights, Memory of Slavery, and Ethnic Identification in Contemporary Brazil." In *Africa, Brazil and the Construction of Trans-Atlantic Black Identities*, edited by Livio Sansone, Élisée Soumonni, and Boubacar Barry, 293–318. Trenton, N.J.: Africa World Press.

McCartney, Clem. 1999. "Northern Ireland: The Role of Civil Society." *Conciliation Resources* website, online at www.c-r.org/, accessed November 1, 2008.

Mejía, María del Carmen, and Sergio Sarmiento Silva. 1987. *La lucha indígena: Un reto a la ortodoxia*. Mexico City: Siglo Veintiuno Editores and the National Autonomous University of Mexico.

Mello Rego, General. 1899. *A rebelião praieira*. Rio de Janeiro: Imprensa Nacional.

Meyer, Jean. 1976. *The Cristero Rebellion: The Mexican People between Church and State, 1926–1929*. Cambridge: Cambridge University Press.

———. 1993a. "El anticlericalismo revolucionario: Un ensayo de empatía histórica." In *Las formas y las políticas del dominio agrario: Homenaje a F. Chevalier*, edited by R. Ávila, 284–306. Mexico City: CEMCA / University of Guadalajara.

———. 1993b. "El conflicto religioso en Chihuahua." In *Actas del III Congreso Internacional de Historia Regional*, 356–66. Ciudad Juárez: University of Ciudad Juárez.

———. 2005. *La Cristiada*. 1973. 21st ed. 3 vols. Mexico City: Siglo XXI.

———. 2007. *El conflicto religioso en Oaxaca, 1926–1938*. Oaxaca City: CIESAS / Instituto de Artes Gráficas de Oaxaca.

Miceli, Sérgio. 1984. *Estado e cultura no Brasil*. São Paulo: DIFEL.

Miller, Joseph C. 1988. *Way of Death: Merchant Capitalism and the Angolan Slave Trade, 1730–1830*. Madison: University of Wisconsin Press.

Mintz, Sidney W., and Richard Price. 1992. *The Birth of African-American Culture: An Anthropological Perspective*. 1974. Boston: Beacon Press.

Mitchell, Timothy. 1990. "Everyday Metaphors of Power." *Theory and Society* 19, no. 5: 545–77.

Mondragón, Jorge Mercado. 2004. "El Acuerdo Nacional para el Campo y la política social del gobierno federal." *El Cotidiano* 19, no. 124: 77–85.

Moniz, Edmundo. 1978. *A guerra social de Canudos*. Rio de Janeiro: Civilização Bra-sileira.

Monteiro, Duglas Teixeira. 1974. *Os errantes do novo século: Um estudo sobre o surto milenarista do Contestado*. São Paulo: Livraria Duas Cidades.

Monteiro, John. 1994. *Negros da Terra*. São Paulo: Companhia das Letras.

Montenegro, Abelardo. 1973. *Fanáticos e cangaceiros*. Fortaleza: Editôra Enriqueta Galeano.

Moore, Barrington Jr. 1966. *Social Origins of Dictatorship and Democracy: Lord and Peasant in the Making of the Modern World*. Boston: Beacon.

———. 1978. *Injustice: The Social Bases of Obedience and Revolt*. New York: Pan-theon.

Moore, Donald S. 1998. "Subaltern Struggles and the Politics of Place: Remapping Resistance in Zimbabwe's Eastern Highlands." *Cultural Anthropology* 13, no. 3: 344–81.

Moreno Badajoz, Rocío. 2004. *Impacto social de programas universitarios de inter-vención: El caso de la Sierra de Manantlán*. B.A. thesis, Universidad del Valle de Atemajac, Guadalajara.

Moura, Clóvis. 2000. *Sociologia política da guerra camponesa de Canudos*. São Paulo: Editora Expressao Popular.

Murão, Lais. 1974. "Contestado: A gestação social do messias." *Cadernos* 7: 59–98.

Myscofski, Carole A. 1988. *When Men Walk Dry: Portuguese Messianism in Brazil*. Atlanta: Scholars Press.

———. 1991. "Messianic Themes in Portuguese and Brazilian Literature in the Six-teenth and Seventeenth Centuries." *Luso-Brazilian Review* 28, no. 1: 77–94.

Nahmad, Salomón. 2007. "Situación social y política de México y de Oaxaca al final del gobierno de Vicente Fox y principios del gobierno de Felipe Calderón." *LASA Forum* 38, no. 2: 24–27.

Navarro, Marysa. 1989. "The Personal Is Political: Las Madres de la Plaza de Mayo." In *Power and Popular Protest: Latin American Social Movements*, edited by Susan Eckstein, 241–58. Berkeley: University of California Press.

Naylor, Thomas H., and Charles W. Polzer. 1986. *The Presidio and Militia on the Northern Frontier of New Spain: A Documentary History, Vol.1, 1570–1700*. Tucson: University of Arizona Press.

Nelson, Diane M. 2005. "Life During Wartime: Guatemala, Vitality, Conspiracy, Milieu." In *Anthropologies of Modernity: Foucault, Governmentality, and Life Poli-tics*, edited by Jonathan Inda, 215–47. Oxford: Blackwell.

O'Dogherty, Laura. 1991. "Restaurarlo todo en Cristo: Unión de Damas Católi-cas Mexicanas, 1920–1926." *Estudios de Historia Moderna y Contemporánea de México* 14: 129–53.

O'Hea, Patrick. 1966. *Reminiscences of the Mexican Revolution*. Mexico City: Centro Anglo-Mexicano del Libro.

Okamura, Jonathan Y. 1981. "Situational Ethnicity." *Ethnic and Racial Studies* 4, no. 4: 452–65.

Oliveira, Pedro A. Ribeiro de. 1985. *Religião e dominação de clase: Gênese, estrutura e funcão do catolicismo romanizado no Brasil*. Petrópolis: Editora Vozes.

Oliveira, Roberto Cardoso de. 1964. *Urbanização e tribalismo: A integração dos índios Terêna numa sociedade de classes*. Rio de Janeiro: Zahar.

Oliviera, João. n.d. "Vida e morte do meu padrinho." Santa Brígida: Mayor's office publication.

Olson, Mancur. 1965. *The Logic of Collective Action: Public Goods and the Theory of Groups*. Cambridge: Harvard University Press.

Olvera, Alberto J. 1992. "The Rise and Fall of Union Democracy at Poza Rica, 1932–1940." In *The Mexican Petroleum Industry in the Twentieth Century*, edited by Jonathan Charles Brown and Alan Knight, 63–89. Austin: University of Texas Press.

Ortiz, Renato. 1991. *A morte branca do feiticeiro negro: Umbanda e sociedade Brasileira*. São Paulo: Editora Brasiliense.

Ortner, Sherry B. 1995. "Resistance and the Problem of Ethnographic Refusal." *Comparative Studies in Society and History* 37, no. 1: 173–93.

Osorno, Diego Enrique. 2007. *Oaxaca sitiada: La primera insurrección del siglo XXI*. Mexico City: Editorial Grijalbo.

Otten, Alexandre. 1994. "Apocalíptica popular: uma dimensão da visão escatológica de Antônio Conselheiro." *Religião and Sociedade* 16, no. 3: 64–79.

Paige, Jeffery M. 1975. *Agrarian Revolution: Social Movements and Export Agriculture in the Underdeveloped World*. New York: Free Press.

Paiva, Eduardo França. 2001. *Escravidão e universo cultural na Colônia: Minas Gerais, 1716–1789*. Belo Horizonte: Ed. UFMG.

Palerm, Ángel, ed. 1976. *Aguirre Beltrán: Obra polémica*. Mexico City: Centro de Investigaciones Superiores del Instituto Nacional de Antropología e Historia (Col. SEP-INAH).

Palmié, Stephan. 1995. "Against Syncretism: 'Africanizing' and 'Cubanizing' Discourses in North American Òrìsà Worship." In *Counterworks: Managing the Diversity of Knowledge*, edited by Richard Fardon, 73–94. London: Routledge.

Pang, Eul-Soo. 1981. "Banditry and Messianism in Brazil, 1870–1940." *Proceedings of the Pacific Coast Council on Latin American Studies* 8: 1–23.

Parés, Luis Nicolau. 2005. "The Nagôization Process in Bahian Candomblé." In *The Yoruba Diaspora in the Atlantic World*, edited by Toyin Falola and Matt D. Childs, 185–208. Bloomington: Indiana University Press.

———. 2006. *A formação do candomblé: História e ritual da nação jeje na Bahia*. Campinas: Editora da Unicamp.

Payne, Leigh A. 2000. *Uncivil Movements: The Armed Right Wing and Democracy in Latin America*. Baltimore: Johns Hopkins University Press.

Paz, Renata Marinho. 1998. *As beatas do Padre Cícero: Participação feminina leiga no movimento sócio-religioso de Juazeiro do Norte*. Juazeiro do Norte: Edições IPESC-URCA.

Peel, John D. Y. 1989. "The Cultural Work of Yoruba Ethnogenesis." In *History and*

Ethnicity, edited by Elizabeth Tonkin, Maryon McDonald, and Malcolm Chapman, 198–215. London: Routledge.

———. 2000. *Religious Encounters and the Making of the Yoruba*. Bloomington: Indiana University Press.

Pereira da Costa, Francisco A. 1983. *Anais Pernambucanos*. Vol. 9. Recife: Fundarpe.

Pereira de Berredo, Bernardo. 1989. *Anais Históricos do Estado do Maranhão*. 1749. Rio de Janeiro: Tipo.

Pérez Castañeda, Juan Carlos. 2002. *El nuevo sistema de propiedad agraria en México*. Mexico City: Palabra en Vuelo.

Pérez Ruiz, Maya Lorena. 2002. "Del comunalismo a las megaciudades: El nuevo rostro de los indígenas urbanos." In *La antropología sociocultural en el México del milenio: Búsquedas, encuentros y transiciones*, edited by Guillermo de la Peña and Luis Vázquez León, 295–342. Mexico City: Fondo de Cultura Económica/ Consejo Nacional para la Cultura y las Artes.

Pessar, Patricia R. 1981. "Unmasking the Politics of Religion: The Case of Brazilian Millenarianism." *Journal of Latin American Lore* 7, no. 2: 255–78.

———. 1982. "Millenarian Movements in Rural Brazil: Prophecy and Protest." *Religion* 12: 187–213.

———. 1991. "Three Moments in Brazilian Millenarianism: The Interrelationship Between Politics and Religion." *Luso-Brazilian Review* 28, no. 1: 95–116.

———. 2004. *From Fanatics to Folk*. Durham: Duke University Press.

Pessoa de Mello, Urbano Sabino. 1978. *Apreciação da revolta praieira em Pernambuco*. 1849. Brasília: Senado Federal.

Phillips, Ulrich B. 1929. *Life and Labor in the Old South*. Boston: Little, Brown.

———. 1966. *American Negro Slavery*. Baton Rouge: Louisiana State University Press. Orig. pubd. 1918.

Pinho, Patricia de Santana. 1997. "Revisando Canudos hoje no imaginário popular." *Revista Canudos* 1, no. 1: 173–203.

———. 2004. *Reinvenções da África na Bahia*. São Paulo: Anna Blume.

Pinto, Roque. 2001. "Como a cidade de Salvador empreende a produção do exótico através do texto da baianidade." M.A. thesis, Universidade Federal da Bahia, Salvador.

Pirola, Ricardo Figueiredo. Forthcoming. *Senzala insurgente: Malungos, parentes e rebeldes nas fazendas de Campinas, 1832*. Campinas: Editora da Unicamp.

Pompa, Cristina. 2003. *Religião como tradução: Missionários, Tupi e Tapuia no Brasil colonial*. Bauru: Edusc/Anpocs.

Postero, Nancy Grey. 2006. *Now We Are Citizens: Indigenous Politics in Postmulticultural Bolivia*. Stanford: Stanford University Press.

Powell, Jonathan. 2008. *Great Hatred, Little Room: Making Peace in Northern Ireland*. London: Bodley Head.

Powell, Philip W. 1977. *La guerra chichimeca, 1550–1600*. Mexico City: Fondo de Cultura Económica.

Prandi, Reginaldo. 1991. *Os candomblés de São Paulo (A velha magia na metrópole nova)*. São Paulo: HUCITEC-EDUSP.

Price, Richard. 2003. "O milagre da crioulização: retrospectiva." *Estudos Afro-Asiáticos* 25, no. 3: 383–419.

Puntoni, Pedro. 2002. *A guerra dos bárbaros: Povos indígenas e a colonização do sertão nordeste do Brasil, 1650–1720*. São Paulo: Edusp/Hucitec/Fapesp.

Queiroz, Maria Isaura Pereira de. 1965. *O messianismo no Brasil e no mundo*. São Paulo: Dominus.

Quintas, Amaro. 1985. "O Nordeste, 1825–1850." In *História geral da civilização brasileira*, vol. 2, edited by Sérgio Buarque de Holanda, 193–241. São Paulo: Difel.

Quirk, Robert E. 1973. *The Mexican Revolution and the Catholic Church, 1910–1929*. Bloomington: Indiana University Press.

Quiroga, Vasco de. 1985. *Información en derecho*. Edited by Carlos Herrejón. Mexico City: Secretaría de Educación Pública.

Ramos, Alcida Rita. 1998. *Indigenism: Ethnic Politics in Brazil*. Madison: University of Wisconsin Press.

Recopilación de leyes de los reynos de las Indias. 1987. Edited by Francisco de Icaza Doufour. Mexico City: M. A. Porrúa.

Reina, Leticia. 1987–88. "Las rebeliones indígenas y campesinas (periodo colonial y siglo XIX)." In *La antropología en México: Panorama histórico*, vol. 4, edited by Carlos García Mora and Martín Villalobos Salgado, 517–42. Mexico City: Instituto Nacional de Antropología e Historia.

Reis, João José. 1993. *Slave Rebellion in Brazil: The Muslim Uprising of 1835 in Bahia*. Translated by Arthur Brakel. Baltimore: Johns Hopkins University Press.

———. 2001. "Candomblé in Nineteenth-Century Bahia: Priests, Followers, Clients." *Slavery and Abolition* 22, no. 1: 116–34.

———. 2003. *Rebelião escrava no Brasil: A história do levante dos Malês em 1835*. 1986. 2nd Brazilian edition, revised and expanded from the 1993 English-language edition. São Paulo: Companhia das Letras.

Reis, João José, and Eduardo Silva. 1989. *Negociação e conflito: A resistência negra no Brasil escravista*. São Paulo: Companhia das Letras.

Restrepo, Eduardo, and Arturo Escobar. 2005. "'Other Anthropologies and Anthropology Otherwise': Steps to a World Anthropology Framework." *Critique of Anthropology* 25, no. 2: 99–129.

Reyes Ramos, María Eugenia. 2008. "La oposición al Procede en Chiapas: Un análisis regional." *El Cotidiano* 147: 5–19.

Ribeiro, Darcy. 1970. *Os indios e a civilização*. Rio de Janeiro: Civilizacão Brasileira.

Rios, Ana Maria Lugão, and Hebe Mattos [de Castro]. 2005. *Memórias do cativeiro: Família, trabalho e cidadania no pós-abolição*. Rio de Janeiro: Civilização Brasileira.

Ríos, Julio. 2002. *La Iglesia en Chiapas*. Preface by Jean Meyer. Mexico City: INEHRM.

Rivera Herrejón, Gladys. 2000. "Por qué los ejidatarios están ignorando la reforma del ejido? Dos experiencias en el Centro de México." Paper presented at the 12th International Congress of the Latin American Studies Association, Miami, March 16–18.

Robertson Sierra, Margarita Teresa. 2002. "Nos cortaron las ramas, pero nos dejaron la raíz: Identidad indígena en Ayotitlán." M.A. thesis, El Colegio de Jalisco, Guadalajara.

Robles Berlanga, Héctor Manuel. 2008. "Saldos de las reformas de 1992 al Artículo 27 constitucional." *Estudios Agrarios* 38: 131–50.

Rocha, Elizabeth Guimarães Teixeira. 2005. "O Decreto 4887 e a regulamentação das terras dos remanescentes das comunidades dos quilombos." *Boletim informativo do NUER: Territórios quilombolas: reconhecimento e titulação das terras* 2, no 2: 97–102.

Rocha Pita, Sebastião da. 1980. *História da América Portuguesa*. 1730. São Paulo: Edusp/Itatitaia.

Rodrigues, Raimundo Nina. 1897. "A loucura epidemica de Canudos." *Revista Brasileira* 2: 129–218.

Rojas, Rosa, ed. 1996. *La comunidad y sus recursos: Ayotitlán: ¿desarrollo sustentable?* Guadalajara: Universidad de Guadalajara / Instituto Nacional Indigenista.

Rose, Nikolas. 1999. *Powers of Freedom: Reframing Political Thought*. Cambridge: Cambridge University Press.

Roseberry, William. 1994. "Hegemony and the Language of Contention." In *Everyday Forms of State Formation: Revolution and the Negotiation of Rule in Modern Mexico*, edited by Gilbert M. Joseph and Daniel Nugent, 355–66. Durham: Duke University Press.

———. 1998. "'El estricto apego a la ley': Liberal Law and Communal Rights in Porfirian Pátzcuaro." Paper presented at the 11th International Congress of the Latin American Studies Association, Chicago, Illinois, September 24–26.

———. 1999. "*Para calmar los ánimos entre los vecinos de este lugar*: Community and Conflict in Porfirian Pátzcuaro." Paper presented at the 113th Annual Meeting of the American Historical Association, Washington, January 7–10.

Rudé, George. 1980. *Ideology and Popular Protest*. London: Lawrence and Wishart.

Rummel, Rudolph J. 1994. *Death by Government*. New Brunswick, N.J.: Transaction.

Ruz, Mario Humberto. 1992. "Los rostros de la resistencia: Los mayas ante el dominio hispano." In *Del katun al siglo: Tiempos de colonialismo y resistencia entre los mayas*, edited by María del Carmen León, Mario Ruz, and José Alejos García, 85–162. Mexico City: CONACULTA.

Sahlins, Marshall. 1997. "O 'pessimismo sentimental' e a experiência etnográfica: Por que a cultura não é um 'objeto' em extinção (Part I)." *Mana* 3, no. 2: 103–50.

———. 2002. *Waiting for Foucault, Still*. Chicago: Prickly Paradigm.

Salles, Ricardo. 2008. *E o Vale era o escravo: Vassouras, século XIX: Senhores e escravos no coração do Império*. Rio de Janeiro: Civilização Brasileira.

Salomon, Frank, and Stuart B. Schwartz, eds. 1999. *Cambridge History of the Native*

Peoples of the Americas, Volume III: South America. Parts 1 and 2. Cambridge: Cambridge University Press.

Salvador, Frei Vicente do. 1889. *História do Brasil.* 1627. Rio de Janeiro: Biblioteca Nacional.

Sampaio, Patrícia Melo. 2000. "Desigualdades étnicas e legislação colonial: Pará, c. 1798-c.1820." *Amazônia em Cadernos* 6: 317–43.

Sampaio, Teodoro. 1987. *O Tupi na Geografia Nacional.* 5th ed. São Paulo: Companhia Editora Nacional. Orig. pubd. 1901.

Sanabria, Harry. 2000. "Resistance and the Arts of Domination: Miners and the Bolivian State." *Latin American Perspectives* 27, no. 1: 56–81.

Sánchez de Tagle, Esteban. 2000. "La remodelación urbana de la Ciudad de México en el Siglo XVIII: Una crítica de los supuestos." *Tiempos de América* 5–6: 9–19.

Sansi, Roger. 2001. "Art, Religion, and the Public Sphere in Salvador de Bahia, Brazil." In *Working Papers Series in Latin American Studies.* Chicago: University of Chicago.

———. 2007. *Fetishes and Monuments: Afro-Brazilian Art and Culture in the 20th Century.* New York: Berghahn Books.

Sansone, Livio. 2004. *Negritude sem etnicidade.* Salvador: Edufba/Pallas.

Santa María, Fray Vicente de. 1973. *Relación histórica de la colonización del Nuevo Santander.* Mexico City: Universidad Nacional Autónoma de México.

Santos, Jocélio Teles dos. 2005. *O poder da cultura e a cultura no poder: A disputa simbólica da herança cultural negra no Brasil.* Salvador: Edufba.

———, ed. 2007. *Regularização Fundiária dos Terreiros de Candomblés.* Salvador: CEAO, Sehab/Semur, Fundação Palmares/Seppir.

Santos Gómez, Hugo. 1999. "Conflictos agrarios en la región mixe: Cacalotepec vs. Huayapam." *Estudios Agrarios* 11: 145–60.

Schell, Patience A. 2003. *Church and State Education in Revolutionary Mexico City.* Tucson: University of Arizona Press.

Schultz, Kristin. 2001. *Tropical Versailles.* New York: Routledge.

Schwartz, Stuart B. 1977. "Resistance and Accomodation in Eighteenth-Century Brazil: The Slaves' View of Slavery." *Hispanic American Historical Review* 57, no. 1: 69–81.

———. 1982. "Patterns of Slaveholding in the Americas: New Evidence from Brazil." *American Historical Review* 87, no. 1 (February): 55–86.

———. 1985. *Sugar Plantations in the Formation of Brazilian Society: Bahia, 1550–1835.* Cambridge: Cambridge University Press.

Schwartz, Stuart B., and Frank Salomon. 1999. "New Peoples and New Kinds of People: Adaptation, Readjustment, and Ethnogenesis in South American Indigenous Societies (Colonial Era)." In *Cambridge History of the Native Peoples of the Americas, Vol. III: South America*, part 2, edited by Frank Salomon and Stuart B. Schwartz, 443–501. Cambridge: Cambridge University Press.

Schwartz, Stuart B., and Hal Langfur. 2005. "Tapanhuns, Negros da Terra, and Curibocas: Common Cause and Confrontation between Blacks and Natives in Colonial Brazil." In *Beyond Black and Red: African-Native Relations in Colonial Latin America*, edited by Matthew Restall, 81–114. Albuquerque: University of New Mexico Press.

Schwarz, Roberto. 1992. *Misplaced Ideas: Essays on Brazilian Culture*. London: Verso.

Scott, James C. 1976. *The Moral Economy of the Peasant: Rebellion and Subsistence in Southeast Asia*. New Haven: Yale University Press.

———. 1985. *Weapons of the Weak: Everyday Forms of Peasant Resistance*. New Haven: Yale University Press.

———. 1986. "Everyday Forms of Peasant Resistance." In *Everyday Forms of Peasant Resistance in South-East Asia*, edited by James C. Scott and Benedict Kerkvliet, 5–35. London: Frank Cass.

———. 1987. "Resistance without Protest and without Organization: Peasant Opposition to the Islamic *Zaket* and the Christian Tithe." *Comparative Studies in Society and History* 29: 417–52.

———. 1990. *Domination and the Arts of Resistance: Hidden Transcripts*. New Haven: Yale University Press.

———. 1994. Foreword to *Everyday Forms of State Formation: Revolution and Negotiation of Rule in Modern Mexico*, edited by Gilbert Joseph and Daniel Nugent, vii-xii. Durham: Duke University Press.

Scott, Joan W. 1986. "Gender: A Useful Category of Historical Analysis." *American Historical Review* 91, no. 5: 1053–75.

Seed, Patricia. 1995. *Ceremonies of Possession in Europe's Conquest of the New World, 1492–1640*. Cambridge: Cambridge University Press.

Selka, Stephen. 2008. "The Sisterhood of Boa Morte in Brazil: Harmonious Mixture, Black Resistance, and the Politics of Religious Practice." *Journal of Latin American and Caribbean Anthropology* 13, no. 1: 79–114.

Serra, Ordep. 1995. *Águas do Rei*. Petrópolis: Editora Vozes.

———. 2005. "Monumentos negros: Uma experiência." *Afro-Ásia* 33: 169–205.

Seymour, Susan. 2006. "Resistance." *Anthropological Theory* 6, no. 3: 303–21.

Shukla, Sandhya, and Heidi Tinsman, eds. 2007. *Imagining Our Americas: Toward a Transnational Frame*. Durham: Duke University Press.

Silva, Cristiano Lima da. 2004. "Como se livre nascera: A alforria na pia batismal em S. João Del Rei (1750–1850)." M.A. thesis, Universidade Federal Fluminense, Niterói.

Silva, Lígia Osório. 1996. *Terras devolutas e latifúndio: Efeitos da Lei de 1850*. Campinas: Editora da UNICAMP.

Silva, Vagner Gonçalves da. 1995. *Orixás da metropole*. 1992. Petrópolis: Editora Vozes.

———. 2001. *O antropólogo e sua magia*. São Paulo: EDUSP.

———. 2007. *Intolerância religiosa: Impactos do neopentecostalismo no campo religioso afro-brasileiro*. São Paulo: EDUSP.

Silva Prada, Natalia. 2007. *La política de una rebelión: Los indígenas frente al tumulto de 1692 en la ciudad de México*. Mexico City: El Colegio de México.

Silveira, Renato da. 1988. "Pragmatismo e milagres de fé no Extremo Ocidente." In *Escravidão e invenção da liberdade: Estudos sobre o negro no Brasil*, edited by João José Reis, 166–97. São Paulo: Editora Brasiliense.

Simpson, Eyler. 1937. *The Ejido: Mexico's Way Out*. Chapel Hill: University of North Carolina Press.

Skocpol, Theda. 1979. *States and Social Revolutions*. Cambridge: Cambridge University Press.

Slater, Candace. 1986. *Trails of Miracles: Stories from a Pilgrimage in Northeast Brazil*. Berkeley: University of California Press.

Slenes, Robert W. 1976. "The Demography and Economics of Brazilian Slavery: 1850–1888." Ph.D. diss., Stanford University.

————. 1999. *Na senzala, uma flor: Esperanças e recordações na formação da família escrava—Brasil sudeste, século XIX*. Rio de Janeiro: Nova Fronteira.

————. 2000. "'Malungu, Ngoma vem!' África coberta e descoberta no Brasil." 1991–92. In *Mostra do redescobrimento: Negro de corpo e alma—Black in Body and Soul*, edited by Nelson Aguilar, 212–20. São Paulo: Fundação Bienal de São Paulo/Associação Brasil 500 Anos Artes Visuais.

————. 2002. "The Great Porpoise-Skull Strike: Central-African Water Spirits and Slave Identity in Early Nineteenth-Century Rio de Janeiro." In *Central Africans in the Atlantic Diaspora*, edited by Linda Heywood, 183–208. Cambridge: Cambridge University Press.

————. 2004. "The Brazilian Internal Slave Trade, 1850–1888: Regional Economies, Slave Experience and the Politics of a Peculiar Market." In *The Chattel Principle: Internal Slave Trades in the Americas*, edited by Walter Johnson, 325–70. New Haven: Yale University Press.

————. 2006. "'Tumult and Silence' in Rio de Janeiro, 1848: Central-African Cults of Affliction (and Rebellion) in the Abolition of the Brazilian Slave Trade." Paper presented at the XXVI International Congress of the Latin American Studies Association, San Juan, Puerto Rico, March 15–18.

————. 2007a. "'Eu venho de muito longe, eu venho cavando': Jongueiros cumba na senzala centro-africana." In *Memória do Jongo: As Gravações Históricas de Stanley J. Stein: Vassouras, 1949*, edited by Silvia Hunold Lara and Gustavo Pacheco, 109–56. Rio de Janeiro: Folha Seca.

————. 2007b. "L'arbre *nsanda* replanté: Cultes d'affliction kongo et identité des esclaves de plantation dans le Brésil du Sud-Est entre 1810 et 1888." *Cahiers du Brésil Contemporain* 67–68: 217–313.

————. 2008. "Saint Anthony at the Crossroads in Kongo and Brazil: 'Creolization' and Identity Politics in the Black South Atlantic, ca. 1700/1850." In *Africa, Brazil and the Construction of Trans-Atlantic Black Identities*, edited by Livio Sansone, Élisée Soumonni, and Boubacar Barry, 209–54. Lawrenceville, N.J.: Africa World Press.

Snyder, Richard. 2001. *Politics after Neoliberalism: Reregulation in Mexico*. Cambridge: Cambridge University Press.

Soares, Márcio de Sousa. 2009. *A remissão do cativeiro: A dádiva da alforria e o governo dos escravos nos Campos dos Goitacases, c. 1750–1830*. Rio de Janeiro: Apicuri.

Soares, Mariza. 2000. *Devotos da cor: Identidade étinica, religiosidade e escravidão no Rio de Janeiro, século XVIII*. Rio de Janeiro: Civilização Brasileira.

Sommer, Barbara Ann. 2000. "Negotiated Settlements: Native Amazonians and Portuguese Policy in Pará, Brazil, 1758–1798." Ph.D. diss., University of New Mexico, Albuquerque.

Spicer, Edward H. 1962. *Cycles of Conquest: The Impact of Spain, Mexico and the United States on the Indians of the Southwest, 1533–1960*. Tucson: University of Arizona Press.

———. 1971. "Persistent Ethnicity Systems." *Science* 174, no. 4011: 795–800.

Spitzer, Leo. 1989. *Lives in Between: Assimilation and Marginality in Austria, Brazil, West Africa, 1780–1945*. Cambridge: Cambridge University Press.

Staden, Hans. 1874. *The Captivity of Hans Staden of Hesse in A.D. 1547–1555: Among the Wild Tribes of Eastern Brazil*. 1557. Translated by Albert Tootal and edited by Richard Burton. London: Hakluyt Society.

Starn, Orin. 1992. "'I Dreamed of Foxes and Hawks': Reflections on Peasant Protest, New Social Movements and the Rondas Campesinas of Northen Peru." In *The Making of Social Movements in Latin America: Identity, Strategy and Democracy*, edited by Arturo Escobar and Sonia E. Alvarez, 89–111. Boulder, Colo.: Westview.

Steil, Carlos Alberto. 1996. *Os sertão das romarias: Um estudo antropológico sobre o santúario de Bom Jesus da Lapa, Bahia*. Petrópolis: Editora Vozes.

Stein, Stanley J. 1985. *Vassouras, a Brazilian Coffee County, 1850–1900*. 1958. 2nd ed. Princeton: Princeton University Press.

Stern, Steve J. 2001. "Between Tragedy and Promise: The Politics of Writing Latin American History in the Late Twentieth Century." In *Reclaiming the Political in Latin American History*, edited by Gilbert M. Joseph, 32–77. Durham: Duke University Press.

Stoll, David. 1999. *Rigoberta Menchú and the Story of All Poor Guatemalans*. Boulder, Colo.: Westview Press.

Stolle-McAllister, John. 2005. "What Does Democracy Look Like? Local Movements Challenge the Mexican Transition." *Latin American Perspectives* 32, no. 4: 15–35.

"Sublevación de los indios tzendales: Año de 1713." 1948. *Boletín del Archivo General de la Nación* 19, no. 4: 497–535.

Sweet, David G. 1992. "Native Resistance in Eighteenth-Century Amazonia: the 'Abominable' Mura in War and Peace." *Radical History* 53: 49–80.

Tarrow, Sidney. 1994. *Power in Movement: Social Movements, Collective Actions, and Politics*. Cambridge: Cambridge University Press.

———. 1996. "Social Movements in Contentious Politics: A Review Article." *American Political Science Review* 90, no. 4: 874–83.

Taylor, William B. 1979. *Drinking, Homicide, and Rebellion in Colonial Mexican Villages*. Stanford: Stanford Universty Press.

———. 1987. *Embriaguez, homicidio y rebelión en las poblaciones coloniales mexicanas*. Mexico City: Fondo de Cultura Económica.

———. 1994. "Santiago's Horse: Christianity and Colonial Indian Resistance in the Heartland of New Spain." In *Violence, Resistance and Survival in the Americas*, edited by William Taylor and Franklin Pease, 153–89. Washington, D.C.: Smithsonian Institution.

———. 1996. *Magistrates of the Sacred: Priests and Parishioners in Eighteenth-Century Mexico*. Stanford: Stanford University Press.

Teixeira, Elenaldo. 2001. *O local e o global: Limites e desafios da participação cidadã*. São Paulo: Editora Cortez.

Teles, Edward E. 2004. *Race in Another America: The Significance of Skin Color in Brazil*. Princeton: Princeton University Press.

Thompson, Edward P. 1968. *The Making of the English Working Class*. Rev. ed. Harmondsworth: Pelican Books.

———. 1971. "The Moral Economy of the English Crowd in the 18th Century." *Past and Present* 50: 76–136.

———. 1974. "Patrician Society, Plebean Culture." *Journal of Social History* 7, no. 4: 382–405.

———. 1978a. "The Peculiarities of the English." In *The Poverty of Theory and Other Essays*. New York: Monthly Review. Orig. pubd. 1965.

———. 1978b. "Eighteenth-Century English Society: Class Struggle without Class." *Social History* 3, no. 2: 133–65.

Thompson, Robert Farris. 1981. *The Four Moments of the Sun: Kongo Art in Two Worlds*. Washington: National Gallery of Art.

———. 1984. *Flash of the Spirit: African and Afro-American Art and Philosophy*. New York: Vintage Books.

Thornton, John K. 1988. "On the Trail of Voodoo: African Christianity in Africa and the Americas." *The Americas* 44, no. 3: 261–78.

———. 1991. "African Roots of the Stono Rebellion." *American Historical Review* 96: 1101–13.

———. 1997. "As guerras civis no Congo e o tráfico de escravos: A história e a demografia de 1718 a 1844 revisitadas." *Estudos Afro-Asiáticos* 32 (December): 55–74.

———. 1998a. *Africa and Africans in the Making of the Atlantic World, 1400–1800*. 1992. 2nd ed. Cambridge: Cambridge University Press.

———. 1998b. *The Kongolese Saint Anthony: Dona Beatriz Kimpa Vita and the Antonian Movement, 1684–1706*. Cambridge: Cambridge University Press.

———. 2002. "Religious and Ceremonial Life in the Kongo and Mbundu Areas, 1500–1700." In *Central Africans in the Atlantic Diaspora*, edited by Linda Heywood, 71–90. Cambridge: Cambridge University Press.

Tilly, Charles. 1986. *The Contentious French: Four Centuries of Popular Struggle*. Cambridge: Harvard University Press.

————. 1991. "Domination, Resistance, Compliance . . . Discourse." *Sociological Forum* 6, no. 3: 593–602.

————. 1995. "Contentious Repertoires in Britain, 1758–1834." In *Repertoires and Cycles of Collective Action*, edited by Mark Trangott, 15–42. Durham: Duke University Press.

Tilly, Charles, Louise Tilly, and Richard Tilly. 1975. *The Rebellious Century, 1830–1930*. Cambridge: Harvard University Press.

Tomich, Dale W. 2004. "The Second Slavery: Bonded Labor and the Transformation of the Nineteenth-Century World Economy." In *Through the Prism of Slavery: Labor, Capital and World Economy*, 56–71. Lanham, Md.: Rowman and Littlefield.

Torres, Gabriel, and Joel Cuevas. n.d. "Una historia discordante: el campo jalisciense, entre la modernización y el desarrollo." Unpublished manuscript.

Touraine, Alain. 2005. *Um novo paradigma: Para compreender o mundo de hoje*. Petrópolis: Editora Vozes.

Trouillot, Michael-Rolph. 1988. "Culture on the Edges: Creolization in the Plantation Context." *Plantation Society in the Americas* 5, no. 1: 8–28.

Tully, James. 1995. *Strange Multiplicity: Constitutionalism in an Age of Diversity*. Cambridge: Cambridge University Press.

Tutino, John. 1990. "Cambio social agrario y rebelión campesina en el México decimonónico: El caso de Chalco." In *Revuelta, rebelión y revolución: La lucha rural en México del siglo XVI al siglo XX*, vol. 1, edited by Friedrich Katz, 94–134. Mexico City: Era.

UACI (Unidad de Apoyo a las Comunidades Indígenas). 2000. "Rescate y valoración de los sistemas normativos tradicionales y asesoría jurídica en materia agraria para el Pueblo Nahua de la Sierra de Manantlán." Guadalajara: Universidad de Guadalajara.

Vaca, Augustín. 2006. "Devociones y trabajos de Margarita Gómez González." In *Siete historias de vida: Mujeres jaliscienses del siglo XIX*, edited by Anayanci Fregoso Centeno, 91–121. Guadalajara: Universidad de Guadalajara.

Vainfas, Ronaldo. 1995. *A heresia dos índios: Catolicismo e rebeldia no Brasil colonial*. São Paulo: Companhia das Letras.

Van den Hoogen, Lisette. 1990. "The Romanization of the Brazilian Church: Women's Participation in a Religious Association in Prados, Minas Gerais." *Sociological Analysis* 51, no. 2: 171–88.

Van de Port, Mattijs. 2005. "Sacerdotes midiáticos: O candomblé, discursos de celebridade e a legitimação da autoridade religiosa na esfera pública baiana." *Religião e Sociedade* 25, no. 2: 32–61.

Van Dijk, Rijk, Ria Reis, and Marja Spierenburg, eds. 2000. *The Quest for Fruition through Ngoma: Political Aspects of Healing in Southern Africa*. Oxford: James Currey.

Vangelista, Chiara. 1991. "Los Payaguá entre Asunción y Cuiabá: formación y decadencia de una frontera indígena (1719–1790)." In *Conquesta i Resistencia en la*

Història d'Amèrica, edited by P. García Jordán, 151–65. Barcelona: Universitat de Barcelona.

Vansina, Jan. 1989. "Deep-Down Time: Political Tradition in Central Africa." *History in Africa* 16: 341–62.

———. 1990. *Paths in the Rainforests: Toward a History of Political Tradition in Equatorial África*. Madison: University of Wisconsin Press.

———. 2002. Preface to *Central Africans in the Atlantic Diaspora*, edited by Linda Heywood, xi-xiii. Cambridge: Cambridge University Press.

———. 2004. *How Societies Are Born: Governance in West Central Africa Before 1600*. Charlottesville: University of Virginia Press.

Van Young, Eric. 1992. "El sociópata: Agustín Marroquín." In *Organización y liderazgo en los movimientos populares novohispanos*, edited by Felipe Castro, Virginia Guedea, and José Luis Mirafuentes, 219–54. Mexico City: Universidad Nacional Autónoma de México.

Vasconcelos, José. 1957a. *Obras Completas: Tomo I*. Mexico City: Libreros Mexicanos Unidos.

———. 1957b. *Obras Completas: Tomo II*. Mexico City: Libreros Mexicanos Unidos.

Vidal, Gore. 2004. *Imperial America*. Forest Row: Clairview.

Vieira, Antônio S. J. 1992. "Relação da Missão da Serra de Ibiapaba." 1656. In *Escritos instrumentais sobre os índios*, edited by J. C. Sebe Bom Meihy, 127–31. São Paulo: Educ.

Vilas, Carlos M. 2002. "By Their Own Hands: Lynchings in Contemporary Mexico." *Southwestern Journal of Law and Trade in the Americas* 8, no. 2: 319–20.

Villa, Marco Antonio. 1997. *Canudos: O povo da terra*. São Paulo: Editora Atica.

Vinhas de Queiroz, Mauricio. 1966. *Messianismo e conflicto social*. Rio de Janeiro: Editora Civilação Brasileira.

Viqueira, Juan Pedro. 1995. "Las causas de una rebelión india: Chiapas, 1712." In *Chiapas: Los rumbos de otra historia*, edited by Juan Pedro Viqueira and Mario Humberto Ruz, 103–43. Mexico City: Universidad Nacional Autónoma de México/Centro de Investigaciones y Estudios Superiores en Antropología Social/Centro de Estudios Mexicanos y Centroamericanos/Universidad de Guadalajara.

———. 2002. "¿Qué había detrás del petate de la ermita de Cancuc?" In *Encrucijadas chiapanecas: Economía, religión e identidades*. Mexico City: Tusquets Editores/El Colegio de México.

———. 2005. "La otra bibliografía sobre los indígenas de Chiapas." *Nuevos Mundos*. http://nuevomundo.revues.org/, accessed November 1, 2008.

———. 2007. "Gerónimo Saraos, fiscal y vicario rebelde: La red de poderes indios durante la sublevación de Cancuc, Chiapas, en 1712." In *La resistencia en el mundo maya*, edited by María del Carmen Valverde, 65–105. Mexico City: Universidad Nacional Autónoma de México.

Viveiros de Castro, E. 1993. "Histórias ameríndias (resenha de *História dos Índios no Brasil*, Manuela Carneiro da Cunha, ed.)." *Novos Estudos do Cebrap* 36:22–33.

Vos, Jan de. 1994. *Vivir en frontera: La experiencia de los indios de Chiapas*. Mexico City: Centro de Investigaciones y Estudios Superiores en Antropología Social and Instituto Nacional Indigenista.

Wafer, Jim. 1991. *The Taste of Blood: Spirit Possession in Brazilian Candomblé*. Philadelphia: University of Pennsylvania Press.

Walker, Charles F. 1999. *Smouldering Ashes: Cuzco and the Creation of Republican Peru, 1780–1840*. Durham: Duke University Press.

Walzer, Michael. 1992. *Just and Unjust Wars*. New York: Basic Books.

Warman, Arturo. 1976. . . . *Y venimos a contradecir: Los campesinos del oriente de Morelos y el estado nacional*. Mexico City: Centro de Investigaciones Superiores del INAH.

Warman, Arturo, and Arturo Argueta, eds. 1993. *Movimientos indígenas contemporáneos en México*. Mexico City: Miguel Ángel Porrúa and UNAM-CIIH.

Weiner, Annette B. 1992. *Inalienable Possessions: The Paradox of Keeping-While-Giving*. Berkeley: University of California Press.

Weinstein, Barbara. 2006. "Inventing the 'Mulher Paulista': Politics, Rebellion, and the Gendering of Brazilian Regional Identities." *Journal of Women's History* 18, no. 1: 22–49.

Welch, Stephen. 1993. *The Concept of Political Culture*. Basingstoke: Macmillan.

Werneck Sodré, Nelson. 1965. *História Militar do Brasil*. Rio de Janeiro: Civilização Brasileira.

Whitehead, Neil. 1990. "Carib Ethnic Soldiering in Venezuela, the Guianas, and the Antilles, 1492–1820." *Ethnohistory* 37, no. 4: 357–85.

———. 1993. "Ethnic Transformation and Historical Discontinuity in Native Amazonia and Guayana, 1500–1900." *L'Homme* 33, nos. 126–28: 285–305.

Williams, Raymond. 1977. *Marxism and Literature*. Oxford: Oxford University Press.

———. 1981. *Culture*. London: Fontana Press.

Wolf, Eric R. 1969. *Peasant Wars of the Twentieth Century*. New York: Harper and Row.

Womack, John Jr. 1969. *Zapata and the Mexican Revolution*. New York: Knopf.

Worsley, Peter. 1957. *The Trumpet Shall Sound*. London: MacGibbon and Kee.

Ximénez, Fr. Francisco. 1999. *Historia de la provincia de San Vicente de Chiapa y Guatemala de la orden de predicadores*. 5 vols. Tuxtla Gutiérrez: Consejo Estatal para la Cultura y las Artes de Chiapas.

Yashar, Deborah J. 2005. *Contesting Citizenship in Latin America: The Rise of Indigenous Movements and the Postliberal Challenge*. Cambridge: Cambridge University Press.

Zaluar, Alba. 1973. "Sobre a lógica do catolicismo popular." *Dados* 11: 173–93.

Zamora, Stephen, José Ramón Cossío, Leonel Pereznieto, José Roldán-Xopa, and David Lopez. 2004. *Mexican Law*. Oxford: Oxford University Press.

Zárate, Margarita. 1998. *En busca de la comunidad: Identidades recreadas y organi-*

zación campesina en Michoacán. Zamora: El Colegio de Michoacán and Universidad Autónoma Metropolitana.

———. 2007. "Women Who Know How to Talk: Gender, Women, Political Participation and Multiculturalism in Mexico." In *Women, Ethnicity, and Nationalisms in Latin America*, edited by Natividad Gutiérrez Chong, 145–68. Aldershot: Ashgate.

About the Contributors

HELGA BAITENMANN is an independent researcher and associate fellow of the Institute for the Study of the Americas, London University.

MARCUS J. M. DE CARVALHO is a professor of history at the Federal University of Pernambuco.

FELIPE CASTRO GUTIÉRREZ is a professor of history at the Institute of Historical Research of the National Autonomous University of Mexico.

GUILLERMO DE LA PEÑA is a professor of anthropology at the Centre for Higher Studies and Research in Social Anthropology in Guadalajara, Mexico.

JOHN GLEDHILL is the Max Gluckman Professor of Social Anthropology at the University of Manchester.

MATTHEW GUTMANN is a professor of anthropology at Brown University.

MARIA GABRIELA HITA is an associate professor of sociology at the Federal University of Bahia.

ALAN KNIGHT is the Professor of the History of Latin America at the University of Oxford.

ILKA BOAVENTURA LEITE is an associate professor of anthropology at the Federal University of Santa Catarina.

JEAN MEYER is a professor of history and director of the journal *Istor* at the Centre for Economic Research and Teaching in Mexico City.

JOHN MONTEIRO is a professor of anthropology at the State University of Campinas.

LUIS NICOLAU PARÉS is an associate professor in the department of anthropology at the Federal University of Bahia.

PATRICIA R. PESSAR is a professor of American studies and anthropology at Yale University.

PATIENCE A. SCHELL is a senior lecturer in Latin American cultural studies in the Department of Spanish, Portuguese and Latin American Studies at the University of Manchester.

ROBERT W. SLENES is a professor of history at the State University of Campinas.

JUAN PEDRO VIQUEIRA is a professor of history at El Colegio de México.

MARGARITA ZÁRATE is an associate professor of anthropology at the Metropolitan Autonomous University in Mexico City.

Index

Abu-Lughod, Lila, 6–7, 283, 291, 341

African cultural heritage, 21, 23, 109–14

Afro-Brazilian religions. *See* Candomblé

agency, 161–62, 208–9, 306–7

agrarian reform in Mexico, 208, 214, 219, 231; alternative land grants, 298; new laws governing, 297–98; new types of, 296–301; postrevolutionary, 290–92, 296, 298–99. *See also* Unión de Comuneros "Emiliano Zapata"

amparo (land rights suits) as resistance, 208, 290–91; alternative land grants and, 297–98; boundary disputes and, 295–98; factionalism and, 294–96, 301; intragovernmental disputes and, 292–93; new agrarian laws and, 297–98; new types of land reform caused by, 296–97, 301; selective land purchases and, 299–300; subaltern-elite dichotomy and, 293–94, 301

anthropology, 4, 28–29, 51, 325, 350–51

anticlericalism, 169, 185, 189–90. *See also* Cristero Rebellion; Union of Mexican Catholic Ladies

antisyncretism movement, 153–54

Argentinian food riots (2001), 3

Asamblea Popular de los Pueblos de Oaxaca (APPO), 316, 319–21

assimilation and resistance, 144–48

Auyero, Javier, 3

Ayotitlán, 206; ancient origins of, 239, 248; belief in ancestors (los señores) in, 238–39; community workshops and, 237–39; *ejido* of, 235; ethnic identity and, 232, 234–35, 246–47; ethnogenesis of, 239, 247; land rights fight of, 234–36; Manantlán Biosphere Reserve and, 233, 236–37, 240–41, 242; religious festivals of, 239; Sierra de Manantlán setting of, 232–33; testimonies of Ayotitlán subjectivities, 239–48; traditional arts and crafts of, 238; traditional medical practices of, 238; University of Guadalajara researchers and, 236–38, 240

Bahia (Brazilian state), 269; tourism and Candomblé in, 144, 150–52; urban housing reform in, 270–71

Bairro da Paz: alliances between community actors in, 285; associations and community in, 282–83; black youth groups and, 281–82, 285–86; Catholic Church and, 278–79; Center for Studies and Social Action and, 273; Conselho de Moradores (resident council) and, 277–78; crèches in, 275–76; ethnogenesis in, 275; Evangelicals and, 279–81; hidden resistance in, 283–86; Ladê Padê Mim (Candomblé terreiro), 279–80; Malvinas invasion in, 273–74; new types of community leadership in, 277–82; Plaza of Decisions in, 274–75; religious networks in, 278–81; resistance and power relations in, 283–87; subaltern official transcripts in, 286–87; tourism and development and, 271–72; as "urban quilombo," 207

Bastide, Roger, 145–46

JOHN GLEDHILL is the Max Gluckman Professor of Social Anthropology and Co-Director of Centre for Latin American Cultural Studies at the University of Manchester. He is the author of several books: *Neoliberalism, Transnationalization, and Rural Poverty: A Case Study of Michoacán, Mexico* (1995); *Power and Its Disguises: Anthropological Perspectives on Politics* (1994); and *Casi Nada: A Study of Agrarian Reform in the Homeland of Cardenismo* (1991). He has edited *Corporate Scandal: Global Corporatism against Society* (2004); and (with Barbara Bender and Mogens Trolle Larsen) *State and Society: The Emergence and Development of Social Hierarchy and Political Centralization* (1988).

PATIENCE SCHELL is a Senior Lecturer in Latin American Cultural Studies, University of Manchester. She is the author of *Church and State Education in Revolutionary Mexico City* (2003) and editor (with Stephanie Mitchell) of *The Women's Revolution in Mexico, 1910–1953* (2007).

Library of Congress Cataloging-in-Publication Data
New approaches to resistance in Brazil and Mexico /
John Gledhill and Patience A. Schell, eds.
p. cm.
Includes bibliographical references and index.
ISBN 978-0-8223-5173-3 (cloth : alk. paper)
ISBN 978-0-8223-5187-0 (pbk. : alk. paper)
1. Protest movements—Brazil. 2. Protest movements—
Mexico. 3. Social change—Brazil. 4. Social change—
Mexico. I. Gledhill, John. II. Schell, Patience A.
(Patience Alexandra), 1970–
HN283.5.N49 2012
322.40981—dc23 2011035970